Models, Numbers, and Cases

D0885824

MODELS, NUMBERS, AND CASES

Methods for Studying International Relations

Edited by
Detlef F. Sprinz
and Yael Wolinsky-Nahmias

THE UNIVERSITY OF MICHIGAN PRESS
Ann Arbor

2011   2010   2009   2008   7   6   5   4

A CIP catalog record for this book is available from the British Library.

Library of Congress Cataloging-in-Publication Data

Models, numbers, and cases : methods for studying international
relations / edited by Detlef F. Sprinz and Yael Wolinsky-Nahmias.
p.   cm.
Includes bibliographical references and index.
ISBN 0-472-09861-6 (cloth : alk. paper) —
ISBN 0-472-06861-X (Paper : alk. paper)
1. International relations—Research—Methodology.   I. Sprinz,
Detlef F.   II. Wolinsky-Nahmias, Yael, [date]

JZ1234.M63   2004
327'.072—dc22   2003021557

ISBN 978-0-472-09861-3 (cloth : alk. paper)
ISBN 978-0-472-06861-6 (Paper : alk. paper)

Contents

Contents

Part III. Formal Methods

Preface

The study of international relations has undergone a dramatic transformation in method and substance over the last three decades in keeping with developments in the social sciences and world events. The proliferation of statistical and formal methods of analysis has been striking, alongside more systematic employment of qualitative case studies. Also in recent years, new areas of research have emerged, such as international environmental politics, and IR scholars have broadened their interest from the study of war to a better understanding of international cooperation. The improvements in methodological sophistication, the emergence of new areas of inquiry, and the increasing scholarly emphasis on international political economy create a need and an opportunity to evaluate the role of methodology in the development of the field.

Books on methodology in the social sciences often deal abstractly with the principles and problems of conducting research. With this book we introduce readers to the three major methodological approaches in political science—case studies, quantitative research, and formal analysis—but we also show how these methods and the debates surrounding them are relevant to specific areas of study in international relations. The volume examines how these methods have been applied to the study of three major sub-fields of international relations: international political economy, international environmental policy, and security studies. It introduces readers to the logic of each method and to the trade-offs that inevitably arise when choosing a particular method to tackle a research problem in international politics. It is our hope for this volume that these candid evaluations of the strengths and weaknesses of the different methods will encourage continued dialogue among scholars in different subfields of international relations and more widespread employment of multimethod approaches. We believe that methodological pluralism is a key to progress in the field and that methodological diversity is the surest route to continued improvements in theory and explanation in the study of international relations.

The idea for this book originated in conversations between the editors during the 1997 annual meeting of the International Studies Association (ISA) in Toronto, Canada. We followed up these conversations with invitations to a distinguished group of international relations scholars to write papers evaluating the application of a particular research method in their substantive fields of expertise. This collection of papers was presented and discussed in three specially convened panels at the 2000 annual meeting of ISA in Los Angeles. During that conference we also organized a workshop for the authors with the help of a generous ISA Workshop Grant. The workshop gave us further opportunity to discuss our views about causality, selection bias, testing, and other methodological issues, and to explore ways to address different perspectives about these issues in the book. Exchanges among the authors continued throughout the drafting, reviewing, and revision of the volume as we read one another's chapters and held candid conversations over e-mail.

This book is aimed for use in advanced undergraduate and graduate courses as well as for scholars interested in international relations methodology. A few suggestions on how to read the book: Reading the book in its entirety will provide readers with a comparative perspective on the application of different research methods across subfields, and give them a concise primer on some key substantive debates in these fields. While we do recommend a complete reading, the book can also be read more selectively by methodological part or by substantive field. For instance, readers can choose to focus on how a particular method has been applied in several subfields of international relations. This focus on a particular method may be especially useful for classes on research methods. Alternatively, readers interested in one substantive subfield can compare how different methods have been applied in that field, which may be useful for classes that focus on that substantive subfield, such as international political economy. Finally, an introductory methods course might give priority to the first chapters of each part, which offer an overview of each method, and supplement these core chapters with a sample of other chapters tailored according to the focus of the course.

We have been very fortunate to receive the support of several friends and colleagues. We thank Jon Hovi, Harold Jacobson, David Lake, Edward Mansfield, Charles Myers, Duncan Snidal, and Arild Underdal for their valuable comments and advice. Yael Wolinsky-Nahmias thanks Dennis Chong for many conversations that helped shape the book and for helpful comments on several chapters. We are also greatly indebted to two reviewers who have provided us with very thoughtful (and amazingly detailed) comments.

Students at the University of Potsdam, Germany, who read several versions of the manuscript during the fall terms of 2000 and 2002 helped us make the book more accessible to readers.

For their excellent research assistance we thank Roshen Hendrickson, So Young Kim, Christy Lions, Christina Nystrom, and Dale Vieregge at Northwestern University. At the Potsdam-Institute for Climate Impact Research, we were also fortunate to rely on able research and administrative assistance by Martin Weiß and Jan Tiessen for the compilation of the first draft of the book. Subsequently, Marco Overhaus assisted with the appendix and kept the logistics in shape until Anja Bauer took over—thanks to her tireless efforts, we completed the final drafts of the manuscript on time. Subsequent invaluable help with indexing and logistics was provided by Christy Lions, Christina Nystrom, and Dale Vieregge at Northwestern University.

Three editors at the University of Michigan Press have provided important support and advice. During the earlier stages of this project Charles Myers, then acquisition editor for Law and Political Science, helped us develop the idea for the book and shape its initial form. His interest in the project was a source of encouragement at the time we needed it most. Jeremy Shine replaced Myers in 2000 and ably guided the book through the review process. We are also grateful to Jim Reische, the current editor for Law and Political Science, who helped us through the final stages of the book.

Our deepest gratitude goes to the authors. Their continued support, wisdom, promptness, and cheerful attitude made this project both possible and enjoyable.

We are grateful for the financial support we have received from several sources. We thank the International Studies Association, and in particular Thomas J. Volgy, Executive Director of ISA, for the 1999 Workshop Grant, which allowed us to convene an author's workshop at the 2000 annual meeting. Carlo Jaeger, head of the Department of Global Change and Social Systems at the Potsdam Institute, kindly provided financial support for the Potsdam-based assistants from the EUROPA Project. Detlef

Sprinz is also grateful to the European Centre for Analysis in the Social Sciences, University of Essex, England, and the Department of Political Science at the University of Oslo for the stimulating intellectual environments they provided during his work on this book. Yael Wolinsky-Nahmias thanks the Department of Political Science at Northwestern University, the Gordon S. Fulcher Fund, and the John D. and Catherine T. MacArthur Fund for their generous research support.

We would also like to thank Linda Murray, an artist from Maine, whose painting graces the cover of the book. The title of the painting, "Choices," captures in essence what this book is about. The painting itself beautifully portrays the hopes and uncertainties that accompany the decisions we make in our lives.

Finally, Detlef Sprinz thanks Galina and Lara for their never-ending encouragement of and patience with this book as well as for their love, which energized him throughout this venture across continents. Yael Wolinsky-Nahmias thanks her family, especially Tamar and Dan, who have helped her in ways too numerous to mention, for all their smiles, love, and support.

Detlef Sprinz,   Yael Wolinsky-Nahmias
Berlin and Potsdam   Evanston, IL

1. Introduction: Methodology in International Relations Research

Detlef F. Sprinz and Yael Wolinsky-Nahmias

Studies of international relations try to explain a broad range of political interactions among countries, societies, and organizations. Whether studying war and peace or exploring economic cooperation or environmental conflict, research on international politics requires a systematic approach to identifying fundamental processes and forces of change. In response to increased economic interdependence and other profound changes in the international system during the last few decades, the analysis of international relations (IR) has expanded in three main directions. First, scholars have tackled new issues, including international environmental politics, international ethics, and globalization. Second, new methods have emerged (e.g., two-level game analysis and spatial analysis), and the scope of methodologies has broadened to include greater use of rational choice models and statistical methods. Third, scholars have become increasingly specialized both in their respective subfields and in their use of various methodologies. These developments have undoubtedly enriched IR research by drawing attention to additional areas of study, such as compliance with international treaties and the explanation of civil wars, and by changing how researchers analyze these subjects.

At the same time the combination of new research themes, greater methodological diversity, and increased subfield specialization has overshadowed common methodological concerns among IR scholars. While general courses on research methodology are now standard in the political science curriculum at both the advanced undergraduate and graduate levels, specific treatments of methodological problems in the analysis of international relations are still comparatively rare. This volume aims to fill this gap by presenting theoretical and empirical studies that address central methodological issues as they have emerged in substantive subfields of international relations research. The authors explore the application of three methods of research—case studies, quantitative analyses, and formal methods[1]—to the study of international political economy, international environmental politics, and international security. The authors also discuss how these methods have influenced key debates in international relations such as whether and why democratic countries are unlikely to fight each other.

Following many years of debate on *which* method is best for studying international relations, this book is written in a very different spirit. It argues that a serious dialogue across different methodological approaches and subfields will generate a better understanding of the advantages and limits of different methods and will lead to more fruitful research on international relations.

Leading scholars of the field have elaborated on the need for a more robust discourse on methodology in international relations. Two former presidents of the International Studies Association, Michael Brecher and Bruce Bueno de Mesquita, have recently attempted to stimulate such a dialogue. In his 1999 presidential address to the International Studies Association, Brecher stated that the field must become more tolerant of competing paradigms, models, methods, and findings. He emphasized the importance of both cumulation of knowledge and cross-methods research. Bueno de Mesquita outlined the comparative advantages of the three major methods used in international relations (case study, quantitative, and formal methods) and suggested that "scientific progress is bolstered by and may in fact require the application of all three methods."

This book offers a unique combination of an introduction to these three methodological approaches *and* an examination of their application to substantive research in international relations. It emphasizes the merits of employing case study, quantitative analysis, and formal methods in IR research and the trade-offs involved in using each method. Each method is first introduced, then followed by separate chapters illustrating the application of the particular method to three subfields of international relations: international political economy, international environmental politics, and international security.

These subfields were chosen for several reasons. International security has been at the heart of the traditional study of international relations and remains a core subfield. Some of the main intellectual challenges in the study of international relations center on international security, beginning with the study of war and its causes at the individual (leader), state, and international system levels. Over the past half century, scholars have expanded the range of questions in security studies to include analysis of nuclear deterrence, civil wars, international alliances, and the effects of different types of domestic regimes on the likelihood of engaging in war (the democratic peace thesis).

International political economy (IPE) is another central subfield of international relations. Much current scholarship on international politics deals with questions of international political economy, including the politics of international trade and monetary relations. Many studies in this field focus on foreign economic policy-making, but broader definitions of the field also include the study of international institutions and cooperation.[2] International political economy has been at the center of the modern study of international relations owing largely to the growing importance of economic interactions among countries and to the flourishing global economy since the end of World War II.

International environmental politics is a relatively new subfield that has emerged with the growing importance of global and transboundary environmental issues including climate change, transboundary air pollution, and threats to the world's biodiversity. Its significance derives from the possibility that perfectly routine human activities now have the potential to destroy the basis of life on a global scale. Students of the field seek to explain the behavior and motivations of both traditional participants in policy-making, such as governments and international organizations, and nontraditional players, especially the burgeoning number of international nongovernmental organizations who now play a prominent role in international environmental politics. Given the emerging status of this field, a timely discussion of methodological problems and lessons from other fields can facilitate a more coherent research agenda.

Theory and Methodology

There are three main issues that can help to evaluate the intellectual progress of an academic field. The first issue is the set of empirical phenomena and questions being studied; the second issue is the state of theoretical development; and the third is the methodology used to form theoretical claims and test their empirical implications. This book focuses on the issue of methodology, but also addresses the question of how methodology informs both theoretical and empirical debates. The links between theory and methodology are complex and require some elaboration.[3]

Theory is defined by the *American Heritage Dictionary* (1985) as

> systematically organized knowledge applicable in a relatively wide variety of circumstances, esp. a system of assumptions, accepted principles, and rules of procedure devised to analyze, predict, or otherwise explain the nature or behavior of a specified set of phenomena.

Theory provides clear and precise explanations of important phenomena. It focuses scholarly attention on puzzles that set the research agenda for students of the field. Ideally, theory should also offer a set of testable and falsifiable hypotheses, thus encouraging systematic reevaluation of its main arguments through different research methods.

Methodology refers to systematically structured or codified ways to test theories. Methodology is particularly useful in the context of a progressive research program where hypotheses lend themselves to falsification. Given a range of assumptions about the properties of actors and their interactions, various hypotheses can be deduced and, ideally, corroborated—or rejected—by empirical case studies or in quantitative research. Methodology can also help expand the scope of received theories. For example, game theory offers additional insights into strategic interactions between players. Formal models can also be used to examine the internal validity of theories (see chaps. 10, 14).

Theory and methodology are most beneficial when they accompany each other for the advancement of knowledge. While theory provides explanations for particular phenomena based on specific assumptions, purely axiomatic knowledge, turned into theories, is rarely useful in explaining "real-world politics." Theoretical arguments have to be augmented with systematic methods of testing that help guard against chance and selection bias. Besides formal models, it is mainly case study research that can generate new hypotheses to advance theory building. Both case studies and quantitative methods are often used to test propositions. Carefully crafted research designs permit the assessment of regularities between variables, detect their limitations (e.g., scope of the relationship in time and space), and point to the possibility of generalization and replicability of the findings.

Political methodology has undergone many changes over the last century. King (1991) offered a five-part history of political methodology during the twentieth century. He describes how research was first based on direct empirical observations; subsequently, the "behavioral revolution" of the mid-1960s led to a sharp increase in empirical-quantitative analyses as large data sets became available in the late 1960s and 1970s. In the late 1970s and 1980s, political scientists borrowed quantitative and formal methods from other disciplines, especially economics. Finally, since the 1980s political science methodologists have improved existing methods and developed new tools specifically geared to answering political science questions.

The history of quantitative studies in international relations resembles that of political science at large, but since the 1970s case study methodology has also proliferated in international relations, particularly in studies that reach into the comparative politics field. In addition, the growth of rational choice approaches first in economics and subsequently in political science has now had a marked impact on the study of international politics. Since the 1980s, both mathematical models and rational choice approaches have contributed to the development and refinement of central ideas in the field such as hegemonic stability theory and the democratic peace (Goldmann 1995; Wæver 1998). During the 1980s and 1990s, constructivist, poststructuralist, and postmodern approaches to international relations also emerged, although it remains debatable whether these approaches actually have developed a methodology of their own.

In order to gain more insight about the prevalence of different methodological approaches in international relations, we surveyed all articles published in several leading journals in the field between 1975 and 2000. The survey included articles published in the *American Political Science Review*,[4] *International Organization, International Security*,[5] *International Studies Quarterly*, the *Journal of Conflict Resolution*, and *World Politics* (see fig. 1).[6]

The articles were classified into five categories:[7]

1. Descriptive analysis
2. Case studies
3. Quantitative (statistical) analysis

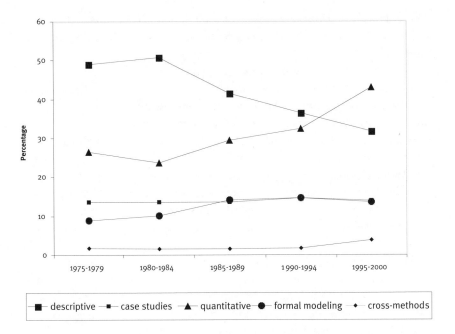

Fig. 1. Trends in methodology of international relations research (1975–2000).
(Data from *American Political Science Review*, vols. 69–94; *International Organization*, vols. 29–54; *International Security*, vols. 1–25; *International Studies Quarterly*, vols. 19–44; *Journal of Conflict Resolution*, vols. 19–44; and *World Politics*, vols. 27–52.)

4. Formal modeling
5. Cross-methods studies

The broad trajectory over the period between 1975 and 2000 (grouped as five-year intervals with the exception of the most recent group which comprises six years) demonstrates important methodological trends in international relations. The most profound trend evident in figure 1 is the continuing decline in the number of articles using a descriptive-historical approach. While in the late 1970s about half of all the articles published in these journals lacked any methodological component, in the late 1990s less than one-third of the articles surveyed could be classified as such. This trend reflects an important development in the way IR scholars conduct their research, and it supports the notion that international relations as a field has become more methods-oriented than before. In particular, *International Studies Quarterly, International Security,* and *World Politics* all currently publish significantly fewer articles that pursue a descriptive-historical approach than twenty-five years ago. For instance, during the late 1970s over 70 percent of the articles published in *World Politics* applied a descriptive or historical approach, while in late 1990s this ratio declined to less than 30 percent. Another interesting finding is the fairly constant frequency of articles using case studies, which has remained roughly steady at around 13 percent throughout the last quarter century.

In contrast, there has been a sharp increase in the number of articles using quantitative, formal, or a combination of both methods. Among articles published in the surveyed journals, the proportion of statistical studies rose from 26 percent during the late 1970s to 43 percent during the late 1990s. This trend is most pronounced in *International Organization and World Politics.* Edward Mansfield found a similar increase in the frequency of statistical analysis in articles on international political economy (see chap. 7, this vol.). It is remarkable that close to half of all articles recently published in these six prominent journals used quantitative methods of research. This trend reflects the growing importance IR scholars place on systematic analysis of political precesses and world events. This trend can also be partly explained by the greater availability of data sets and methodological training of graduate students.

Overall, the number of articles using formal methods increased from less than 9 percent during the late 1970s to 14 percent in the late 1990s. While *International Organization, International Studies Quarterly,* and *World Politics* all currently publish more articles using formal methods than they did twenty-five years ago, the rate of increase is greatest in journals that have traditionally published more quantitative work, specifically the *Journal of Conflict Resolution* and the *American Political Science Review.* Game theory is becoming more influential in the study of international politics although articles using formal methods still constitute a relatively small portion of IR publications (on par with case study analysis).

The survey of these leading journals also shows that few scholars in the field employ multimethod research. Less than 4 percent of all articles published during the late 1990s in the journals surveyed combined two methodological approaches. Cross-method analysis obviously requires more training (or alternatively, cross-field collaboration). However, it allows scholars to investigate alternative explanations, compensate for weaknesses in each of these methods, and corroborate research results.

Plan of the Book

The book is organized around three methodological approaches to the study of international relations: case studies, quantitative analyses, and formal methods. Each methodological part begins with an introductory essay that presents an overview of the method and explains its advantages and its limitations. The introductory chapter is followed by several chapters that focus on applications of the respective method in different subfields of international relations, namely, international political economy, international environmental politics, and international security. These chapters evaluate the contribution of the various methods to central debates in the field and to theory building. They do so by discussing the literature and elaborating on specific methodological issues. Table 1 details the structure of the book and the authors of the respective chapters.

The chapters are united in their emphasis on exploring common methodological concerns and providing a critical evaluation of central ideas from a methodological perspective. Each chapter also offers a list of five studies for further reading. The conclusion, titled "Methodological Pluralism," discusses problems that are common to different methods and addresses in more detail cross-methods research. Reading the book in its entirety will provide the readers with a comparative perspective on the application of different research methods across subfields of international relations. The book can also be read more selectively as each chapter stands on its own merits; in addition, the book can be read by methodological part or by substantive field. For instance, readers can choose to focus on how a particular method has been applied in several subfields of international relations. This focus on a *particular* method may be more useful for classes on research methods (reading by row in table 1). Alternatively, readers interested in a particular subfield can compare how the different methods have been applied in that particular field (reading by column). Such reading of the book is most useful for classes in a particular subfield; for instance, students in a class on international political economy will benefit from reading about the application of the three different methodological approaches in their subfield. Finally, an introductory course may choose to use the first chapters of each part to obtain an overview of each method, together with a sampling of the applications chapters tailored to the focus of the course.[8]

The first part of the book examines the application of case study methods to the analysis of international political economy, international environmental politics, and international security studies. The introductory chapter by Andrew Bennett reviews both the design and application of case study methods in international relations research (chap. 2). Bennett explains the logic of various case study methods and shows how different designs can contribute to the development of contingent generalizations or "typological theories." He illustrates how to choose between case study methods on the basis of their relative strengths and weaknesses. Bennett argues that case studies, when developed to their full potential, can aid in the generation of new theories. The chapter also provides guidance about the criteria to use for selecting cases and deciding on the number of variables to be studied. Bennett concludes by stressing the complementary nature of case study methods, statistical analysis, and formal methods.

Following the introductory chapter on case study methodology, John Odell reviews the intellectual development of case study analysis in the subfield of international political economy (chap. 3). The chapter discusses various forms of single case studies, including the "method of difference,"

TABLE 1.   Organization of the Book

Methodological Domain	Introductory Chapter	International Political Economy	International Environmental Politics	International Security
Part I: Case Study Methods	Bennett (chap. 2)	Odell (chap. 3)	Mitchell and Bernauer (chap. 4)	Kacowicz (chap. 5)
Part II: Quantitative Methods	Braumoeller and Sartori (chap. 6)	Mansfield (chap. 7)	Sprinz (chap. 8)	Huth and Allee (chap. 9)
Part III: Formal Methods	Snidal (chap. 10)	Milner (chap. 11), Conybeare (chap. 12)	Kilgour and Wolinsky-Nahmias (chap. 13)	Kydd (chap. 14)

and explains both the advantages and limitations of these methods. Using central studies in the field, ranging from E. E. Schattschneider's classic *Politics, Pressures, and the Tariff* (1935) to Richard Haass's *Economic Sanctions and American Diplomacy* (1998), Odell shows how qualitative research has been instrumental in developing theories of international political economy. He argues that case studies may support a theoretical relationship but do not provide proof of causality. Therefore, he stresses the value of using statistical methods to complement empirical case studies.

In chapter 4, Ronald Mitchell and Thomas Bernauer examine the application of case study methods to the study of international environmental policy and outline procedures for designing and conducting qualitative case studies. They discuss the problems inherent in analyzing small samples. The chapter offers ways to increase validity and reliability in small-n studies by disaggregating cases into multiple events or observations. Mitchell and Bernauer suggest that in order to advance positivist case study research in international environmental policy and more broadly in international relations, scholars must aim to derive testable hypotheses with clearly identified variables and values.

The first part of the book concludes with Arie Kacowicz's review of case study methods in international security studies (chap. 5). Kacowicz describes the contribution of empirical case study to ongoing debates in international relations, such as the democratic peace thesis. He identifies limitations of the method of difference and discusses recurring issues in the application of case studies such as selection bias and endogeneity problems. Kacowicz proposes several strategies for overcoming the methodological limitations of case studies and recommends using case studies to generate conditional theoretical statements. Finally, Kacowicz evaluates how case study analysis has advanced research on international security.

Part 2 of the book focuses on the use of quantitative methods in IR research. In their introductory chapter, Bear Braumoeller and Anne Sartori observe that quantitative methods allow researchers to draw inferences about the world by applying the laws of probability to the available data. While the statistical method facilitates summarizing relevant quantitative information in a compact way, it also requires careful evaluation of reliability and validity of measures and inferences. Most important, statistical methods render simultaneous testing of competing and complementary hypotheses in a precise way. Braumoeller and Sartori discuss two common shortcomings in the application of statistical methods, namely, (1) weak theoretical foundations underlying model specifications and (2) errors in inference, especially confusion over the distinction between statistical and substantive significance. Nevertheless, Braumoeller and Sartori show that quantitative methods, when properly employed, can summarize a wealth of information in an accessible form and provide a rigorous means of testing theory.

In chapter 7, Edward Mansfield reviews how quantitative methods have been applied in the study of international political economy. He first highlights the important role of these methods and their growing use. About 45 percent of the articles published on international political economy in a sample of leading journals subscribe to quantitative methods—roughly the same proportion reported for international relations at large (fig. 1, this chap.). By focusing mainly on the literature on international trade, Mansfield shows how a progression of theoretical interests has shaped the explanation of a nation's trade, including hegemonic stability theory, the effect of military alliances, and the interaction between military alliances and preferential trading arrangements. Mansfield recommends that more attention be given to the functional form of the relationship between variables and to developing reliable measures of key concepts of international political economy.

Detlef Sprinz reviews the quantitative research on international environmental policy in chapter 8. He covers studies of ecological modernization, the effects of international trade on the environment, environmental regulation, environmental security, and the effectiveness of international regimes. He summarizes common methodological problems in the field and provides examples of multimethod research on international environmental policy. Sprinz points to the absence of large databases that would facilitate cumulative research on basic questions in this realm, such as the effects of domestic regime type on democratic environmental performance.

Inspired by the reasoning of game theory, Huth and Allee develop a logical progression of stylized games to illustrate how quantitative research in international security studies could advance in the future (chap. 9). Their sequence includes a dispute initiation game, a challenge of the status quo game, and subsequently a negotiation or a military escalation game. Using this sequence of games, the authors highlight several methodological challenges in the study of international security and provide advice on ways to overcome selection effects and the lack of independence of observations both over time and cross-sectionally. Huth and Allee maintain that more attention should be placed on developing better measures of core concepts.

Part 3 of the book examines the application of formal methods to the study of international politics. In his introductory chapter, Duncan Snidal discusses the reasons for using models to study international relations (chap. 10). Snidal views formal modeling as complementary to other research methods. He emphasizes that successful modeling depends on the model being closely linked to important theoretical and substantive questions. While models always simplify reality, Snidal argues that models foster progress by allowing us to draw deductive inferences—thus leading to more precise theories. Snidal then illustrates the evolution of modeling in international relations by considering a developmental sequence of simple models starting with Richardson's arms race model. He shows how the limitations of previous models inspired new directions and more effective modeling, especially game modeling, leading to a more precise analysis of competition and cooperation between states.

Following Snidal's introductory chapter, Helen Milner provides an overview of formal methods approaches to the study of international political economy (chap. 11). Milner begins by defining the field of international political economy to include studies that address economic and political variables at the international level. Milner notes that rational choice methods have been an integral part of international political economy research, dating back to Hirschman's (1945) *National Power and the Structure of Foreign Trade.* Milner reviews how rational choice theory has been applied in three major areas of international political economy: hegemonic stability theory; international trade and monetary policy-making; and international institutions and cooperation. Milner argues that the use of formal methods in these areas has been limited but fruitful, leading to progress in the development of IR theory. She also suggests that using formal methods to study international political economy can create a better discourse with international economics.

In chapter 12, John Conybeare explains the logic of the microeconomic approach to the study of international relations. Following a brief introduction to the principles of microeconomics, Conybeare shows how models of supply and demand can be applied to a variety of foreign policy issues such as war, peace, and trade liberalization. He argues that microeconomics can help organize information in ways that facilitate theory testing. The chapter also suggests that microeconomic models provide better explanations of some phenomena than alternative IR theories such as the hegemonic stability theory. Finally, Conybeare points to several additional areas of IR in which the application of microeconomic approaches can improve current research.

Marc Kilgour and Yael Wolinsky-Nahmias evaluate the potential contribution of game-theoretic methods to the study of international environmental policy (chap. 13). They argue that although the application of game theory to international environmental politics is new, its focus on strategic interactions lends it particularly well to central issues in global environmental governance. Kilgour and Wolinsky-Nahmias discuss both cooperative and noncooperative game theory and show how game models provide insights into the likelihood, stability, and fairness of possible solutions to environmental conflicts. A general deterrence model is used to illustrate game modeling and is applied to water conflicts in the Middle East. The article also discusses how two-level game models improve our understanding of international environmental negotiations by addressing domestic constraints. Finally, the authors evaluate the challenges and limitations of employing game-theoretic methods in the study of international environmental politics.

In chapter 14, Andrew Kydd argues that formal models are suited to security studies because the field focuses on situations with a small number of actors who have high stakes and long familiarity with the strategic problems they face. To illustrate, Kydd presents a simple bargaining model based on the work of Fearon (1995) and Schultz (1999), and applies it to the India-Pakistan dispute over Kashmir. By delineating rational responses to uncertainty and to the role of signaling, Kydd shows how formal analysis has greatly improved our understanding of the origins of war. Kydd also discusses the contribution of game theory to other central debates in the field, including the democratic peace, arms races, and alliances.

In the concluding chapter, the editors, Detlef Sprinz and Yael Wolinsky-Nahmias, reflect on how the three methods (empirical case studies, statistical analyses, and formal methods) have advanced our knowledge of central issues in international relations. We discuss some of the methodological challenges raised in the book and address the opportunities and challenges of cross-methods analysis. We suggest a few thoughts about new methodological developments and how they may affect future research on international relations.

In summary, this book introduces the main methods of research in international relations and addresses a broad range of questions, from how empirical case studies of international relations can be designed to overcome methodological challenges to how quantitative analysis can be integrated with formal methods to advance IR research. It discusses limitations and trade-offs in using case studies, statistical analysis, and formal methods in the study of international relations and evaluates applications of these methods in studies of international political economy, international environmental politics, and security studies. We hope that the book will generate a dialogue among scholars who specialize in different issue areas and will enhance the ability of researchers to conceptualize, theorize, and better understand trends and changes in international politics.

Notes

We would like to thank Roshen Hendrickson and So Young Kim for their research assistance.

1. We chose to focus on these three methods because these are the most common methods used in IR research.

2. Helen Milner (chap. 11) suggests that studies of international institutions and cooperation should be thought of as part of the field of international political economy if they involve the study of economic variables.

3. Books on methodology in the social sciences do not always distinguish between theory and methodology. For example, some consider "quantitative studies" and "formalized rational choice" either a "metatheoretical orientation" or "theoretical position" (Wæver 1998, 701–3). More generally, some social science methodology books, in particular in Europe, restrict themselves to a philosophy-of-science perspective—at the expense of more modern methodological considerations for social science research.

4. We also reviewed the statistical data excluding *American Political Science Review (APSR)* because the journal publishes political science research not limited to the study of international relations. We found that excluding *APSR* led to higher ratios of formal and statistical articles, but the reported trends remain the same.

5. *International Security* began publishing in 1976, therefore we surveyed the period 1976–2001.

6. The authors thank So Young Kim for her research assistance for this survey.

7. The classification is based on the following criteria: "Descriptive analysis" includes articles based on historical analysis that lack clearly detectable methodol-

ogy; "Case studies" include articles that use any of the research approaches discussed in chapter 2 and a justification for the case selection; "Quantitative analysis" ranges from simple correlation/covariance analysis and factor analysis to more sophisticated regression analysis; "Formal modeling" ranges from soft rational choice theory, simulation, and game-theoretic models to more sophisticated formal analysis that includes a mathematical proof; and "Cross-methods" analysis includes articles that combine at least two methodologies (mostly quantitative and formal analyses).

8. The book can also be read in conjunction with other books that have a different focus. One of the prominent books on methodological problems in the social sciences is *Designing Social Inquiry* by Gary King, Robert O. Keohane, and Sidney Verba (1994). It considers general methodological problems of social inquiry such as research design and causal inference (but it does not focus on issues that are of particular importance to the study of international relations). Another valuable book in the area of methodology, more specific to international relations, is Daniel Frei and Dieter Ruloff's *Handbook of Foreign Policy Analysis* (1989), which covers mostly formal and statistical approaches to the study of foreign policy. Other books that discuss theories and methodologies of international politics include Patrick M. Morgan's *Theories and Approaches to International Politics* (1987) and Michael Don Ward's *Theories, Models, and Simulations in International Relations* (1985). These books, however, were published during the late 1980s or early 1990s. A more recent edited volume that offers a reflective evaluation of methodology in international studies is Frank P. Harvey and Michael Brecher's *Evaluating Methodology in International Studies* (2002).

References

Brecher, M. 1999. ISA Presidential Address. *International Studies Quarterly* 43 (2): 213–64.

Bueno de Mesquita, B. 2002. Domestic Politics and International Relations. *International Studies Quarterly* 46 (1): 1–9.

Fearon, J. D. 1995. Rationalist Explanations for War. *International Organization* 49:379–414.

Frei, D., and D. Ruloff. 1989. *Handbook of Foreign Policy Analysis: Methods for Practical Application in Foreign Policy Planning, Strategic Planning, and Business Risk Assessment.* Dordrecht: Martinus Nijhoff.

Geddes. B. 2003. *Paradigms and Sand Castles.* Ann Arbor: University of Michigan Press.

Goldmann, K. 1995. Im Westen Nichts Neues: Seven International Relations Journals in 1972 and 1992. *European Journal of International Relations* 1 (2): 245–58.

Haass, R. N., ed. 1998. *Economic Sanctions and American Diplomacy.* Washington, DC: Brookings Institution Press.

Harvey, F. P., and M. Brecher, eds. 2002. *Evaluating Methodology in International Studies.* Ann Arbor: University of Michigan Press.

Hirschman, A. 1945. *National Power and the Structure of Foreign Trade.* Berkeley: University of California Press.

King, G. 1991. On Political Methodology. In *Political Analysis: An Annual Publication of the Methodology Section of the American Political Science Association,* edited by J. A. Stimson. Ann Arbor: University of Michigan Press.

King, G., R. O. Keohane, and S. Verba. 1994. *Designing Social Inquiry: Scientific Inference in Qualitative Research.* Princeton: Princeton University Press.

Lakatos, I. 1986. Falsification and the Methodology of Scientific Research Programmes. In *Criticism and the Growth of Knowledge,* edited by I. Lakatos and A. Musgrave. Cambridge: Cambridge University Press.

Morgan, P. M. 1987. *Theories and Approaches to International Politics: What Are We to Think?* New Brunswick, NJ: Transaction Publishers.

Schattschneider, E. E. 1935. *Politics, Pressures, and the Tariff.* Englewood Cliffs, NJ: Prentice-Hall.

Schultz, K. A. 1999. Do Democratic Institutions Constrain or Inform? Contrasting Institutional Perspectives on Democracy and War. *International Organization* 53 (2): 233–66.

Wæver, O. 1998. The Sociology of a Not So International Discipline: American and European Developments in International Relations. *International Organization* 52 (4): 687–727.

Ward, M. D., ed. 1985. *Theories, Models, and Simulations in International Relations: Essays and Research in Honor of Harold Guetzkow.* Boulder: Westview.

Part I. Case Study Methods

2. Case Study Methods: Design, Use, and Comparative Advantages

Andrew Bennett

There is a growing consensus among social scientists that research programs advance more effectively through the iterative or collaborative use of different research methods than through the use of any one method alone. Making the most of the synergies among research methods requires an understanding of the relative comparative advantages, trade-offs, and limitations of each method and an ability to translate between different methods. The comparative advantages of case study methods include identifying new or omitted variables and hypotheses, examining intervening variables in individual cases to make inferences on which causal mechanisms may have been at work, developing historical explanations of particular cases, attaining high levels of construct validity, and using contingent generalizations to model complex relationships such as path dependency and multiple interactions effects. Particularly important is the ability to identify new hypotheses, which case studies can do through a combination of deduction and induction.

Recurrent trade-offs in the use of case study methods include the problem of case selection and the danger of selection bias, which can have more severe consequences in case studies than in statistical studies, and the tension between parsimony and richness in selecting the number of variables and cases to be studied. In addition, case study findings are usually contingent and can be generalized beyond the type of case studied only under specified conditions, such as when a case study shows that a variable is not a necessary condition or a sufficient condition for an outcome, or when a theory fails to fit a case that it appeared most likely to explain. Potential limitations of case studies, though not inherent in every one, include indeterminacy or inability to exclude all but one explanation, lack of independence of cases, and the impossibility of perfectly controlling case comparisons.

The inherent limitations of case study methods include their relative inability to render judgment on the frequency or representativeness of particular cases and their weak capability for estimating the average "causal weight" of variables. These are inferential processes for which case studies are not designed and cannot be used except in a rudimentary manner. Fortunately, these inherent limitations correspond almost exactly with the comparative advantages of statistical methods, which give various measures of frequency and can estimate the expected causal weight of a variable.

This chapter defines and explicates case study methods and details their comparative advantages and limitations. It then more briefly reviews the strengths and limits of formal models and statistical methods. This analysis substantiates the conclusion that the comparative advantages of case study methods are complementary to those of statistical methods and formal models. It concludes with suggestions for increasing multimethod collaboration among researchers to make the best possible use of this complementarity.

Overview of Case Study Methods

Defining *Case* and *Case Studies*

A *case* is often defined as a "phenomenon for which we report and interpret only a single measure on any pertinent variable" (Eckstein 1975). This wrongly implies, however, that each case has only one observation on the dependent variable but many independent variables. If this were true, it would present an inherent problem of indeterminacy, or an inability to choose among competing explanations for a case.[1] Yet each "case" in fact has a potentially large number of observations on intervening variables and may allow several qualitative measures of various dimensions of the independent and dependent variables, so case studies do not necessarily suffer from indeterminacy (King, Keohane, and Verba 1994, 225; Campbell 1975, 179, 181–82). I therefore follow the definition of a *case* as an instance of a class of events of interest to the investigator (George 1979a), such as an instance of revolution, type of governmental regime, kind of economic system, or personality type. A *case study* is thus the investigation of a well-defined aspect of a historical happening that the investigator selects for analysis, rather than a historical happening itself. The Soviet revolution, for example, is an instance of civil conflict, war termination (the Soviet pullout from World War I), the role of personality in politics, and so on. The investigator decides which class of events, which facets of the Soviet revolution, and which variables to focus upon.[2]

There is also potential for confusion among the terms *comparative methods, case study methods,* and *qualitative methods.* I use the term *case study methods* to refer to both within-case analysis of single cases and comparisons among a small number of cases, as most case studies involve both kinds of analysis due to the limits of either method used alone. Even single-case studies usually draw implicit comparisons to wider groups of cases. As for the term *qualitative methods,* this is sometimes used to encompass both case studies carried out with a neopositivist view of the philosophy of science and those implemented with a postmodern or interpretive view. In the present chapter I use the term *case study* to refer only to studies that aspire to causal explanations, setting aside those interpretivist and postmodernist analyses that eschew such explanations or view them as unattainable.

Types of Theory-Building Contributions of Case Studies

Within this general definition of case studies, there are many types of case studies. Some methodological texts focus on theory-testing cases at the expense of theory development. It is important to keep in mind, however, that there are several kinds of contributions to theory, including the generation of new hypotheses (the "logic of discovery") as well as the testing of existing ones (the "logic of confirmation"). In addition, there are several kinds of research objectives, including not only the development of generalized theories but the *historical explanation* of particular cases, that is, explanation of a sequence of events that produce a particular historical outcome in which key steps in the sequence are in turn explained with reference to theories or causal mechanisms. Case studies can contribute to all of these kinds of theory building, as Arend Lijphart (1971) and Harry Eckstein (1975) indicated in their similar taxonomies of different kinds of case studies, outlined in table 1 (from George 1979a).

TABLE 1. Equivalent Terms for Types of Case Studies

Arend Lijphart	Harry Eckstein
Atheoretical case study	Configurative-ideographic case study
Interpretative case study	Disciplined-configurative case study
Hypothesis-generating case study	Heuristic case study
Deviant case study	(No comparable term or concept)
Theory-confirming/infirming case study	Crucial, most likely, least likely test cases

Apart from the first type, which is simply a kind of chronological narrative, case studies have an explanatory or theory-building purpose. "Interpretive" or "disciplined configurative" cases use theoretical variables to provide historical explanations of particular cases. In other words, they use theories to show that in the particular historical circumstances of the case, the outcome was to be expected. Heuristic case studies seek to generate new hypotheses inductively. "Deviant" cases, or cases whose outcomes are not predicted or explained well by existing theories, can be particularly useful in identifying new or left-out variables. Finally, researchers can use case studies to test whether extant theories accurately explain the processes as well as the outcomes of particular cases. Herein, I use Eckstein's terminology, which is more common, with the addition of Lijphart's term for the study of "deviant" cases.

Within-Case Methods of Analysis

Process Tracing

There are three methods of within-case analysis: process tracing, congruence testing, and counterfactual analysis.[3] Process tracing focuses on whether the intervening variables between a hypothesized cause and observed effect move as predicted by the theories under investigation. Put another way, process tracing looks at the observable implications of putative causal mechanisms in operation in a case, much as a detective looks for suspects and for clues linking them to a crime. The goal is to establish which of several possible explanations is consistent with an uninterrupted chain of evidence from hypothesized cause to observed effect. The power of process tracing arises from the fact that it requires continuity and completeness in explaining a case (although there are pragmatic limits on the ability or need to examine the infinite "steps between steps" in a temporal process). If even a single significant step in a hypothesized process is not as predicted, the hypothesis must be modified, sometimes trivially and other times substantially, if it is to explain the case. If, for example, 98 of 100 dominoes standing in a straight line knock one another over but the 99th domino does not fall or strike the final domino, we need a separate explanation for why the 100th domino has fallen.

This contrasts sharply with statistical methods, which rely on probabilistic associations but do not require continuity or completeness in any given case. In this sense, process tracing is different from the notion of "pattern matching" outlined by Donald Campbell (1975). Campbell does not elaborate in any detail on what he means by "pattern matching," but he indicates that it involves finding similar patterns or sequences in different cases, and he does not define it to include an analysis of the full sequence of events in either case. This is potentially an important form of inference that combines elements of cross-case comparison with some degree of within-case analysis, but it does not require full continuity or completeness and hence cannot constitute a historical explanation of either case. The distinction is analogous to the difference between finding common short sequences in a long strand of DNA that may offer clues to its operation (pattern matching) and attempting to explain how the full strand operates to express itself in the life form to which the DNA belongs (process tracing).

In any particular study, there can be a deductive element to process tracing, an inductive element, or both. Deductively, the researcher uses theories to predict the values of intervening variables in a case and then tests these predictions. This may require filling in the predictions that underspecified theories should make in a case, and it is important to trace the predicted processes of alternative hypotheses as well as those of the main hypothesis of interest. Inductively, the researcher should be open to unexpected clues or puzzles that indicate the presence of left-out variables. This can lead to the development of new hypotheses.

One common misconception here is that it is always illegitimate to derive a hypothesis from a case and then test it against the same case. In fact, it may be possible to develop a hypothesis from a case and then test it against *different evidence* in the same case. Detectives, of course, do this all the time: clues may lead to a new "theory of the case," which prompts the detective to look for "new" evidence in the case that had previously been ignored or considered irrelevant. If the new evidence fits the prediction of the new theory, this is considered an independent corroboration.[4]

Process tracing is not infallible. Measurement error and omitted variables can lead to incorrect inferences in process tracing just as they can in statistical methods. There are also practical limits on our ability to observe or trace processes in all of their nearly infinite detail and to establish fully continuous sequences. The requisite evidence may not be available at key steps in the process, and even where evidence is available, we may not have the time to go through all of it. Yet by insisting that we establish explanations that document the intervening variables and processes through which the hypothesized independent variables are purported to have brought about the observed outcome, process tracing differs from and complements statistical inferences. Although no case study is undertaken in the infinite level of detail that would be needed to establish a *fully* continuous process, case study explanations are open to challenge if they are inconsistent with the finest level of detail that is observable. For example, if a rational choice theory posits that an individual should have gone through a rational calculation that led to a certain behavior, but it can be shown in a case study that the individual's thinking process was actually very different from that posited by the theory, then the theory cannot constitute a satisfactory explanation of the case even if its predicted outcome is consistent with the observed outcome.

Congruence Testing

In congruence testing, the researcher focuses on the values of the independent and dependent variables rather than the intervening variables. Here, the researcher tests whether the predicted value of the dependent variable, in view of the values of the case's independent variables, is congruent with the actual outcome in the case. Congruence tests are usually less conclusive than process tracing because in the social sciences we usually lack precise models of the value that the individual variables, individually and collectively, should produce in the dependent variable. In this sense, congruence tests in a single case or a small number of cases are a less reliable version of statistical tests of covariation or estimates of partial correlations among a large number of cases. Still, congruence tests may be able to rule out proposed necessary or sufficient conditions, and they may weaken the plausibility of particular historical explanations of cases.

Counterfactual Analysis

Counterfactual analysis inverts the standard mode of inference for empirical testing of assertions such as "x in a specified case was necessary for y." This assertion poses a logically equivalent counterfactual, namely, "if not-x had occurred in the case, then not-y would have occurred." Analogously, a claim that a variable x is sufficient for an outcome y, whether made for all y or only for specific contexts, can be assessed by looking at the equivalent counterfactual, "not-y could occur only if not-x." Interest in counterfactual analysis has increased in recent years (Fearon 1991; Tetlock and Belkin 1996). At the same time, there is an obvious danger of confirmation bias and spuriousness if counterfactual analysis is carried out in an undisciplined way.

Philip Tetlock and Aaron Belkin have devised a useful taxonomy of counterfactual analyses. These include "idiographic case-study counterfactuals," which focus on points of supposed historical contingency in individual cases, and "nomothetic counterfactuals," which apply well-defined theories to specific antecedent counterfactual conditions. These authors argue that an especially important type of counterfactual combines these two, bringing together in-depth knowledge of particular cases with strong theories about the consequences of particular values of a variable to produce convincing accounts of what should have been true if one variable in a case had assumed a particular value. They illustrate this with the example of dinosaur extinction (1996, 6–11): If an asteroid of a size sufficient to cause climatic change had struck the earth 65 million years ago, what testable implications should be observable in contemporary geologic evidence? This combines the known specifics of the dinosaur extinction case with theories on asteroid impacts to produce testable assertions, and it thus moves from the counterfactual to the factual. The difficulty of applying this to the social sciences, as they note, is that we generally lack "idiographic-nomothetic syntheses of comparable scope and sweep in world politics" (11).

Tetlock and Belkin also offer sensible advice on criteria for defining good counterfactual analyses, including clarity in defining the variables, minimization of the necessary rewriting of history, and consistency with established theories and statistical findings. Most important, they suggest that good counterfactuals must have testable implications in the factual world (1996, 18). They also note that if we find a causal argument plausible but its equivalent counterfactual argument implausible, or vice versa, we must reconcile the asymmetry in our thinking. This can help identify double standards, inconsistent causal reasoning, and hindsight bias (13). Subject to these criteria, counterfactual analysis is a useful tool in the explanation of individual cases and can provide a check on confirmation bias rather than an open license to rewrite history.

Research Design Tasks

There are five research design tasks common to both single and comparative case studies, many of them common to statistical studies as well (George 1979a; George and McKeown 1985). First, the researcher must define the research objective, including the class of events to be explained, the alternative hypotheses under consideration, and the kind of theory building to be undertaken. Second, the researcher must specify the independent, dependent, and intervening variables and decide which of these are to be controlled for and which are to vary across cases or types of cases. Third, the researcher selects the cases to be studied, possibly assisted by the typological space that results from the specification of the variables and alternative hypotheses. Fourth, the researcher should consider how best to describe variance in the independent and dependent variables, considering not only individual variables but also types of cases, or combinations of variables, and the sequential pathways that characterize each type. Finally, the researcher specifies the structured questions to be asked of each case in order to establish the values of the independent, intervening, and dependent variables.

An example from my own work illustrates how these tasks were accomplished in one study.[5] I chose to study Soviet and Russian military interventionism and to try to explain the puzzle of why such interventionism appeared to increase in the 1970s, decrease in the 1980s, and increase once again in the mid-1990s. I first had to define *interventionism*, the propensity for intervention, as distinct from actual military *interventions*. This required defining in a general way what constituted an inviting or uninviting "opportunity" for military intervention, which I did by looking at a typology of situational factors. I also compared opportunities in which the Soviet Union or Russia intervened to analogous opportunities in which they did not intervene, and I compared Soviet interventions in particular countries to later Soviet withdrawals from those same countries. I also decided to focus on one subtype of intervention: the high end of the scale involving the direct use of Soviet or Russian troops or commanders.

For the alternative explanations of patterns in Soviet-Russian interventionism, I included standard theories from the IR literature based on the systemic, domestic, organizational, and individual levels, as well as theories based on the arguments of area experts and policymakers. The explanation that interested me most was that Soviet and Russian leaders learned lessons from their ongoing experiences that made them more willing to resort to military intervention in the 1970s, less so in the 1980s, and more so once again in the mid-1990s.[6] I specified the variables for each of the alternative explanations and carried out both congruence and process-tracing tests on each explanation. Explanations based on changes in the balance of military forces, for example, were consistent with the rise of Soviet interventionism in the 1970s, but not with its decline in the 1980s when Soviet forces were still strong or with its resurgence in 1994 when Russian forces were weak. For the "learning" explanation, eight specific beliefs on the efficacy of using force were listed, such as beliefs on whether "balancing" or "bandwagoning" is the most likely response by others to the use of force. I also defined corresponding behaviors, such as the intensity of efforts to get other regional states or national liberation movements to bandwagon with Soviet-Russian efforts.

After considering for study more than a dozen cases of interventions, noninterventions, and withdrawals, I chose to examine the Soviet-Cuban intervention in Angola in 1975, the Soviet intervention in Afghanistan in 1979, the ongoing occupation of Afghanistan through the 1980s, the withdrawal from Afghanistan in 1989, and the Russian intervention in Chechnya in 1994. I was assisted in this process by a chart outlining my preliminary knowledge on how each of the possible cases for study fit with respect to their values on the seven independent variables identified by the hypotheses. This helped ensure that the cases I chose included wide variation in both the independent and dependent variables. It also made clear which other cases might have been included, thereby "leaving up the scaffolding" for future researchers to build upon or future critics to question (King, Keohane, and Verba 1994). This is an important aspect of research design that is seldom adequately carried out.

I also used my preliminary knowledge of the cases to select from among the cases that history provided the ones that yielded the most analytical leverage on my research objective and that best fit a strong "most similar cases" research design. Since the learning hypothesis focused on a path-dependent historical process, I chose cases that covered the entire historical period from 1973 (the lead-up to Soviet intervention in Angola) to 1996 (the peak of modern Russia's first intervention in Chechnya). I also included cases of different types of intervention, such as direct intervention (Afghanistan, Chechnya) and proxy intervention (Angola). Also, the before-and-after cases of intervention in and withdrawal from Afghanistan provided a most-similar-case comparison that controlled for many variables, such as intrinsic geographic importance. Controlling for other variables that changed over time, such as U.S. policy, was done through a combination of case comparisons and process tracing. Thus, as is common, the research design included both within-case analysis of every case and cross-case comparisons.

The questions asked of each case included those that established the values of the independent and intervening values for each hypothesis and the outcome of the case. For the learning hypothesis, the case studies tested whether stated Soviet and Russian beliefs changed in response to experience and were congruent with Soviet behavior. They also tested whether the patterns and timing of changes in stated beliefs fit the dynamics predicted by theories of individual, organizational, and governmental learning. A particularly important test was whether individuals' stated beliefs fit better with their apparent material interests, as many explanations argued they should, or with the experiences and information to which individuals were exposed, as learning theory predicted. Finally, the study designated fifty-five key Soviet and Russian officials whose stated views were traced through public statements, archival documents, interviews, and memoirs.[7]

The actual case studies found substantial changes in stated beliefs over time that correlated closely with actual Soviet-Russian behavior. I was also able to trace these changes of beliefs to ongoing Soviet-Russian experiences in the use of force and to show that beliefs were often correlated more closely with individuals' experiences than with their bureaucratic or material interests. Many military officers who fought in Afghanistan, for example, strongly protested the use of Russian troops in Chechnya, even to the point of losing their jobs and ending their careers. These conclusions constituted strong evidence for the general applicability of learning theory, as in many respects the closed Soviet system was a least likely case for learning. The cases studied did not include any crucial cases, however, as U.S. policy responses and Soviet-Russian domestic politics were also broadly consistent with changes in Soviet behavior.

Single-Case Research Designs

Within the context of general research design tasks, there are specific considerations that apply to single and comparative case studies. Some methodologists have downplayed the theory-building contributions that can be made by single-case research designs (King, Keohane, and Verba 1994, 209–11). In contrast, most case study researchers have argued that single-case studies can provide tests that might strongly support or impugn theories. Many influential research findings in political science have come from single-case studies that presented anomalies for accepted theories.[8]

An important single-case research design is the study of crucial, most likely, or least likely cases that pose severe tests of theories. Harry Eckstein developed the idea of a "crucial case," or a case that *must closely fit* a theory if one is to have confidence in the theory's validity, or, conversely, *must not fit* equally well any rule contrary to that proposed" (1975, emphasis in original). Because true crucial cases were rare in Eckstein's view, he pointed to the alternative of "most likely" and "least likely" cases. A most likely case is one that is almost certain to fit a theory if the theory is true for any cases at all. The failure of a theory to explain a most likely case greatly undermines our confidence in the theory. A least likely case, conversely, is a tough test for a theory because it is a case in which the theory is least likely to hold true. Eckstein's conception is a useful starting point on theory testing in case studies, but it is at best incomplete because he does not address whether the cases in question are most or least likely for competing theories, or whether these theories predict the same outcome as the theory of interest or a different outcome altogether. Thus, a more complete version of Eckstein's insight would be that a theory is most strongly supported when it makes a clear prediction on the outcome or process of a case, all other theories make clear predictions that we should not find this outcome or process, and the first theory is corroborated in the case. Conversely, if both our theory of interest and the alternative theories make the same prediction on the outcome or process of a case, but this prediction proves wrong, then the theory of interest is strongly impugned because its failure cannot be explained away by the operation of other theories or mechanisms.[9] Single-case studies that fit either of these situations can greatly increase or decrease our confidence in a theory or require that we alter its scope conditions, although we can never entirely rule out the possibility that the outcome or process of the case was caused by probabilistic processes analogous to those of quantum mechanics.

Another important single-case research design is the study of a deviant or outlier case. Research on deviant cases can help inductively identify variables and hypotheses that have been left out of existing theories. Deviant cases may also uncover measurement errors that may exist in less extreme forms in other cases.

Single-case study designs can fulfill the other theory-building purposes identified by Lijphart and Eckstein as well. Idiographic studies, while often disdained, may provide data for later more theoretically oriented case studies. Also, a study of a newly defined puzzle or phenomenon might begin with a fairly open-ended effort—sometimes called "soaking and poking" in the data—to generate hypotheses that can then be tested more systematically.[10]

Comparative Methods

Mill's Methods and Most-Similar and Least-Similar Case Comparisons

Comparisons between cases are a powerful source of causal inferences but also a potential source of inferential errors. One mode of case comparisons is Mill's method of agreement, in which the investigator looks for the potentially causal antecedent conditions that are the same between two cases that have the same outcome. Ideally, these would turn out to be necessary conditions. Thus, if we compared the following two cases using Mill's method of agreement, we might infer that the variable A is causally related to the outcome Y, as it is the only independent variable common to the two cases.

Mill's Method of Agreement

	Independent Variables	Dependent Variable
Case 1	A B C D E	Y
Case 2	A F G H I	Y

This method of agreement corresponds, somewhat confusingly, with what has been called the "least similar cases" research design. If, for example, we find that teenagers are "difficult" in both tribal societies and industrialized societies, we might be tempted to infer that it is the nature of teenagers rather than the nature of society that accounts for the difficulty of teenagers (Przeworski and Teune 1970).

In Mill's method of difference, the investigator would look for antecedent conditions that differ between two cases that have different outcomes, and they would judge that those antecedent conditions that were the same despite differing outcomes could not be sufficient to cause either outcome. In the following example (where ~A represents "not A") the researcher would draw the inference that the variable A was causally related to the outcome because it is the only one that varies when the outcome varies.

Mill's Method of Difference

	Independent Variables	Dependent Variable
Case 1	A B C D E	Y
Case 2	~A B C D E	~Y

This corresponds with the "most similar case" research design (Przeworski and Teune 1970). It has also been called the method of "controlled comparison," because if two cases in fact are the same in all but one independent variable, then we have the functional equivalent of a controlled experiment. The practical limitation here, of course, is that two cases are almost never identical in all but one independent variable (George 1979a).[11]

In actual practice, case study researchers almost never draw conclusions on the basis of Mill's methods alone because these methods require demanding and unrealistic assumptions in order to provide nonspurious inferences. One key limitation of Mill's methods, which Mill himself identified, is that they cannot work well in the presence of equifinality (George 1982). A condition of equifinality, or what Mill called a "plurality of causes," holds when the same outcome can arise through different pathways or combinations of variables. Thus, when equifinality is present, there might be no single necessary or sufficient variable for a phenomenon: it might be that either ABC or DEF causes Y, and that none of the variables A through F is by itself sufficient to cause Y. In such circumstances, pairwise comparisons of cases might lead us wrongly to reject variables that can cause an outcome in conjunction with some contexts but not others, and it might also lead us to accept a confounding variable as causal rather than recognizing that its relationship to the outcome is spurious.

Thus Mill's methods can work well at identifying causal relations only under three conditions that are impossible to realize fully in practice. First, the causal relations being investigated must be deterministic regularities involving conditions that by themselves are either necessary or sufficient for a specified outcome. This implies that there can be no causally relevant interaction effects. Second, all variables that contributed causally to the outcome would have to be identified and included in the analysis. Third, cases that represent the full range of all logically and socially possible causal paths must be available for study (Little 1998; George and McKeown 1985).

Because these requirements are unrealistic, case study researchers use Mill's methods in only a very general and preliminary way to identify potentially relevant variables, but they then rely heavily on process tracing to compensate for the evident weakness of Mill's methods (Mahoney 1999).[12] For example, when it is not possible to find cases similar in all but one independent variable and the dependent variable, process tracing can test whether each of the potentially causal variables that differ between the imperfectly matched cases can be ruled out as having causal significance.[13]

Structured, Focused Comparison of Cases and the Development of Typological Theories

In response to the limitations of Mill's methods and controlled comparison, Alexander George (1979a, 1979b) systematized case study procedures and developed the method of "structured focused case comparisons." In this method, the researcher systematically (1) specifies the research problem and the class of events to be studied; (2) defines the independent, dependent, and intervening variables of the relevant theories; (3) selects the cases to be studied and compared; (4) decides how best to characterize variance in the independent and dependent variables; and (5) formulates a detailed set of standard questions to be applied to each case.

In addition, consistent with his emphasis on equifinality, George argued that case studies could be especially useful in developing what he called "typological theories," or contingent generalizations on *"the variety of different causal patterns* that can occur for the phenomena in question [and] *the conditions under which each distinctive type of causal patterns occurs"* (1979a, emphasis in original). He advocated a kind of "building block" approach to the development of theories. In this approach, each case, while rendered in terms of theoretical variables, might prove to be a distinctive pathway to the outcome of interest. Typological theories treat cases as *configurations* of variables that may involve complex interactions among all of the variable values in the case. While statistical methods can model interactions effects as well, this puts added pressure on the sample size necessary to be confident in one's results, and statistical studies rarely model interactions among *all* the variables acting together, as a typological theory may do.

Typological theories make less restrictive assumptions about case comparisons than Mill's methods. Specifically, typological theorizing assumes that if cases within the same type, or with the same mix of independent variables, have different outcomes on the dependent variable, the difference in the outcome is due to measurement error or left-out variables, not to the type of probabilistic relations theorized in quantum physics. This addresses a common misinterpretation of case study methods, namely, that they assume or require restrictive forms of determinism (Lieberson 1992). It is certainly true that all forms of case comparison are much stronger sources of inference when a variable is a necessary or sufficient condition for a particular outcome. But it is also true that some forms of case comparison require more deterministic assumptions than others, and most case study researchers appear to assume that equifinality is a common condition in social life (Ragin 1987). The minimal assumptions of typological theory are in fact similar to those of the statistical researchers who interpret the "error term" in their equations as including measurement error or left-out variables.[14] This assumption sets aside a third possibility, which can never be definitively ruled out, namely, that the error term can also represent a fundamentally stochastic element analogous to the irreducible probabilism of quantum mechanics.

Comparative Advantages of Case Study Methods

Case study methods have considerable comparative advantages relative to statistical methods or formal models (Collier 1993). These include the operationalization and measurement of qualitative variables (construct validity), the heuristic identification of new variables or hypotheses, the examination of potential causal mechanisms within particular cases or contexts, the historical explanation of cases, and the incorporation of complex relations like equifinality and path dependency into typological theories.

Construct Validity

One of the greatest strengths of case studies is the opportunity to achieve high levels of construct validity, or the ability to measure in a case the indicators that best represent the theoretical concept we intend to measure. Many of the variables of interest to researchers, such as democracy, power, and political culture, are notoriously difficult to operationalize and measure. What constitutes a "democratic" procedure in one cultural context might be profoundly undemocratic in another. Thus, it is important to carry out "contextualized comparison," that is, comparison that "self-consciously seeks to address the issue of equivalence by searching for *analytically equivalent* phenomena—even if expressed in substantively different terms—across different contexts" (Lock and Thelen 1998, 11). This requires detailed consideration of contextual variables, which is extremely difficult to carry out in statistical studies but common in case studies. Whereas statistical studies run the risk of "conceptual stretching" if they lump together dissimilar cases to get a higher sample size (Sartori 1970), case studies move in the opposite direction, refining concepts with a higher level of validity but doing so at the cost of producing generalizations applicable only over a smaller number of cases. Put in other terms, there is a trade-off between achieving a high level of construct validity, which is easier to do in case studies, and establishing a high level of external validity, or the ability to apply findings across a wide population of cases, which statistical studies are better suited to doing.[15]

Because case studies can achieve high construct validity, statistical research is not only usefully preceded by case study research to identify relevant variables, it is often followed by case study work that focuses on deviant cases and further refines concepts (Collier 1998). For example, after

34

a range of statistical studies suggested that democracies do not fight other democracies, case study researchers started to explore which aspects of democracy—democratic values, democratic institutions, the transparency of decision making in democracies, and so on—might be responsible for this apparent "inter-democratic peace" (George and Bennett 2004). Should these case studies indicate, to take a hypothetical example, that a free press and transparency are more important factors than competitive elections in producing an interdemocratic peace, then statistical databases that weighted competitive elections heavily in the definition of democracy will have to be redone, and new statistical tests performed.

Generating New Theories

Case studies can also heuristically identify new variables and hypotheses. This can take place through the study of deviant cases, as noted earlier, but it also happens in the ordinary course of fieldwork, such as archival research and interviews with participants, area experts, and historians. The popular refrain that observations are theory-laden does not mean that they are theory-determined. When a case study researcher asks a participant, "Were you thinking x when you did y," and they get the answer, "No, I was thinking z," they may have a new variable demanding to be heard. Statistical methods lack any counterpart for this process; some methods of "data mining" or "exploratory data analysis" can be used to identify potentially relevant variables, but even these methods can use only data that is already coded into data sets, or data that someone has already identified as sufficiently useful to be worth coding. Statistical studies that do not involve archival work or interviews to measure or code variables have no inductive means of identifying new variables, although deductive theorizing, whether by a researcher using statistical methods or a formal modeler, can also identify new variables.[16]

Making Inferences Regarding Causal Mechanisms

Case studies can use process tracing to examine in detail the observable implications of hypothesized causal mechanisms in individual cases. Causal mechanisms can be defined as the ultimately unobservable entities or structures that operate in specific contexts to generate the phenomena that we observe in the physical or social world.[17]

Thus, as the philosopher David Hume famously argued, we cannot directly observe theories or causal mechanisms. As noted earlier, process tracing, like all methods (even experimental ones), does not allow direct or infallible assessment of causal mechanisms as there is always the danger of measurement error, specification error, and omitted variables. Hume also noted, however, that we have several *sources of inference* on the operation of hypothesized causal entities, so that our inferences on underlying causal mechanisms, while fallible, are not mere guesswork. Some of the sources of inference that Hume pointed to—constant conjunction and congruity (similarity in size)—relate to statistical methods, but others—temporal succession and contiguity—relate more directly to process tracing.[18] The detailed tracing of sequential processes among spatially and/or temporally contiguous entities in a single case is a fundamentally different source of inference from the assessment of correlations among cases. Process tracing involves examining the hypothesized causal sequences that a theory and its associated causal mechanisms predict should have taken place in a case, then determining whether the intervening variables along these pathways, or those predicted by alternative explanations, were in fact extant in the case. This provides a basis for inference on whether the hypothesized explanation can or cannot be ruled out as a historical explanation for the case, which in turn allows inferences on the more general scope conditions of the theories under investigation (a theory that fails to explain a "most likely case," for example, is strongly impugned).

It is the demand for a high level of detail and continuity in explaining an individual historical case that distinguishes process tracing from statistical analysis. As noted previously, the finding that 98 of 100 dominoes have knocked one another over in sequence is not enough to establish that the 99th domino caused the 100th to fall. In this regard, process tracing is quite different from the "manipulation account" of causal inference, in which the value of one variable is manipulated in a controlled experiment to provide a basis for causal inference. Process tracing is useful primarily in nonexperimental studies of historical cases, where controlled experiments are impossible. It can still be useful even in experimental settings, however, as a check on possible sources of error or failure to fully control all of the differences between two trials of an experiment. It can also be useful as a supplement to statistical studies of nonexperimental data by providing a check on possibly spurious interferences and giving evidence on causal direction, or helping to discern which of two correlated variables appears to be causing the other by temporally preceding it. By combining deductive inquiry—what should I expect to see in the detailed processes in a case if a theory is true?—and inductive inquiry—how might I explain the unanticipated sequences or processes that I find in the case?—process tracing is a powerful source of inference. The inductively derived insights that arise in a case can be distinguished from mere storytelling if they can be explained by extant theories or if they lead to additional novel predictions about the processes in the case or in other cases that are then empirically verified.

To take one example from the medical sciences, scientists have been confident for many years on the basis of statistical analysis of nonexperimental data in humans and experimental data in animal studies that smoking cigarettes increases the likelihood of contracting lung cancer. But this data did not provide much insight into the microlevel causal mechanisms that linked the act of smoking to the outcome of cancer. Nor did it offer explanations of individual cases of lung cancer, as nonsmokers can contract lung cancer as well. Only recently has an improved understanding of cellular-level mechanisms begun to fill in the missing linkages between smoking and cancer. This knowledge has been fostered by pathology studies of individual cases of both human and animal subjects, analogous to process tracing, and of how healthy and cancerous cells and organs changed over time. This improved understanding may eventually improve our ability to predict which individuals are most likely to contract cancer if they smoke, who may be at low risk of cancer despite smoking, and who may be at high risk of cancer despite not smoking. An individual who defied the odds in either direction would be a prime candidate for closer pathology studies (process tracing) that might lead to new insights about the underlying mechanisms.

Historical Explanation of Cases

Conversely, not only can we use a case study to explore causal mechanisms, we can use causal mechanisms to give historical explanations of cases. Historical explanation is quite different from the development and testing of variable-centered theories based on the statistical study of a large number of cases. In historical explanation, the researcher uses theories at each step of a historical process to show how the variables made subsequent steps and the ultimate outcome likely under the historical circumstances of the case (Roberts 1996). This is quite different from establishing statistical generalizations. As statistical researchers readily acknowledge, correlation does not imply causality, and a statistically significant correlation does not necessarily "explain" any or all of the cases upon which it is based. It is not enough to know, for example, that an individual fitting specified relationships to a murder victim is more likely than most to have committed the murder. The prosecutor needs to establish empirically that means, motive, and opportunity existed in this particular case. Ideally, they need a complete and uninterrupted chain of evidence, using forensic, psychological, and other theories to bolster each point in the chain, establishing how the crime was likely have been done by the accused, together with evidence and theoretical explanations that help rule out other likely suspects. Process tracing allows this kind of analysis in individual cases.

Process tracing is thus similar in some respects to standard techniques of writing diplomatic or political history, and there has been an active and growing dialogue between case study researchers and historians.[19] Historians often use theories implicitly to explain rather than merely describe events, and they frequently generalize, though usually only to limited domains of time and space. Yet the purposes, methods, and writings of historians and political scientists remain quite different. As Jack Levy argues, historians seek to understand single unique events, the *milieu et moment,* while political scientists aim to generalize about classes of events; historians tend to favor complex explanations, while political scientists aim for elegant and parsimonious explanations. Historians construct narrative-based explanations; political scientists construct theory-based explanations. Political scientists are explicit about their theoretical assumptions and causal argument; historians are more implicit.[20]

Levy notes that these distinctions are best understood as lying on a continuum, and case study methods are closer to the writing of history than are other political science methods. Yet the difference remains that case study researchers in political science are interested in the theory-based explanation of individual cases for the purposes of generalizing to other cases, while for historians the explanation of individual cases is a primary goal in itself.

Addressing Complex Causal Relations

A final advantage of case studies is their ability to accommodate complex causal relations such as equifinality, complex interactions effects, and path dependency (Ragin 1987).[21] If equifinality holds and there are several paths or combinations that can lead to the same outcome, a typological theory can provide contingent generalizations on each path or combination, and case studies can examine the processes of each. Similarly, by treating cases as configurations of variables, rather than seeking partial correlations among specified variables, case studies can capture complex interactions effects and model path-dependent relationships. The ability to address complexity comes at a price, however, as the more contingent and fine-grained a typological theory, the less parsimonious it becomes and the fewer the cases to which it applies.

Limitations and Trade-offs in the Use of Case Studies

Case Selection Biases and Confirmation Biases

One of the most common critiques of case study methods is that they are prone to "selection bias" (Achen and Snidal 1989; Geddes 1990). Selection bias, in statistical terminology, occurs "when some form of selection process in either the design of the study or the real-world phenomena under investigation results in inferences that suffer from systematic error" (Collier and Mahoney 1996, 59). Such biases can occur when the researcher selects cases that represent a truncated sample along the dependent variable of the relevant universe of cases (Collier and Mahoney 1996, 60; King, Keohane, and Verba 1994, 128–32). In statistical research, the standard presentation of selection bias suggests that a truncated sample typically understates the strength of the relationship between the independent and dependent variables. In other words, it reduces the magnitude of the estimated beta coefficients; Huth and Allee note that in some instances selection biases can also reverse the sign of the coefficients in statistical studies (see chap. 9, this vol.). This is why statistical researchers are recurrently admonished not to select cases on the dependent variable (Collier and Mahoney 1996, 60).

Practitioners and analysts of case study methods, however, have argued that cases selected on the dependent variable can test whether a variable is necessary for the selected outcome (Dion 1997; Collier 1995; Goertz and Starr 2003, 30). If a variable hypothesized to be necessary for a specified outcome can be shown to have been absent in even a single case in which the outcome occurred, then this case can disprove the claim that the variable is a necessary condition for the outcome. In addition, in the early stages of a research program, selection on the dependent variable can serve the heuristic purpose of identifying the potential causal paths and variables leading to that dependent variable. Later, when this first stage of research has clarified the causal model, this model can be tested against cases in which there is variation on the dependent variable.[22] Of course, ideally, researchers would have the functional equivalent of a controlled experiment, with controlled variation in independent variables and resulting variation in dependent variables. However, the requisite cases for such research designs seldom exist.[23]

Statistical views of the problem of selection bias also understate the most severe and the most common kinds of selection biases in qualitative research. The potential case study selection bias with the most damaging consequences arises from a form of confirmation bias: selecting only those cases whose independent *and* dependent variables vary as the favored hypothesis suggests and ignoring cases that appear to contradict the theory. This type of selection bias can occur even when the traditional warnings against selection bias have not been violated; that is, even when there is variation on both independent and dependent variables, and even when this variation covers the full range of values that these variables can assume. Rather than understating the relationship between independent and dependent variables, this selection bias can understate or overstate the relationship, and it is particularly misleading when the results are overgeneralized to wider populations (Collier and Mahoney 1996, 71–72). Thus, researchers need to be extremely careful in generalizing results from case study designs that include only "present-present" and "absent-absent" cases; that is, they should look hard for similar cases in which the independent variable of interest is present but the predicted effect is absent and for those in which the independent variable is absent but the dependent variable is present.

While this is the most dangerous kind of selection bias, it is also usually easy to identify and avoid. Several other potential biases are more common in case study selection. These include selection of cases based on extreme values of the variables, on the availability of evidence, or on cases' "intrinsic" historical importance. Each of these criteria for case selection has value for some research goals. Looking at cases with extreme values on the variables, for example, can allow studying particular causal mechanisms in especially stark or obvious forms (Van Evera 1997, 42–49). However, there is also a risk in emphasizing these criteria to the exclusion of other standards. Selection of cases based on extreme values may lead to overgeneralization if researchers are not vigilant in reminding others (and themselves) that they are working on an extremely truncated sample (Collier and Mahoney 1996, 71). Selection of historically "important" or easily researched cases is less useful for theory building than the selection of cases that are likely to be the most theoretically informative such as deviant, most likely, or most similar cases.[24]

In addition to contributing to case selection biases, confirmation biases can affect the selection and interpretation of evidence within cases. This can lead to competing or contradictory interpretations by different researchers studying the same case. It is important to guard against this problem by explicitly considering a wide range of alternative explanations for a case and doing systematic process-tracing on these alternatives. Also, whenever researchers modify a historical explanation to better fit a case, they should endeavor wherever possible to find some novel facts that the new explanation also fits and to place more confidence in modifications that do lead to new and empirically verified facts.[25]

Potential Indeterminacy

Particular case studies may suffer from indeterminacy, or an inability to exclude all but one explanation of a case on the basis of the available process-tracing evidence from that case (Njolstad 1990). When this occurs, it may still be possible to narrow the number of plausible explanations, and it is also important to indicate as clearly as possible the extent to which the remaining hypotheses appear to be complementary, competing, or incommensurate in explaining the case.

One version of the problem of indeterminacy has been widely misapplied to case study methods. This is the "degrees of freedom" problem, which is one kind of indeterminacy that can afflict statistical studies. The degrees of freedom problem arises in statistical work when there are more independent variables than cases, so that it becomes impossible to find coefficient estimates for the variables. Thus, when a researcher has many independent variables but only one or a few observations on the dependent variable, the research design is indeterminate. Some analysts have thus suggested that case studies inherently suffer from a degrees of freedom problem since they have many variables and few "cases" (Achen and Snidal

1989, 156–57). An important misinterpretation arises on this issue, however, from using definitions of *case, variable,* and *observation* that are excessively narrow. Earlier I criticized the definition of a case as a phenomenon in which we report only one measure on any pertinent variable. It is this misguided definition, plus inattention to the potential for process tracing, that leads to the conclusion that case studies suffer from an inherent degrees of freedom problem. In fact, as noted previously, an entity may have many different dimensions or contrast classes rather than providing a "single observation." An apple, for example, has a certain color, texture, sugar content, flavor, and so on; we might aggregate these into a single index defining a "good" apple, but this is different from capturing the many distinct qualities of the apple. In addition, within a single case there are many possible process-tracing observations along the hypothesized causal paths between independent and dependent variables. A causal path may include many necessary steps, and they may have to occur in a particular order. Defining and observing the steps along the hypothesized causal path can lead to "a plethora of new observable implications for a theory" and circumvent the degrees of freedom problem (King, Keohane, and Verba 1994, 119–20; Campbell 1975). There is still the possibility, noted earlier, that a particular case study will be indeterminate in discerning which of several competing hypotheses apply. This is more appropriately described as an indeterminacy problem rather than a degrees of freedom problem, however, as it is more a matter of how the evidence in a particular case matches up with competing hypotheses than a mechanical issue of the number of cases and the number of variables.

Lack of Representativeness

Statistical methods require a large sample of cases that is representative of and allows inferences about an even wider population of cases. To get a representative sample, such studies often rely on random selection of cases. While useful and necessary in statistical studies, these requirements and practices are inappropriate and counterproductive when extended to case study methods (King, Keohane, and Verba 1994, 124–27).

Case study researchers do not aspire to select cases that are "representative" of large and diverse populations, and they ordinarily cannot make claims that their findings are applicable to such populations, with the partial exception of case studies that show that a theory failed to explain its most likely case or that disprove purported necessary or sufficient conditions (McKeown 1999). Case study researchers are usually more interested in finding out the conditions under which specified outcomes occur and the mechanisms through which they occur than the frequency with which those conditions and their outcomes arise (George and Bennett 2004). Researchers often select cases with the goal of providing the strongest possible inferences on particular theories or of using deviant cases to help identify left-out variables. In either research design, the cases selected are intentionally and necessarily unrepresentative of wider populations, and researchers must be careful to point out that they seek only contingent generalizations that apply to cases that are similar to those under study (George and Smoke 1989; George and Bennett 2004). To the extent that there is a "representativeness" problem, it is more accurately presented as a problem of overgeneralization that arises if case study researchers or their readers extend research findings to types of cases unlike those actually studied.[26]

In this regard, case studies involve a trade-off between generalizability and specificity. Rich generalizations in the social sciences often apply only to small and well-defined populations or subtypes, whereas theories that apply to broader populations are usually not very specific. In part, choices between rich but narrow generalizations and less specific but broadly applicable generalizations depend on aesthetic decisions about the kind of theory one prefers and pragmatic considerations such as whether the theory is to focus on "manipulable variables" that policymakers can change to affect outcomes. Choices between broad or deep theorizing can also reflect theoretical assumptions about the complexity of the world. If the researcher believes that similar causal relations hold for large populations and that there are limited interactions effects, then broad theories may prove fruitful, and they may even be fairly rich as well. If multiple interactions effects are present, on the other hand, then only highly contingent theorizing for small and well-defined subpopulations may be possible.[27]

Potential Lack of Independence of Cases

Another issue concerns whether cases are independent of one another. Here again, there is a particular statistical version of this problem that does not apply to case studies, and a more fundamental version that does. In a statistical study, if a correlation is the result not of the hypothesized relationship under consideration but of learning or diffusion from one case to the others, then the additional cases do not provide as much new information as if they were fully independent of one another, so in effect the sample size is smaller than if the cases were independent (George 1982, 19–23; King, Keohane, and Verba 1994, 222; and see Huth and Allee, chap. 9, this vol., for a related discussion of this issue in the context of statistical methods). This is sometimes referred to as Galton's problem. In case studies, there is a danger that the researcher will fail to identify a lack of independence between cases, but this danger does not manifest itself as a problem related to the sample size or number of cases studied, and it is not necessarily amplified by the intentional selection of cases based on a preliminary knowledge of their variables (indeed, such intentional selection may be designed specifically to assess the independence of cases or the diffusion processes among them). As Alexander George has argued, the question of whether the independence of cases is a relevant consideration is not a question that can be answered "on a priori grounds; the answer surely depends on the research objectives of a particular study, what theory or hypothesis is being developed, and how the comparison of cases is structured" (1982, 21). As George notes, process tracing can inductively uncover linkages between cases and reduce the dangers of any unanticipated lack of independence of cases. When learning or diffusion processes are anticipated or uncovered and taken into account, they need not undercut the value of studying partially dependent cases. Indeed, only cases that are perfectly dependent provide no additional information (King, Keohane, and Verba 1994, 222). Moreover, as George points out, case study methods can be particularly effective at examining precisely the kinds of path-dependent learning and diffusion processes that give rise to Galton's problem (George 1982, 21).

Other limitations of case study methods require only brief mention. Case studies are better at determining the scope conditions under which variables have an effect than estimating the magnitude of that effect. This latter task of assessing the causal "weight" or causal effect of variables is better performed through statistical studies. Case study researchers also face a trade-off between doing richly detailed studies of a small number of cases versus seeking broader generalizations across a larger number of cases. Often the best approach is for each researcher to focus in detail on a small but well-defined subset of cases or types of cases, while making comparisons to existing research in the same research program so that the field as a whole incrementally fills out the typological space.

In sum, critiques of case study methods through the prism of statistical concepts have often misconstrued the strengths and weaknesses of case studies. On the issues of degrees of freedom, "representativeness," independence of cases, and the use of Mill's methods, case studies are generally stronger than their critics have suggested. On the question of case selection and selection bias, standard statistical critiques have overstated some methodological problems but understated others. The two most constraining limits of case study methods are the problem of getting a range of cases for study that covers many of the possible causal paths or types and the problem of interpreting outcomes and processes that are consistent with more than one theory. Both of these problems have received less attention because they do not fit as readily into statistical terms (for exceptions see Little 1998; Ragin 1987; Lieberson 1992; Njolstad 1990).

Comparative Strengths and Limitations of Formal Models and Statistical Methods

To underscore the essential complementarity of the leading methods in political science, it is useful to review briefly the comparative advantages of formal models and statistical methods. The comparative advantages of formal models center on their rigorous deductive logic. Deductive logic can be useful in elucidating the dynamics of causal mechanisms, and it can lead to counterintuitive hypotheses that can then be tested. Well-known examples include the literatures on collective action dilemmas, principal-agent relations, problems of credible commitment, two-level games, gatekeeping, veto points, and tipping points. Limitations of formal models include presence of multiple equilibria, the potential for path dependencies, and the possibility of self-denying prophecies (that is, understanding of the model itself can lead to changes in behavior, though this problem is not unique to formal models). Of course, formal modeling is not an empirical method and must be linked to either case studies or statistical studies to provide empirical tests.[28]

The primary advantages of statistical methods include their ability to estimate the average explanatory effects of variables, their ability to analyze the representativeness or frequency of subsets of the data collected, their visual display, and the high degree of replicability of studies using the same database. Limitations of standard statistical methods include the challenges they face in identifying new variables, dealing with multiple conjunctural causality or equifinality, devising conceptually valid operationalizations of qualitative variables, and providing or testing historical explanations of individual cases. Some of these limitations may be inherent in statistical methods, while others may involve trade-offs that could ease somewhat with the development of more sophisticated statistical techniques. Notably, these advantages and limitations are almost precisely the converse of ones associated with case study methods, which are poor at partial correlations and measures of frequency but good at identifying new variables, dealing with complex causal relations, and devising and testing historical explanations.

The Outlook for Increased Multimethod Collaborative Research

As the editors to this volume conclude, the increasingly evident complementary relationship between case studies, statistical methods, and formal modeling has begun to lead toward more multimethod and collaborative research. Because case studies, statistical methods, and formal modeling are all increasingly sophisticated, however, it is difficult for a single researcher to be adept at more than one set of methods while also attaining a cutting-edge theoretical and empirical knowledge of his or her own field. As a result, much multimethod work is collaborative. Encouraging such cooperative efforts will require that political science departments do not discriminate against multiauthored works in their hiring and promotion decisions, as they currently often do. This will raise the problem of evaluating the work of individual contributors to multiauthored works, but in many other fields (particularly the medical and physical sciences) multiauthored works are common. One means of apportioning credit for such works, which is often done in books but could be extended to articles, is to provide a brief footnote that outlines which parts of a work were done primarily by one author or another and which were fully collaborative.

Collaboration can also take place sequentially if researchers work to build on findings generated by those using different methods. For example, statistical analysis might identify outliers or deviant cases, and case studies can investigate why these cases are deviant (Ness 1985). Case studies can also look at the "average" or "representative" cases identified in statistical studies to test and refine the hypothesized causal mechanisms behind the correlations or patterns observed and provide a check on whether a correlation is spurious and on potential endogeneity. Statistical studies, in turn, can assess the general applicability of causal mechanisms uncovered by case studies, and statistical studies might identify strong patterns that can be used to structure the study of individual cases. Similarly, proposed formal models can be tested in case studies to see if their hypothesized causal mechanisms were in fact in operation. This eschews the "as if" assumption made by some formal modelers, namely, the argument that actors did not need to actually go through the posited decision process as long as the model correctly predicts outcomes "as if" actors went through the hypothesized processes. Such "as if" assumptions are inconsistent with causal explanations that refer to causal mechanisms, as these explanations are open to challenge if they can be shown to be inconsistent with processes observed at a lower level of analysis or in finer detail.[29] Case studies can also inductively identify variables and theories that can then be formalized in models.

Both kinds of collaboration require that even as they become expert in one methodological approach, scholars must also become aware of the strengths and limits of other methods and capable of an informed reading of their substantive results. If proficiency in the cutting-edge techniques of all three methods is an unrealistic goal for most mortals, an achievable goal would be proficiency as a producer in one method and an informed reader capable of using and critiquing research using the other two methods. This requires that graduate curricula offer sequences of courses leading up to the highest levels of current professional practice in all three methods and that departments require a reading proficiency in all three methods.[30]

Conclusions

At a high level of generality, the successors of the positivist tradition who employ case study methods, statistical methods, and formal models share an epistemological logic of inference. They all agree on the importance of testing theories empirically, generating an inclusive list of alternative explanations and their observable implications, and specifying what evidence might infirm or affirm a theory. On the methodological level, however, what is useful or necessary for one method, such as random selection of cases in a statistical study, may be unnecessary or even counterproductive in another, such as case studies. This creates an obligation for researchers to learn how to translate between the various methods and to understand their respective strengths and limitations. More important, it creates an opportunity that has not yet been fully or efficiently realized. The comparative advantages of the respective methods are profoundly different, but this allows the strengths of one method to compensate for the weaknesses of another.

Recommended Readings

Brady, H., and D. Collier. 2003. *Rethinking Social Inquiry: Diverse Tools, Shared Standards.* Berkeley, CA: Berkeley Institute of Governmental Studies Press; and Latham, MD: Rowman and Littlefield.

George, A. L., and A. Bennett. 2004. *Case Studies and Theory Development.* Cambridge: MIT Press.

Little, D. 1998. *Microfoundations, Method, and Causation: On the Philosophy of the Social Sciences.* New Brunswick, NJ: Transaction.

Mahoney, J., and D. Rueschemeyer, eds. 2003. *Comparative Historical Analysis in the Social Sciences.* Cambridge: Cambridge University Press.

Ragin, C. 2000. *Fuzzy Set Social Science.* Chicago: University of Chicago Press.

Van Evera, S. 1997. *Guide to Methods for Students of Political Science.* Ithaca: Cornell University Press.

Notes

1. In statistical terms, this problem of "too many variables, too few observations" is known as the "degrees of freedom problem."

2. For further discussion of the issues of defining "what is this event a case of?" and "given this phenomenon, is this event a case of it?" see Ragin and Becker (1992).

3. Strictly speaking, congruence testing may involve explicit or implicit comparisons to other cases, and counterfactual analysis involves comparison to a hypothetical case, so process tracing is the only method that is purely within-case.

4. This is also a standard practice in the physical sciences. For example, we might use plant records to develop a theory that a large meteorite caused a case of mass dinosaur extinction, and then test this theory against other geological evidence on the possible impact of a large meteor at the time in question (King, Keohane, and Verba 1994). Similarly, we might develop a historical explanation of a

political process from available evidence in a case and then predict what evidence we should find from archives once they are opened (Wohlforth 1998).

5. Bennett (1999). I choose my own work in part because it is difficult to evaluate fully the research design decisions made by others on substantive issues in which one is not an expert.

6. The book's chapter on learning theory includes a typological theory on the different paths that learning can take depending on such factors as the strength of the state and of civil society (Bennett 1999, 108–12).

7. For excellent advice on carrying out these kinds of field research, see Thies (2002) and Murphy (1980).

8. Rogowski (1995) gives several examples, including Lijphart (1975).

9. For a similar view, see Van Evera (1997). In practice, few cases pose such clearly decisive tests, but it is still important for researchers to indicate the severity of the test a case poses for a theory.

10. Eckstein also suggests that a "plausibility probe" might be undertaken to give a preliminary estimate of a theory's explanation of a case before a more intensive and costly study is undertaken. This should not be misinterpreted, however, as a means of "lowering the bar" for a new hypothesis; rather, it is an opportunity to judge if further study is warranted and to adapt the theoretical framework for a more systematic test against additional evidence from within the case.

11. Another of Mill's methods, "concomitant variation," relies upon observed covariations in the strength of variables. In Mill's example of this method, one might observe the covariation between the level of the tides and the phases of the moon and assume that there is some causal connection. Concomitant variation is thus related to the statistical logic of partial correlations, and, like Mill's other methods, it is vulnerable to spurious inferences unless restrictive conditions are satisfied.

12. A more flexible variant of Mill's methods is Charles Ragin's method of qualitative comparative analysis (QCA) (1987). This method relies on Boolean algebra to make pairwise comparisons of cases, or types of cases, and relaxes some of the assumptions necessary for the direct use of Mill's methods. QCA allows for the possibility of equifinality, a key advance over Mill's methods, but QCA still requires sufficiency at the level of conjunctions of variables to reach definitive results, and it requires the inclusion of all causally relevant variables to prevent spurious inferences. In addition, the results of QCA are unstable in that adding a single new case or changing the coding of one variable can radically change the results of the analysis (Goldthorpe 1997, 20 nn. 8, 9). For these reasons, Ragin warns against the "mechanical" use of QCA for causal inference (1987, 98), and his later work on fuzzy logic is in some sense an effort to relax the requirements of QCA. In short, with QCA, as with Mill's methods, it is necessary to supplement case comparisons with process tracing of cases in order to relax the restrictive and

unrealistic assumptions necessary for definitive results from comparisons alone (Rueschemeyer and Stephens 1997, 60–61).

13. For an example of using process tracing to rule out residual differences between cases as being causal, see James Lee Ray (1995), *Democracies and International Conflict,* 158–200.

14. King, Keohane, and Verba (1994, 59 n. 12) suggest that most statisticians use deterministic working assumptions in this regard.

15. Similarly, Paul Huth and Todd Allee (chap. 9, this vol.) note the trade-off between careful measurement of variables in a small number of cases versus less precise measurement over a large number of cases. Ronald Mitchell and Thomas Bernauer (chap. 4, this vol.) addresses the closely related issue of internal validity, or the ability to discern that an observed correlation between variables in a case is in fact causal (in part by achieving high construct validity, reducing measurement error, and excluding alternative explanations). They note that "internal validity is a precondition for external validity" and argue that case studies can achieve high internal validity through process tracing. They also concur, however, that selecting cases to control for certain variables limits the range of cases to which one can generalize, except to the extent that the results of "hard cases" or tough tests, such as the failure of a theory to fit its most likely case or the ability of a theory to explain even a least likely case, can be generalized.

16. Questionnaires with open-ended questions may also turn up new variables, and scholars critiquing a piece of statistical research may suggest possible omitted variables as well. There are thus some means of identifying omitted variables in statistical research, though they are quite limited in studies that use only preexisting databases.

17. On this and other definitions of causal mechanisms, see James Mahoney (2001).

18. On Hume and sources of causal inference, see Marini and Singer (1988).

19. Elman and Elman (2001).

20. Jack Levy (2001, 40).

21. This advantage may be relative rather than absolute. Statistical methods can model several kinds of interactions effects, although they can do so only at the cost of requiring a larger sample size, and models of nonlinear interactions rapidly become complex and difficult to interpret. It is possible that new statistical methods may be able to improve upon the statistical treatment of equifinality and interactions effects, and at least narrow the gap in the treatment of this issue. (Braumoeller 2002)

22. Case study researchers in many instances should make comparisons between the subset of cases or types studied and the larger population, where there is more variance on the dependent variable (Collier and Mahoney 1996, 63). Some-

times, such comparisons can be made to existing case studies in the literature, or the researcher might include "mini" case studies, or less in-depth studies, of a wide number of cases in addition to full studies of the cases of greatest interest. To say that such comparisons are often useful for many research goals, however, is very different from arguing that they are always necessary for all research goals.

23. A related issue is whether foreknowledge of the values of variables in cases, and perhaps researchers' cognitive biases in favor of particular hypotheses, necessarily slant the selection of case studies. However, selection with some preliminary knowledge of cases allows much stronger research designs, as cases can be selected with a view toward whether they are most likely, least likely, or crucial. Selecting cases in this way can strengthen, rather than undermine, the severity of the process-tracing test of a theory. Also, within-case analysis often leads to the finding that the researcher's (or the literature's) preliminary knowledge of the values of the independent and dependent variables was incomplete or simply wrong, and case study researchers sometimes conclude that none of the proposed theories is an adequate explanation of a case (Campbell 1975). In addition, intentional selection of cases can benefit from knowledge of the findings of existing studies, and it can be guided by estimations of whether the theories of interest are strong and previously tested or new and relatively weak (Laitin 1995, 456).

24. Van Evera in fact offers many criteria for selecting the most theoretically informative cases, including cases with large within-case variance, cases about which competing theories make opposite and unique predictions, cases that are well-matched for controlled comparisons, outlier cases, and cases whose results can be replicated. These criteria present fewer complications than those of extreme values, data availability, and intrinsic importance.

25. This is the methodological standard emphasized by Lakatos (1970).

26. In some instances, critiques of particular case studies have overstated the problems of representativeness and selection bias by assuming that these studies have purported to offer generalizations that cover broad populations, whereas in fact these studies carefully circumscribed their claims to apply them only to cases similar in well-specified respects to those studied. Collier and Mahoney (1996, 80–87) make this critique of Barbara Geddes's (1990) review of case studies and selection bias.

27. This is similar to the question of whether the "unit homogeneity" assumption is theorized to be applicable to a large and diverse population or only to small and well-defined populations with regard to the processes under study. Two units are defined as homogenous whenever "the expected values of the dependent variables from each unit are the same when our explanatory variable takes on a particular value" (King, Keohane, and Verba 1994, 91).

28. Additional strengths and limitations attend to that subset of formal mod-

els that focus on rational choice theories. There is a tendency in the literature to conflate formal and rational choice models, but it is possible to have formal models based on cognitive processes other than rational ones, such as prospect theory.

29. See, for example, Bates, Greif, Levi, Rosenthal, and Weingast (1998).

30. A reading proficiency does not require equal numbers of courses in each method; one course each in case study methods and formal modeling might be sufficient, while several courses in statistics may be necessary. According to a survey of graduate curricula that I have undertaken, however, many top departments require one or more courses in statistics, but courses in qualitative methods and formal modeling are seldom required and sometimes not even offered (Bennett, Barth, and Rutherford 2003). In part to address this imbalance, the interuniversity Consortium on Qualitative Research Methods now sponsors a two-week training institute in these methods at Arizona State University, analogous to the University of Michigan's summer institute in statistical methods (see http://www.asu.edu/clas/polisci/cqrm/), 2003.

References

Achen, C., and D. Snidal. 1989. Rational Deterrence Theory and Comparative Case Studies. *World Politics* 41 (2): 143–69.

Bates, R., A. Greif, M. Levi, J. Rosenthal, and B. Weingast. 1998. *Analytic Narratives*. Princeton: Princeton University Press.

Bennett, A. 1999. *Condemned to Repetition? The Rise, Fall, and Reprise of Soviet-Russian Military Interventionism, 1973–1996*. Boston: MIT Press.

Bennett, A., A. Barth, and K. Rutherford. 2003. Do We Preach What We Practice? A Survey of Methods in Political Science Journals and Curricula. PS: *Political Science and Politics* 36 (3): 373–78.

Braumoeller, B. F. 2003. Causal Complexity and the Study of Politics. *Political Analysis* 11 (3): 209–33.

Campbell, D. T. 1975. "Degrees of Freedom" and the Case Study. *Comparative Political Studies* 8 (2): 178–94.

Collier, D. 1993. *The Comparative Method. in Political Science: The State of the Discipline II*. Edited by A. W. Finifter. Washington, DC: APSA.

———. 1995. Translating Quantitative Methods for Qualitative Researchers: The Case of Selection Bias. *American Political Science Review* 89:461–66.

———. 1998. Comparative Method in the 1990s. APSA-CP Newsletter 9 (1).

Collier, D., and J. Mahoney. 1996. Insights and Pitfalls: Selection Bias in Qualitative Research. *World Politics* 49 (1): 56–91.

Dion, D. 2003. Evidence and Inference in the Comparative Case Study. In *Neces-*

sary Conditions: Theory, Methodology, and Applications, edited by G. Goertz and H. Starr, 95–112. Boulder: Rowman and Littlefield.

Eckstein, H. 1975. Case Study and Theory in Political Science. In *Handbook of Political Science,* vol. 7, *Strategies of Inquiry,* edited by F. Greenstein and N. Polsby. Reading, MA: Addison-Wesley Press.

Elman, C., and M. F. Elman, eds. 2001. *Bridges and Boundaries: Historians, Political Scientists, and the Study of International Relations.* Cambridge: MIT Press.

Fearon, J. D. 1991. Counterfactuals and Hypothesis Testing in Political Science. *World Politics* 43 (2): 169–95.

Geddes, B. 1990. How the Cases You Choose Affect the Answers You Get: Selection Bias in Comparative Politics. *Political Analysis* 2:31–50.

George, A. L. 1979a. Case Studies and Theory Development: The Method of Structured, Focused Comparison. In *Diplomacy: New Approaches in History, Theory, and Policy,* edited by P. G. Lauren. New York: Free Press.

———. 1979b. The Causal Nexus between Cognitive Beliefs and Decision-Making Behavior. In *Psychological Models in International Politics,* edited by L. Falkowski. Boulder: Westview.

———. 1982. Case Studies and Theory Development. Manuscript, Stanford University.

George, A. L., and A. Bennett. 2004. *Case Studies and Theory Development.* Cambridge: MIT Press.

George, A. L., and T. J. McKeown. 1985. Case Studies and Theories of Organizational Decision Making. In *Advances in Information Processing in Organizations,* edited by R. Coulam and R. Smith. Greenwich, CT: JAI Press.

George, A. L., and R. Smoke. 1989. Deterrence and Foreign Policy. *World Politics* 41 (2): 170–82.

Goertz, G., and H. Starr, eds. 2003. *Necessary Conditions: Theory, Methodology, and Applications.* Lanham, MD: Rowman and Littlefield.

Goldthorpe, J. 1997. Current Issues in Comparative Macrosociology. *Comparative Social Research* 16:1–26.

King, G., R. O. Keohane, and S. Verba. 1994. *Designing Social Inquiry: Scientific Inference in Qualitative Research.* Princeton: Princeton University Press.

Laitin, D. D. 1995. Disciplining Political Science. *American Political Science Review* 89 (2): 454–56.

Lakatos, I. 1970. Falsification and the Methodology of Research Programmes. In *Criticism and the Growth of Knowledge,* edited by I. Lakatos and A. Musgrave. Cambridge: Cambridge University Press.

Levy, J. S. 2001. Explaining Events and Developing Theories: History, Political Science, and the Analysis of International Relations. In *Bridges and Boundaries,* edited by C. Elman and M. F. Elman. Cambridge: MIT Press.

Lieberson, S. 1992. Small N's and Big Conclusions: An Examination of the Reasoning in Comparative Studies Based on a Small Number of Cases. In *What Is a Case? Exploring the Foundations of Social Inquiry,* edited by C. Ragin and H. Becker. Cambridge: Cambridge University Press.

Lijphart, A. 1971. Comparative Politics and the Comparative Method. *American Political Science Review* 65 (2): 682–93.

———. 1975. *The Politics of Accommodation: Pluralism and Democracy in the Netherlands.* Berkeley: University of California Press.

Little, D. 1998. *Microfoundations, Method, and Causation.* New Brunswick, NJ: Transaction.

Lock, R., and K. Thelen. 1998. Problems of Equivalence in Comparative Politics: Apples and Oranges Again. APSA-CP: 9–15.

Mahoney, J. 1999. Nominal, Ordinal, and Narrative Appraisal in Macro-Causal Analysis. *American Journal of Sociology* (3): 1154–96.

———. 2001. Beyond Correlational Analysis: Recent Innovations in Theory and Method. *Sociological Forum* 16 (3): 575–93.

Marini, M., and B. Singer. 1988. Causality in Social Sciences. In *Sociological Methodology 1988,* edited by C. Clogg. Washington, DC: American Sociological Science Association.

McKeown, T. J. 1999. Case Studies and the Statistical World View. *International Organization* 53 (1): 161–90.

Murphy, J. 1980. *Getting the Facts: A Fieldwork Guide for Evaluators and Policy Analysts.* Santa Monica: Goodyear.

Ness, G. 1985. Managing Not-So-Small Numbers: Between Comparative and Statistical Methods. *International Journal of Comparative Sociology* 26:1–13.

Njolstad, O. 1990. Learning from History? Case Studies and the Limits to Theory-Building. In *Arms Races: Technological and Political Dynamics,* edited by O. Njolstad. Los Angeles: Sage.

Przeworski, A., and H. Teune. 1970. *The Logic of Comparative Social Inquiry.* New York: Wiley.

Ragin, C. 1987. *The Comparative Method: Moving beyond Qualitative and Quantitative Strategies.* Berkeley: University of California Press.

Ragin, C., and H. Becker. 1992. Introduction. In *What Is a Case? Exploring the Foundations of Social Inquiry,* edited by C. Ragin and H. Becker. Cambridge: Cambridge University Press.

Ray, J. L. 1995. *Democracy and International Conflict: An Evaluation of the Democratic Peace Proposition.* Columbia: University of South Carolina Press.

Roberts, C. 1996. *The Logic of Historical Explanation.* University Park: Pennsylvania State University Press.

Rogowski, R. 1995. The Role of Theory and Anomaly in Social-Scientific Inference. *American Political Science Review* 2:467–70.

Rueschemeyer, D., and J. Stephens. 1997. Comparing Historical Sequences: A Powerful Tool for Causal Analysis. *Comparative Social Research* 16:55–72.

Sartori, G. 1970. Concept Misformation in Comparative Politics. *American Political Science Review* 64:1033–53.

Tetlock, P. E., and A. Belkin, eds. 1996. *Counterfactual Thought Experiments in World Politics: Logical, Methodological, and Psychological Perspectives.* Princeton: Princeton University Press.

Thies, C. 2002. A Pragmatic Guide to Qualitative Historical Analysis in the Study of International Relations. *International Studies Perspectives* 3 (4): 351–72.

Van Evera, S. 1997. *Guide to Methods for Students of Political Science.* Ithaca: Cornell University Press.

Wohlforth, W. 1998. Reality Check: Revising Theories of International Politics in Response to the End of the Cold War. *World Politics* 50 (4): 650–80.

3. Case Study Methods in International Political Economy

John S. Odell

Research on the world political economy relies heavily on qualitative methods, but we scholars could generate greater value from many of our case studies. This chapter is addressed to the advanced student and others who wish to learn how case studies can contribute to theory building in international political economy (IPE). It illustrates both single case methods and the comparative method of difference and what they have contributed to this domain of international relations. This chapter supplements the previous one by identifying additional types of case study that could be used outside IPE as well as inside, and it says more about how to conduct some types. It adds perspectives to the assessment of case studies' advantages and disadvantages that chapter 2 began.

Case study methods have dominated the IPE subfield over the past three decades. Case studies have illuminated virtually every subject investigated by international political economists, with examples in imperial expansion (Eyck 1958; Wolff 1974; Rosen and Kurth 1974; Fieldhouse 1973), interdependence and war (Papayoanou 1997; Paris 1997), world depressions (Kindleberger 1973; Gourevitch 1986; Eichengreen 1992), trade wars, policy decisions, and negotiations (Schattschneider 1935; Destler, Fukui, and Sato 1979; Conybeare 1987; Hart, Dymond, and Robertson 1994; Mayer 1998), monetary policies and negotiations (Moggridge 1969; Feis 1966; Kapstein 1989; Goodman 1992; Oatley and Nabors 1998), interest group pressures on economic policies (Kindleberger 1951; Milner and Yoffie 1989; Schamis 1999), efforts to form and change regional and larger international economic regimes and organizations (Gardner 1956; Winham 1986; Milner 1997; Moravcsik 1998 and works cited there), the influence of these organizations on state goals and behavior (Martin 1992; Finnemore 1996), multinational corporations and governments (Moran 1974), regulation, deregulation, and privatization (Vogel 1996; Kessler 1998), globalization and liberalization in developing and postcommunist countries (Shirk 1994; Haggard and Webb 1996; Haggard and Maxfield 1996; Snyder 1999; Burgess 1999), economic sanctions, and environmental cooperation (treated in various chapters in this book).

What counts as a case can be as flexible as the researcher's definition of the subject. By a *case* I mean an instance of a class of events or phenomena of interest to the investigator, such as a decision to devalue a currency, a trade negotiation, or an application of economic sanctions. One could select three cases defined as decisions by three different countries to devalue their currencies. Or three events in the history of a single country could be defined as three cases. Furthermore, within a single case study, however defined, multiple observations of theoretically relevant variables normally can be made. Selecting one case of a phenomenon need not mean making only one theoretically relevant observation.

The terms *qualitative* and *case study* are used by diverse scholars who disagree on epistemological basics. This chapter, like the rest of this book, operates from the foundation of what could be called pragmatic positivism, the mainstream epistemology in U.S. social science. Many other sources introduce qualitative methods practiced by adherents of humanistic and other philosophies of knowledge (for example, Geertz 1973; Denzin and Lincoln 1994; Puchala 1995; Alker 1996 and works cited there).

Single Case Designs

The single case study is actually a family of research designs. The following types are distinct but not mutually exclusive. A particular work can fit more than one category.

The Descriptive Case Study

One common type aims only to document an important event for the possible benefit of later policymakers, scholars, and other citizens. Some are written by participants after the event or by historians (e.g., Feis 1966; Hart, Dymond, and Robertson 1994; Paemen and Bensch 1995). These works make little effort to engage scholarship already published on the general subject and little effort to generalize to other cases. Such works can be influential. They may create memorable analogies that later practitioners use to identify pitfalls to avoid and strategies that work. They may stimulate scholars to think of new analytical ideas, and their evidence may be used in evaluating theories. But the generation of these wider benefits depends largely on others. This chapter will concentrate hereafter on studies conducted at least partly for the purpose of contributing directly to theory building.

The Preliminary Illustration of a Theory

Another common type aims to illustrate a theoretical idea. It puts concrete flesh on the bare bones of an abstract idea in order to help readers see its meaning more clearly and to convince them that the idea is relevant to at least one significant real-world instance. This type of study does not examine alternative interpretations of the case or attempt to judge which are more valuable or appropriate. Keohane (1984) introduces the theory that states form international regimes because a regime can supply information and otherwise reduce the transaction costs of reaching subsequent agreements. Chapter 9 of his study presents the case of the International Energy Agency, formed by the industrial democracies in response to the oil shock of the early 1970s, to illustrate the theory's applicability.

The Disciplined Interpretive Case Study

Many cases are selected for investigation because they are recent or seem intrinsically important. Major events such as wars, the onset of the Great Depression, the creation of the Bretton Woods institutions, and decisions to change domestic economic institutions have probably sent history down a different track from what it otherwise would have followed. Understanding crucial break points is as important as testing any hypothesis that might be valid between them. But a case study need not be limited to reporting the facts or to an intuitive understanding of such a turning point.

The disciplined interpretive case study interprets or explains an event by applying a known theory to the new terrain. The more explicit and systematic the use of theoretical concepts, the more powerful the application.

Although this method may not test a theory, the case study shows that one or more known theories can be extended to account for a new event. This type of research will interest critics as well as defenders of the theories, even those who care little about the particular event. This type of case study cannot fairly be called atheoretical nor its broader contributions nil.[1] As Harry Eckstein notes, "Aiming at the disciplined application of theories to cases forces one to state theories more rigorously than might otherwise be done." (1975, 103).[2] As a result of this conceptual work, the author may often be able to generate new suggestions for improving the theory as well.

An example from IPE concerns the 1971 decision by the United States to suspend the dollar's convertibility into gold and achieve a dollar depreciation in the currency markets (Odell 1982, chap. 4; with apologies for citing my own work). First I explicated five general perspectives for explaining changes in any government's foreign economic policy. None of these perspectives was completely unheard-of, but using them together in a case study forced me to sharpen, refine, and contrast them. I formulated an international market perspective for explaining government actions, as distinct from prescriptions based on pro-market thinking. Another theoretical perspective emphasizing policymakers' subjective beliefs was synthesized from psychology, security studies, and scattered ideas in economic history. I then used the five refined perspectives to construct an interpretation of the 1971 policy change and concluded that the market, power, and ideas perspectives identified the most powerful sources of policy change. The international currency market for the dollar had dropped into deficit; U.S. power relative to other states had slipped; and there had been a striking shift in policy predispositions at the top of the Nixon administration, especially in early 1971.[3]

Most events are consistent with more than one interpretation. One general risk of this method is selective reconstruction of the event to support a favored theory, by underplaying evidence inconsistent with the theory or supporting an alternative. A check against this risk is faithful presentation of one or more of the most powerful alternative theories, combined with interrogation of the evidence to check each. Doing so also makes an interpretive case study disciplined.

Having done this, we all prefer not only to report a list of the important factors but also to say which ones were more important. Assigning weights to different causes rigorously is difficult, however, when observing only a single case. One way to discipline private intuition is to add explicit counterfactual argument (see chap. 2, this vol.).[4] Concretely, conduct a mental experiment. Ask how much difference it would have made to the result if factor C had taken a different value, assuming all else had been the same. Spell out the most plausible chain of reasoning to a conclusion about what would have happened. Increase plausibility by relying on well-established theoretical generalizations if any can be found. Observe other actual cases in which C was different. Bring to bear any other relevant known facts and theories about human behavior. This procedure is analogous to comparing the case with a second observed case; the reference point here is an imagined rather than observed case. Repeat this counterfactual question with other causal factors, one at a time. Then ask whether it is plausible that any one of these changes would have produced a greater effect than changes in the other causes. In some situations many observers may agree that the effects of a change in one particular cause would have swamped those of changes in other causes.

Counterfactual argument is only speculation, but it is common, though often not explicit, throughout scholarship and political debate. When an author says, "a hegemonic power structure in 1945 was necessary to reopen a liberal world economy," the statement must mean that if the power structure had not been hegemonic in 1945—a counterfactual—a liberal world economy would not have reopened. When an author claims, "IMF actions made things worse during the 1997 financial crisis," the implication is that had the IMF acted differently, the results would have been better. A single case study that presents counterfactual thought experiments explicitly and carefully is likely to convince more readers than assertion or private intuition would.

A disciplined interpretive case study can usefully complement formal and statistical research. When a formal model has suggested hypotheses for testing, and even after large-n quantitative tests have provided confirmation, there always remains the question whether the causal mechanism suggested by the theory was actually responsible for connecting the measured cause with the measured effect variable in any case. Other mechanisms are always conceivable. Statistical tests are always qualified by the assumption that no omitted variable would have biased the conclusions. A thorough case study can investigate these questions in detail, checking whether events unfolded according to the proposed model in at least one case, while also checking for rival interpretations and omitted considerations. A rigorous case study that confirms the theory leaves it stronger that it was before.

For example, aggregate data in Lisa Martin's *Coercive Cooperation* (1992) provide strong support for the hypothesis (among others) that cooperation among states to impose economic sanctions will increase dramatically when an international institution calls on them to cooperate. One chapter (among others) adds a case study of economic sanctions imposed against Argentina during the 1982 conflict with Great Britain over the Falkland/Malvinas Islands. After the UK-imposed sanctions, London sought cooperation from allied governments. Martin's interpretation holds that the institutions of the European Community, and linkages between the sanctions issue and EC budget negotiations, were decisive in achieving and maintaining cooperation from increasingly reluctant partners.

The Hypothesis-Generating Case Study

A case study begun for any purpose can become a hypothesis-generating case study as well. One of the most valuable contributions of any method would be the generation of a new hypothesis that turned out to be valid or generated fresh lines of investigation. E. E. Schattschneider's *Politics, Pressures, and the Tariff* (1935), a case study of how the famous 1930 Hawley-Smoot Tariff Act was enacted, proved to be highly influential in later U.S. political economy. For years it was cited as authority for the view that U.S. trade policy results from pressure groups running amok in Washington. Charles Kindleberger (1973) inquired why the Great Depression was so wide, so deep, and so prolonged. The lesson of the interwar experience, Kindleberger concluded, was "that for the world economy to be stabilized, there has to be a stabilizer, one stabilizer" (305). When in 1929 "the British couldn't and the United States wouldn't" supply the public good of leadership, down went the interests of all (292). This case study stimulated other scholars to think of the influential hegemony theory of international economic stability (discussed in this book's chaps. 7 and 11, also on IPE).

The Least-Likely (Theory Confirming) Case Study

Let us shift now to methods that select a single case not for its novelty or intrinsic interest but for its ability to contribute to theory building. It is unlikely that any single case study will be able, alone, to prove or disprove a theory decisively.[5] Probably the closest a single case study can come to approximating a neutral test would be when the researcher selects an extreme case that is highly unlikely to confirm it, and finds that even this case does so. Such a least-likely case study would provide strong support for the inference that the theory is even more likely to be valid in most other cases, where contrary winds do not blow as strongly.

Edward Morse's thesis in *Foreign Policy and Interdependence in Gaullist France* (1973)[6] is that increasing modernization and interdependence transform foreign policy, making it less nationalistic and more cooperative. Observing a breakdown of the distinction between foreign and domestic policy, he directs attention to domestic social structure as the primary determinant of foreign policy. What country case might be least likely to confirm such a thesis? President Charles de Gaulle's famous nationalism stands out among industrial states of his time. De Gaulle defended the primacy of foreign policy over domestic policies and, during the 1960s, attempted to use foreign economic policy to maintain independence from the monetary system led by the United States. During a run on the French franc in November 1968, he proudly declared that the franc would not be devalued. Europe's economy was becoming more closely integrated, however, as governments implemented the Common Market. Domestic student protests of 1968 had accelerated an erosion of the franc's underpinnings. Even de Gaulle's determined effort proved futile. Shortly after President Pompidou succeeded him in 1969, France devalued the franc and accepted the U.S. scheme to create a new form of money in the International Monetary Fund. If even Gaullist France yields to interdependence, is it not likely that many other governments will do the same?

The "plausibility probe" is a weaker form for a like purpose. The researcher conducts a single case study only to check the plausibility of a theory, using a case that may not be especially difficult for the theory. One might even select a case whose circumstances are thought to be favorable to the theory, as a pilot study before undertaking a more extensive evidence gathering effort. If this probe does not confirm the theory's plausibility, resources can be better directed; if it does, a more comprehensive and costly test can be undertaken with greater confidence. If the case chosen is not especially difficult for the theory, however, then it alone will not support as strong a claim.

The Most-Likely (Theory Infirming) Case Study

If a theory were invalid, the most powerful single case to show that would be one that disconfirmed it even though conditions seem to make the case unusually favorable for the theory. If the theory failed even in a most-likely case, this evidence would provide strong support for the expectation that it would fail even more clearly in less hospitable circumstances.

I do not know of a published IPE study that exemplifies this logical type perfectly. As an approximation, consider dependency theory with its thesis that dependency of a less developed country on the world capitalist system retards or even reverses its development. The 1959 Cuban revolution was a sharp break with the world capitalist system, and so the case of Cuba before and after 1959 would seem to be likely, if any would, to support a thesis implying that dependency retards development. Evidence that Cuba did not experience improvement in development terms would be more telling against this theory than evidence from most countries that did not make as clear a break (Cuba experienced some improvements along with many disappointments).[7] Again, even an extreme historical case will be subject to more than one interpretation. Here the dependentista might attribute disappointments to the fact that the United States worked aggressively to undermine revolutionary Cuba after 1960, or to avoidable errors by the Castro government.

This chapter does not cover all types of case study that appear in IPE. The problem-solving case study is designed to help solve a particular problem rather than mainly to contribute to theory. Robert Rothstein's *Global Bargaining* (1979) inquires why the North-South commodity trade negotiations of the 1970s achieved so little and what could be done to improve such negotiations. Richard Haass's *Economic Sanctions and American Diplomacy* (1998) reports eight single case studies of sanctions attempts and draws lessons for future policy. Publications of this type are widespread, and the problem-solving design deserves a set of guidelines of its own.[8] Still other case studies are written for teaching purposes and often deliberately purged of analysis in order to put the burden on the student.

Process tracing in a general sense is involved in writing almost any case study. Virtually all case studies entail documenting some dynamic process—a process of decision, policy change, depression, conflict, negotiation, or the spread of norms. Bennett (chap. 2, this vol.) also refers to process tracing in a narrower sense to mean a possible way to test hypotheses within a single case.

The Method of Difference

Between single case methods on one end of the spectrum and large-n statistical methods on the other stand comparative case methods. They combine the benefits of the case study with the analytical leverage that comes from comparison. J. S. Mill's method of difference proceeds "by comparing instances in which the phenomenon does occur with instances in other respects similar in which it does not" (1970).[9] Some applications begin with a hypothesis linking a cause C with an effect E. Two or more cases are selected to illustrate a difference in C. If the observed cases differed in C and differed as expected in the supposed effect E but were similar in all other relevant respects, then by elimination one could infer that the reason for the E difference must have been the difference in C.

More often, theory is not used to guide case selection. The researcher is interested primarily in E, chooses two or more cases to illustrate variance in E, such as a success and a failure in attempts at economic cooperation, and investigates what antecedents could have produced the difference. This variant, the retrospective contrast, carries the risk that research will uncover a host of differences between the cases, each of which could have explained E. Such a study provides weaker support for any one hypothesis than a design that selected a set of cases that eliminated at least some hypotheses by matching on those conditions.

Actual comparative studies vary by degrees in these matters. When less thought is given to rival interpretations at the design stage and less effort is invested in selecting cases for analytical reasons, the support for the main conclusion is usually weaker. The more thoroughly case selection matches other important variables, the more rigorous and convincing the support for the central hypothesis. As an additional remedy, a subsequent project could select cases so as to hold a rival causal variable D invariant or to focus on D in its own right.[10]

Examples

The Protestant Ethic and the Spirit of Capitalism is an early IPE example of historical comparison with limited attention to controlling for alternative interpretations. Weber observed in 1904 that what he called the peculiar modern rational form of capitalism had developed only in the West, not in India or China (E). He famously contended that the key reason (C) was the presence in the West of Calvinist theology, which, for believers, translated into devotion to work, ascetic personal habits, and accumulating wealth as a moral calling. Weber reported that in Germany, business leaders and skilled workers were overwhelmingly Protestant. He raised but discounted the alternative interpretation that inheritance accounted for Protestant dominance of business. He noted that a smaller proportion of Catholic (than Protestant) college graduates prepared for middle-class business careers, favoring more humanistic education (1958, 35–40). Generally, though, this essay did not deliver what today would be considered thorough controlled comparisons. Weber did not set forth a comprehensive framework identifying alternative causes, nor did he select cases for study so as to match them according to these variables. The essay stimulated a chorus of critics as well as admirers.[11]

Great Britain's first negotiation to join the Common Market (in the early 1960s) failed, while the second (in the late 1960s) succeeded (E). In another retrospective contrast, Robert Lieber (1970) conducts thorough investigations of the processes inside Britain and between Britain and the European Economic Community (EEC) during the two episodes (among other things). He concludes that greater domestic politicization of the British process in the second case turned the decision into a matter of national foreign policy and diluted the earlier influence of agricultural groups on London's negotiating position. In case 1, these groups had elicited pledges from the Macmillan government for conditions to protect agriculture that proved unacceptable to the Six (123, 130). In case 2, greater politicization diminished pressure group influence, and Harold Wilson's negotiators made their application relatively free of restrictive conditions (271). By observing two contrasting cases, Lieber was in a much stronger position to support valid conclusions about the relationship between politicization and pressure group influence, which illuminated the difference between international impasse and agreement, than if he had looked only at one case. Moreover, in this design certain key variables were essentially constant, including the key states and their institutions and many of the issues. No pair of cases ever rules out every conceivable rival interpretation, of course. For instance, Britain's trade was also shifting increasingly away from the former empire and toward the Continent (Cohen 1977).

One hypothesis in my *Negotiating the World Economy* (2000)[12] holds that gains from a threatening, value-claiming bargaining strategy will diminish as domestic divisions undermine the credibility of the government threat. Chapter 6 supports this hypothesis with two contrasting case studies chosen from the second Reagan administration in 1985–86, in both of which the U.S. economic negotiator used a threatening strategy. The cases differ as to cause and as to supposed effect. In the first, U.S. constituents expressed significant opposition to carrying out the threat, and the U.S. negotiator gained less abroad. In the second, few U.S. constituents expressed opposition to implementing the threat, and the U.S. negotiator gained more abroad.

These cases are matched with respect to five other variables thought to be relevant to bargaining outcomes. Since the negotiations occurred during the same period, there was no difference in the relevant international institutions, U.S. domestic political institutions, or the degree to which the U.S. government was divided. The same president was in office and the same negotiator used the same strategy in each. The threatened party was not less powerful in the second case. In fact, the European Community (in the second case) was more powerful than Brazil, yet Washington gained more from the EC. Moreover, in the Brazil case the main causal variable shifted later in the negotiation (U.S. constituents fell into line behind Reagan's hard line), and almost immediately the Brazilian government made its one substantive concession to Washington. Thus at least five rival theoretical challenges to the main inference can be rejected by virtue of matched case selection.[13]

Assessment

Single and comparative case methods have been so popular because they offer several significant advantages relative to statistical methods.[14] This assessment section adds political economy examples as well as several original points to those made in the previous chapter. First, qualitative studies are equal or superior for generating valid new theory. The ultimate goal is valid theory, of course, not just any theory. More comprehensive and more detailed contact with concrete instances of the events and behavior about which we wish to generalize helps sharpen distinctions and stimulates fresh concepts, typologies, and hypotheses. Kindleberger's investigation of the Great Depression is a prominent IPE example. The farther we move from direct observation of the people we wish to understand—for instance, by importing hypotheses from other fields—the greater the risk of generating a theory that turns out to be invalid for this domain.

Second, case methods allow stronger empirical grounding for a hypothesis in the cases observed than statistical methods can provide for the same cases. Case methods provide greater assurance that the hypothesis is valid in those cases. One clear IPE illustration is the study of European economic sanctions against Argentina in connection with the Falklands/Malvinas controversy (Martin 1992). The author first provides formal models and statistical tests based on ninety-nine economic sanction attempts in history. One of the ninety-nine data points is the Falklands case. Martin constructs quantitative indicators for the degree of cooperation among sanctioners and for six possible causal variables. These aggregate data indicate a significant general relationship between cooperation and, among other things, whether an international institution had called on its members to cooperate. While the data provide strong, original support for the generalizations reported, the statistical method by its nature restricts us to observing a limited slice of the Falklands case, and even these aspects only as filtered through standardized indicators. We cannot see any of the facts that had to be omitted. Some risk of omitted variable bias is inherent in statistical methods. Case methods complement them by allowing the researcher to check for additional rival interpretations. By tracing the process chronologically as it unfolded within the EC structure, and by considering previously omitted facts and views as well, the case study leaves us with greater confidence that the hypothesis is valid and salient for the Falklands case. Of course, case methods provide no evidence that the hypothesis is valid in unobserved cases, which is where large-n statistical methods have a relative advantage.

More often IPE case studies are conducted before any aggregate data on the same theoretical relationship have been analyzed. If, in that situation, thorough case studies establish strong empirical support for a hypothesis in a few instances, they give greater confidence that the theory is worth testing over a large number of cases.

Third, one of the most telling attractions of case studies is that they are generally more insightful than the alternatives for empirically studying processes. The world political economy is moved along by means of many significant processes, such as technological innovation, business collusion, market equilibration, electoral competition, the interstate exercise of influence, bargaining, communication, conflict, learning, institutional change, and regional integration and disintegration. Several examples have already been mentioned, such as the process of bringing the United Kingdom into the European Common Market, the process through which the United States changed its international monetary policy in 1971, and the economic conflict and negotiation process between the United States on one side and Brazil and the European Community on the other in 1985 through 1987. No meaningful large-n quantitative data exist for describing many processes—such as technological innovation or negotiation or institutional change—in the sense of measuring a series of events forming a pattern that occurs many times. Those curious about the processes of technological or management innovation in business firms turn to case studies as well.

Structures are certainly important, but given their relative stability, they alone are unable to explain much variation that occurs within the same structures, as IPE literature has shown repeatedly. Moreover, when structures and institutions have changed, case studies have provided our best empirical knowledge of how those changes came about. They have shown, for example, how successive rounds of multilateral trade negotiations gradually changed the institutions of the world's trading system.[15] Each of the studies mentioned does more than describe a process. But of course we must describe them before we can analyze, compare, and generalize about them. While it might be possible theoretically to generate large-n quantitative data on processes of interest to international political economists, few have found ways to do so.

Fourth, a thorough case study naturally preserves and reports more information about that case than a statistical study covering the same case. Fuller reporting makes it more likely that readers will construct alternative interpretations of the same events and generate new hypotheses. Reporting this information also provides researchers with materials that can be used later to construct quantitative indicators.

The method of difference offers two additional advantages relative to single case designs. A well-selected contrast between cases that are similar in several ways creates an interesting puzzle. More important, variation in the cause and the effect, plus the elimination of some competing interpretations by case selection, supplies more rigorous support for a causal hypothesis than most single case studies, or multiple case studies that have not been selected to control for competing interpretations. This method provides more convincing empirical grounding for a causal inference than all except perhaps the least-likely and most-likely single case designs.

Disadvantages

Case methods also entail several inherent disadvantages relative to statistical methods. Chapter 2 identified four possible problems. This section, reflecting slightly different judgments, will identify three general disadvantages plus one that is specific to the comparative method of difference. The first, given that most case studies work with far fewer observations than most statistical studies, is that we do not know how accurately and neutrally the few selected observations represent the set of events the theory refers to. The scholar can define that set widely or narrowly. But even if a theory pertains only to a certain class of events, the claim to have supported a theory implies some effort to generalize beyond the particular observations studied. The least-likely and most-likely designs can help reduce the effects of this problem of representativeness. But even if this remedy succeeds, a larger number of observations from the theoretical population will provide even more convincing tests and support.

Second, qualitative methods are less precise. Because numbers are not assigned to measure the values of variables, case methods cannot measure those variables as precisely or permit as precise a calculation of the magnitude of an effect or the relative importance of multiple causes. This is one of the most obvious advantages of statistics. The sanctions study can illustrate again: if Martin's book had been limited to case studies, she would have been unable to support such precise theoretical claims and tests as the book does report. Her statistical methods compensated for these shortcomings of case studies. Unfortunately, greater precision always comes at a price. The validity of the precise statistical conclusions is compromised to the degree that the variables as measured fall short of reflecting the respective theoretical constructs perfectly, and also to the degree that the analysis has omitted variables that could not be measured. All social scientists face this trade-off, and they lack consensus about which goal should be compromised the most.

This being said, qualitative methods could be deployed with greater precision than is common. Case authors could pin themselves down with operational definitions of key concepts and construct ordinal scales for measuring their variations qualitatively. A process under study could, for instance, be divided conceptually into stages, with each stage concept defined precisely and operationally. Then a description of one case of this process, accomplished by coding that case with these rules, would be more precise and disciplined than is usually found. Such a qualitative study could contribute its method to later studies on different cases. Greater precision would allow more convincing comparisons and contrasts across cases, and it would become easier to look for general patterns and greater accumulation in analysis. As an IPE example, Haggard and Maxfield (1996) investigate why developing countries liberalized their financial systems in recent years. This qualitative analysis of four country case studies is strengthened by use of a twelve-value scale of financial internationalization.

Third, for these reasons, most case methods are at a relative disadvantage when it comes to testing a theory, including (in my view) one that claims to identify a causal mechanism. Specialists disagree somewhat on the value of case methods for testing theories. Their differences may reflect the fact that the idea of rigorous, neutral testing has more than one dimension, and different specialists emphasize different dimensions. One aspect is how many observations the theory has passed, or how representative and unbiased the sample is. A second dimension is how precise the measurement is. The looser a concept's effective meaning, the easier it is to make it fit more cases. And if measurement is not uniform across cases, claims of similarity or contrast across cases are weakened. On these two dimensions, statistical methods have a relative advantage. A third dimension is how many rival interpretations have been eliminated by the analysis. Here the case study is able to explore more alternative interpretations, including what is often called the context, more thoroughly than the statistical study, in the cases studied by each. The case study can also check in more detail for the sequences of events or mechanisms that the theory assumes and connect the cause to the effect, which statistical studies often cannot observe as well. The relative advantage of case methods in this respect mitigates their overall disadvantage for testing.

This reasoning also suggests a way to make a single case study more rigorous as a test of hypothesis C. The disciplined interpretive case study can introduce alternative hypotheses explicitly, stating each independently of the case's facts. The analyst can then compare the expectations of each theory with the facts of the case (if the theories' expectations are precise enough to be checked empirically) and ask whether the case confirms any of them more than any other. A case study that provides such challenges approximates a test more closely than one that does not.

Another technique for mitigating this weakness, not yet seen in IPE studies to my knowledge, is Donald Campbell's multiple implications technique (1975). Campbell suggests improving on the discipline offered by single-site studies by using the key theory to predict other aspects of the case, as many as possible, besides the dependent variable of greatest interest. Ask, "If this theory is valid, what *else* should one expect to see?" Suppose our hypothesis says that opening a developing or postcommunist country to international liquid capital flows will strengthen the political influence within that country of existing holders of liquid assets, making it more likely that they will press for and get their government to open further and resist efforts to close the border again. Campbell would ask, "If that is so, what other changes should result?" Should greater influence by this class also lead to changes in tax regulations in their favor? By thus expanding the "implication space," the scholar gains more data points at which the theory could succeed or fail, all within the single case study. For Campbell, data collection should include keeping a box score of the theory's hits and misses. A theory should be rejected if it does not pass most of these tests. If it does not, the scholar might attempt to formulate and test a better theory in the same way on the same case.

The least-likely and most-likely case studies and the comparative method of difference are other ways to strengthen the inference that can be drawn with respect to hypothesis C. Bennett (chap. 2, this vol.) mentions other techniques for testing theories in a single case study. Yet all case methods are still at an inherent disadvantage on the first two dimensions. Authors of case studies are well advised to be cautious in making the ambitious claim that these methods alone have convincingly "tested" a theory. A slightly more modest claim to have "provided strong support for a causal inference that needs further inquiry" will provoke fewer objections.[16]

The method of difference has special limitations. Because the historical record never provides a set of cases that are perfectly matched on all other relevant variables, this method by itself cannot prove with perfect certainty that no rival factor other than C has any role in producing E. History always seems to allow some factor D that could also have contributed to E in the cases chosen. This method by itself also provides no way to disentangle complex interaction effects among variables.

A few critics have blown up this method's limitations into a wholesale rejection, which seems exaggerated considering that no other method is free of limitations either. Lieberson declares flatly that Mill's methods of agreement and difference "cannot be applied to historical and comparative studies in which the researcher is limited to a small number of cases" (1994, 1225; 1991). George and McKeown (1985), citing Cohen and Nagel (1934), complain that the method is beset by formidable difficulties. Bennett (chap. 2, this vol.) says this method has unrealistic requirements. It says the study must handle every possible causal variable and must find cases that represent every logically possible causal path.

These requirements would be necessary only for an investigator who claimed to prove causality with perfect certainty. Mill was writing in 1843 primarily about the logic of natural science experiments and did think he was describing a method for arriving "with certainty at causes" (1900, 282). Early positivists like Nagel also construed science this way. But during the twentieth century most philosophers of science and scientists, including many in natural science, abandoned this goal as unrealistic. No social science method, including case studies with process tracing or the congruence procedure, can aspire to prove general causality with airtight certainty. Statistical studies rarely include every conceivable causal variable either, and so their findings can be accepted only on the assumption that inclusion of an omitted variable would not change them. Caveats must also be attached to experimental findings. Formal modeling cannot generate any results without strong and sometimes unrealistic assumptions, and the results' empirical significance is unknown until evidence is collected and analyzed by one of these empirical methods. The method of difference in this chapter means a social science approximation to Mill's idea understood through today's mainstream theory of knowledge. This method is as realistic as any other in this book as long as we avoid making excessive claims in its name. In fact its contributions have improved on those of the many published case studies that lack explicit comparison. Future method-of-difference studies could improve on those of the past by adding complementary techniques to offset its limitations. For example, counterfactual analysis might support the argument that C would have led to E in these cases even if D had not been present. Another remedy is to conduct a sequence of such studies concentrating on different causes. Scholars can combine the power of comparison with the advantages of the case study as long as they acknowledge this method's limitations with appropriate caveats.

Conclusion

In the past three decades political science scholars of the world political economy have relied on case study methods more than any other empirical methods, and using them they have made widespread contributions to our understanding. Case studies have generated new theoretical ideas that were later tested and refined, such as the hegemony theory. Likewise, the case of the 1978 Bonn G-7 economic summit stimulated Robert Putnam to devise his influential metaphor of the two-level game (1988). Keohane developed and illustrated his seminal application of transaction cost economics to international cooperation partly by means of a case study of the International Energy Agency. Theories of economic policy rooted in market liberalism and domestic political structures have battled each other on the terrain of case studies (e.g., Katzenstein 1978; Cowhey 1993; Keohane and Milner 1996). Studies in Mexico, Brazil, and Ghana developed and critiqued dependency theory (e.g., Gereffi 1978; Evans 1979; Ahiakpor 1985). Power theorists have used case studies in the GATT and the international communication regimes to defend their claims, including innovations compared with earlier theories (e.g., Grieco 1990; Krasner 1991). Case studies have contributed to our understanding of the effects of changing policy ideas—ideas such as free trade (Kindleberger 1975), exchange rate flexibility (Odell 1982), Keynesianism (Hall 1989), developmentalism (Sikkink 1991), and environmentalism (Haas 1992)—on national and international economic policies. Comparative case methods have deepened our knowledge of relations between domestic politics and the international economic negotiation process (e.g., Evans, Jacobson, and Putnam 1993; Wolf and Zangl 1996). Case comparisons have supported institutional explanations for developing countries' relative success and failure in economic and democratic reforms (Haggard and Webb 1996).

Many other case studies less known for direct theoretical contributions have laid down a base of empirical knowledge of major institutional changes and other processes and have educated subsequent theorists and provided them raw material. These works have documented crucial historical tipping points like the spread of nineteenth-century imperialism (Fieldhouse 1973), the 1925 restoration of the pound sterling to its prewar parity (Moggridge 1969), the enactment of the 1930 U.S. Hawley-Smoot Tariff Act, and creation of the Bretton Woods institutions (Gardner 1956).

No one would argue that we would be better off without the knowledge we have gained from these historical case studies, limited to what could be known through formal models and large-n statistical tests.

Case study methods offer appealing advantages and suffer from significant limitations relative to statistical methods, in IPE just as in other subject areas. The most general implication is familiar but still inescapable, in my opinion. Neither family is sufficient. Claims made on the basis of either alone should always carry appropriate qualifications. Statistics compensate for the shortcomings of case studies, and case studies offset the weaknesses of statistics. Students should be alert to the possibility that many established scholars have committed themselves exclusively to one type of method because they feel more comfortable with its shortcomings than those of the alternatives, rather than because any method is free of imperfections. Aspiring researchers should seek education in both qualitative and quantitative methods. I believe educators should reconsider any required methods course that is biased against either family or else offer an alternative to it. Established analysts should resist the temptation to discriminate against one family as a means of promoting another and should learn from both.

Recommended Readings

Evans, P., H. Jacobson, and Robert Putnam, eds. 1993. *Double-Edged Diplomacy: International Bargaining and Domestic Politics.* Berkeley: University of California Press.

Kindleberger, C. 1973. *The World in Depression, 1929–1939.* Berkeley: University of California Press.

Martin, L. L. 1992. *Coercive Cooperation: Explaining Multilateral Economic Sanctions.* Princeton: Princeton University Press.

Milner, H. V. 1988. *Resisting Protectionism: Global Industries and the Politics of International Trade.* Princeton: Princeton University Press.

Odell, J. S. 2000. *Negotiating the World Economy.* Ithaca: Cornell University Press.

Notes

1. Contrast Lijphart (1971, 692).

2. Verba (1967) calls this method a "disciplined configurative approach." For an alternative meaning of interpretive case studies, see Geertz (1973).

3. Other examples of this method include Spar (1992), Finnemore (1996), and Berejekian (1997).

4. For elaboration see Bennett (chap. 2, this vol.), McClelland (1975), Fearon (1991), and Tetlock and Belkin (1996). The latter warn of dangers of bias in making counterfactual arguments and develop explicit criteria for accepting or rejecting them.

5. This section draws on Lijphart (1971) and Eckstein (1975). The final section of this chapter returns to the question of testing theories with case studies.

6. Morse (1973). This paragraph refers to chapter 5.

7. LeoGrande (1979) finds that Cuba's international economic dependency was lower in the postrevolutionary period than before, but that it remained highly dependent on the USSR in some senses. This study does not investigate other indicators of development.

8. See Maxwell (1996) for some leads.

9. Mill (1970), taken from Mill (1843), book 3, chap. 8, "of the four methods of experimental inquiry." Strictly speaking, Mill was writing primarily about the experimental method in natural sciences like chemistry. Here, *method of difference* means a social science approximation with the same core comparative logic but using case studies.

10. See Odell (2001) for more guidance on how to implement this method.

11. Samuelsson (1957) marshals evidence contradicting the Puritanism thesis. Marshall (1982) faults Weber for not showing direct evidence on leaders' and workers' motives, as distinct from evidence from Calvinist theological writings, and for failing to raise alternative interpretations for evidence about workers.

12. An earlier version was published as Odell (1993).

13. For examples of this method on monetary policies, see McNamara (1998) and Odell (1988).

14. For a fuller statement of my assessment please see Odell (2001).

15. See Winham (1986) on the Tokyo round and Paemen and Bensch (1995) on the Uruguay round. On the ups and downs of the International Coffee Organization, see Bates (1997).

16. Eckstein (1975) defended the argument that single case studies are valuable for testing theories. The "congruence procedure" discussed by George and McKeown (1985) is intended to test a single causal theory using "within-case observations" rather than controlled comparison. Van Evera (1997) and Bennett and George (1997) expand on this idea. This proposal has not, to my knowledge, been followed by many examples in IPE.

References

Ahiakpor, J. C. W. 1985. The Success and Failure of Dependency Theory: The Experience of Ghana. *International Organization* 39:535–53.

Alker, H. R., Jr. 1996. *Rediscoveries and Reformulations: Humanistic Methodologies for International Studies.* Cambridge: Cambridge University Press.

Bates, R. H. 1997. *Open-Economy Politics: The Political Economy of the World Coffee Trade.* Princeton: Princeton University Press.

Bennett, A., and A. L. George. 1997. Developing and Using Typological Theories in Case Study Research. Annual convention of the International Studies Association, Toronto.

Berejekian, J. 1997. The Gains Debate: Framing State Choice. *American Political Science Review* 91:789–805.

Burgess, K. 1999. Loyalty Dilemmas and Market Reform: Party-Union Alliances under Stress in Mexico, Spain, and Venezuela. *World Politics* 52:105–34.

Campbell, D. T. 1975. "Degrees of Freedom" and the Case Study. *Comparative Political Studies* 8 (2): 178–94.

Cohen, B. J. 1977. Great Britain. In *Economic Foreign Policies of Industrial States,* edited by W. F. Kohl. Lexington, MA: D. C. Heath.

Cohen, M. R., and E. Nagel. 1934. *An Introduction to Logic and Scientific Method.* New York: Harcourt, Brace.

Conybeare, J. A. C. 1987. *Trade Wars: The Theory and Practice of International Commercial Rivalry.* New York: Columbia University Press.

Cowhey, P. F. 1993. Domestic Institutions and the Credibility of International Commitments: Japan and the United States. *International Organization* 47:299–326.

Denzin, N. K., and Y. S. Lincoln, eds. 1994. *Handbook of Qualitative Research.* Thousand Oaks, CA: Sage.

Destler, I. M., H. Fukui, and H. Sato. 1979. *The Textile Wrangle: Conflict in Japanese-American Relations, 1969–1971.* Ithaca: Cornell University Press.

Eckstein, H. 1975. Case Study and Theory in Political Science. In *Handbook of Political Science,* vol. 7, *Strategies of Inquiry,* edited by F. Greenstein and N. Polsby. Reading, MA: Addison-Wesley Press.

Eichengreen, B. 1992. *Golden Fetters: The Gold Standard and the Great Depression, 1919–1939.* New York: Oxford University Press.

Evans, P. 1979. *Dependent Development: The Alliance of Multinational, State, and Local Capital in Brazil.* Princeton: Princeton University Press.

Evans, P. B., H. K. Jacobson, and R. D. Putnam, eds. 1993. *Double-Edged Diplomacy: International Bargaining and Domestic Politics.* Berkeley: University of California Press.

Eyck, E. 1958. *Bismarck and the German Empire.* London: Allen and Unwin.

Fearon, J. D. 1991. Counterfactuals and Hypothesis Testing in Political Science. *World Politics* 43 (2): 169–95.

Feis, H. 1966. *1933: Characters in Crisis.* Boston: Little, Brown.

Fieldhouse, D. K. 1973. *Economics and Empire, 1830–1914.* Ithaca: Cornell University Press.

Finnemore, M. 1996. *National Interests in International Society.* Ithaca: Cornell University Press.

Gardner, R. N. 1956. *Sterling-Dollar Diplomacy: Anglo-American Collaboration in the Reconstruction of Multilateral Trade.* Oxford: Clarendon.

Geertz, C. 1973. *The Interpretation of Cultures.* New York: Basic Books.

George, A. L., and T. J. McKeown. 1985. Case Studies and Theories of Organizational Decision Making. In *Advances in Information Processing in Organizations,* edited by R. Coulam and R. Smith. Greenwich, CT: JAI Press.

Gereffi, G. 1978. Drug Firms and Dependency in Mexico: The Case of the Steroid Hormone Industry. *International Organization* 32:237–86.

Goodman, J. B. 1992. *Monetary Sovereignty: The Politics of Central Banking in Western Europe.* Ithaca: Cornell University Press.

Gourevitch, P. 1986. *Politics in Hard Times.* Ithaca: Cornell University Press.

Grieco, J. M. 1990. *Cooperation among Nations: Europe, America, and Non-Tariff Barriers to Trade.* Ithaca: Cornell University Press.

Haas, P. M. 1992. Special Issue: Knowledge, Power, and International Policy Coordination. *International Organization* 46 (1).

Haass, R. N., ed. 1998. *Economic Sanctions and American Diplomacy.* Washington, DC: Brookings Institution Press.

Haggard, S., and S. Maxfield. 1996. The Political Economy of Financial Internationalization in the Developing World. *International Organization* 50:35–68.

Haggard, S., and S. B. Webb. 1996. *Voting for Reform: Democracy, Political Liberalization, and Economic Adjustment.* New York: ICS Press and the World Bank.

Hall, P. A., ed. 1989. *The Political Power of Economic Ideas: Keynesianism across Nations.* Princeton: Princeton University Press.

Hart, M., B. Dymond, and C. Robertson. 1994. *Decision at Midnight: Inside the Canada-US Free-Trade Negotiations.* Vancouver: UBC Press.

Kapstein, E. B. 1989. Resolving the Regulator's Dilemma: International Coordination of Banking Regulation. *International Organization* 43:323–47.

Katzenstein, P., ed. 1978. *Between Power and Plenty.* Madison: University of Wisconsin Press.

Keohane, R. O. 1984. *After Hegemony: Cooperation and Discord in the World Political Economy.* Princeton: Princeton University Press.

Keohane, R. O., and H. V. Milner, eds. 1996. *Internationalization and Domestic Politics.* Cambridge: Cambridge University Press.

Kessler, T. P. 1998. Political Capital: Mexican Financial Policy under Salinas. *World Politics* 51:36–66.

Kindleberger, C. P. 1951. Group Behavior and International Trade. *Journal of Political Economy* 59:30–46.

————. 1973. *The World in Depression, 1929–1939*. Berkeley: University of California Press.

————. 1975. The Rise of Free Trade in Western Europe, 1820–1875. *Journal of Economic History* 35:20–55.

Krasner, S. D. 1991. Global Communications and National Power: Life on the Pareto Frontier. *World Politics* 43:336–66.

LeoGrande, W. 1979. Cuban Dependency: A Comparison of Pre-Revolutionary and Post-Revolutionary International Economic Relations. *Cuban Studies* 9:1–28.

Lieber, R. J. 1970. *British Politics and European Unity: Parties, Elites, and Pressure Groups*. Berkeley: University of California Press.

Lieberson, S. 1991. Small N's and Big Conclusions: An Examination of the Reasoning in Comparative Studies Based on a Small Number of Cases. *Social Forces* 70:307–20.

————. 1994. More on the Uneasy Case for Using Mill-Type Methods in Small-N Comparative Studies. *Social Forces* 72:1225–37.

Lijphart, A. 1971. Comparative Politics and the Comparative Method. *American Political Science Review* 65 (2): 682–93.

Marshall, G. 1982. *In Search of the Spirit of Capitalism: An Essay on Max Weber's Protestant Ethic Thesis*. New York: Columbia University Press.

Martin, L. L. 1992. *Coercive Cooperation: Explaining Multilateral Economic Sanctions*. Princeton: Princeton University Press.

Maxwell, J. A. 1996. *Qualitative Research Design: An Interactive Approach*. Thousand Oaks, CA: Sage.

Mayer, F. W. 1998. *Interpreting NAFTA: The Science and Art of Political Analysis*. New York: Columbia University Press.

McClelland, P. 1975. *Causal Explanation and Model Building in History, Economics, and the New Economic History*. Ithaca: Cornell University Press.

McNamara, K. R. 1998. *The Currency of Ideas: Monetary Politics in the European Union*. Ithaca: Cornell University Press.

Mill, J. S. 1900. *A System of Logic*. New York and London: Harper and Brothers.

————. 1970. Two Methods of Comparison. In *Comparative Perspectives: Theories and Methods,* edited by A. Etzioni and F. L. Dubow. Boston: Little, Brown.

Milner, H. V. 1997. *Interests, Institutions, and Information: Domestic Politics and International Relations*. Princeton: Princeton University Press.

Milner, H. V., and D. B. Yoffie. 1989. Between Free Trade and Protectionism: Strategic Trade Policy and a Theory of Corporate Trade Demands. *International Organization* 43:239–72.

Moggridge, D. E. 1969. *The Return to Gold, 1925: The Formulation of Economic Policy and Its Critics*. Cambridge: Cambridge University Press.

Moran, T. H. 1974. *Multinational Corporations and the Politics of Dependence: Copper in Chile.* Princeton: Princeton University Press.

Moravcsik, A. 1998. *The Choice for Europe: Social Purpose and State Power from Messina to Maastricht.* Ithaca: Cornell University Press.

Morse, E. L. 1973. *Foreign Policy and Interdependence in Gaullist France.* Princeton: Princeton University Press.

Oatley, T., and R. Nabors. 1998. Redistributive Cooperation: Market Failure, Wealth Transfers, and the Basle Accord. *International Organization* 52:35–55.

Odell, J. S. 1982. *U.S. International Monetary Policy: Markets, Power, and Ideas as Sources of Change.* Princeton: Princeton University Press.

———. 1988. From London to Bretton Woods: Sources of Change in Bargaining Strategies and Outcomes. *Journal of Public Policy* 8:287–316.

———. 1993. International Threats and Internal Politics: Brazil, the European Community, and the United States, 1985–1987. In *Double-Edged Diplomacy: International Bargaining and Domestic Politics,* edited by P. B. Evans, H. K. Jacobson, and R. D. Putnam. Berkeley: University of California Press.

———. 2000. *Negotiating the World Economy.* Ithaca: Cornell University Press.

———. 2001. Case Study Methods in International Political Economy. *International Studies Perspectives* 2:161–76.

Paemen, H., and A. Bensch. 1995. *From the GATT to the WTO: The European Community in the Uruguay Round.* Leuven: Leuven University Press.

Papayoanou, P. A. 1997. Economic Interdependence and the Balance of Power. *International Studies Quarterly* 41:113–40.

Paris, R. 1997. Peacebuilding and the Limits of Liberal Internationalism. *International Security* 22:54–89.

Puchala, D. J. 1995. The Pragmatics of International History. *Mershon International Studies Review* 39 (Supplement 1): 1–18.

Putnam, R. D. 1988. Diplomacy and Domestic Politics. *International Organization* 42 (3): 427–60.

Rosen, S., and J. Kurth, eds. 1974. *Testing Theories of Economic Imperialism.* Lexington, MA: D. C. Heath Lexington Books.

Rothstein, R. L. 1979. *Global Bargaining: UNCTAD and the Quest for a New International Economic Order.* Princeton: Princeton University Press.

Samuelsson, K. 1957. *Religion and Economic Action.* New York: Basic Books.

Schamis, H. E. 1999. Distributional Coalitions and the Politics of Economic Reform in Latin America. *World Politics* 51:236–68.

Schattschneider, E. E. 1935. *Politics, Pressures, and the Tariff.* Englewood Cliffs, NJ: Prentice-Hall.

Shirk, S. L. 1994. *How China Opened Its Door: The Political Success of the PRC's Foreign Trade and Investment Reforms.* Washington, DC: Brookings Institution.

Sikkink, K. 1991. *Ideas and Institutions: Developmentalism in Brazil and Argentina.* Ithaca: Cornell University Press.

Snyder, R. 1999. After Neoliberalism: The Politics of Reregulation in Mexico. *World Politics* 51:173–204.

Spar, D. L. 1992. Co-Developing the FSX Fighter: The Domestic Calculus of International Co-Operation. *International Journal* 47:265–92.

Tetlock, P. E., and A. Belkin, eds. 1996. *Counterfactual Thought Experiments in World Politics: Logical, Methodological, and Psychological Perspectives.* Princeton: Princeton University Press.

Van Evera, S. 1997. *Guide to Methods for Students of Political Science.* Ithaca: Cornell University Press.

Verba, S. 1967. Some Dilemmas in Comparative Research. *World Politics* 19:111–27.

Vogel, S. K. 1996. *Freer Trade, More Rules: Regulatory Reform in the Advanced Industrial Countries.* Ithaca: Cornell University Press.

Weber, M. 1958. *The Protestant Ethic and the Spirit of Capitalism.* New York: Charles Scribner's Sons.

Winham, G. R. 1986. *International Trade and the Tokyo Round Negotiation.* Princeton: Princeton University Press.

Wolf, D., and B. Zangl. 1996. The European Economic and Monetary Union: "Two-Level Games" and the Formation of International Institutions. *European Journal of International Relations* 2:355–93.

Wolff, R. 1974. *The Economics of Colonialism: Britain and Kenya, 1870–1930.* New Haven: Yale University Press.

4. Beyond Story-Telling: Designing Case Study Research in International Environmental Policy

Ronald Mitchell and Thomas Bernauer

Scholars have employed a range of methods to explore international environmental politics and policy (IEP). A small, but increasing, number have approached the subject quantitatively (Sprinz and Vaahtoranta 1994; Underdal 2001; Mitchell 2002a). Most, however, have used qualitative methods. In doing so, they have varied in whether their goals are descriptive (what did happen?), predictive (what will happen?), normative (what should happen?), or explanatory (what made this happen?). Like the rest of the international relations community, IEP scholars also vary in theoretical proclivities, ranging along the constructivist-rationalist continuum (Ruggie 1998). Scholars' different goals and proclivities have also led to debates about what qualitative research can, and should try to, accomplish. These debates are unlikely to be resolved soon, nor do we aspire to do so here. We believe that IEP scholars are more likely to understand the complexities of IEP accurately and fully if they use, as a community if not as individuals, a range of methods.

Our goal is to aid those IEP students and scholars who, at least some of the time, use qualitative methods to pursue explanatory goals within a rationalist paradigm. Descriptive analyses of existing international environmental issues, processes, negotiations, or agreements and prescriptive analyses of alternative policies clearly play important political and intellectual roles in IEP. Our argument is limited to noting that they usually contribute little to our understanding of causal relationships. For ease of exposition and to clarify that our argument is not intended to extend to all qualitative scholarship, we use QER (qualitative, explanatory, rationalist) to refer to the explanatory and rationalist subset of qualitative scholars and approaches. For these scholars, we seek to identify general principles to emulate and pitfalls to avoid in qualitative studies aimed at drawing causal inferences regarding independent and dependent variables from one or a small set of IEP cases that can be generalized to a larger class of cases.

After a brief look at the opportunities and challenges of case study research in IEP we outline six steps that promote the drawing of systematic, rigorous, and theoretically and empirically informative conclusions from qualitative research in this area. We introduce the reader to some key problems and possible solutions in qualitative case study research. However, the focus of this chapter is primarily on empirical applications of this method in IEP. Qualitative case study research is treated in more generic terms by Bennett (chap. 2, this vol.). We are motivated by our view that case studies of IEP too frequently make methodological errors that lead to unnecessarily weak or inaccurate conclusions. Rather than highlight the many available examples of such errors, we seek to identify positive empirical or hypothetical examples of how researchers have or could have avoided such errors.

Opportunities and Challenges of Causal Research in IEP

Causal analysis is central to much IEP research, if only because most scholars working in the field bring to their research a normative commitment to reducing human degradation of the environment. To actualize that commitment through research that links knowledge to action requires the researcher to identify causes of environmentally harmful outcomes with sufficient accuracy that governmental or private decision makers using their findings can be confident regarding which actions will avert such outcomes and under which conditions. It involves carefully identifying the political, economic, and social forces that cause international environmental problems; why some environmental problems get internationalized while others do not; and why solutions are devised for some international problems but not for others. It also engages questions of why some intergovernmental, corporate, and nongovernmental policies and behaviors mitigate these problems while others do not and what determines global society's success at evaluating and improving its attempts to protect the global environment (Mitchell 2002b).

Although similar questions inform research on security, international political economy, and human rights, the character of international environmental policy presents somewhat different opportunities and challenges to qualitative research. Interstate governance is less centralized than in any of these other arenas—several hundred multilateral agreements and hundreds more bilateral agreements have been established, most involving their own secretariats and with surprisingly little coordination across treaties or regimes (Mitchell in press). In regime formation and effectiveness research, the availability of numerous cases has facilitated edited volumes that evaluate multiple regimes (Sand 1992; Haas, Keohane, and Levy 1993; Keohane and Levy 1996; Brown Weiss and Jacobson 1998; Victor, Raustiala, and Skolnikoff 1998; Young 1998, 1999; Miles et al. 2001). The best of these and related works produce relatively rigorous comparative case studies, but many could be described more accurately as parallel analysis. In part this reflects the nature of multiauthor edited volumes, but it also reflects a deeper belief of many IEP researchers that differences in the nature of the underlying environmental problems preclude meaningful comparison across environmental problems or the social efforts to mitigate them. Recent work has begun to engage this assumption, taking up the task of defining metrics, identifying cases, and developing data in ways that would allow meaningful comparisons and inclusion in a common database for quantitative study (Breitmeier et al. 1996; Helm and Sprinz 2000; Miles et al. 2001; Mitchell 2002a; Young 2001).

International environmental politics also poses different challenges than other issues in the lack of consensus regarding what constitutes policy effectiveness, a dependent variable for many researchers working in the field (Mitchell 2002b). As in other arenas, some view negotiation of an international agreement as evidence of meaningful cooperation, while others believe compliance is necessary. Unlike most other areas, however, there has been ongoing debate in the subfield regarding whether even compliance is an appropriate object of study, since compliance is neither a necessary nor sufficient condition to achieve what many scholars consider to be the ultimate goal of international environmental cooperation, namely, significant environmental improvement. We illustrate and attempt to address these and related challenges in the rest of this chapter.

Performance Criteria and Research Steps

The literature on designing and carrying out systematic, rigorous QER research (George and Bennett 2004; Tetlock and Belkin 1996; Yin 1994, 54–101; King, Keohane, and Verba 1994; Ragin 1994) points to five criteria (phrased in table 1 as questions) that characterize innovative contributions to our understanding of the sources of variation in IEP. Meeting these criteria necessitates attention to the six tasks discussed later. Although delineated in logical order, research rarely does, and often should not, proceed in linear fashion; high-quality research often requires an iterative path through these steps. But those conducting QER research should address each of these tasks explicitly to produce findings that compel, convince, and contribute.[1]

Identifying an Important Theoretical Question

Innovative QER research on IEP should address existing theoretical debates in the field while attending to current policy concerns (King, Keohane, and Verba 1994, 15). Research efforts should target unresolved debates, untested theoretical claims including those about the merits of unassessed policy "innovations," or previously uninvestigated relation-

TABLE 1. Criteria for High Quality QER Research

Criteria	Question
Construct validity	Does the collected empirical information accurately capture the concepts or variables contained in the theoretical model or propositions nominally being investigated?
Internal validity	Does the analytic method demonstrate that, for each hypothesized causal relationship, observed variation in the independent variable correlates with observed variation in the dependent variable, and that no other variables provide a more plausible explanation of variation in the dependent variable?
External validity	Has the researcher accurately identified the boundary between the class of cases to which the findings can be validly generalized and beyond which valid generalizations are unlikely?
Reliability	Could other researchers replicate the research techniques used, e.g., data collection and analytic methods, and, having done so, arrive at the same results?
Progressive research	Does the research contribute to a larger, cumulative research program?

ships. Appropriate targeting of research questions requires a sophisticated understanding of existing theory and existing empirical patterns.

Familiarity with extant theoretical literatures helps the researcher identify whether variation in a particular variable is considered of interest to other scholars, identifies the factors that explain that variation or are explained by it, and allows a researcher to frame research questions in ways that help build a progressive research program while engaging appropriate scholarly communities (Lakatos 1970). Early scholarship in IEP often assumed issues were undertheorized because no one had explicitly sought to explain the phenomena of interest. Research on IEP has come of age over the last decade, however. Extensive theoretical work already exists regarding the roles of nongovernmental actors and movements in IEP (Lipschutz and Conca 1993; Princen and Finger 1994; Wapner 1996; Dawson 1996; Clapp 1998), the domestic sources of international environmental policy (Schreurs and Economy 1997; O'Neill 2000; DeSombre 2000), international regime formation (Susskind, Siskind, and Breslin 1990; Lipschutz 1991; Sjostedt 1993; Young and Osherenko 1993; Meyer et al. 1997; Young 1998), and international regime effects (Sand 1992; Haas, Keohane, and Levy 1993; Keohane and Levy 1996; Brown Weiss and Jacobson 1998; Victor, Raustiala, and Skolnikoff 1998; Young 1998, 1999; Miles et al. 2001).

At this point, there is no dearth of theories susceptible to evaluation with QER methods. Even scholars interested in exploring previously uninvestigated issues in IEP can begin by identifying how general theories of international relations—for example, realism, institutionalism, critical theory, constructivism—have answered the central research issue, or would answer it given the core principles of their theoretical arguments. Thus, early scholarship on environmental regime compliance derived predictions from broader theories of international relations rather than "starting new" (Young 1989, chap. 3; Haas 1990, chap. 2; Mitchell 1994, chap. 2). Most scholars now start from the assumption that general theories of international relations apply as well to IEP as to other policy domains, and use evidence that they do not to support such conclusions as military or economic power and interests explain less variation in IEP outcomes than in security or that prevailing theories are less generalizable than claimed, rather than that no relevant theory exists.

Empirical puzzles provide a useful way to frame QER research. Highlighting a contradiction between outcomes predicted by theory and those actually observed engages the reader and grounds theory. Puzzles can also stem from competing theoretical explanations for the same outcome, from untested theoretical predictions, or from the absence of any theories purporting to explain an observed outcome. Puzzles that use a particular outcome as a way of generating a debate between competing theories are particularly valuable since their findings are assured of refuting one theory and lending support to another or refuting both, regardless of the particular empirical findings. Testing one theory's prediction without a competing theory's prediction is riskier: the researcher cannot know beforehand whether cases selected will disconfirm a theory and so may end up with results that fail to falsify a theory yet, by definition, cannot prove it and, because of the small number of observations in QER research, cannot even provide strong support for it (Popper 1968).

Defining the research in terms that view the case(s) studied as instances in a larger class of cases (see Bennett, chap. 2, this vol.) is also crucial to QER analysis of IEP.[2] Thus, Princen's (1996) argument that the ivory trade ban established a norm against purchasing ivory was of interest not simply to those concerned about rhinos and elephants because he framed it as an example of how bans establish ecological norms more effectively than other policies. Several edited volumes (Young and Osherenko 1993; Haas, Keohane, and Levy 1993; Keohane and Levy 1996; Brown Weiss and Jacobson 1998; Victor, Raustiala, and Skolnikoff 1998) also show how case studies contribute to cumulative knowledge when cases with substantive appeal are analyzed as examples of larger classes of cases. In short, successful QER studies in IEP must match a generalizable theoretical question with a corresponding empirical one (Stinchcombe 1968).

Given such a theoretical foundation, QER research in IEP usually fits into one of three possible modes. Researchers can attempt to explain change in a specified dependent variable (DV), being initially agnostic about whether any particular factor was its major cause. Thus, the Social Learning Group set out to understand why "social learning" (defined as improvement in a society's ability to manage environmental risks) occurred in specific countries with respect to certain environmental problems at particular points in time but not in other countries, with respect to other problems, or at other times. They attributed the observed variation to a complex interplay of ideas, interests, and institutions, rather than any one factor (2001a, 2001b). Researchers may also specify both independent variables (IVs) and dependent variables at the outset. Much of the work to date on regime compliance and effectiveness has taken this shape, finding that international environmental regimes influence environmental policies and behaviors only under specified conditions (Brown Weiss and Jacobson 1998; Victor, Raustiala, and Skolnikoff 1998; Miles et al. 2001). A collection of QER studies of international environmental aid found that it had its intended effect only infrequently (Keohane and Levy 1996). Current research on global environmental science assessments demonstrates that their influence on international politics depends on their being simultaneously salient, legitimate, and credible to multiple audiences (Mitchell et al. forthcoming). Finally, researchers can analyze the effects of a specific IV, as evident in much of Oran Young's recent work that seeks to examine the full range of effects of international environmental regimes, examining direct and indirect effects, effects that are internal to the problem being addressed and external to it, and effects that are intended and positive as well as those that are unintended and negative, an approach also followed by those interested in the pathologies of international organizations (Young 1999, 15; Barnett and Finnemore 1999).

Developing Hypotheses and Identifying Variables

Efforts to draw causal inferences in IEP requires that hypotheses "can be shown to be wrong as easily and quickly as possible" and that criteria for what constitutes falsification be identified before research begins (King, Keohane, and Verba 1994, 100). In developing hypotheses, the researcher must carefully identify independent, control, and dependent variables, their potential values, and their theorized causal relationships.[3] Consider an effort to apply QER methods to the claim that "a country's culture influences how likely it will be to join an environmental regime." The DV (regime membership) and IV (culture) are clear, as are the potential values of the DV (ranging from extremely likely to extremely unlikely), but the values of the IV are not. To make this hypothesis falsifiable, the researcher must categorize "culture" into at least two values that she predicts correspond to higher and lower likelihoods of membership. Whether categorized as indigenous and nonindigenous; strongly environmental, weakly environmental, and nonenvironmental; or by some other taxonomy, evaluating this hypothesis requires defining categories for culture.

Most recent work on regime compliance and effectiveness carefully specifies both the predicted influence of each IV on the DV and potential causal pathways or mechanisms by which these variables may be operating (Brown Weiss and Jacobson 1998; Young and Osherenko 1993; Young 1999; Wettestad 1999; Miles et al. 2001). Extant theory is crucial in developing hypotheses and designing a convincing study, since it identifies which IVs need to be evaluated (and which do not) to explain variation in a DV convincingly. Familiarity with previous research, both theoretical and empirical, clarifies which variables should be included as controls or evaluated as alternative explanations of the DV, and it also clarifies effective and convincing ways to observe or operationalize all the variables in the study. In short, familiarity with earlier work identifies which variables to include and how to include them, as well as which variables can be ignored as not relevant to the study at hand.

Much QER research in IEP seeks to identify the one or more independent variables that caused the observed variation of a dependent variable in a particular case from the plethora of other potentially explanatory variables. Identifying such causal inferences requires that the researcher evaluate more observations than independent variables. Recalling Bennett's distinction between cases and observations (chap. 2, this vol.), note that it does not require multiple cases. Many single case studies draw well-supported inferences by making multiple observations of the IVs and DV in their case over time. Others have developed compelling findings by carefully constructing counterfactuals that are sufficiently plausible to serve as additional "observations" (Biersteker 1993; Fearon 1991). The key point here is that to identify the influence of a single IV on a DV requires at least two observations—we believe a minimal standard for claiming that A caused B involves demonstrating that A and B were observed together but also that not-A and not-B were observed together. Many case studies in IEP and elsewhere that are unconvincing because they demonstrate only that A and B were observed together could be significantly improved by the simple process of adding evidence that B was observed only after A had come to pass.

Indeed, case studies of single nongovernmental organizations (NGOs), single negotiations, or single regimes become quite convincing when they explicitly identify the several, sometimes numerous, potential observations within that case. Young and his colleagues call these observations "snapshots," examining both regime structure (the IV) and behavior patterns (the DV) at various points in a single regime's development to show both the conditions under which and pathways by which regime change leads to behavior change (Young 1999). Similarly, Parson examines different periods in the stratospheric ozone regime (a single case) to demonstrate that scientific assessments had decisive influence on international policy during the regime's formation but that technology assessments that drew heavily on private-industry expertise drove the rapid adaptation of the regime thereafter (2002, 2003). The quality of a QER study depends on whether the researcher selects her cases and observations in ways that allow her convincingly to evaluate its hypotheses.

Selecting Cases and Observations

Careful case and observation selection that reflects prior theory and research lies at the heart of QER research in IEP. Indeed, we believe that the choices of whether to study one or more than one case, which case or cases to study, and how many observations of each case to make are as important as which questions are asked and which variables are included. In a QER study of IEP, the number and appropriateness of case selection and observation selection determine, even before research has begun, whether the researchers will be able to make a convincing argument about the hypotheses being tested. The researchers must choose which, and how many, cases and observations to make in light of how many IVs they seek to analyze. Adding another case or observation can either allow analysis of an additional IV or strengthen the analysis of the IVs already selected for study. We believe that IEP research progresses faster from studies that provide strong support for the hypotheses they evaluate rather than those that evaluate many hypotheses. Good scholarship is defined by the quality of analysis, not the quantity of analyses.

The quality of a QER study and its ability to identify specific effects of one or more independent variables is enhanced by the criteria used to select cases and observations. Cases and observations should be selected to ensure they provide data appropriate to the hypotheses being evaluated; the primary IV of interest varies across observations, while other IVs do not; and the number of observations exceeds the number of IVs that vary across those cases and observations. Assuming the quality of observations can be maintained, more observations are preferable to fewer. Observations also should be selected based on variation in the IVs of interest, "without regard to the values of the dependent variable," to avoid biasing the selection process in favor of the hypothesis but without selecting cases that exhibit no variation in the DV (King, Keohane, and Verba 1994, 142–46).

A particularly common threat to case selection in IEP arises from the understandable and appropriate desire to contribute to current policy debates. This desire produces an independent (but often inappropriate) precommitment to studying a particular case. Unfortunately, initiating research by selecting a case because of substantive interests or letting this case dictate the research question often produces results with neither theoretical nor policy value. Frequently, theoretically hot questions cannot be answered using politically hot cases. Thus, although scholars and practitioners are currently quite interested in regime effectiveness, studies of headline issues—climate change, desertification, deforestation—cannot provide useful insights into how to design regimes effectively because these cases have not yet produced data that could be used in service of this question. Likewise, QER studies that sought to evaluate the influence of free trade on environmental quality could only begin to use NAFTA (signed in 1993) as a case in the late 1990s, after NAFTA-related data became available (Thompson and Strohm 1996). Instead of analyzing hot issues, scholars concerned with contributing to current policy debates are better served by selecting historical cases that provide internally valid results but that, by intention, generalize particularly well to those cases of policy concern.

Isolating one IV's influence on a DV from another requires selecting observations, whether multiple observations of a single case or single observations of multiple cases, in which the IV of interest varies while the other IVs that may also influence the DV do not. Drawing convincing causal inferences requires, first of all, an unbiased assessment of the association between independent and dependent variables across observations— if there is no association between a hypothesized IV and a specific DV, change in this IV cannot be a cause of change in the DV. As a basic principle, researchers must include at least one observation for every value of the independent variable. Consider a hypothesized relationship between an IV that can have the values A and not-A, and a DV that can have the values B and not-B. To infer from the data that "A caused B," the minimum requirements would be to show that (1) in one observation, B is present when A is present, (2) in a similar observation (i.e., ceteris paribus), B is absent when A is absent, and (3) A preceded B in time (Fearon 1991). This has implications for whether one needs multiple cases or can conduct the analysis with multiple observations from a single case: evaluating the "culture-regime participation" proposition mentioned earlier most likely requires at least two cases of different cultures, since culture, however categorized, is not something that is likely to vary quickly over time.

Convincing inferences by the QER researcher are fostered by selecting observations that show other potentially explanatory variables did not vary (i.e., control variables). Analyzing a single environmental issue as composed of several observations, either by observing variables in different time periods or in different subissue areas, provides a strong argument that most variables did not vary across the comparison. This is particularly useful when an alternative explanatory variable, had it varied across the observations, would have explanatory priority. For example, Mitchell (1994) compared oil company compliance with two different but contemporaneous rules within a single international regime regulating oil pollution. This strategy ensured that economic influences (particularly oil prices, which would have trumped regime influences) had equivalent effects over compliance with both rules and could therefore be excluded as explanations of the observed differences in compliance with the different rules.

Or, consider the proposition that trade liberalization causes convergence of environmental standards across countries. In this proposition, the relevant class is all cases of "trade liberalization," and an observation is defined by a pair of countries with some given level of trade. To evaluate the effect of trade liberalization requires comparing at least two such observations, one of which exhibits more liberalization than the other. The proposition predicts that the environmental standards of the countries with more liberalization among them will look more similar (their environmental standards will have converged more) than those with less liberalization. But, since two countries' environmental policies may converge because they face the same transboundary environmental problem (rather than because of trade liberalization), the observations selected should ensure the environmental problem is local and varies significantly in magnitude across the two countries. The comparison then can occur between observations of a single pair of countries before and after an increase in liberalization, observations of two pairs of countries that have different levels of liberalization at a given point in time, or observations of both types. The first approach keeps most country-specific variables constant, the second keeps most time-specific variables constant, and the third allows an analysis that takes account of the influence of both country-specific and time-specific variables. Evidence of greater policy similarity in addressing local environmental problems in liberalized settings than in nonliberalized ones supports the proposition. The first (change over time) approach allows evaluation of whether initially disparate national policies became more similar after liberalization, allowing us to concentrate our search for explanations among those, presumably few, variables that also changed at approximately the same time as the liberalization.

The notion that comparisons occur across observations, rather than cases, helps facilitate causal evaluations. Whether or not the real world of IEP provides observations that meet the criteria just mentioned, careful counterfactual analysis can prompt the collection of additional evidence that strengthens the conclusions of the study (Tetlock and Belkin 1996, 16–37; Fearon 1991; Dessler 1991). The analyst seeks to carefully identify whether and how the world would have been different had the independent variable of interest had a different value. For example, case studies on the effectiveness of international environmental regimes often ask questions such as how sulfur dioxide emissions in Western Europe would have evolved if the regime on long-range transboundary air pollution had not been established (Levy 1995).

A study's internal and external validity are also strengthened by seeking out "hard cases" in which the values of theoretically important control variables (CVs) are "distinctly unfavorable" to the hypothesis being tested (Young 1992, 165). Selection of observations should not only hold potentially explanatory variables constant, but should do so at values that make it unlikely the DV would have the value predicted by the IV of interest. This approach makes it less likely that evidence supporting the hypothesized relationship will be found but ensures such evidence, if found, provides stronger support of that hypothesis, since it was found true in an unlikely context (see, for example, Mitchell 1994; Haas 1990, 214; Young 1989). Also, such an approach strengthens the generalization of the case to other cases where the control variables had values more favorable to the IV of interest's influence on the DV.

Selecting cases and observations using these guidelines requires initial knowledge of possible cases. Gaining such knowledge usually requires discussions with other scholars, scanning primary and secondary literatures, and sometimes conducting one or more pilot studies. Following the guidelines discussed here can be painful: analysts often must drop cases to which they are emotionally attached and in whose analysis considerable and unre-trievable time and resources have already been invested, add cases or observations not yet investigated, or completely reanalyze cases and observations already studied. Yet, these steps are crucial to the eventual quality of the findings.

Linking Data to Propositions

To collect data, the analyst must identify appropriate proxies of the study's theoretical constructs (Levy, Young, and Zürn 1995; Bernauer 1995; Young 1992; Dessler 1991, 339). Variables must be operationalized to correspond well to the relevant theoretical constructs (construct validity). General theories seek to explain outcomes across an array of cases and define variables nonspecifically. Yet, constructing falsifiable predictions requires defining variables in ways that help empirical identification of the values of and relationships among variables. For example, Sprinz and Vaah-toranta conceive of interests in international environmental policy as consisting of a state's "environmental vulnerability" and "abatement costs," operationalizing them for ozone depletion as skin cancer rates and CFC consumption (1994, 89). Although these proxies fail to capture the conceptual richness of ecological vulnerability or abatement costs, they correspond reasonably well to these concepts and can be readily observed. Given the difficulties of operationalizing complex conceptual constructs and variables (Homer-Dixon 1996), it often helps to identify and collect data on a variety of indicators of a variable. Even if one has low confidence that any one of multiple indicators captures the true value of a conceptual variable, if all those indicators point in the same direction for that variable it can strengthen the confidence in the study's claims.

Examining different proxies may also lead to new theoretical insights. Victor, Raustiala, and Skolnikoff's (1998) analysis of various indicators of "implementation" documented that formal legal compliance with environmental treaties is often high whereas behavioral effectiveness, measured as whether a regime alters actor behavior, is low. By contrast, they found informal commitments associated with less compliance but more effectiveness, opening up an avenue for innovative explanations of variation across different indicators for effectiveness. QER studies also can identify variables initially considered unimportant and excluded from the original research design. A healthy tension can exist between the structure imposed by delineating the relationships among IVs, DVs, and CVs before the study begins and, when linking data to propositions, an open-mindedness to factors not captured within the boundaries of this initial structure. For example, the finding that capacity conditions environmental treaty effectiveness was an inductive conclusion from the evidence rather than an affirmation of a deductive hypothesis in Haas, Keohane, and Levy's book (1993).

Clear definitions and operationalizations of variables allow the researcher to gather data representing the values for each IV, CV, and DV. Sources of data include the primary and secondary literature, documents, electronic databases, structured or open interviews and surveys, or direct or participant observation. QER research often combines qualitative and quantitative data. For example, in examining whether a particular international agreement reduced pollution levels, a researcher may seek quantitative and qualitative evidence of changes in pollution levels, changes in pollution control technologies, exogenous economic trends that might produce changes in pollution levels, as well as information on decision makers' and activists' views on whether and why pollution levels changed over time and how the agreement contributed to these reductions (Bernauer 1996).

Examining Explanatory Pathways

Procedures for analyzing qualitative data are less well-established and less well-accepted than procedures for quantitative research. That said, the simple rules of systematically comparing predicted and observed values of the DV, qualitatively estimating associations between key variables, constructing empirical narratives to evaluate theoretical arguments more directly, and assessing rival hypotheses promotes solid inference (see, for example, Ragin 1994). The best approach for using empirical evidence to evaluate a theory is to identify clearly what the theory under investigation would predict about that DV's value given the values of the IVs and CVs for each observation, temporarily ignoring any knowledge about the value of the DV. The failure of observed DV values to match predicted DV values indicates that the theory fails to explain the variation across the observations in question, that it deals with a necessary but not sufficient condition for the DV to have the predicted value, or that it lacks explanatory power more generally.[4]

A table of the values of each variable for each observation imposes beneficial rigor on the analysis. Each row constitutes an observation with columns showing the values of each IV and CV, the value predicted for the DV given the values of the IVs and CVs, and the observed values of the DV. Such a table makes explicit the researcher's interpretation of what theory predicts in each observation, and it clarifies whether the IVs and DV covary as predicted. If they do, then the analyst needs to determine whether the covariation is evidence of a causal relationship or simply spurious covariation, which may involve including the values of other CVs in the chart to check for their covariation with the DV. Demonstrating that control variables actually were held constant (or had values that theory predicts would cause the DV to have a different value than that observed) refutes rival hypotheses that those variables caused the observed variation in the DV. If the control variables assumed as constant actually varied, the researcher should reevaluate her analytic strategy. Gathering more observations allows evaluation of whether the IV and/or (what was originally considered a) control variable explain the DV's variation. In this and other instances, change in CVs requires careful attention to ensure that a presumed control variable is not an important cause of change in the DV.

Consider a study evaluating how scientific consensus influences the outcome of international environmental negotiations. The independent variable might be defined as "level of scientific consensus on the causes of an environmental problem" with potential values of high or low; and the dependent variable as "negotiation of international environmental agreement" with potential values of yes or no. Evaluating this hypothesis requires—as a starting point—comparing one observation exhibiting high consensus regarding an environmental problem's causes with another exhibiting low consensus. Four types of results might arise: (1) a negotiated agreement in the first but not the second; (2) a negotiated agreement in the second but not the first; (3) negotiated agreements in both; and (4) no negotiated agreement in either. In results (3) and (4), no association between the two variables appears to exist. Result (1) provides initial support that scientific consensus may facilitate negotiation of an agreement, while result (2) provides initial support that scientific consensus may inhibit negotiation of an agreement.

Having found covariation between the IV of interest and the DV (with CVs held constant), the researcher should identify how the IV explains variation in the DV. Such a narrative will usually combine theoretical reasoning with empirical evidence on hypothesized "causal mechanisms" that connect IVs and the DV. As Alexander George notes, this involves subjecting the observations "in which that correlation appears to more intensive scrutiny, as the historian would do, in order to establish whether there exists an *intervening process,* that is, a causal nexus, between the independent variable and the dependent variable" (1979, 46). QER research has an advantage over quantitative methods in this regard, since it allows disaggregated and in-depth analysis of such mechanisms (Dessler 1991, 352). Detailed process tracing is more than mere storytelling (George 1979). Examining causal pathways helps demonstrate a linkage between an IV and a DV by taking advantage of the fact that a theory regarding an IV usually has several, and often many, observable implications beyond simply the value of the DV. Process tracing involves evaluating available evidence to see if it supports these additional implications that the IV explains change in the DV. Thus, to evaluate whether a given case supports Homer-Dixon's claim that environmental degradation causes acute conflict requires demonstrating not merely that environmental degradation was followed by acute conflict but that environmental degradation was followed by natural resource scarcity, which was followed by increased migration, which was followed by exacerbated rivalries between immigrants and indigenous populations, which was followed by the observed conflict (1991, 85–86; 1996).

Quantitative methods exist to evaluate such pathways, but collecting this level of information for more than a few cases often exceeds available resources. QER methods therefore complement quantitative methods. Internal validity is enhanced if alternative explanations are considered and found "less consistent with the data and/or less supportable by available generalizations" (George 1979, 57–58). Standard theoretical explanations of variation in the DV provide a list of likely suspects for these rival hypotheses. As already noted, careful selection of cases and observations should have eliminated many of these variables by holding them constant. The researcher should evaluate explicitly whether remaining rival variables provide a better or simpler explanation of the observed variation in the DV. She also should give the benefit of the doubt to these rival explanations if those explanations have strong previous support. For example, one explanation of why governments negotiated and signed the Montreal Protocol in 1987 contends that scientific consensus, stimulated mainly by the discovery of the ozone hole, was the proximate cause of negotiating success (Haas 1992). Making this claim requires refuting the rival claim that governments completed the agreement in response to Dupont (the world's leading producer of CFCs) and, later, other producers removing their objections to the agreement for economic, not scientific or environmental, reasons (Parson 2003). Notably, the rival arguments can be compared based on their predictions of when, as well as whether, agreement would be reached. Similarly, Bernauer and Moser (1996) evaluated whether the Rhine protection regime caused decreased pollution levels by developing several plausible narratives leading from the presumed cause to the observed outcome. Process tracing via open interviews with decision makers, analysis of pollution and regulatory data, and review of the secondary literature showed that transboundary regulation probably caused only a fraction of the pollution reduction. Interviews in particular showed that a secular decline in heavy industries and coal mining along the Rhine, and a general greening of domestic politics, also appeared to correlate with pollution reductions, making them more likely and plausible explanatory factors. Their careful evaluation of rival hypotheses allowed these analysts to avoid inaccurately attributing causal power to the international regime.

If the observations and cases selected allow too many plausibly explanatory variables to vary—a situation QER researchers often find themselves in—they face the difficult task of partitioning explanatory power between two or more IVs. Evaluating the implications of competing explanatory variables against available evidence often helps here. For example, both epistemic community and industry pressure arguments seem to explain the content of the Montreal Protocol. Closer consideration, however, suggests that the inclusion of various ozone depleting substances in the Montreal Protocol reflected the epistemic community's influence, while the Protocol's focus on alternatives involving new chemicals rather than nonchemical technologies reflected industry's influence. With sufficient observations, the analyst can examine whether the covariance of one IV with the DV is more consistent across different subsets of observations than the covariance of the other IV with the DV. Although the number of observations in a study is usually too small to build a strong argument to choose between the two alternatives, such an analysis makes the most of the available data.

The foregoing discussion highlights a unique risk of QER research on IEP: no fallback position exists if no evidence of the hypothesized causal relationship is found. The need to exclude observations that vary in explanatory variables other than the IV of interest runs the risk that, if the IV of interest does not explain variation in the DV, the researcher will have to (1) examine new cases to see if, under other conditions, the hypothesized relationship does exist or (2) collect new data from the cases studied to determine whether other variables previously considered unimportant actually contributed to the observed variation in the DV.[5] Many scholars can recount studies involving carefully selected cases and observations that simply failed to allow development of a compelling account that could exclude other factors as explanations of variation in the DV.

Generalizing to Other Cases

Finally, QER researchers on IEP should evaluate whether their findings are relevant to cases not investigated.[6] Assessing external validity forges links with broader debates. If the cases and observations studied differ in significant ways from most cases in a class, accurate generalization becomes difficult. Even if they can be generalized, convincing policymakers to adopt or reject a particular policy (or scholars to accept or reject a particular theory) requires demonstrating that the conditions in the cases studied are sufficiently similar to those in the targeted policy area to warrant the expectation that the same explanatory relationships will operate there.

It can be argued that case studies provide less foundation for generalization than quantitative analyses. In a quantitative, large-N study, the pursuit of internal validity usually also ensures that the results apply to a range of cases, both because they apply to the range of cases included in the study and because when findings are derived from observations and cases that exhibit considerable variation in other variables, it is more likely that they apply to a broader set of cases. High-quality quantitative analysis can identify both the average association of the IV with the DV over a range of CV values as well as interactive effects between the IV and various CVs (Mitchell 2002a). In contrast, most QER studies document the association between an IV and a DV for only a single value of any given CV, a CV that is likely to be different in many cases to which the researcher might want to generalize.

Consider a quantitative and a qualitative study of how NGO activism influences the chances of regime formation. Imagine that the only variable that theory suggests needs to be controlled for is the existence of a hegemon (Young 1983). Assuming the availability of sufficient cases with and without NGO activism, with and without hegemons, and with and without regimes, the quantitative analyst could identify the average impact NGOs had on regime formation and might be able to determine whether this impact was larger when a hegemon was absent and smaller when a hegemon was present. In contrast, the qualitative analyst, knowing that hegemony would likely confound causal inference, would seek to hold hegemony constant, selecting "hard cases" where hegemons were absent since they are alleged to facilitate regime formation. The qualitative study should find the same strong influence of NGOs on regime formation as the quantitative study found among cases in which hegemons were absent. The qualitative study would have developed a clearer sense of exactly how the NGOs fostered regime formation. Although the analyst should not bluntly claim that "NGOs play a major role in regime formation," she could claim that "these cases support the view that NGOs facilitate regime formation when no hegemon is available." Having made this argument with these observations, she might then go on to explore whether NGOs are likely to facilitate regime formation when a hegemon is available or if they have no real influence in that situation. Had she selected cases where hegemons (which promote regime formation) were present, however, both the internal validity and external validity of the study would be more limited.

Given internally valid findings, analysts can increase external validity in three ways. First, they can add cases and observations in which CVs have different values. Second, they can select hard cases (see previous discussion as well as Bennett, chap. 2, and Odell, chap. 3, this vol.). Third, they can select cases and observations that take advantage of the types of variation examined in past studies. By literal or theoretical replication of other cases, choosing cases to evaluate how different values of control variables influence the relationship of the IV and the DV, the researcher can contribute to a progressive research program that collectively establishes generalizable results through joint analysis of a larger set of cases (Yin 1994). In sum, the researcher should be cautious in generalizing. Assessing external validity requires determining how the values at which CVs were held constant affected the influence of the IV on the DV and on how well the values of those CVs match other cases and observations in the class of cases being studied.

Conclusion

More of our knowledge of international environmental politics to date has come from qualitative, explanatory, and rationalist studies than from quantitative or formal studies, and that is likely to remain true for the foreseeable future. Yet, methodologies for drawing inferences from small numbers of cases and observations remain underdeveloped and too rarely appear on political science syllabi. The plethora of poorly constructed QER studies in the IEP literature testifies to the difficulty of designing and conducting them well. To address this, we have outlined six steps crucial to rigorous QER research in IEP. We recognize that other qualitative approaches have much to offer the study of IEP and urge others to provide guidelines for good research within those traditions.

Good IEP research in what we have called the qualitative, explanatory, rationalist (or QER) tradition begins by identifying an important and compelling research question. The analyst then transforms this question into testable hypotheses, explicitly delineating variables and their possible values. Having done this, choices about the number and type of cases and observations provide a crucial, but all too often ignored or poorly implemented, basis for identifying associations between independent and dependent variables, drawing causal inferences from such findings, and generalizing those findings to other cases. Cases and observations should be selected to facilitate the researcher's urge to develop or evaluate a theory, avoiding the temptation to explore politically hot or personally interesting cases unless they also can answer theoretically important questions. QER research requires sufficient familiarity with existing theory to identify the independent and control variables considered most important to variation in the dependent variable. Simple tables can help identify the degree to which observed variation in the DV corresponds (ceteris paribus) to variation predicted by theory. Process tracing of other observable linkages between the IV and DV can strengthen claims that those relationships are causal and not just correlational. Finally, the researcher should clearly identify the class of cases to which the findings can (and cannot) be appropriately generalized.

In QER research on IEP, systematic evaluation of hypothesized relationships must be restricted to very few IVs and CVs. Even with a solid research design, comparing the effects of more than one IV on the DV is much harder than with multivariate statistical analysis. Moreover, explanations derived from QER studies are often difficult to generalize. The frequently encountered view that QER studies are an "easy way out" for students and scholars deterred by the technicalities of statistics is highly erroneous. As the difficulties discussed here clarify, deriving valid and interesting inferences from a QER study requires at least as much care and thought as doing so from a quantitative analysis. Those undertaking QER studies are well advised to follow Mark Twain's admonition to "put all your eggs in the one basket and—WATCH THAT BASKET" (1894, 15). The procedures outlined here can reduce the risks. We believe that researchers attentive to these steps can improve the rigor of their work, contributing to the growing effort to understand how international environmental problems arise; when, why, and how they can be resolved; and how we can better manage our social, political, and economic behaviors to have fewer detrimental impacts on the environment.

Recommended Readings

Brown Weiss, E., and H. K. Jacobson, eds. 1998. *Engaging Countries: Strengthening Compliance with International Environmental Accords.* Cambridge: MIT Press.

Haas, P. M., R. O. Keohane, and M. A. Levy, eds. 1993. *Institutions for the Earth: Sources of Effective International Environmental Protection.* Cambridge: MIT Press.

Miles, E. L., A. Underdal, S. Andresen, J. Wettestad, J. B. Skjaerseth, and E. M. Carlin, eds. 2001. *Environmental Regime Effectiveness: Confronting Theory with Evidence.* Cambridge: MIT Press.

Victor, D. G., K. Raustiala, and E. B. Skolnikoff, eds. 1998. *The Implementation and Effectiveness of International Environmental Commitments.* Cambridge: MIT Press.

Young, O. R., ed. 1999. *Effectiveness of International Environmental Regimes: Causal Connections and Behavioral Mechanisms.* Cambridge: MIT Press.

Notes

This chapter is a substantially revised version of Ronald B. Mitchell and Thomas Bernauer, "Empirical Research on International Environmental Policy: Designing Qualitative Case Studies," *Journal of Environment and Development* 7 (1): 4–31, March 1998. The authors would like to express their appreciation to Detlef Sprinz and Yael Wolinsky-Nahmias, as well as to Peter Haas, Andrew Bennett, Harold Jacobson, Peter Moser, Roy Suter, Arild Underdal, and two anonymous reviewers of the *Journal of Environment and Development* for extremely helpful comments on earlier drafts of this article. Ronald Mitchell's work was supported by a

Sabbatical Fellowship in the Humanities and Social Sciences from the American Philosophical Society.

1. These steps draw extensively from the work of Tetlock and Belkin (1996); King, Keohane, and Verba (1994); George (1979); Eckstein (1975); and other scholars of qualitative research methodology.

2. Members of dissertation committees as well as discussants on panels at scientific conferences regularly ask questions such as "And what is this a case of?" Too frequently, however, the answers reveal a failure to consciously address this question early on in the research process.

3. George and Bennett (1997) have argued that case studies can be particularly useful for developing "typological theory" in which the case study helps to establish the different categories of phenomena as well as their causal relationships.

4. Of course, the first two of these possibilities can and should have been addressed by careful selection of cases to allow more determinate testing of the theory chosen for study.

5. The QER researcher must designate an independent variable of interest at the outset of the study, then face the problem of having "no findings" if variation in that independent variable is not associated with variation in the dependent variable. The quantitative researcher, by contrast, can select cases and observations that exhibit considerable variation in all the independent variables, developing an explanatory argument around whichever independent variables show strong associations with the dependent variable.

6. Many constructivists argue that the importance of contextual contingency demands a healthy skepticism about even limited generalizations.

References

Barnett, M. N., and M. Finnemore. 1999. The Politics, Power, and Pathologies of International Organizations. *International Organization* 53 (4): 699–732.

Bernauer, T. 1995. The Effect of International Environmental Institutions: How We Might Learn More. *International Organization* 49 (2): 315–77.

———. 1996. Protecting the Rhine River against Chloride Pollution. In *Institutions for Environmental Aid: Pitfalls and Promise,* edited by R. O. Keohane and M. A. Levy. Cambridge: MIT Press.

Bernauer, T., and P. Moser. 1996. Reducing Pollutions of the Rhine River: The Influence of International Cooperation. *Journal of Environment and Development* 5 (4): 391–417.

Biersteker, T. 1993. Constructing Historical Counterfactuals to Assess the Consequences of International Regimes: The Global Debt Regime and the Course of the Debt Crisis of the 1980s. In *Regime Theory and International Relations,* edited by V. Rittberger. New York: Oxford University Press.

Breitmeier, H., M. A. Levy, O. R. Young, and M. Zürn. 1996. *The International Regimes Database as a Tool for the Study of International Cooperation.* Laxenburg, Austria: International Institute for Applied Systems Analysis.

Brown Weiss, E., and H. K. Jacobson. 1998. *Engaging Countries: Strengthening Compliance with International Environmental Accords.* Cambridge: MIT Press.

Clapp, J. 1998. The Privatization of Global Environmental Governance: ISO 14000 and the Developing World. *Global Governance* 4 (3): 295–316.

Dawson, J. 1996. *Eco-Nationalism.* Durham: Duke University Press.

DeSombre, E. R. 2000. *Domestic Sources of International Environmental Policy: Industry, Environmentalists, and U.S. Power.* Cambridge: MIT Press.

Dessler, D. 1991. Beyond Correlations: Toward a Causal Theory of War. *International Studies Quarterly* 35 (3): 337–55.

Eckstein, H. 1975. Case Study and Theory in Political Science. In *Handbook of Political Science,* vol. 7, *Strategies of Inquiry,* edited by F. Greenstein and N. Polsby. Reading, MA: Addison-Wesley.

Fearon, J. D. 1991. Counterfactuals and Hypothesis Testing in Political Science. *World Politics* 43 (2): 169–95.

George, A. L. 1979. Case Studies and Theory Development: The Method of Structured, Focused Comparison. In *Diplomacy: New Approaches in History, Theory, and Policy,* edited by P. G. Lauren. New York: Free Press.

George, A. L., and A. Bennett. 1997. Developing and Using Typological Theories in Case Study Research. International Studies Association Conference, Toronto.

———. 2004. *Case Studies and Theory Development.* Cambridge: MIT Press.

Haas, P. M. 1990. *Saving the Mediterranean: The Politics of International Environmental Cooperation.* New York: Columbia University Press.

———. 1992. Banning Chlorofluorocarbons. *International Organization* 46 (1): 187–224.

Haas, P. M., R. O. Keohane, and M. A. Levy, eds. 1993. *Institutions for the Earth: Sources of Effective International Environmental Protection.* Cambridge: MIT Press.

Helm, C., and D. Sprinz. 2000. Measuring the Effectiveness of International Environmental Regimes. *Journal of Conflict Resolution* 44 (5): 630–52.

Homer-Dixon, T. 1991. On the Threshold: Environmental Changes as Causes of Acute Conflict. *International Security* 16 (2): 76–116.

———. 1996. Strategies for Studying Causation in Complex Ecological Political Systems. *Journal of Environment and Development* 5 (2): 132–48.

Keohane, R. O., and M. A. Levy, eds. 1996. *Institutions for Environmental Aid: Pitfalls and Promise.* Cambridge: MIT Press.

King, G., R. O. Keohane, and S. Verba. 1994. *Designing Social Inquiry: Scientific Inference in Qualitative Research.* Princeton: Princeton University Press.

Lakatos, I. 1970. Falsification and the Methodology of Research Programmes. In *Criticism and the Growth of Knowledge,* edited by I. Lakatos and A. Musgrave. Cambridge: Cambridge University Press.

Levy, M. A. 1995. International Cooperation to Combat Acid Rain. In *Green Globe Yearbook: An Independent Publication on Environment and Development,* edited by H. O. Bergesen, G. Parmann, and Ø. B. Thommessen. Oxford: Oxford University Press.

Levy, M. A., O. R. Young, and M. Zürn. 1995. The Study of International Regimes. *European Journal of International Relations* 1 (3): 267–330.

Lipschutz, R. D. 1991. Bargaining among Nations: Culture, History, and Perceptions in Regime Formation. *Evaluation Review* 15 (1): 46–74.

Lipschutz, R. D., and K. Conca, eds. 1993. *The State and Social Power in Global Environmental Politics.* New York: Columbia University Press.

Meyer, J. W., D. J. Frank, A. Hironaka, E. Schofer, and N. B. Tuma. 1997. The Structuring of a World Environmental Regime, 1870–1990. *International Organization* 51 (4): 623–29.

Miles, E. L., A. Underdal, S. Andresen, J. Wettestad, J. B. Skjaerseth, and E. M. Carlin, eds. 2001. *Environmental Regime Effectiveness: Confronting Theory with Evidence.* Cambridge: MIT Press.

Mitchell, R. B. 1994. *Intentional Oil Pollution at Sea: Environmental Policy and Treaty Compliance.* Cambridge: MIT Press.

———. 2002a. A Quantitative Approach to Evaluating International Environmental Regimes. *Global Environmental Politics* 2 (4): 58–83.

———. 2002b. International Environment. In *Handbook of International Relations,* edited by W. Carlsnaes, T. Risse, and B. Simmons. Thousand Oaks, CA: Sage.

———. In press. International Environmental Agreements: A Survey of their Features, Formation, and Effects. *Annual Review of Environment and Resources* 28.

Mitchell, R. B., W. C. Clark, D. W. Cash, and F. Alcock, eds. Forthcoming. *Global Environmental Assessments: Information, Institutions, and Influence.* Cambridge: MIT Press.

O'Neill, K. 2000. *Waste Trading among Rich Nations.* Cambridge: MIT Press.

Parson, E. A. 2002. The Technology Assessment Approach to Climate Change. *Issues in Science and Technology* 18 (4): 65–72.

———. 2003. *Protecting the Ozone Layer: Science and Strategy.* Oxford: Oxford University Press.

Popper, K. 1968. *The Logic of Scientific Discovery.* New York: Harper and Row.

Princen, T. 1996. The Zero Option and Ecological Rationality in International Environmental Politics. *International Environmental Affairs* 8 (2): 147–76.

Princen, T., and M. Finger. 1994. *Environmental NGOs in World Politics: Linking the Local and the Global.* New York: Routledge.

Ragin, C. C. 1994. *Constructing Social Research: The Unity and Diversity of Method.* Thousand Oaks, CA: Pine Forge Press.

Ruggie, J. G. 1998. What Makes the World Hang Together? Neo-Utilitarianism and the Social Constructivist Challenge. *International Organization* 52 (4): 855–85.

Sand, P. H., ed. 1992. *The Effectiveness of International Environmental Agreements: A Survey of Existing Legal Instruments.* Cambridge, UK: Grotius.

Schreurs, M. A., and E. Economy, eds. 1997. *The Internationalization of Environmental Protection.* Oxford: Oxford University Press.

Sjostedt, G., ed. 1993. *International Environmental Negotiation.* Newbury Park, CA: Sage.

Social Learning Group, ed. 2001a. *Learning to Manage Global Environmental Risks.* Vol. 1, *A Functional Analysis of Social Responses to Climate Change, Ozone Depletion, and Acid Rain.* Cambridge: MIT Press.

———. 2001b. *Learning to Manage Global Environmental Risks.* Vol. 2, *A Comparative History of Social Responses to Climate Change, Ozone Depletion, and Acid Rain.* Cambridge: MIT Press.

Sprinz, D., and T. Vaahtoranta. 1994. The Interest-Based Explanation of International Environmental Policy. *International Organization* 48 (1): 77–105.

Stinchcombe, A. L. 1968. *Constructing Social Theories.* New York: Harcourt, Brace, and World.

Susskind, L. E., E. Siskind, and J. W. Breslin, eds. 1990. *Nine Case Studies in International Environmental Negotiation.* Cambridge: MIT-Harvard Public Disputes Program.

Tetlock, P. E., and A. Belkin, eds. 1996. *Counterfactual Thought Experiments in World Politics: Logical, Methodological, and Psychological Perspectives.* Princeton: Princeton University Press.

Thompson, P., and L. A. Strohm. 1996. Trade and Environmental Quality: A Review of the Evidence. *Journal of Environment and Development* 5 (4): 363–88.

Twain, M. 1894. *The Tragedy of Pudd'nhead Wilson; and, the Comedy, Those Extraordinary Twins.* Hartford: American Publishing Company.

Underdal, A. 2001. Conclusions: Patterns of Regime Effectiveness. In *Environmental Regime Effectiveness: Confronting Theory with Evidence,* edited by E. L. Miles, A. Underdal, S. Andresen, J. Wettestad, J. B. Skjaerseth, and E. M. Carlin. Cambridge: MIT Press.

Victor, D., K. Raustiala, and E. B. Skolnikoff. 1998. *The Implementation and Effectiveness of International Environmental Commitments.* Cambridge: MIT Press.

Wapner, P. 1996. *Environmental Activism and World Civic Politics.* Albany: State University of New York Press.

Wettestad, J. 1999. *Designing Effective Environmental Regimes: The Key Conditions.* Cheltenham, UK: Edward Elgar.

Yin, R. K. 1994. *Case Study Research: Design and Methods.* Thousand Oaks, CA: Sage.

Young, O. R. 1983. Regime Dynamics: The Rise and Fall of International Regimes. In *International Regimes,* edited by S. D. Krasner. Ithaca: Cornell University Press.

————. 1989. *International Cooperation: Building Regimes for Natural Resources and the Environment.* Ithaca: Cornell University Press.

————. 1992. The Effectiveness of International Institutions: Hard Cases and Critical Variables. In *Governance without Government: Change and Order in World Politics,* edited by J. N. Rosenau and E.-O. Czempiel. New York: Cambridge University Press.

————. 1998. *Creating Regimes: Arctic Accords and International Governance.* Ithaca: Cornell University Press.

————, ed. 1999. *Effectiveness of International Environmental Regimes: Causal Connections and Behavioral Mechanisms.* Cambridge: MIT Press.

————. 2001. Inferences and Indices: Evaluating the Effectiveness of International Environmental Regimes. *Global Environmental Politics* 1 (1): 99–121.

Young, O. R., and G. Osherenko, eds. 1993. *Polar Politics: Creating International Environmental Regimes.* Ithaca: Cornell University Press.

5. Case Study Methods in International Security Studies

Arie M. Kacowicz

The use of case study methods in research on international security offers a number of advantages to investigators but also involves challenges and limitations. In this chapter, I assess the merits and limits of case study methods in the study of international security. First, I discuss the idea that case study methods can be regarded as a methodological middle ground between positivists and constructivists. Second, I assess practical challenges and methodological problems in the field of international security. Third, I summarize important findings and contributions of several seminal works in the field that use case study methods.

Case study methods, as Bennett specifies (chap. 2, this vol.), include both the single case study method (Eckstein 1975, 85) and the comparative method (Lijphart 1971, 691; George 1997, 1). Single case studies provide tests that might strongly support or impugn theories in a single event. Conversely, the comparative method employs a systematic analysis of a small number of cases, or a small N (Collier 1993, 105), in order to test competing hypotheses, develop new theories, draw "lessons of history," and generalize across cases (George 1979, 43, 50). The use of the comparative method with a small number of case studies allows for a controlled, structured, and focused analysis (see George 1979, 1991; George and Smoke 1974; Kacowicz 1994; Rock 1989). Alternatively, the use of the comparative method can be less structured and more interpretative, as in recent empirical work by constructivist scholars (see Katzenstein 1996a; Finnemore 1996; Adler and Barnett 1998).

The major advantages of case study methods include the following: (1) operationalization of qualitative variables, which allows the attainment of high levels of conceptual validity; (2) identification of new variables or hypotheses and the testing and refinement of those already existing; (3) examination of causal mechanisms within individual cases, including unveiling causal processes in nonevents; (4) construction of historical and detailed explanations of particular cases through in-depth examination; and (5) analysis of complex causal relations through contingent generalizations and typological theories[1] in instances of equifinality and path dependency (see Bennett 1999, 3; 2000; Collier 1993; Bennett and George 1997c, 8, 12; Eckstein 1975, 80; George 1979, 61; Ragin 1994, 81; Maoz 2002, 2–3).

However, case study methods pose several methodological problems, including (1) case-selection bias; (2) potential indeterminacy as related to the trade-off between parsimony and richness in the selection of the number of variables and cases to be studied; (3) limited explanatory range, due to the impossibility of addressing covariation and causal effects, especially in single case methods; (4) potential lack of independence of cases, and limited external validity and reliability, all of which undermine the possibility of generalization; and (5) endogeneity and tautological circles (see Bennett 2000; Collier 1993; Yin 1984, 21–22; Ray 1995, 153–54; Van Evera 1997, 51, 53; King, Keohane, and Verba 1994, 118–19; Bennett and George 1997c, 9).

Case Studies as a "Middle Ground"?

A cursory review of qualitative research in international security reveals that many authors have adopted a soft positivist stance. This approach is quite different from the standards that both formal theorists and statistical/correlational analysts apply in their research and also from the recommendations of King, Keohane, and Verba (1994) for a unified logic of causal inference. In international security, as in other fields of international relations and social science, causal and/or statistical inferences are difficult to make and consequently the rules of scientific inference cannot always be realistically applied. In other words, there seems to be a dialectical relationship between the use of case studies for the development of typological theories and the use of these theories in turn to design case study research and select cases, which involves both inductive inferences and deductive theorizing (Bennett and George 1997b, 34–35).

An interesting question is whether the use of case studies as a soft positivist method can create a methodological bridge between neorealists, who attempt to account for scientific progress on the basis of an objective representation of reality, and constructivists, who emphasize interpretive understandings, "thick descriptions," and the social construction of reality. The debate between positivists and constructivists centers on the role of culture, ideas, and norms in explaining political reality in international security. Neorealists, and to a lesser extent neoliberals, have been challenged in recent years by their inability to explain the end of the Cold War and the emergence of a post–Cold War security order (Katzenstein 1996b, 9). The dissatisfaction with realist explanations of state behavior has led constructivist scholars to emphasize the role of norms, ideas, values, and culture in explaining international security, in juxtaposition to materialist and rationalist theories (Desch 1998, 149). For instance, Katzenstein focuses on the norms, identity, and culture associated with "national security," challenging predominant explanations of national security as a function of the state interests (1996b, 1).

The use of case studies in international security is linked to this important debate. Positivists have traditionally applied qualitative methods, including the single case study and the comparative method alongside formal and quantitative methods to evaluate their theoretical claims about international security. Moreover, some positivists have even explored certain aspects of national security with reference to "social facts," such as strategic beliefs (Snyder 1991) or balances of threat (Walt 1987; 1996, 340), though they have subordinated the causal force of social facts to their materialistic or rationalistic views (Katzenstein 1996b, 26–27). Interestingly, constructivists have also turned to comparative analysis of case studies to illustrate their theoretical arguments in empirical terms. There seems to be a growing constructivist research agenda regarding central puzzles in international security, including the balance of threat, security dilemmas, neoliberal institutionalist accounts of cooperation under anarchy, and the liberal theory of democratic peace (Hopf 1998, 186–92).

Among the authors reviewed here those who explicitly use the method of structured comparison turn to contingent generalizations and typological or tentative theories instead of lawlike generalizations. For instance, George and Smoke (1974) propose a typological theory regarding deterrence failure, partially derived from the analysis of eleven case studies between 1948 and 1963 in which the United States either applied a deterrence strategy or considered applying it to assist weaker allies and neutral states. Yet, these authors' three discerned patterns of deterrence failure (fait accompli attempt, limited probe, and controlled pressure) suggest contingent generalizations rather than unequivocal causal relationships or full-fledged deductive theories. Similarly, in his edited volume on limited wars, George suggests several types of "inadvertent wars" in order to understand how some diplomatic crises have ended in war even though neither side wanted or expected this at the outset (1991, xi).

Some scholars are also aware that applying a comparative research design in case studies of international security cannot offer a conclusive test of their theories, since interpretations are far from definitive. For instance, Snyder explores the issue of overextension among the great powers across five historical cases. He concludes that "the cases constitute a preliminary test, subject to further historical and theoretical scrutiny" (1991, 65). Similarly, in my book on peaceful territorial change, because it is difficult to test the model with ten explanatory variables (six background conditions and four process variables) across only four case studies, I have combined the comparative method with a preliminary quantitative methodology (Kacowicz 1994).

In even more explicit terms, many constructivists reject a priori the possibility of attempting hard science or even suggesting contingent generalizations. For instance, since there may be too many rather than too few plausible generalizations that describe the causes and effects of international norms on international security, Katzenstein and his colleagues (1996) reject the possibility of sorting and testing rival hypotheses about the links among norms, identity, and national security on the grounds that social norms can operate in a wide variety of ways (Kowert and Legro 1996, 495).

Adler and Barnett (1998) have resurrected Karl Deutsch's concept of "pluralistic security communities" in their edited volume. This is a pivotal concept for international security studies. It implies that community can exist at the international level, that security politics is profoundly shaped by community, and that those states dwelling within an international community might develop a peaceful disposition in their mutual relations.

Adopting a constructivist viewpoint and employing process-tracing analysis (within-case analysis), they present in their book a rich array of nine case studies that exhibit different path-dependent "tracks" (434–35). However, they refrain from attempting strong generalizations, justifying their methodological abstinence as follows: "Because the contextual socio-cognitive and material conditions that give birth to security communities vary from case to case, security communities will exhibit different path dependence 'tracks,' and therefore researchers are unlikely to identify a 'master variable'" (434–435). Thus, their reticence about generalizing across cases situates their work closer to that of postpositivists who give up on any theoretical effort in the social sciences.

Similarly, Katzenstein (1996a) and Finnemore (1996), who classify themselves as constructivists, also use qualitative methodologies, namely, the analysis of detailed case studies. In each of these volumes, the authors try to compare and/or draw some conclusions from their cases. However, their comparative method is usually neither structured nor focused. There seems to be an inherent problem of underspecification in their analysis, since constructivists seldom specify the existence, let alone the precise nature or value, of causal variables and pathways. Indeed, constructivists face an inherent methodological dilemma: the more focused and structured their theory, the more they distance themselves from the possibility of maintaining the ontological openness (and looseness) that characterizes their interpretive method (Hopf 1998, 197). In this sense, the common usage of case studies blurs the methodological distance between positivists and constructivists. To paraphrase Adler's article on constructivism (1997), the use of case studies becomes a kind of methodological middle ground between soft positivists and conventional constructivists even though the substantive differences remain the same.

Methodological Challenges in the Use of Case Studies

This section addresses practical methodological challenges and problems associated with the use of case studies in international security. I first examine the problems of case-selection bias and endogeneity in case studies of international security (also see Bennett, chap. 2, this vol.). Then I discuss process tracing as a useful tool that approximates the case study methodology to the empirical work of diplomatic historians.

Case-Selection Bias and Endogeneity

The reluctance to turn to contingent generalizations among some constructivists who use case study methods is complicated by other problems that are common to both constructivists and soft positivists: case-selection bias, endogeneity, and a serious limitation to external validity.

Selection bias seems to be inescapable in the use of case study methods in international security studies, especially in research designs of single cases or only two cases. If selection bias is unavoidable, researchers should follow two sensible rules of thumb. First, they should select cases that best serve the purposes of their inquiry. Second, they should select cases that maximize the strength and number of tests for their theories and hypotheses (Van Evera 1997, 78).

A review of relevant books on international security reveals that selection bias is very common and that many of the authors tend to follow these two rules of thumb. For instance, in Lustick's study of state expansion and contraction (1993) he selects three cases for comparison—Israel, the West Bank, and the Gaza Strip (beginning in 1967); Britain and Ireland (1834–1922); and France and Algeria (1936–62). In his words, "these are the best-known historical cases of democratic states faced with major territorial problems located 'between' secession and decolonization" (46). Yet, there is not much variation in the dependent variable here. Similarly, Levite, Jentleson, and Berman choose six cases of protracted military interventions to discern the motivations for intervention's three analytical stages: "getting in, staying in, and getting out" (1992, 16). Again, there is not much variation in the dependent variable here, since all of the cases selected experienced all three stages of military intervention.

Selection bias in terms of arbitrary selection of some cases is present in studies of different issues in international security: extended deterrence and deterrence failure (George and Smoke 1974; Jervis, Lebow, and Stein 1985); crisis management and inadvertent wars (George 1991); the link between revolutions and war (Walt 1996); imperialism and overexpansion of great powers (Snyder 1991); nuclear crises in the Cold War (Lebow and Stein 1994); rapprochement and the transition from war to peace between great powers (Rock 1989); appeasement (Rock 2000); peaceful territorial change (Kacowicz 1994); zones of peace in the Third World (Kacowicz 1998); stable peace among nations (Kacowicz et al. 2000); the initiation of war by weaker powers (Paul 1994); and the ideology of the offensive (Snyder 1984).

The problem of selection bias is even more acute in security studies performed by constructivist scholars, who tend to neglect methodological purism and, unlike their positivist colleagues, often do not explicitly justify their criteria for case selection (see Katzenstein 1996a; Finnemore 1996; Adler and Barnett 1998). Thus, from a strictly methodological perspective, though constructivists should be applauded for their pluralism and openness, they should be encouraged to be more rigorous in their research designs and cross-case comparisons.

Another problem affecting the quality of research design in case studies of international security is endogeneity, where "the values our explanatory variables take on are sometimes a consequence, rather than a cause, of our dependent variable" (King, Keohane, and Verba 1994, 185). The direction of causality in many phenomena of international security studies, such as the link between democracy and peace, is difficult to ascertain. In his study on revolutions and war, Walt recognizes that "revolutions lead to war, but war in turn affects the revolutions" (1996, 16). In assessing the conditions that explain the maintenance of long periods of regional peace in the Third World, I have been criticized for suggesting that satisfaction with the territorial status quo is a necessary condition for an international zone of peace, while at the same time it is a consequence or reflection of that peace (Kacowicz 1998; Steves 1999, 790). Constructivists that use case study methods do not consider endogeneity as a methodological problem at all but rather a methodological reflection of "structuration processes" in which agents and structures in international relations mutually constitute and affect each other (Dessler 1989). The use of detailed case studies can help to deal with the problem of endogeneity in a satisfactory fashion.

The Imperfect Method of Difference and the Panacea of Process Tracing

Much of the discussion of case study methods has focused on the research design of controlled comparisons using John Stuart Mill's "method of difference" (comparing two or more cases that are similar in every respect but one). However, this requirement is not always realistic due to the difficulties of finding two almost identical cases in real life, and so case study methods have to rely heavily on within-case analysis as a way of evaluating claims about causal processes (George and McKeown 1985, 24).

In international security studies, there is widespread reference to the method of process tracing as the potential panacea for comparing historical cases that exhibit complex causal processes. For instance, Lustick refers to "the opportunity to compare the conditions under which the relationships between Britain and Ireland, and France and Algeria, moved across the thresholds of state-building and state contraction" (1993, 50). For George and Smoke, the study of extended deterrence in U.S. foreign policy includes the examination of each case in some depth: "all cases are approached by asking identical questions. The investigator is able to uncover similarities among cases that suggest possible generalizations; and to investigate the differences in a systematic matter" (1974, 96). For Levite, Jentleson, and Berman (1992), the focus of their edited volume on protracted military interventions is examining "a common set of questions asked of each case at each stage of three levels of analysis: the international system, the domestic context of the intervening state, and the 'indigenous terrain' of the target state" (1992, 16). In Elman's critical study of the democratic peace, "each chapter tests the applicability and the explanatory power of the democratic peace theory against particular historical episodes. We look to see whether the decision-making process corroborates the causal logic of the theory and its various predictions" (1997a, 42). Walt's study on revolutions and war compares the "process-tracing of the relationship between each revolutionary stage and its main foreign interlocutors for at least ten years after the revolution" (1996, 15–16). For Snyder, in his study of strategic beliefs and overextension, the use of process tracing is an indirect way to measure causal variables. Thus, to determine whether the political system is cartelized, Snyder observes the political process to see if groups behave as if they were in a cartelized system (1991, 61). Adler and Barnett, in their study of security community, explicitly use process tracing: "tracing historically the material and cognitive conditions that shape the evolution and institutionalization of the security community" (1998, 434–35). In Rock's study of great power rapprochement, the use of process tracing enables him not only to identify "the various factors motivating and influencing individual decision-makers and public opinion" but also to "discover their interactive effects and assess their relative significance" (1989, 20).

Case Study Methods in International Security Studies

Thus, given the inherent difficulties of selection bias, endogeneity, and setting a perfect or almost perfect comparison in the "method of difference," process tracing has become a more feasible strategy for designing case study research in international security, whether in a single case or by a comparison of several cases. Intuitively, this methodological strategy is not very different from (if not identical to) a detailed and careful historical analysis as performed by diplomatic historians. The overlap between a deep and detailed analysis performed by a historian and a structured comparison of a few case studies as performed by a political scientist is evident in the superb studies by Stephen Rock about great power rapprochement at the turn of the twentieth century (1989) and appeasement (2000). This is a good example of the need to link international security studies and diplomatic history, as is advocated in the edited volume of Elman and Elman (2001).

The Utility of Case Studies for Studying International Security

This section discusses a few relevant books on international security that have employed case study methods, both single cases and structured-focused comparisons. I will also demonstrate how the use of case studies can *complement* the findings of other methods, such as quantitative research, as in the case of the literature on democratic peace.

Single Case Studies

Although King, Keohane, and Verba (1994, 209–11) have questioned the possible theoretical contributions of a single case research design, the use of one or two case studies can serve important heuristic purposes, provide a plausibility probe or testing for competing theories, and be quite revealing about the strength of a theory (especially if these are "crucial cases") (see Lijphart 1971; Eckstein 1975). The following examples from the Cold War are illustrative of substantial findings derived from the use of cases that proved to be crucial for the understanding of a given historical period.

In 1971, Graham Allison wrote *Essence of Decision: Explaining the Cuban Missile Crisis*. This is probably the best example of a single case as a disciplined-configurative case study. The research design develops and tests three conceptual models of decision making in order to explain U.S. and

Soviet behavior during the Cuban missile crisis (1971, 3–5). Thus, the book can be treated as a single case study (the Cuban missile crisis) or as three case studies (as instances of the same event), each of which uses one of the frames of reference or models in searching for answers to the major questions of the Cuban missile crisis (v): Why did the Soviet Union place strategic offensive missiles in Cuba? Why did the United States respond with a naval quarantine in Cuba? Why did the Soviets withdraw eventually? The single case study (or three variations of it) is supposed to give us an approximate answer to those questions and to illustrate the three decision-making frameworks. The result is a pathbreaking work in international security and in political science in general.

A second example of a seminal study on the Cold War is Lebow and Stein's study on two nuclear crises during the Cold War (the Cuban missile crisis of 1962 and the Yom Kippur War crisis of October 1973). The authors explore the contradictory consequences of nuclear threats and weapons and show that strategies of deterrence and compellence were more provocative than restraining, so that they actually prolonged the Cold War (1994, ix). Lebow and Stein's research design of two "crucial cases" serves heuristic purposes in a disciplined-configurative way, while at the same time providing a rich historical analysis, through process tracing, that might be relevant for other cases as well. Thus, in their ambitious formulations, the authors claim that "by looking through the window of these two crises at the broader superpower relationship, we can learn lessons that will be applicable to the prevention, management, and resolution of international conflict beyond the Cold War" (4–5).

Structured-Focused Comparisons

Structured-focused comparisons have been very popular among authors of international security studies who use case study methods, as mentioned earlier. Two important examples of this method are Alexander L. George and Richard Smoke's *Deterrence in American Foreign Policy: Theory and Practice* (1974) and Alexander George's *Avoiding War: Problems of Crisis Management* (1991).

Deterrence in American Foreign Policy examines and critiques deterrence theory and deterrence policy as applied by the U.S. government between the end of World War II and the Cuban missile crisis of 1962. The book includes eleven case studies that epitomize the most serious crises during the Cold War (the Berlin Blockade of 1948–49; the outbreak of the Korean War; the Chinese intervention in Korea; Korea and Indochina in 1953–54; the Taiwan Strait crisis of 1954–55; the Hungarian Revolution of 1956; deterrence in the Middle East in 1957–58; the Quemoy crisis of 1958; the Berlin crises of 1958–59 and 1961; and the Cuban missile crisis of 1962). Instead of a formal theory of deterrence, the authors suggest an alternative, typological theory of deterrence.

According to George and Smoke, the use of case studies fulfills two major functions. First, it provides an empirical basis for the theoretical refinement and formulation of deterrence. Second, the case studies offer historical explanations for the outcomes of major deterrence efforts of the Cold War period (1974, 105). In this sense, the process tracing illustrated in those cases represents an early example of the link between political science and diplomatic history.

In 1991, Alexander George and his contributors provided a comprehensive and systematic analysis of the phenomenon of "inadvertent wars" in *Avoiding War: Problems of Crisis Management.* Similarly to the 1974 study, by focusing on the failures and successes of crisis management, the case studies (or "case histories") provide an empirical background for developing generic knowledge about the phenomenology of inadvertent wars and the causal dynamics of crisis escalation to inadvertent wars (9–10). The cases include the Crimean War; World War I; the U.S.-China war in Korea; the Arab-Israeli War of 1967; the Suez War of 1956; the Berlin Blockade of 1948–49; the Cuban missile crisis of 1962; the Sino-Soviet border crisis of 1969; the War of Attrition between Israel and Egypt in 1969–70; and the Arab-Israeli War of October 1973. Through the method of structured-focused comparison the authors draw generalizations about principles and strategies of crisis management, extrapolating toward more contemporary instances such as the reference to the Iraqi invasion of Kuwait in 1990.

Among the wide array of studies that have adopted the structured-focused comparison, some authors employ a more rigorous approach, following the advice of George (1979). Those studies include, among others, the study of protracted military interventions (Jentleson and Levite 1992, 11); the link between revolutions and wars (Walt 1996); overexpansion of imperialistic policies of great powers (Snyder 1991); the rapprochement between great powers (Rock 1989); the study of appeasement (Rock 2000); and the problem of peaceful territorial change (Kacowicz 1994). A common thread running through those books is the deliberate (if not always successful) attempt by the authors to specify and justify their case selection, to design their case study method in a scientific (or quasi-scientific) manner, and to draw cross-case comparisons according to the formulated design (see Maoz 2002).

Other authors comparing case studies have followed the method of structured-focused comparison more loosely. Those include studies about state expansion and contraction (Lustick 1993); democratic peace (Elman 1997b); the impact of norms in the international society (Finnemore 1996); the culture of national security (Katzenstein 1996a); security communities (Adler and Barnett 1998); zones of peace in the Third World (Kacowicz 1998); and stable peace among nations (Kacowicz et al. 2000).

Case Study Methods and
the Democratic Peace Research

From the early 1960s through the late 1980s empirical research on democratic peace utilized statistical methods to test for a possible correlation between domestic regime types and war (or peace). Yet, as the focus of the research program began to shift from whether such a correlation exists to why it exists, the advantages of using case studies to test specific causal mechanisms and alternative explanations of the democratic peace became more evident (Layne 1994; Owen 1994; Ray 1995; see esp. Elman 1997b; Owen 1997). Statistical studies have been useful in testing for the empirical existence of an interdemocratic peace (Maoz and Abdolali 1989; Maoz and Russett 1993; Ray 1995). Conversely, explaining why such a peace might exist could best be addressed through the detailed examination of the decision-making processes in historical case studies, trying to understand why democracy mattered, if at all, for war and peace decisions (Bennett and George 1997a, 4–5; Elman 1997a, 33; see also Ray 1995, 158–59). Yet the argument for using case studies as a *test* of the democratic peace thesis is controversial in itself: critics of case study methods point out that the theory of democratic peace explains only patterns and trends of interstate behavior, not individual foreign policy choices. Hence, the examination of a limited number of case studies cannot be used either to prove or to disprove the general theory (see Elman 1997a, 45), due to the inherent pitfalls of the method, including case selection bias and indeterminacy.

Moreover, the use of case studies to test the democratic peace thesis has led to contradictory and inconclusive results, as reflected in the empirical work of Layne (1994), Owen (1994, 1997), and Elman (1997b). Using the process-tracing method, Layne (1994, 13) tests the robustness of democratic peace theory's causal logic by focusing on "near misses," specific cases in which democratic states had both opportunities and reasons to fight each other but did not. In his analysis, balance of power, not democratic peace, provides the most compelling explanation of why war was avoided. Owen (1994, 1997) tests propositions from existing democratic peace theories on twelve historical cases (using process tracing as well and researching two of the cases studied by Layne). However, Owen reaches opposite conclusions. In his analysis, ideas embedded in liberal democracies provide the causal mechanism that prevent democracies from going to war against one another (1994, 123). Finally, the picture that Elman draws in her edited volume after comparing international crises between democratic, mixed, and nondemocratic dyads—using the same method, including process tracing—is at best inconclusive: "democratic peace theory is neither completely invalid nor universally applicable" (1997c, 503). However, according to Elman, the relative advantages of using case studies are clear. Comparative case study research design "can help us to identify the reasons why democracy generates pacific international outcomes; specify the circumstances under which a liberal peace might break down; and assess the extent to which foreign policy makers act in ways that are consistent with the theory's propositions" (1997b, viii–xi). All in all, using case study methods—both within-case analysis (process tracing) and cross-case comparisons—can illuminate the causal mechanism of the democratic peace idea, even though causal arguments are difficult to prove.

Summary and Conclusions

The methodological debate among scholars of international security poses qualitative methods in juxtaposition to both statistical analysis and formal modeling. This debate can be illustrated by the "rational deterrence debate." As George and Smoke point out (1974, 1989), early works in security studies, focusing on the nuclear deterrence between the United States and the Soviet Union at the height of the Cold War, offered little empirical support for their conclusions and prescriptions. Thus, the comparative case study method was explicitly designed to counter these ahistorical and formal approaches. By focusing on concrete historical examples, the comparative method of structured-focused comparison sought to develop a more appropriate and "policy-relevant" deterrence theory (George and Smoke 1974, 616–42). In more specific terms, George and Smoke (1989) argue that the logic of formal "rational deterrence theory" is flawed for several reasons. It cannot be operationalized, since there is no key concept to single out; the absence of a challenge to deterrence can be spuriously scored as a deterrence success; situational analysis is crucial; and the theory cannot define its own scope and relevance. In turn, formal theorists maintain that there has always been a trade-off between analytical power and historical description. In their view, case study methods cannot avoid selection bias when focusing on cases that involve failures of deterrence. Moreover, one should not confuse empirical generalizations with theories. In other words, theories cannot be derived from case studies (Achen and Snidal 1989).

Despite their inherent pitfalls, case study methods have remained a popular and useful tool to further our understanding of international security. The following points are critical when considering these methods.

- Case study methods have an important role in illuminating the current ontological, epistemological, and methodological debates in the field of international relations in general and more specifically in the study of international security.
- When we turn to a research design of empirical studies in international security, we cannot always keep the pristine logic of inference as suggested by King, Keohane, and Verba (1994), especially in relation to methodological problems such as selection bias and even endogeneity. We have to compromise stern methodological premises with the limitations and constraints of the complex reality we want to understand and explain.
- Like many other authors in this volume, I call here for a pluralist and eclectic use of different methodologies to enrich the quality of

our empirical research. In other words, since qualitative, quantitative, and formal methods complement (rather than contradict) each other, diverse methodologies should be used in security studies. For instance, in my study of peaceful territorial change, I applied a two-step methodology, starting from a large historical sample of successful and unsuccessful cases of peaceful territorial change since 1815 ($N = 100$) and then turning to the comparative method of four case studies, according to a structured-focused comparison (Kacowicz 1994, 10).

- My plea for pluralism and possible convergence is not confined only to the methodological realm. Thus, I argue here that the use of case studies seems to offer a middle ground between soft positivists and conventional constructivists, who intensively use process-tracing methods and similar historical analysis of detailed cases.

- The case study methods in international security are far from being methodologically ideal. At the same time, they have offered us a rich variety of tools for a better understanding of our complex reality. The analysis of international relations should center upon the most important substantial issues or *problematiques,* such as war and peace. Case study methods, because of their emphasis on specific historical events, have the advantage of focusing researchers' attention on the historical and empirical reality that they are interested in understanding and explaining.

Recommended Readings

Allison, G. T. 1971. *Essence of Decision: Explaining the Cuban Missile Crisis.* Boston: Little, Brown.

Elman, M. F., ed. 1997. *Paths to Peace: Is Democracy the Answer?* Cambridge: MIT Press.

George, A. L., and R. Smoke. 1974. *Deterrence in American Foreign Policy: Theory and Practice.* New York: Columbia University Press.

Lebow, R. N., and J. G. Stein. 1994. *We All Lost the Cold War.* Princeton: Princeton University Press.

Yin, R. K. 1984. *Case Study Research: Design and Methods.* Beverly Hills, CA: Sage.

Notes

I would like to thank Galia Press-Bar-Nathan, Orly Kacowicz, and the editors for their comments and suggestions in previous drafts of this essay.

1. Conceptual generalizations that help categorize different items, without the rigor of causality. For more on this issue see Andrew Bennett and Alexander L. George (1997b), Developing and Using Typological Theories in Case Study Research, paper presented at the 38th Annual Convention of the International Studies Association in Toronto, March 18–22.

References

Achen, C., and D. Snidal. 1989. Rational Deterrence Theory and Comparative Case Studies. *World Politics* 41 (2): 143–69.

Adler, E. 1997. Seizing the Middle Ground: Constructivism in World Politics. *European Journal of International Relations* 3:319–63.

Adler, E., and M. Barnett, eds. 1998. *Security Communities.* Cambridge: Cambridge University Press.

Allison, G. T. 1971. *Essence of Decision: Explaining the Cuban Missile Crisis.* Boston: Little, Brown.

Bennett, A. 1999. Causal Inference in Case Studies: From Mill's Methods to Causal Mechanisms. APSA Annual Meeting, Atlanta.

————. 2000. Case Study Methods: Design, Use, and Comparative Advantages. 41st Annual Convention of the International Studies Association, Los Angeles, California.

Bennett, A., and A. L. George. 1997a. Case Study Methods and Research on the Democratic Peace. APSA Annual Meeting, Washington, DC.

————. 1997b. Developing and Using Typological Theories in Case Study Research. Annual Convention of the International Studies Association, Toronto, March 18–22.

————. 1997c. Process Tracing in Case Study Research. MacArthur Foundation Workshop on Case Study Methods, Belfer Center for Science and International Affairs, Harvard University.

Collier, D. 1993. The Comparative Method. In *Political Science: The State of the Discipline II,* edited by A. W. Finifter. Washington, DC: APSA.

Desch, M. C. 1998. Culture Clash: Assessing the Importance of Ideas in Security Studies. *International Security* 23:141–70.

Dessler, D. 1989. What's at Stake in the Agent-Structure Debate? *International Organization* 43:441–73.

Eckstein, H. 1975. Case Study and Theory in Political Science. In *Handbook of*

Political Science, vol. 7, *Strategies of Inquiry,* edited by F. Greenstein and N. Polsby. Reading, MA: Addison-Wesley Press.

Elman, C., and M. F. Elman, eds. 2001. *Bridges and Boundaries: Historians, Political Scientists, and the Study of International Relations.* Cambridge: MIT Press.

Elman, M. F. 1997a. Introduction: The Need for a Qualitative Test of the Democratic Peace Theory. In *Paths to Peace,* edited by M. F. Elman. Cambridge: MIT Press.

———, ed. 1997b. *Paths to Peace: Is Democracy the Answer?* Cambridge: MIT Press.

———. 1997c. Testing the Democratic Peace Theory. In *Paths to Peace,* edited by M. F. Elman. Cambridge: MIT Press.

Finnemore, M. 1996. *National Interests in International Society.* Ithaca: Cornell University Press.

George, A. L. 1979. Case Studies and Theory Development: The Method of Structured, Focused Comparison. In *Diplomacy: New Approaches in History, Theory, and Policy,* edited by P. G. Lauren. New York: Free Press.

———, ed. 1991. *Avoiding War: Problems of Crisis Management.* Boulder: Westview Press.

———. 1997. The Role of the Congruence Method for Case Study Research. 38th Annual Convention of the International Studies Association, Toronto.

George, A. L., and T. J. McKeown. 1985. Case Studies and Theories of Organizational Decision Making. In *Advances in Information Processing in Organizations,* edited by R. Coulam and R. Smith. Greenwich, CT: JAI Press.

George, A. L., and R. Smoke. 1974. *Deterrence in American Foreign Policy: Theory and Practice.* New York: Columbia University Press.

———. 1989. Deterrence and Foreign Policy. *World Politics* 41 (2): 170–82.

Hopf, T. 1998. The Promise of Constructivism in International Relations Theory. *International Security* 23:171–200.

Jentleson, B. W., and A. E. Levite. 1992. The Analysis of Protracted Foreign Military Intervention. In *Foreign Military Intervention,* edited by A. E. Levite, B. W. Jentleson, and L. Berman. New York: Columbia University Press.

Jervis, R., R. N. Lebow, and J. G. Stein. 1985. *Psychology and Deterrence.* Baltimore: Johns Hopkins University Press.

Kacowicz, A. M. 1994. *Peaceful Territorial Change.* Columbia: University of South Carolina Press.

———. 1998. *Zones of Peace in the Third World: South America and West Africa in Comparative Perspective.* Albany: SUNY Press.

Kacowicz, A. M., Y. Bar-Siman-Tov, O. Elgstrom, and M. Jerneck, eds. 2000. *Stable Peace among Nations.* Lanham, MD: Rowman and Littlefield.

Katzenstein, P. J., ed. 1996a. *The Culture of National Security: Norms and Identity in World Politics.* New York: Columbia University Press.

———. 1996b. Introduction: Alternative Perspectives on National Security. In

The Culture of National Security, edited by P. J. Katzenstein. New York: Columbia University Press.

King, G., R. O. Keohane, and S. Verba. 1994. *Designing Social Inquiry: Scientific Inference in Qualitative Research.* Princeton: Princeton University Press.

Kowert, P., and J. Legro. 1996. Norms, Identity, and Their Limits: A Theoretical Reprise. In *The Culture of National Security,* edited by P. J. Katzenstein. New York: Columbia University Press.

Layne, C. 1994. Kant or Cant: The Myth of the Democratic Peace. *International Security* 19:5–49.

Lebow, R. N., and J. G. Stein. 1994. *We All Lost the Cold War.* Princeton: Princeton University Press.

Levite, A. E., B. W. Jentleson, and L. Berman, eds. 1992. *Foreign Military Intervention: The Dynamics of Protracted Conflict.* New York: Columbia University Press.

Lijphart, A. 1971. Comparative Politics and the Comparative Method. *American Political Science Review* 65 (2): 682–93.

Lustick, I. S. 1993. *Unsettled States, Disputed Lands: Britain and Ireland, France and Algeria, Israel and the West Bank-Gaza.* Ithaca: Cornell University Press.

Maoz, Z. 2002. Case Study Methodology in International Studies. Manuscript, Tel-Aviv University, Department of Political Science.

Maoz, Z., and N. Abdolali. 1989. Regime Type and International Conflict. *Journal of Conflict Resolution* 33:3–35.

Maoz, Z., and B. Russett. 1993. Normative and Structural Causes of Democratic Peace, 1946–86. *American Political Science Review* 87 (3): 624–38.

Owen, J. M. 1994. How Liberalism Produces Democratic Peace. *International Security* 19:87–125.

———. 1997. *Liberal Peace, Liberal War: American Politics and International Security.* Ithaca: Cornell University Press.

Paul, T. V. 1994. *Asymmetric Conflicts: War Initiation by Weaker Powers.* Cambridge: Cambridge University Press.

Ragin, C. C. 1994. *Constructing Social Research: The Unity and Diversity of Method.* Thousand Oaks, CA: Pine Forge Press.

Ray, J. L. 1995. *Democracy and International Conflict: An Evaluation of the Democratic Peace Proposition.* Columbia: University of South Carolina Press.

Rock, S. R. 1989. *Why Peace Breaks Out: Great Power Rapprochement in Historical Perspective.* Chapel Hill: University of North Carolina Press.

———. 2000. *Appeasement in International Politics.* Lexington: University Press of Kentucky.

Snyder, J. 1984. *The Ideology of the Offensive: Military Decision-Making and the Disasters of 1914.* Ithaca: Cornell University Press.

———. 1991. *Myths of Empire: Domestic Politics and International Ambitions.* Ithaca: Cornell University Press.

Steves, F. 1999. Book Review of "Zones of Peace in the Third World." *Millennium* 28:789–91.

Van Evera, S. 1997. *Guide to Methods for Students of Political Science.* Ithaca: Cornell University Press.

Walt, S. M. 1987. *The Origins of Alliances.* Ithaca: Cornell University Press.

———. 1996. *Revolution and War.* Ithaca: Cornell University Press.

Yin, R. K. 1984. *Case Study Research: Design and Methods.* Beverly Hills, CA: Sage.

Part II. Quantitative Methods

6. The Promise and Perils of Statistics in International Relations

Bear F. Braumoeller and Anne E. Sartori

Students of international relations who are considering investing the time and effort necessary to learn statistics would be justified in first asking exactly what the statistical method is capable of doing. The answer can be summed up in a single sentence: it permits the researcher to draw inferences about reality based on the data at hand and the laws of probability. The ability to draw inferences is immensely helpful in assessing the extent to which the empirical expectations generated by theories are consistent with reality. It is also helpful in uncovering interesting questions or puzzles (e.g., Zinnes 1980) which occur when evidence is inconsistent with prior theoretical expectations.

In the sections that follow we attempt to highlight both the promise and the perils of the use of statistics in the pursuit of a better understanding of international political behavior. We do not aim to survey the vast literature in international relations that uses statistics; rather, we refer to particular works to illustrate our points. First, we discuss the advantages of the statistical method. These include the ability to aggregate information from large numbers of cases and to use the laws of probability to generalize well beyond those cases; the ability not just to describe associations among phenomena but to calculate the probabilities that such associations are the product of chance; and—as a direct result—the ability to gain a better understanding of the sources of human behavior in international affairs.

Despite our enthusiasm about applying statistical methods to international affairs in theory, we are cognizant of its shortcomings in practice. The shortcomings that concern us most are not the oft-stated worries of many quantitative researchers—failures to satisfy regression assumptions, the need to ensure adequate levels of internal and external validity in our measures, and so on.[1] Such topics are covered at length in statistics and econometrics texts and need not be recited here. Rather, we are particularly concerned about a more fundamental problem: the widespread use of statistics with inadequate attention to the goal of *testing theories of international behavior*. In the following sections, we discuss two classes of shortcomings. The first pertains to the widespread neglect of the development of theory prior to the specification of a statistical model: statistical tests of theories usually have little worth unless the theories that they test are solid. The second concerns the process of deriving inferences from data, the finer points of which are too often neglected.

Advantages of the Statistical Method

One advantage of the statistical method is that it permits political scientists to aggregate information from a tremendous number of cases. This advantage is perhaps so obvious that its importance is often overlooked. To comprehend its magnitude we need only imagine trying to make sense of a thousand surveys of individual attitudes, beliefs, voting behavior, and so on, *without* the aid of statistics. The ability to extract even basic summary statistics from such a mass of data is immensely valuable: even something as unsophisticated as a sample mean—say, per capita GNP—conveys a wealth of information in compact and understandable form.

The ability to aggregate information is a potent stimulus for theorizing. Theory development often begins when a researcher uncovers an empirical puzzle that remains unexplained by prior theory. Such a puzzle leads to a search for an explanation and eventually to new or better-developed theory. A puzzle can emerge from a single case, but the researcher often would like to know whether or not it indicates a more widespread pattern of behavior. Only statistics can provide the answer to this question.[2] For example, statistical analyses indicate that a number of pairs of states (e.g., India and Pakistan) engage in a disproportionate number of wars (Goertz and Diehl 1992). The empirical discovery of this phenomenon, which the literature terms "enduring rivalry," has led to a number of attempts to explain the behavior of this set of dyads (e.g., Vasquez 1995; Bennett 1998; Diehl and Goertz 2000): what is it that makes states become rivals; why do rivals fight so often; and how do rivalries end?

The use of statistics also makes the terms of a given debate more explicit. Inference requires assumptions, whether implicit or explicit; statistics force scholars to be quite explicit about the nature of at least some assumptions. Transparency is valuable both because assumptions should be as clear as possible and because one can compensate for violated assumptions if they are understood.[3]

In addition to standards of inference, the use of statistics necessarily entails standards of evidence. Even the most scrupulous researcher can be hard-pressed to avoid selecting only the evidence that would support his or her theory. Here, too, standardization is an asset; the need for coding procedures forces the researcher to be explicit about criteria for measurement and mitigates the human tendency to notice only trends that are consistent with the theory under investigation. Quantification can be a considerable boon to both reliability and validity: in the former case, explicit tests of reliability can flag unacceptably noisy measures, while in the latter, details of the coding process make it clear what is and is not being measured.[4] For example, the Polity IV democracy index is an aid to scholars because the coding rules are specific and reliability can be calculated.

Statistical techniques also permit us to assess the claim that observed associations among variables are due to chance. Such assessments are critical to the testing of theory, and they are often very difficult to make. The statistical method can make the task almost trivially easy. For example, the extent to which any given Third World country votes with the United States in the UN will naturally vary from year to year; as a result, it can be difficult to determine whether an increase or decrease following a change in domestic political regime is an indicator of realignment or simply the product of random fluctuation. Absent the ability to assess the odds that such fluctuations are due to chance, analysts could argue endlessly over their substantive significance.[5] Hagan (1989) addresses this question by testing to determine whether mean voting scores under a given regime differ significantly from mean voting scores under its successor; in about half of the eighty-seven cases he examines, he finds that random fluctuation is a highly improbable ($p < 0.05$) explanation for the difference in voting patterns across regimes. Although statistical testing does not answer the question with perfect certainty, it gives far more precise answers than could otherwise be obtained. In so doing it dramatically narrows potential areas of disagreement.

By answering the question of whether observed associations are the plausible result of chance, the statistical method also permits us to draw causal inferences. Using statistics, one can investigate ancillary associations implied by a posited causal process and assess the probability that these associations are due to chance.[6] Because international relations scholars constantly seek to understand why actors behave as they do, this ability is perhaps the method's greatest contribution to the discipline. To continue the preceding example, one might wonder not just whether a given country's UN votes coincide to a greater or lesser degree with those of the United States but why. One obvious possibility would be that American foreign aid, to put it crudely, buys votes: American leaders use foreign assistance to induce cooperation. If this is the case, increases in American aid should be followed by an increased coincidence of votes in the UN on issues considered to be important by the United States. Wang (1999) tests this hypothesis by examining the voting records of sixty-five developing countries from 1984 to 1993 and finds that an increase in American foreign aid generally precedes an increase in voting alignment; moreover, the positive relationship between the two is very unlikely (again, $p < 0.05$) to be the result of chance. Absent statistical techniques, the effects of American aid could be debated one anecdote at a time without any conclusion in sight. Even the most meticulous case selection and comparison could never produce such precise results.

A final strength of the statistical method is the fact that it conveys the ability to test two explanations against one another with remarkable precision. For example, while tests of realist and of domestic-political explanations of conflict typically limit themselves to ruling out chance associations, Clarke (2001) tests realism against two domestic-political explanations and finds that realism "either does as well as the rival or better than the rival" theory (28).[7]

Potential Pitfalls

Despite the power of the statistical method, statistical evidence sometimes is far from persuasive. This failure typically stems from misunderstanding or ignorance of the underlying purpose of the method. It is critical for users of statistical techniques to realize that statistical models are models of human behavior and that, as a result, the assumptions that underlie them are substantively nontrivial. Common assumptions—such as simple additivity among variables—constitute theoretical assertions about how reality works, and the prevalence of unreflective assumptions in statistical research has contributed to a widespread perception among formal modelers that statistical research is theoretically unsophisticated (see, e.g., Morton 1999, 3, 16–24 and passim). It need not be. In the following sections, we focus upon two sets of common errors, which we call errors of specification and errors of inference.

Errors of Specification

In order to convey useful information about the world, statistical tests must relate meaningfully to the causal mechanisms implied by the theories that they purport to evaluate. Failure to do so constitutes an error of specification. Three such errors are, in our view, of paramount importance. First, empirical researchers often spend too much effort calculating correlations with little or no attention to theory. Second, theory itself often is weak and difficult to test because it is too imprecise or too shallow. Finally, empirical researchers often impose a statistical model on the theory instead of crafting a model to test the theory. Under any of these circumstances, even the most sophisticated statistical techniques are futile.

The large literature on the democratic peace illustrates both the benefits of using statistics and the pitfalls of doing so with too little theory. Several studies demonstrated a relationship between democracy and peace and explained the relationship between the two by offering two theories, one based on liberal norms (e.g., Doyle 1986; Russett 1993) and the other based on the domestic political structure of democratic states (e.g., Rummel 1979; Morgan and Campbell 1991; Bueno de Mesquita and Lalman 1992).[8] Debate over whether or not there was, in Gertrude Stein's words, a "there there" ensued, with authors arguing both pro and con.[9] Researchers developed and tested additional hypotheses based on the generic notion of cooperation among democracies, yielding additional empirical insights.[10] Occasionally, they derived implications from the theories that would allow them to be tested against each other.[11] The result was an unusually comprehensive corpus of literature describing the behavior of democratic states.

The development of theory, however, proceeded at a much slower pace than the proliferation of statistical associations: with the exception of David Lake's (1992) article, which offered an explanation based on the relative rent-seeking behavior of democratic and nondemocratic states, variants of structural and normative theories dominated the study of democracies and peace for well over a decade. Recently, three additional contenders—the informational theory forwarded by Kenneth Schultz (1999), the institutional variant laid out by Bueno de Mesquita et al. (1999), and the evolutionary learning approach of Cederman (2001)—have rekindled interest in the democratic peace phenomenon. They have also raised an issue that may have widespread implications for the studies that preceded them: the question of what the independent variable should be. Although both the ability to generate audience costs and the existence of a broad constituency are correlated with democracy, for example, the correlations are not equal to one.[12] The development of new theory has brought to light the possibility that scores of books and articles have based their conclusions on measurements of the wrong causal variable.[13]

Unfortunately, simply paying attention to theory is not enough: many international relations theories are too imprecise or shallow to be subjected to tests against other theories. When a theory is imprecise, a wide range of relationships between independent and dependent variables is consistent with the theory. In the extreme, an imprecise theory may be entirely unfalsifiable. For example, as Lake and Powell (1999, 23) note, Waltzian neorealism suggests that states respond in one of two contradictory ways when confronted with a powerful adversary in a multipolar system: they either balance against an aggressive state or bandwagon with that state (Waltz 1979). If we see states balancing (or bandwagoning), is this behavior consistent with realism? Theoretically, the answer is yes, so that neither finding falsifies the theory. Similarly, the hypothesis that bipolarity is associated with the prevalence of peace is vague and untestable; only when polarity is carefully defined (see Wagner 1993) is this hypothesis falsifiable. In some cases, making a theory precise is merely a question of operationalizing variables. In others, as with polarity, lack of precision corresponds to inadequate definitions and is a weakness in the theory itself.

When a theory is shallow, it has testable implications, but only one or two. It may explain a broad range of phenomena, but it fails to explain even a few details of any one type of event. For example, scholars often use the Prisoners' Dilemma game to model international relations (see Snidal, chap. 10, fig. 2, this vol.). The Prisoners' Dilemma is a striking analogy, and it has been a useful step in theory development. The insights scholars glean from it are applicable to a broad range of problems.[14] Unfortunately, the trade-off in this case is depth.[15]

Because of its simplicity, a two-by-two game yields few implications about any specific substantive situation. Researchers usually derive implications from game-theoretic models by performing "comparative statics": they vary some feature of a model, usually the players' payoffs, and determine how the logical implications of the game change as a result. However, a two-by-two game has few elements that can be varied in this way; it portrays only one decision by each actor and four possible outcomes.

For example, a researcher might use the Prisoners' Dilemma game (Snidal, chap. 10) to investigate whether or not states' possession of nuclear weapons affects the probability of war. He or she might assume that states' payoffs differ depending upon whether or not both states have nuclear weapons. Perhaps, if both states possess nuclear weapons, mutual noncooperation represents nuclear war and is each state's least-preferred outcome. If so, then one testable implication of the game is that the states are more likely to cooperate (less likely to go to war) if they have nuclear weapons than if they do not.[16]

However, the model has few other implications since it has few components besides these payoffs to vary. Thus, the model cannot be tested against those alternative theories that also imply that jointly nuclear dyads are more peaceful. It can be tested only against the null hypothesis that the possession of nuclear weapons does not affect the probability of war. Shallow theory requires attention to theory development first. Statistical tests can do little to increase our understanding of the situation and must come later, when their empirical force can be brought to bear at the point of greatest theoretical leverage.

The final specification problem that we will discuss is inattention to the causal process or processes that generated the data. Correct specification of functional form requires close attention to theory, and widespread reliance on canned econometric techniques still tempts users to rely on statistical convention rather than theoretical logic. The form of a statistical test should be derived from the form of the theory, not vice versa. As a consequence, the ability to find a statistical test suitable for one's theory is crucial; the ability to design such a test when one does not exist would be ideal. Toward these ends we cannot overemphasize the importance of wide and deep familiarity with both mathematics and statistics. The old adage about hammers and nails is appropriate: when the only tool you have is regression, the world has a surprising tendency to look linear and additive. Possession of a larger and more diverse methodological tool kit alleviates

135

this problem to some degree, of course, but being up to date on the latest advances in maximum likelihood, Markov chain Monte Carlo, or Hilbert space methods will be of little use if the researcher gives insufficient attention to the choice of an estimator that is appropriate to the theory at hand and the causal process that generated the data. Another, equally obvious lesson is equally critical: *think about the theory.*

Attention to theory is not the only way to guard against misspecification, however. At times the data can suggest a markedly different functional form, perhaps one consistent with a different theory altogether, and an inattentive researcher can easily miss such a signal. As Anscombe (1973) pointed out, statistical models can be imposed on the data and can fit the data fairly well, even if their functional forms grossly misrepresent the relationship of interest. Table 1 and figure 1 demonstrate this point graphically: The regression results in table 1 suggest a significant linear relationship between Y and X, but they could have been generated by any one of the four data sets graphed in figure 1. In an era in which data sets can be obtained in moments and regressions run even more quickly, this underscores a fundamental lesson: *look at the data.*

The eyeball test is part of the intricate interplay between theory and data that occurs in skillful application of the scientific method. By thinking about the variables, the researcher often can anticipate the functional form that he or she sees in the data. For example, the relationship between the balance of forces and the probability that a state starts a war probably is not linear; moving from a 2-to-1 balance to a 3-to-1 balance probably has more of an effect than moving from a 100-to-1 to 101-to-1 balance. Thus, one might posit that the log of the military balance captures the hypothesized relationship better than the military balance itself. Never-

TABLE 1. Relationship between Y and X

Y	Coef.	S.E.	t	$P > |t|$	95% Conf. Interval	
X	0.500	0.118	4.24	0.002	0.233	0.767
Constant	3.000	1.125	2.67	0.026	0.455	5.545

$n = 11$	$R^2 = 0.667$
$F(1,9) = 17.98$	Adj. $R^2 = 0.629$
Prob $> F = 0.002$	Root MSE = 1.237

Source: From Anscombe (1973)

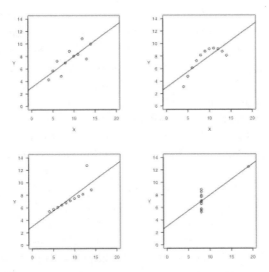

Fig. 1.   Four data sets consistent with results in table 1

theless, in theorizing, one may miss important nonlinearities. A look at the data can provide a useful reminder that inadequate attention has been given to functional form.

The overall message is simple: statistical tests should correspond to theory that is well-developed. Toward this end, the use of formal theory can be especially useful in that it prompts careful thinking and forces the researcher to specify many important aspects of the situation under study. For example, a game-theoretic model requires the basic elements of theory: assumptions about which actors are important to the outcome being explained, what they care about and how strongly (the utility that they receive if various outcomes occur), the choices that are available to them, the order in which they can make choices, and the relationship of choices to outcomes. Game-theoretic models also must specify the information available to actors and their beliefs about any information about which they are uncertain. Varying any of these raw elements of the model produces implications about the relationships between the element (independent variable) and the action taken or outcomes (dependent variable).[17] Without any of the raw elements, the model cannot be solved. Thus, the researcher cannot deduce implications without specifying the required

137

assumptions. The statistical method does not force the user to provide, or even to think very hard about, any of these important elements of theory, nor does formal theory force the user to think about some of the intricacies of empirical testing or to say anything about the real world. Because each provides what the other lacks, the combination of the two methods constitutes a potent tool for inquiry.

Nevertheless, formalization is not a panacea for the problem of incomplete theory. The Prisoners' Dilemma model reveals three steps that the researcher must take in order to create testable (falsifiable) theory. First, whether the model is formal or verbal, the empirical researcher must specify precisely the real-world correspondents of the raw elements of the model. In the Prisoners' Dilemma example (Snidal, chap. 10, this vol.), the researcher must start by specifying what "cooperate" and "not cooperate" mean in the substantive problem at hand—possibly "no new arms" or "increase arms." He or she also must specify the real-world factors that constitute utility for a given actor. Which factors determine how much the states benefit from a state of mutual disarmament? How much do they like or dislike the other outcomes? Like the Prisoners' Dilemma, many models can be used to explain several real-world situations. Nevertheless, research would progress more rapidly if game theorists in particular were more specific about some of the possible real-world referents of their models.

Second, while simplicity is a virtue, the model must be complex enough to capture an explanation of an interesting phenomenon. We emphatically agree with the edict often attributed to Einstein that "everything should be made as simple as possible, but not simpler."

Third, the researcher often must resolve indeterminacy in a model before turning to empirical tests. Some game-theoretic models imply that a large number of outcomes are logically possible (corresponding to different equilibria). This indeterminacy does not make the models useless: they still narrow down the set of behaviors expected in a given situation. However, it does raise questions for empirical testing. For example, as Duncan Snidal discusses (chap. 10, this vol.), if the Prisoners' Dilemma is played repeatedly and players care sufficiently about the future, then many types of cooperative outcomes are possible (and mutual defection also is possible). Which outcome should the researcher expect to find in the real world? Game theory contains some tools for narrowing down the set of likely outcomes (called "equilibrium refinements"). However, multiple equilibria often remain, and some refinements seem worse than arbitrary.

Two equilibria of the same game can encompass very different substantive stories about the players' interactions. For example, some equilibria of repeated games specify that players forever punish those who decide not to act in a certain way. When a game-theoretic model leads to multiple equilibria, our preference is to consider each as its own explanation, with its own set of empirical implications.[18] If the results of statistical tests are inconsistent with the implications of an equilibrium, then that equilibrium is ruled out as an explanation for the outcome under investigation. Of course, researchers similarly can test different versions of the same, indeterminate verbal theory. For example, they can test a multiplicity of realisms. As with game-theoretic models, researchers should be up-front about the indeterminacy of the general model and about the specifics of the version that they are testing.

Game-theoretic modeling does not do away with the need to think about functional form and the nature of the error term. Researchers are increasingly considering how best to test the implications of game-theoretic models,[19] and international relations research is making progress on this front (see Signorino 1999a, 1999b; Smith 1999; Lewis and Schultz 2003; Sartori 2003). However, much work remains to be done. One thorny question is the extent to which factors outside the formal model (which is always quite simple), but thought to be theoretically important, should be considered in the statistical tests. For example, models are simplifications, and the error structure that comes literally from the model may not be the theorist's true best guess about the error in the underlying data-generating process. As the work on testing formal models progresses, it is our hope that researchers will continue to pay attention to the data as well as to theory. While the game-theoretic model may imply particular assumptions about the functional form and/or distribution of the error term, it is important to think about and look at the data before carrying these assumptions to the statistical model.

Errors of Inference

The two classes of problems that we have just discussed limit the extent to which statistical tests accurately assess the implications of a theory. A final set—not, we should emphasize, one that is unique to statistical methods—concerns the extent that tests of a given theory reveal information about reality. This problem is a marked tendency to ignore some of the thornier problems involved in integrating data into larger-scale explanations. In particular, the complexity of the role that data play in the broader enterprise of theory testing is rarely appreciated. To put it more bluntly, statistics can take the place of thinking.

The first way in which statistics can do so is via the blind application of statistical significance to judge the importance of a variable. Although the notion of statistical significance is immensely useful, its abuse can lead to a multitude of sins. There is a persistent tendency to focus on statistical significance (the probability that an observed relationship between X and Y occurred by chance) without paying attention to substantive significance (the magnitude of the relationship between changes in X and changes in Y).

A data set with 50,000 observations, for example, permits us to uncover even the most minute relationships among variables and demonstrate that they were unlikely to have occurred by chance. Such relationships may, however, provide only very weak support for the theory under consideration. A novice statistician who ran the analysis reported in table 2 might enthusiastically report very strong findings—a relationship between X and Y that is significant at the $p < 0.01$ level!—without ever realizing, as the data cloud in figure 2 makes clear, that the substantive relationship between the two is virtually nil.[20]

The relationship between the magnitude of a coefficient and substantive significance depends upon the problem at hand. There is no good quantitative rule for determining substantive significance. For example, assume that a researcher found that joint democracy decreased the probability of war from 0.03 to 0.001. One might be tempted to see this as an insubstantial decrease of 2.9 percentage points in the probability of the occurrence of war. However, given the extreme rarity of war, that seemingly minor decrease would imply that jointly democratic dyads experienced

TABLE 2. A Significant Regression Coefficient with 50,000 Observations

Y	Coef.	S.E.	t	$P > |t|$	95% Conf. Interval	
X	0.013	0.004	2.94	0.003	0.004	0.022
Constant	0.0007	0.004	0.15	0.881	−0.008	0.010

$N = 50,000$	$R^2 = 0.0002$
$F_{(1,49998)} = 8.64$	Adj. $R^2 = 0.0002$
Prob $> F = 0.003$	Root MSE = 1.0018

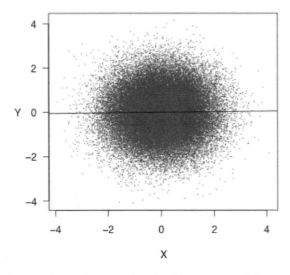

Fig. 2. Scatterplot of data summarized in table 2, with estimated regression line

one-thirtieth as much war as other dyads. In our opinion, this particular result would be extremely substantively important, because of its implications for both theory and policy. In general, what counts as substantively significant depends on the substance.

Political methodologists have succeeded in killing off widespread abuse of the R^2 coefficient (see Achen 1977) by distinguishing between degree of correlation and substantive significance, but this subtler form of confusion remains. The only good news is that, despite its tenacity, this tendency is at least decreasing. A survey of 211 articles on international relations from the past decade of some of the field's top journals[21] revealed that, prior to 1996, only 16.4 percent of the quantitative articles discussed substantive significance, but after that point 38.8 percent contained such discussions.

Moreover, much of the field seems to forget that the choice of a significance level for rejecting the null hypothesis is arbitrary. A better way to judge the certainty of one's results when the baseline is the null is simply to calculate the probability that an observed result is nonzero due to chance. Finding that this probability is 6 percent rather than 5 percent should decrease one's confidence in a study's finding only trivially. Unfortunately, researchers and journals often apply the "5 percent rule" and relegate such findings to the trash can.

Finally, levels of statistical significance are based on the assumption that a single test has been carried out on a single data set. Running multiple tests, or running the same set on different data sets, invalidates this assumption, and significance levels are therefore incorrect. Mock and Weisberg (1992) provide an amusing example of this point by examining the *Washington Post*'s assertion, based on data from the 1985–87 General Social Survey (GSS), that there is a relationship between an individual's partisanship and his or her zodiac sign. In fact, they demonstrate that such a relationship exists and is significant at the $p < 0.10$ level.[22] They then expand the sample to eleven separate years and demonstrate that there is only a significant relationship between sign and partisanship in one of them (1985). The probability of finding at least one significant relationship in eleven attempts, as they point out, is 0.69: far from being surprising, a result like the 1985 one is precisely what should be expected due to chance variation.

Few political scientists who utilize the statistical method would argue with the preceding example; even fewer, unfortunately, are mindful of its implications for the researcher who runs eleven regressions and finds one significant relationship. Most researchers can point to one or two colleagues whom they suspect of mining data sets behind closed doors until significant results appear.[23] The variables rarely are zodiac signs, but the associations uncovered in this fashion are no less silly. Worse, publication bias is pervasive: nonresults typically do not make it to print (of the 211 articles in the previous survey, just 10, or 4.7 percent, reported only null results), and as a result insignificant relationships may be discarded or ignored until a significant one happens along.

We have pointed to an unfortunate tendency among scholars of international relations to judge the importance of results by statistical rather than substantive significance. The second way in which statistics take the place of thinking is that researchers simply accept or reject a theory by examining one data set to assess whether or not the effect of one variable on another can reliably be distinguished from zero.[24] The implications of a nonzero coefficient for the status of a theory are not always clear, and practitioners typically pay far too little attention to this rather critical issue. To those who believe along with Lakatos (1970) that theory A should be retained until superior theory B is found, simply accepting or rejecting theories seriatim based on whether or not variables have nonzero effects can constitute a sin of omission. Lakatos asserts that a theory should be retained despite empirical anomalies until a better theory can be found. If one is a

Lakatosian, therefore, the ultimate way to assess a theory's performance is to compare its success to that of another theory; this sometimes, but not always, can be accomplished by determining that particular variables that a theory points to have nonzero effects. To those who take a more Bayesian view of comparative theory testing, the degree to which various theories are believed to be true depends not on the results of a single statistical analysis but rather on the cumulation of results over time. Either way, it makes no sense simply to look at a parameter and its associated standard error and either accept or reject a theory based on their values.

However, investigating the match between a particular theory and data is often a useful exercise during what may be a long period of theory development. Most theories have multiple implications that can be taken as working hypotheses. Determining how likely variables are to have the signs that the theory implies provides useful information for refinement of the theory. In most cases, the data are consistent with some of the theory's implications and inconsistent with others. The researcher refines the theory, taking into account the results of the data analysis, and tests the new version by examining the new set of implications using a new data set. At the same time, empirical regularities uncovered during this period can give rise to alternative explanations that can also be developed and (ultimately) tested. While the researcher can compare the relative success of two or more theories during the early stages of theory development, such an exercise can also be counterproductive: it can distract the researcher from the many important issues involved in carefully testing the theory at hand.

When researchers do compare the relative usefulness of two or more theories, they often pay insufficient attention to how this should be done. Theories are generally assumed to be competing rather than potentially complementary parts of a larger theory, though there is no particular reason for this to be the case. Moreover, even if they are competing explanations, it is not at all clear that the way to compare them is to include variables representing each in an additive statistical equation. Doing so, though it comports with standard statistical practice, assumes that their effects cumulate in an additive fashion, which is probably not a reasonable representation of the either-or logic of evaluating competing theories.[25]

Finally, attempts to compare competing theories often result in a sin of commission—a decision to throw every plausible causal variable into the regression equation. Adding large numbers of variables often takes the place of careful investigation of the effect of the few variables truly relevant to the theory (Achen 2002). Moreover, if the variables that the competing theory suggests are important happen to be correlated in the sample with the variables of primary interest, then including these "control" variables can lead to incorrect conclusions about the primary theory being tested. In the absence of formal theory, Achen (2002) suggests "A Rule of Three" (ART): no more than three independent variables in a statistical specification. While informed opinion will surely differ regarding exactly how many independent variables should be permitted in a given equation, we agree that "garbage can" models—those with many independent variables and weak or absent microfoundations—represent a threat to inference that is currently underappreciated.

In short, it is often asserted or implied that theories have been proven correct by a successful rejection of the null hypothesis despite the inherent difficulty (some would say impossibility) of gauging precisely *how much* support for a theory is implied by support for a hypothesis that is consistent with it.[26] Here, we must confess, it is often far easier to criticize than to propose solutions, but the absence of solutions has become dangerously comfortable.

Even if researchers are meticulous in avoiding all of the pitfalls described earlier, they are typically unaware of a final threat to inference: simple computer error. In a series of articles, Bruce McCullough has endeavored to assess the reliability of commonly used econometric software,[27] and Micah Altman and Michael P. McDonald (2001) have extended these analyses to include the software packages most frequently used by political scientists. The results are the stuff of nightmares. One respected software package produced *t*-statistics that were half of the correct value when performing maximum likelihood analysis; another produced incorrect regression results when the names of the variables were too long. Few software packages were deemed entirely reliable for even fairly straightforward tasks. Therefore, when possible, it seems advisable to attempt to replicate findings using a different statistics package to avoid the possibility that important findings (or nonfindings) are simply artifacts of a bug in a particular statistics package.

So Why Bother?

We have stressed that statistical analyses are just one step in the scientific method of the study of international relations. While statistics can and should be used to generate stylized facts, the most common underlying goal of research that uses statistics is to test and evaluate theories of international phenomena. Unfortunately, much research strays far from this goal in practice because the researcher fails to specify the theory carefully before testing it, because the statistical model conforms poorly to the theory, or because the researcher uses statistical "tests" without concern for their underlying meaning or relation to the theory.

Given the preceding discussion, students of international relations may wonder whether the expenditure in time and effort to learn statistical methods is worth the payoff. Our answer is an immediate yes. It is important not to make the best the enemy of the good: our critiques here are of ways in which international relations researchers often use the method rather than of the method itself. While the statistical method is of little value without theory, so, too, is theory insignificant without empirical tests. Absent empirical tests, we might work forever developing fundamentally incorrect theories.

The statistical method conveys tremendous advantages to the scholar wishing to test explanations of international events. It permits generalization, compels specificity, and conveys information with unparalleled precision. As recent issues of *Political Analysis* and the growing body of working papers amassed at the Society for Political Methodology website attest, increasingly sophisticated statistical methods are rapidly improving our ability to extract information from data, and the amount of data available to us continues to increase. In short, statistics provide a way of evaluating our understanding of the world that is simply unavailable via other means.

Recommended Readings

Statistical texts roughly in order of increasing difficulty

Gonick, L., and W. Smith. 1993. *The Cartoon Guide to Statistics.* New York: Harper Perennial. For students who find the prospect of mathematics horrifying, this book provides a remarkably gentle introduction up to the level of regression analysis.

Achen, C. H. 1982. *Interpreting and Using Regression.* Newbury Park, CA: Sage. This book provides invaluable advice to the student wishing to use regression in a thoughtful manner.

King, G. 1989. *Unifying Political Methodology.* Cambridge: Cambridge University Press. Reprint, Ann Arbor: University of Michigan Press, 1998. This book provides an introduction to maximum-likelihood estimation, which forms the basis of many current statistical models in political science.

Greene, W. H. 2002. *Econometric Analysis.* Upper Saddle River, NJ: Prentice Hall. This book covers many of the key topics of statistical analyses at an intermediate level.

Morton, R. B. 1999. *Methods and Models: A Guide to the Empirical Analysis of Formal Models in Political Science.* Cambridge: Cambridge University Press. A useful book for students wishing to pursue the idea of testing formal models.

Notes

1. This chapter assumes that the reader has at least an introductory knowledge of statistics. Those readers who do not are encouraged to see the recommended readings at the end of the chapter for definitions of terms. For definitions of external and internal validity, see Campbell and Stanley (1963).

2. In common terminology, statistical analyses can lead to the discovery of "empirical regularities" that could be explained by theory.

3. See, e.g., Kennedy (1998).

4. Reliability and validity assessment are often covered in passing in statistics books; for more specific treatments see Carmines and Zeller (1979) and Litwin (1995). Few international relations scholars assess reliability or validity, a fact that is quite striking given the manifest threats to both presented by their data.

5. We differ here from Clarke (2001), who argues that chance always is an uninteresting alternative explanation.

6. Lest we be misunderstood: correlation should never be equated with causation. Nevertheless, correlation provides valuable evidence in assessing claims of causation, as the following example demonstrates.

7. While Clarke's study is of nonnested models, researchers can compare nested models using simple, well-known techniques such as F-tests.

8. The literature on the democratic peace is vast, and we do not attempt to review all relevant works here. For further summary of the normative and structural theories, see Russett (1993).

9. See, e.g., Farber and Gowa (1995), Layne (1994), Spiro (1994), and Russett (1995). For a detailed case-by-case assessment of conflicts deemed dangerous to the finding, see Ray (1995).

10. Examples abound. See, for example, Dixon (1994) on democracy and the settlement of conflict, Simon and Gartzke (1996) on democracy and alliance, and Maoz and Russett (1993) on democracy and both involvement in and escalation of militarized interstate disputes (MIDs).

11. For an attempt to do precisely this, as well as an elaboration of one of the present authors' views on the subject, see Braumoeller (1997). The reader would

be justified in inferring that we can claim only limited impartiality on this point (limited, that is, to the other author).

12. For example, if relative size of constituency is the driving force behind the democratic peace, the Nineteenth Amendment produced a dramatic effect on the causal variable of interest. By most measures, however, the United States is not considered to have been half as democratic before women were allowed to vote as it was subsequently.

13. This possibility existed even in the case of structural and normative theories (Braumoeller 1997, fn. 7), but norms and structure are arguably more closely related to democracy. Nevertheless, Morgan and Campbell (1991) make this point with regard to the structural-constraints school and attempt to determine whether constrained states are more peaceful than others. Their results are discouraging for structuralists but quite encouraging for proponents of empirically informed theoretical progress.

14. See, for example, Oye (1986).

15. Some readers may argue that depth is about details, that taken to an extreme, our argument suggests that political scientists should examine the details of individual cases rather than develop theory. We are decidedly in favor of developing theory.

16. Technically, the game implies that mutual noncooperation never will occur in this situation. Usually, researchers translate the deterministic implications of game-theoretic models into probabilistic hypotheses about the world. In varying the payoffs so as to generate a testable implication of the Prisoners' Dilemma, one is comparing outcomes when the two-by-two game is a Prisoners' Dilemma to one in which the game has some other name; however, most of the structure of the situation remains the same.

17. We discussed the most common method of deriving implications, varying the payoffs, earlier in the chapter.

18. See Sartori (2004) for an example. Of course, the reasonableness of considering equilibria as competing explanations depends upon the model.

19. It is particularly encouraging that the National Science Foundation has a new program, "Empirical Implications of Theoretical Models," designed to encourage advances on this subject.

20. The data were simulated: $Y = Xb + e$, $X \sim N(0,1)$, $e \sim N(0,1)$, $b = 0.01$.

21. The *American Political Science Review, American Journal of Political Science, International Studies Quarterly, International Security, International Organization,* and *World Politics* were examined; we are grateful to Doug Stinnett for his careful research assistance.

22. Libras are most likely (30.1 percent) to be Republicans, while those born under the sign of Aquarius are most likely (49 percent) to be Democrats.

23. One of the authors was horrified when, at a recent conference, a speaker

proudly reported having come up with statistically significant results on the first attempt. One wonders how many it usually takes.

24. Researchers often make such a determination by a formal hypothesis test against the null that a variable in question has no effect.

25. Space constraints prohibit a more detailed discussion of these points; interested readers will find them developed more fully in Braumoeller (2003) and Clarke (2001).

26. From a Bayesian point of view the answer to this question hinges on prior probabilities, which in turn depend critically on the number of theories that could potentially be correct. Popper (1959), for example, holds that there are an infinite number of potential theories; that none can therefore have a positive prior probability; and that the failure to reject one of them therefore provides only an infinitesimally small increment in posterior probability. Another position, forwarded by Jeffreys (1961, 10) among others, is that the number of potential theories should be limited to those that have actually been asserted. Though the infinity-of-alternatives problem is thereby "solved" in the sense that positive prior probabilities can be assigned and the extent to which evidence supports one theory over its competitors can be calculated, it is not solved in the sense that the *correct* prior probabilities can be assigned: designation of priors tends to be arbitrary, true priors remain unknown (and perhaps unknowable), and the number of theories that have actually been forwarded, while reasonable as a minimum, constitutes an arbitrary and certainly conservative guess.

27. See especially McCullough (1998, 1999) and McCullough and Vinod (1999).

References

Achen, C. H. 1977. Measuring Representation: Perils of the Correlation Coefficient. *American Journal of Political Science* 21 (4): 805–15.

———. 2002. Towards a New Political Methodology. Microfoundations and Art. *Annual Review of Political Science* 5:423–50.

Altman, M., and M. P. McDonald. 2001. Choosing Reliable Statistical Software. *PS: Political Science and Politics* 24 (3): 681–88.

Anscombe, F. J. 1973. Graphs in Statistical Analysis. *American Statistician* 27 (1): 17–21.

Bennett, D. S. 1998. Integrating and Testing Models of Rivalry Duration. *American Journal of Political Science* 42 (4): 1180–99.

Braumoeller, B. F. 1997. Deadly Doves: Liberal Nationalism and the Democratic

Peace in the Soviet Successor States. *International Studies Quarterly* 41 (3): 375–402.

———. 2003. Causal Complexity and the Study of Politics. *Political Analysis* 11 (3): 209–33.

Bueno de Mesquita, B., and D. Lalman. 1992. *War and Reason: Domestic and International Imperatives.* New Haven: Yale University Press.

Bueno de Mesquita, B., J. D. Morrow, R. M. Siverson, and A. Smith. 1999. An Institutional Explanation of the Democratic Peace. *American Political Science Review* 93 (4): 791–807.

Campbell, D., and J. C. Stanley. 1963. *Experimental and Quasi-Experimental Designs for Research.* Boston: Houghton Mifflin.

Carmines, E. G., and R. A. Zeller. 1979. *Reliability and Validity Assessment.* Sage University Papers Series. Quantitative Applications in the Social Sciences, 07–17.

Cederman, L. 2001. Back to Kant: Reinterpreting the Democratic Peace as a Macrohistorical Learning Process. *American Political Science Review* 95 (1): 15–32.

Clarke, K. 2001. Testing Nonnested Models of International Relations: Reevaluating Realism. *American Journal of Political Science* 45 (3): 724–44.

Diehl, P. F., and G. Goertz. 2000. *War and Peace in International Rivalry.* Ann Arbor: University of Michigan Press.

Dixon, W. 1994. Democracy and the Peaceful Settlement of International Conflict. *American Political Science Review* 88 (1): 14–32.

Doyle, M. 1986. Liberalism and World Politics. *American Political Science Review* 80 (4): 1151–71.

Farber, H. S., and J. Gowa. 1995. Polities and Peace. *International Security* 20 (2): 123–46.

Goertz, G., and P. F. Diehl. 1992. The Empirical Importance of Enduring Rivalries. *International Interactions* 18 (2): 151–63.

Hagan, J. D. 1989. Domestic Political Regime Changes and Third World Voting Realignments in the United Nations, 1946–84. *International Organization* 43 (3): 505–41.

Jeffreys, S. H. 1961. *Theory of Probability.* Oxford: Clarendon.

Kennedy, P. 1998. *A Guide to Econometrics.* Cambridge: MIT Press.

Lakatos, I. 1970. Falsification and the Methodology of Research Programmes. In *Criticism and the Growth of Knowledge,* edited by I. Lakatos and A. Musgrave, 91–195. Cambridge: Cambridge University Press.

Lake, D. A. 1992. Powerful Pacifists: Democratic States and War. *American Political Science Review* 86 (1): 24–37.

Lake, D. A., and R. Powell. 1999. International Relations: A Strategic-Choice

Approach. In *Strategic Choice and International Relations,* edited by D. A. Lake and R. Powell, 3–38. Princeton: Princeton University Press.

Layne, C. 1994. Kant or Cant: The Myth of the Democratic Peace. *International Security* 19 (2): 5–49.

Lewis, J. B., and K. A. Schultz. 2003. Limitations to the Direct Testing of Extensive Form Crises Bargaining Games. *Political Analysis* 11 (4): 345–67.

Litwin, M. S. 1995. *How to Measure Survey Reliability and Validity.* Beverly Hills, CA: Sage.

Maoz, Z., and B. Russett. 1993. Normative and Structural Causes of Democratic Peace, 1946–86. *American Political Science Review* 87 (3): 624–38.

McCullough, B. D. 1998. Assessing the Reliability of Statistical Software: Part I. *American Statistician* 52 (4): 358–66.

———. 1999. Assessing the Reliability of Statistical Software: Part II. *American Statistician* 53 (2): 149–59.

McCullough, B. D., and H. D. Vinod. 1999. The Numerical Reliability of Econometric Software. *Journal of Economic Literature* 37 (2): 633–65.

Mock, C., and H. F. Weisberg. 1992. Political Innumeracy: Encounters with Coincidence, Improbability, and Chance. *American Journal of Political Science* 36 (4): 1023–46.

Morgan, T. C., and S. H. Campbell. 1991. Domestic Structure, Decisional Constraints, and War: So Why Kant Democracies Fight? *Journal of Conflict Resolution* 35 (2): 187–211.

Morton, R. B. 1999. *Methods and Models: A Guide to the Empirical Analysis of Formal Models in Political Science.* Cambridge: Cambridge University Press.

Oye, K. A. 1986. *Cooperation under Anarchy.* Princeton: Princeton University Press.

Popper, K. R. 1959. *The Logic of Scientific Discovery.* New York: Basic Books.

Ray, J. L. 1995. *Democracy and International Conflict: An Evaluation of the Democratic Peace Proposition.* Columbia: University of South Carolina Press.

Rummel, R. J. 1979. *War, Power, and Peace: Understanding Conflict and War.* Beverly Hills, CA: Sage.

Russett, B. 1993. *Grasping the Democratic Peace.* Princeton: Princeton University Press.

———. 1995. And Yet It Moves. *International Security* 19 (4): 164–75.

Sartori, A. E. 2003. An Estimator for Some Binary-Outcome Selection Models without Exclusion Restrictions. *Political Analysis* 11 (2): 111–38.

———. 2004. *Deterrence by Diplomacy.* Princeton: Princeton University Press (forthcoming).

Schultz, K. A. 1999. Do Democratic Institutions Constrain or Inform? Contrasting Institutional Perspectives on Democracy and War. *International Organization* 53 (2): 233–66.

Signorino, C. S. 1999a. Statistical Analysis of Finite Choice Models in Extensive Form. Manuscript, University of Rochester.

———. 1999b. Strategic Interaction and the Statistical Analysis of International Conflict. *American Political Science Review* 93 (2): 279–98.

Simon, M. W., and E. Gartzke. 1996. Political System Similarity and the Choice of Allies: Do Democracies Flock Together, or Do Opposites Attract? *Journal of Conflict Resolution* 40 (4): 617–35.

Smith, A. 1999. Testing Theories of Strategic Choice: The Example of Crisis Escalation. *American Journal of Political Science* 43 (4): 1254–83.

Spiro, D. E. 1994. The Insignificance of the Liberal Peace. *International Security* 19 (2): 50–86.

Vasquez, J. 1995. Why Do Neighbors Fight—Proximity, Contiguity, or Territoriality? *Journal of Peace Research* 32 (3): 277–93.

Wagner, H. 1993. What Was Bipolarity? *International Organization* 47 (1): 77–106.

Waltz, K. 1979. *Theory of International Politics.* Reading, MA: Addison-Wesley.

Wang, T. Y. 1999. U.S. Foreign Aid and U.N. Voting: An Analysis of Important Issues. *International Studies Quarterly* 43 (1): 199–210.

Zinnes, D. 1980. Three Puzzles in Search of a Researcher. *International Studies Quarterly* 24 (3): 315–42.

7. Quantitative Approaches to the International Political Economy

Edward D. Mansfield

Over the past few decades, scholars of international relations have displayed a growing interest in the links between politics and economics. Much of the rich and important body of research stimulated by this interest focuses on how political factors shape foreign trade. The literature on this topic has given rise to some of the most influential theories of the international political economy. It also has yielded various empirical tests of these theories, an increasing number of which rely on quantitative methods.

The purpose of this essay is to survey some of the quantitative research conducted on the political economy of international trade. I argue that various aspects of international politics have a potent influence on overseas commerce. This is important because statistical models of trade developed by economists frequently ignore political factors. Omitting such influences can produce biased results and, hence, a misleading set of conclusions about the determinants of foreign commerce.

At the outset, I briefly document the rising use of quantitative methods to study the international political economy. I then discuss how these methods have been used to address a series of core debates over the effects of the distribution of power, political-military alliances, preferential trading arrangements (PTAs), and interstate conflict on international trade. Finally, I consider a number of statistical studies bearing on a closely related topic, the political economy of sanctions.

The Growth of Quantitative Research on the
International Political Economy

The bulk of quantitative research in the field of international relations has addressed issues of political-military security. Consequently, it is easy to underestimate the amount of quantitative work conducted on the international political economy. Helen Milner (see chap. 11, this vol.) points out that the field of international political economy is only about three decades old. Since its inception, statistical work has made an important contribution to this field and has constituted a fair portion of the research published on it in leading journals.

To get a rough sense of how much quantitative research has been conducted on the international political economy and whether the amount of such research has changed over time, I surveyed the articles published between 1970 and 1999 in the *American Political Science Review, American Journal of Political Science, International Organization, International Studies Quarterly, Journal of Conflict Resolution, Journal of Politics,* and *World Politics.* These periodicals differ across many dimensions, including the amount of quantitative research they publish, the frequency with which they publish studies of the international political economy, and whether they are geared to scholars of international relations or political scientists in general. Each, however, is a high-quality journal that has served as an outlet for work on the international political economy—defined broadly as the study of the links between states and markets in the global arena (Gilpin 1987; Milner, chap. 11, this vol.). Next, I identified what portion of such articles included some type of statistical analysis. During the 1970s, about 20 percent of the relevant articles contained some statistical evidence; during the 1980s, this figure rose to about 25 percent; and during the 1990s, it jumped to about 45 percent.[1]

Clearly, these figures should be interpreted with considerable caution. For one thing, they pertain to only a fraction of the research on the international political economy, most notably because no account is taken of research published in books. For another thing, these figures obviously depend on both what substantive issues fall under the heading of international political economy and what constitutes a statistical analysis. Nonetheless, they do indicate that quantitative methods have been applied to the study of the international political economy for some time, that these methods have been used with a fair amount of regularity, and that there has been a sharp rise in the amount of quantitative work on the international political economy during the past decade. These findings also reinforce Detlef F. Sprinz and Yael Wolinsky-Nahmias's point (chap. 1, this vol.) that statistical methods have been used with rising frequency throughout the field of international relations over the past few decades.

The Effects of Hegemony on Trade

Much of the quantitative research conducted on the international political economy has focused on the political underpinnings of foreign trade. I evaluate this literature, placing primary emphasis on studies cast at the systemic level of analysis. Systemic studies of international relations stress that the organization of nation-states influences patterns of global outcomes.[2] A system, as Kenneth Waltz (1979) points out, is composed of interacting units and a structure that guides their interaction. The key structural variable in the international system is the global distribution of power. Scholars of the international political economy have placed particular emphasis on one aspect of this distribution: whether there exists a state—referred to as a hegemon—that is powerful enough and willing to single-handedly manage the global system.

Hegemonic stability theorists argue that such a state is necessary to promote economic openness. In their view, the relatively liberal international economy that existed during much of the nineteenth century and after World War II stems from the preponderance of Great Britain during the former era and the United States during the latter one. Furthermore, they attribute the extensive economic instability and commercial closure between World Wars I and II to the absence of a hegemon. Hegemonic stability theorists have advanced two sets of explanations linking hegemony to economic openness. Some of them argue that the establishment and maintenance of an open international economy are fraught with collective action problems. Without a hegemon to resolve these problems and manage international economic relations, the system is likely to break down (Kindleberger 1973). Other hegemonic stability theorists maintain that international economic openness is not a public good; as such, hegemony is not needed to address collective action problems. Instead, openness is inhibited by the fact that states in different positions in the international system have different preferences regarding trade policy. A hegemon is needed to reconcile these disparate preferences and prod protectionist states to engage in commercial liberalization (Gilpin 1987; Krasner 1976).[3]

Although both variants of hegemonic stability theory have been quite influential, they have also been the subject of considerable criticism. Some of these critiques have been lodged on conceptual grounds, challenging the logical underpinnings of the theory. Others have focused on the theory's explanatory power. To assess the explanatory power of hegemonic stability theory, a number of statistical studies have been conducted. The results, however, have been far from uniform, fueling debates about the relationship between hegemony and global trade. In large measure, the differences in these studies' findings stem from disagreements over how to define and measure hegemony and over exactly what outcomes are to be explained.

In one of the first quantitative tests of hegemonic stability theory, John A. C. Conybeare (1983) estimated a series of regressions to evaluate the relationship between the international distribution of power and nominal tariff levels on manufactures in 1902 and in 1971. To measure power in 1902, he relied on each country's gross domestic product (GDP) and population, as well as the ratio of its military expenditures to that of Great Britain. To measure power in 1971, he relied on each country's GDP, the ratio of its military expenditures to that of the United States, and the "geographic diversification of imports . . . and exports" (1983, 448). Conybeare found little evidence that these factors affect national tariff levels. He therefore concluded that hegemonic stability theory does not provide an adequate explanation of trade policy.

Whereas Conybeare conducted cross-sectional analyses of the links between hegemony and national tariff levels, Timothy J. McKeown (1991) conducted a time-series analysis of the relationship between variables associated with hegemony and the ratio of imports to national income for a set of advanced industrial states during the period 1880 to 1987. McKeown analyzed various aspects of the distribution of power: (1) the concentration of naval capabilities among the major powers (a variable discussed at greater length later); (2) the portion of global imports accounted for by the largest importer in the international system ($TCON1$); (3) the portion of global imports accounted for by Great Britain, the United States, France, (West) Germany, and Japan ($TCON5$); (4) the ratio of $TCON1$ to $TCON5$; (5) the ratio of Great Britain's national income to the sum of the national incomes of Great Britain, the United States, France, (West) Germany, and

Japan; and (6) the ratio of U.S. national income to this sum. That these variables had only a modest influence on the ratio of imports to national income led McKeown to share Conybeare's skepticism about the explanatory power of hegemonic stability theory.

Other studies, however, have found more support for the view that hegemony affects the global trading system. For example, Robert Pahre (1999) argues that there has been a hegemon at every point from 1815 to the present, but he distinguishes between periods of benevolent hegemony and periods of malevolent hegemony. Pahre's regression results indicated that hegemony generally has a malign effect on the international political economy. However, he also found that hegemons surrounded by more foes than friends tend to be benevolent and that malevolent hegemony can stimulate cooperative behavior on the part of the remaining states in the international system.

Finally, I have argued (Mansfield 1994) that it is important to distinguish between hegemony (a situation marked by the existence of a preponderant state in the international system) and the concentration of capabilities (which is a function of the number of major powers and the relative inequality of capabilities among them). In a study using least-squares regression to address the effects of these (and other) factors on the level of global trade as a percentage of total global production from 1850 to 1965, I found that hegemony's influence depends heavily on how it is defined and measured. Based on Robert Gilpin's (1987) classifications, hegemony promotes global trade, a result that accords with hegemonic stability theory. Based on Immanuel Wallerstein's (1983) classifications, however, hegemony has no systematic influence on trade. This observed variation in the relationship between hegemony and commercial openness stems from a key difference in these sets of classifications: Gilpin argues that Great Britain remained hegemonic from the conclusion of the Napoleonic Wars until the outbreak of World War I, whereas Wallerstein maintains that British hegemony came to a close roughly forty years prior to World War I. While this is not the place to attempt to resolve the disagreement between Gilpin and Wallerstein,[4] these results starkly illustrate the effects that differences in the definition and measurement of key concepts can have on statistical results and the need to develop measures that are closely linked to the underlying theory being tested.

Furthermore, I found that the concentration of capabilities among the major powers in the international system is strongly related to global trade (Mansfield 1994). Concentration is a continuous variable that ranges from 0 to 1. It approaches 0 as the distribution of capabilities among the major powers grows more uniform; it approaches 1 as this distribution grows increasingly skewed. My results indicate that the ratio of global trade to global production is highest when the level of concentration is either very high or very low, whereas this ratio is lowest when concentration is at an intermediate level. I argued that the U-shaped relationship between concentration and global trade reflects the fact that when the level of concentration is low, market power in the international system is dispersed and states therefore have little ability to use trade barriers to improve their terms of trade. Consequently, foreign commerce tends to be open and the level of global trade tends to be high. As concentration increases, however, so does the market power of the dominant states, creating an incentive for them to impose an optimal tariff, which is likely to depress the flow of trade throughout the system. Yet beyond some level of concentration at which the level of global trade is minimized, increases in concentration promote commerce. When concentration rises to a very high level and a single state (or even a few states) accumulates substantial market power, it has an incentive to forgo the use of an optimal tariff in order to maintain its monopoly power in the international system, to foster economic dependence on the part of smaller trade partners, and to induce political concessions from them.

That the relationship between concentration and global commerce is U-shaped helps to explain the difference between my results and McKeown's, since his tests focus on whether a monotonic relationship exists between these variables.[5] It also underscores Bear F. Braumoeller and Anne E. Sartori's (chap. 6, this vol.) point that close attention needs to be paid to the functional form of relationships in empirical research.

The Effects of Alliances on Trade

In addition to debates over the explanatory power of hegemonic stability theory, there is widespread disagreement about whether it has an adequate theoretical basis. Among the critiques leveled against this theory is that it fails to account for how open international markets affect the security of trade partners (Gowa 1994; Gowa and Mansfield 1993). This line of argument has spawned a number of recent statistical analyses of the relationship between political-military alliances and bilateral trade flows.

Central to the effects of alliances on foreign commerce are the efficiency gains from trade. These gains yield increases in national income that can be used to augment a state's military power. As such, trade generates security externalities, which are uncompensated benefits or costs influencing a country's national security that arise from actions taken by another country or set of states (Gowa 1994). Since the anarchic nature of the international system places pressure on states to attend to the power of others (Waltz 1979), they cannot ignore these security externalities without bearing substantial risks.

States can address the security externalities stemming from commerce by trading more freely with their allies than with their (actual or potential) adversaries. Trade between allies is likely to enhance the security of both parties: the gains from trade accrue to states with common security goals and bolster the aggregate political-military power of the alliance. In contrast, open trade between adversaries produces negative security externalities. A state engaging in trade with an enemy augments the national income of its trading partner, thereby threatening to undermine its own security. Especially among states with sufficient market power to influence their terms of trade, governments therefore are expected to discriminate in their foreign economic policies between allies and adversaries (Gowa 1994).

Private traders and investors have incentives to behave in a manner consistent with these government policies. All other things being equal, trade barriers imposed on a product increase its local price, reducing local demand for it by private traders and other consumers. Since governments are more likely to impose trade barriers on the goods of adversaries than on those of allies, there is likely to be less local demand for an adversary's than an ally's goods.

In addition, many investments by firms are relation-specific: they are made to support a particular transaction with a particular partner (Williamson 1985, 54; Yarbrough and Yarbrough 1992, 25). The cost of shifting relation-specific assets to their best alternative use tends to be high, and the value of these assets depends in part on the continuity of the particular relationship for which they are designed (Williamson 1985, 55). As such, relation-specific investments—and the trade flows they generate—are quite susceptible to opportunistic behavior by foreign governments. Investors face the risk that a foreign government will take actions, like raising trade barriers, that degrade the investment's value.

The specter of governments taking such actions, however, is reduced within an alliance (Mansfield and Bronson 1997). Because open trade among allies promotes the security of members, governments have less incentive to behave opportunistically toward their allies' firms than toward firms of other states. Thus, private agents reduce the likelihood of falling prey to predatory actions by foreign governments—and enhance the expected profitability of overseas investments—by investing in relation-specific assets to service allies' markets. Similarly, governments have incentives to engage in opportunistic behavior toward their adversaries' firms, since doing so helps to redress the security externalities arising from trade. Firms face heightened risks, including the possibility that a foreign government will increase its trade barriers or even expropriate dedicated assets located within its borders, if they make investments to service adversaries' markets. Furthermore, even if a firm prefers to conduct business with its home country's adversaries, its ability to do so can be curtailed by government regulations.

For these reasons, trade flows are likely to be greater between allies than between actual or potential adversaries. Moreover, the effects of alliances are likely to be more pronounced in a bipolar than a multipolar system (Gowa 1994; Gowa and Mansfield 1993). States in a bipolar system tend to be locked into alliances. They have less opportunity to move from one alliance to another than in multipolar systems, where alliances tend to be relatively fluid. Hence, a state liberalizing trade with an ally faces a greater risk in a multipolar than a bipolar system that the ally will realize political-military gains from the commercial relationship and then shift into an opposing alliance. Since the security externalities stemming from free trade are more easily internalized in bipolar alliances than multipolar alliances, the former are more likely to foster open trade than the latter.

To test these arguments, Joanne Gowa and I (Gowa 1994; Gowa and Mansfield 1993) conducted a statistical analysis of the effects of alliances on trade flows between major powers during the twentieth century. It is obvious that trade flows are shaped by various economic and political factors besides alliances. The failure to account for these factors could produce misleading estimates of the influence of alliances on commerce. As such, we relied on the gravity model, which has become a workhorse in empirical studies of the political and economic determinants of bilateral trade flows.[6] This model—which describes trade between any two states as a function of factors influencing the supply of exports and the demand for imports in these states, as well as factors impeding or facilitating commerce between them—usually takes the following form.

$$TRADE_{ij} = \beta_0 \times GDP_i^{\beta_1} \times GDP_j^{\beta_2} \times POP_i^{\beta_3} \times POP_j^{\beta_4}$$
$$\times DIST_{ij}^{\beta_5} \times N_{ij}^{\beta_6} \times e_{ij} \tag{1}$$

In equation (1), $TRADE_{ij}$ is the flow of trade between countries i and j, GDP_i and GDP_j are the gross domestic products of i and j, POP_i and POP_j are the populations of i and j, $DIST_{ij}$ is the geographical distance between i and j, N_{ij} is a set of "noneconomic" factors influencing trade between i and j, and e_{ij} is a lognormally distributed error term. This model is commonly estimated using least-squares regression, after taking the logarithm of each variable.[7]

Various justifications have been offered for the gravity model's multiplicative functional form. One rationale is that as the GDP or the population of either trade partner approaches zero, so too should the amount of trade they conduct (Deardorff 1998). This is captured by expressing equation (1) in a multiplicative rather than a linear form.[8] Furthermore, the gravity model's multiplicative form is convenient, since the coefficients can be directly interpreted as elasticities once the variables are expressed in logarithms.

Equally, a variety of arguments have been advanced for the independent variables included in the gravity model. However, it is widely accepted that a state's capacity to export goods and demand for imports are both directly related to its GDP. The populations of i and j are included in the gravity model as proxies for the size of each country's domestic market. Assuming economies of scale in production, the larger a country's population, the more goods for which it is likely to achieve the minimum scale needed for efficient production without relying on export markets. A more populous country therefore is expected to produce less for export relative to its total production than a less populous country. Similarly, a more populous country is expected to have a greater capacity to satisfy domestic demand with domestically produced goods, and thus a lower demand for imports, than a less populous country.

Distance is included in the gravity model as a proxy for transportation costs. These costs are expected to rise, and hence bilateral trade flows are expected to decrease, as the distance between trade partners increases. For these and other reasons, the gravity model predicts that bilateral trade flows will be directly related to the GDP of i and j, inversely related to the population of i and j, and inversely related to the distance between i and j.

Recall that in equation (1), N_{ij} is a set of noneconomic factors influencing trade between i and j. Gowa and I included a number of such factors in our model of trade, but primary emphasis was placed on the effects of alliances. More specifically, we included one dummy variable indicating whether i and j were members of a bilateral alliance (i.e., an alliance composed of i and j alone) and another dummy variable indicating whether they were members of a multilateral alliance (i.e., an alliance composed of more than these two states). These variables took on values of e (the base of the natural logarithms) if i and j were allied and 1 if they were not. Consequently, the logarithms of these variables—which are what we included in the regression equation since the model is estimated in log-linear form—equaled 1 and 0.

We then estimated this model for nine annual cross-sections during the twentieth century, five of which were during the multipolar era prior to World War II and four of which were during the bipolar era thereafter.[9] We found that the estimated regression coefficient of bilateral alliances was positive in six out of these nine cases; in five instances, it was both positive and statistically significant. Also, the estimated coefficient of multilateral alliances was positive and significant in six cases. Furthermore, we found considerable evidence that allies have conducted more trade during bipolar than multipolar periods. We compared the mean of the regression coefficients of bilateral alliances during the multipolar era to the mean of these coefficients during the bipolar era. We did likewise for the regression coefficients of multilateral alliances. In both cases, a t-test yielded statistically significant evidence that the magnitude of alliances' effects on trade was larger during bipolar than multipolar periods.

The aforementioned study analyzed the effects of alliances on trade flows between major powers. As such, it did not address the extent to which the relationship between alliances and trade depends on whether the commercial partners are major powers. Nor did it examine whether the existence of institutions designed to guide commerce influences the relationship between alliances and trade. We now turn to a discussion of some recent quantitative research on these issues.

Alliances, Preferential Trading Arrangements, and Trade

Among the most important institutions designed to shape commerce are preferential trading arrangements (PTAs), agreements stipulating that states impose lower levels of protection on members' goods than on the goods of third parties. These agreements take on various forms, including free trade areas, customs unions, common markets, and economic unions. Despite the differences among these types of PTAs, all of them grant members' goods preferential access to the market of each participant (Anderson and Blackhurst 1993, 5).

Because many preferential groupings are composed of states located in the same geographic region, the rapid proliferation of these arrangements since World War II has prompted many observers to conclude that economic regionalism is becoming increasingly widespread (Anderson and Blackhurst 1993; Bhagwati 1993; Mansfield and Milner 1999). An initial wave of postwar regionalism occurred during the 1950s and 1960s, spurred by the formation of the European Coal and Steel Community, the European Economic Community, the European Free Trade Association, the Council for Mutual Economic Assistance, and a series of PTAs established by less developed countries. More recently, the creation of the North American Free Trade Agreement, the Mercado Común del Cono Sur (Mercosur), the organization for Asia-Pacific Economic Cooperation, and numerous bilateral trade agreements involving states formerly in the Soviet orbit have contributed to a second wave of regionalism (Bhagwati 1993; Mansfield and Milner 1999). Of course, regionalism is not a phenomenon limited to the period since World War II, but both the number of countries involved in PTAs and the amount of trade they cover have risen to new heights throughout this era (World Trade Organization 1995).

Accompanying the contemporary growth of regionalism has been a surge of interest in how PTAs influence the economic welfare of states and the stability of the multilateral trading system. Existing quantitative research bearing on these topics centers primarily on the effects of preferential arrangements on bilateral trade flows. Studies of this sort usually begin with the gravity model discussed earlier and define N_{ij} (which, recall, is a set of noneconomic factors affecting the flow of trade between states i and j) as a variable or set of variables related to the PTAs in which i and j participate. These analyses generally find that PTAs promote trade

between members, although the strength of these effects varies across preferential arrangements (Aitken 1973; Eichengreen and Irwin 1998; Frankel
1993; Linnemann 1966; Pelzman 1977; Pollins 1989a; Tinbergen 1962).
Such research, however, seldom emphasizes other noneconomic determinants of trade and almost never assesses the effects of political-military
relations.[10] Since preferential trading arrangements often are comprised of
allies, these studies risk confusing the effects of alliances and PTAs. In so
doing, they are likely to yield biased estimates of preferential trading
arrangements' effects on trade flows and, hence, to offer a distorted view of
the political economy of international trade.

To address this issue, Rachel Bronson and I (Mansfield and Bronson
1997) conducted a statistical analysis comparing the effects of alliances and
PTAs on trade flows. We also analyzed whether the interaction between
alliance membership and PTA membership affects commerce, since we
argued that the combination of alliance and a PTA should promote greater
trade between states than either type of institution alone. Besides preferential trading arrangements, the presence of a major power also may influence
the relationship between alliances and trade. More specifically, all alliances
are expected to spur trade among members, but the disproportionate durability of major power alliances is likely to bolster their effect on foreign
commerce because members have reason to discount less heavily the future
benefits arising from intra-alliance trade than members of other alliances.

To test these arguments, we extended the gravity model by adding to it
variables indicating whether states i and j were allies, whether they were
parties to the same PTA, and whether either state was a major power. We
also included the interaction between allies and PTA membership,
between allies and major power status, and between PTA membership and
major power status. Further, we analyzed the lagged value of trade (to
account for any temporal dependence in the data) and control variables
indicating whether the trading partners (1) were at war with one another,
(2) were parties to the General Agreement on Tariffs and Trade, (3) had a
prior colonial relationship, and (4) had command economies. The sample
was made up of all pairs of states for which complete data were available in
1960, 1965, 1970, 1975, 1980, 1985, or 1990. We pooled the data across
these seven years and then estimated our model using ordinary least
squares, after controlling for country-specific and year-specific fixed effects
by including a dummy variable for all but one country and all but one year
in the sample.

The results indicated that alliances and preferential trading arrangements each promote trade, that the effects of alliances are heightened if the trade partners include a major power, and that the combination of an alliance and a PTA generates more commerce than either type of institution by itself. Not only were almost all of these effects statistically significant, they were also substantively large. For example, a change from the absence to the existence of an alliance increases the predicted volume of trade between nonmajor powers by about 20 to 25 percent if they are not members of a common preferential trading arrangement and by roughly 120 percent if they belong to the same PTA. If the trading partners include a major power and are not members of a common preferential trading arrangement, a change from the absence to the existence of an alliance generates about a 20 to 30 percent increase in the predicted flow of commerce. This figure rises to about 130 percent if such partners participate in the same PTA.

Like alliances, preferential trading arrangements exert a sizable influence on trade. A change from the absence to the existence of a preferential grouping yields about a 60 to 65 percent increase in the predicted volume of trade between nonmajor powers that are not allied. The effects of PTAs are more pronounced, however, if the participants are also allies. Under these circumstances, a change from the absence to the existence of a PTA yields almost a 200 percent increase in commerce between nonmajor powers and roughly a 70 percent increase in trade between countries that include a major power.

The Effects of Political Conflict on Trade

A growing number of statistical studies have addressed the effects of political-military relations on trade flows. As discussed earlier, one strand of this literature focuses on the influence of alliances. Another strand centers on the influence of political-military conflict.

Among scholars of international relations, it is widely argued that interstate conflict dampens trade among the belligerents. This argument, for example, is central to the liberal claim that heightened trade inhibits hostilities. Liberals maintain that open trade encourages specialization in the production of goods and services, rendering governments and societal actors dependent on foreign commerce. These actors have an incentive to avoid antagonism with key trading partners, since conflict threatens to disrupt commercial relations and jeopardize the welfare gains from trade. Realists agree that military disputes undermine trade between participants, since a state must consider the contribution that trade with an adversary will make to the foe's ability to prevail in the dispute (that is, the security externalities arising from trade), as well as the related possibility that trade will benefit the adversary more than itself, thereby undermining its own security.[11]

But despite the widespread claim that conflict depresses commerce, it is not hard to locate cases in which states traded with the enemy during hostilities (Barbieri and Levy 1999). Until recently, very little systematic research had been conducted on the extent to which political-military conflict actually affects trade. During the past decade, however, various quantitative studies have addressed this issue.

One set of studies focuses on the effects of political cooperation and conflict on bilateral trade flows. Brian M. Pollins conducted two influential analyses of this topic. In the first study, he analyzed a sample of twenty-five countries during the period from 1960 to 1975 (Pollins 1989a). Pollins started with a gravity model and added a variable indicating the tenor of diplomatic relations between the trade partners, as well as variables indicating whether they participated in the same PTA. He used least-squares regression to estimate this model for each of the sixteen years included in his sample. In every year, there was statistically significant evidence that cooperation promotes trade. In the second study, Pollins (1989b) analyzed the effects of cooperation and conflict on imports by six countries from each of twenty-four primary trade partners during the era from 1955 to 1978. After pooling these observations and controlling for the importer's national income and the price of imports, Pollins again found that cooperative political relations significantly increase the flow of trade.

A second set of studies addresses the effects on trade of militarized interstate disputes (MIDs), which are events where one state threatens, displays, or uses military force against a counterpart (Jones, Bremer, and Singer 1996). James D. Morrow, Randolph M. Siverson, and Tressa E. Taberes (1998, 1999) found that, taken as a group, MIDs had no statistically significant effect on trade flows between major powers throughout the twentieth century. Jon C. Pevehouse and I (Mansfield and Pevehouse 2000) arrived at a similar conclusion based on a study of geographically contiguous pairs of countries and pairs that include a major power during the period since World War II.

A third set of studies considers the effects of war on trade. In one analysis, for example, I (Mansfield 1994) found that major power wars significantly reduced the amount of global trade (as a percentage of global output) over the period from 1850 to 1965. Furthermore, Gowa and I (Gowa 1994; Gowa and Mansfield 1993) assessed the effects of war in our analyses of alliances and trade between major powers. Of the nine cross-sections we examined, there were only two in which a pair of states included in our sample was at war. In one of these cases, war's estimated effect on commerce was inverse and statistically significant; in the other case, it was direct and not significant. Bronson and I (Mansfield and Bronson 1997) also included war in our model of alliances, PTAs, and trade. The estimate of this variable's coefficient was negative and statistically significant, indicating that belligerence dampens trade.

Taken together, this body of research suggests that the effects of conflict on trade grow stronger as hostilities become more intense.[12] That MIDs (which, recall, include acts ranging from threats of force to wars) have little bearing on trade and that wars tend to depress trade implies that disputes in which force is not used have little effect on commerce.[13] In the same vein, as the degree of political-military cooperation rises, so does the level of interstate trade. Trade partners that have close diplomatic relations, a formal political-military alliance, or many of the same allies engage in considerably more commerce than partners that have less cooperative relations (Gowa 1994; Gowa and Mansfield 1993; Mansfield and Bronson 1997; Morrow, Siverson, and Tabares 1999; Pollins 1989a, 1989b).

The Political Economy of Sanctions

At the outset of this chapter, I mentioned that most quantitative work on the international political economy cast at the systemic level of analysis has focused on trade. Surprisingly little research of this sort has addressed other areas of economic activity, such as international finance, foreign direct investment, or foreign aid. Over the past decade, however, a number of statistical studies have been conducted on the international political factors influencing economic sanctions, and it is useful to review this literature before concluding.

Most theoretical and empirical work on sanctions has focused on identifying the conditions that promote their effectiveness. Such research has been divided over whether effectiveness should be evaluated solely in terms of the damage these policy instruments impose on a target (i.e., the state or states at which sanctions are directed) or whether the clarity and strength of the signals conveyed about the sender (i.e., the state or states imposing sanctions) also influence their effectiveness (Baldwin 1985; Hufbauer, Schott, and Elliott 1990). A central issue for both views, however, is how to coordinate multilateral sanctions. In order to maximize the economic damage to a target, it is generally necessary for states to band together, since a sender acting alone rarely possesses the market power needed to inflict substantial damage on a target. In order to heighten the clarity and magnitude of a sanction's signal, it is often useful for senders to act in concert.

One of the initial efforts to study the factors giving rise to multilateral cooperation on economic sanctions was made by Lisa L. Martin (1992). She began by developing three models of cooperation. First, the coincidence model is based on liberal explanations of cooperation. Each sender has an unconditional interest in imposing sanctions. The problem they face, however, is how to distribute the attendant costs of doing so and reaching agreement on the appropriate type and extent of sanctions. Second, the coercion model stems from realist theories. In it, one actor prefers to sanction a target, even if that means doing so unilaterally. Consequently, other prospective senders have reason to free ride on this actor's efforts unless it furnishes some inducement to gain their cooperation. Third, the coadjustment model is a neoliberal institutional framework in which each sender would benefit from the imposition of sanctions, but none of them has an incentive to act unilaterally. Since each sender worries about the implications of acting alone if its counterparts become free riders, the senders collectively impose a suboptimal level of sanctions unless there is a means (like an international institution in which they all participate) to facilitate policy adjustment among them.

To test these models, Martin conducted a series of quantitative analyses covering the period from 1945 to 1989. Relying on Gary Clyde Hufbauer, Jeffrey J. Schott, and Kimberly Ann Elliott's (1990) well-known data on sanctions, she examined three measures of the extent of cooperation among senders in each episode: (1) the percentage of the target's total foreign trade that it conducts with the senders (omitting its trade with the primary sender), (2) a four-point measure of the extent of cooperation developed by Hufbauer, Schott, and Elliott, and (3) the number of senders. To explain these aspects of cooperation, Martin focused on variables tapping key features of the coincidence, coercion, and coadjustment models. She used

167

ordinary least squares regression to analyze the first measure of cooperation since it is a continuous variable, an ordered probit specification to analyze the second measure since it is ordered and nominal, and event-count models to analyze the number of states imposing sanctions.

The results of these analyses strongly indicated that cooperation is more likely and more extensive among senders that belong to the same international institution, a finding that is consistent with the coadjustment model. However, she also found considerable evidence that cooperation rises as the costs borne by the major sender increase—which accords with the coercion model—and limited evidence that senders cooperate more when the target receives assistance from third parties during a sanctions episode—which is consistent with the coincidence model. Hence, Martin's study provides a good deal of support for neoliberal institutional and realist explanations of economic sanctions and some weaker support for liberal explanations.

Whereas Martin focused on the factors influencing cooperation on sanctions, two other quantitative studies have analyzed the extent to which sanctions succeed. In the first one, T. Clifton Morgan and Valerie L. Schwebach (1997) examined the conditions under which sanctions lead a target to change policy without the sender resorting to force. They developed a model suggesting that sanctions should have only a modest impact on the target's behavior during disputes, except in cases where the costs to the target are quite substantial. Instead, the political power and resolve of states generally should be more potent influences on foreign policy.

Like Martin, Morgan and Schwebach used Hufbauer, Schott, and Elliott's data on sanctions to test this argument, although their analysis spanned a longer period of time (1914 to 1990) than hers. However, Morgan and Schwebach recognized that relying solely on these data could introduce a selection bias if the same factors that affect whether states become involved in sanctions also influence the outcome of sanctions. For this reason and in order to analyze their hypothesis that whether sanctions are imposed has relatively little influence on the outcome of disputes, they supplemented Hufbauer, Schott, and Elliott's sample of sanctions with a set of interstate crises in which sanctions were not imposed. Morgan and Schwebach considered two features of disputes, events that include both sanctions episodes and interstate crises.

First, they addressed whether a dispute led to war and found very little evidence that sanctions affect escalation of this sort. Second, they analyzed whether the settlement of disputes ending peacefully favored the initiator, the target, or neither party. Using polytomous logistic regression—since this dependent variable is trichotomous—Morgan and Schwebach found that sanctions have neither a statistically significant nor a substantively large effect on dispute outcomes. Power relations, however, have a strong influence on conflicts, with stronger states achieving more favorable settlements than their weaker counterparts. Finally, Morgan and Schwebach examined those cases where sanctions were imposed and found that as the associated costs to a target rise, so does the probability that the sender will achieve a favorable settlement. As the costs to the sender increase, its likelihood of obtaining a favorable settlement declines. But while the effects of these costs were statistically significant, they seemed to be substantively small, leading Morgan and Schwebach to conclude that sanctions are rarely useful policy instruments.

In another study addressing the political economy of sanctions, Daniel W. Drezner (1999) argued that political-military relations influence which states senders target and when sanctions are most likely to succeed. He claims that states are less likely to sanction political-military allies than adversaries, but that it is harder to successfully sanction adversaries than allies. Crucial to Drezner's argument is the greater expectation of future conflict among adversaries than among allies. Due to this expectation, states worry more about the long-term implications of acquiescing—including the reputational consequences of backing down and how the distribution of gains and losses from the sanctions will affect their security—when they are sanctioned by an adversary. One upshot of his theory is that the targets of sanctions will make fewer concessions to adversaries than to allies.

To test this hypothesis, Drezner followed Martin (1992), Morgan and Schwebach (1997), and others in using Hufbauer, Schott, and Elliott's data on sanctions. Relying on a sample composed of cases in which sanctions were imposed between 1914 and 1990, he began by analyzing the magnitude of the concessions targets made. Since this measure is ordered and nominal, the analysis was conducted using an ordered probit model. The results indicate that as political relations between states grow warmer (hostile), targets are increasingly (decreasingly) willing to make concessions. Equally, targets that realign politically just before or during sanctions episodes make fewer concessions to senders. These results support Drezner's claims. So do the findings derived from an analysis of the duration of sanctions, which furnishes strong evidence that states impose shorter sanctions on allies than on adversaries.

Furthermore, Drezner generates some additional evidence that bears on the studies discussed earlier in this section. First, while Morgan and Schwebach find that power relations have a potent influence on whether the sender or the target achieves a more favorable settlement, Drezner concludes that such relations also influence the duration of sanctions. As a sender grows stronger relative to a target, sanctions are imposed for longer periods of time. His results also indicate, however, that power relations have no statistically significant effect on the magnitude of the concessions made in response to sanctions. Second, all three studies show that the economic costs to participants influence sanctions. Martin finds that multilateral cooperation among senders rises as the costs to the major sender increase. Morgan and Schwebach report that as the sanction-related costs to a state increase, its prospect of achieving a favorable settlement dips, although the magnitude of this effect may not be very sizable. Drezner's results indicate that as the difference between the target's costs and the sender's costs grows larger, the target tends to make bigger concessions and the episode becomes shorter. Third, whereas Martin provides considerable evidence that international institutions stimulate cooperation among senders, Drezner produces equally strong evidence that such cooperation reduces the concessions made by targets. Taken together, then, these studies seem to indicate that cooperation among states imposing multilateral sanctions may undermine their effectiveness, a result that is at odds with the received wisdom and that merits further attention in future research.[14]

Conclusions

For centuries, scholars have displayed a lively interest in the factors guiding international trade. Most studies of this issue have focused on the economic determinants of foreign commerce. However, the widespread recognition that political factors also shape international exchange has generated rising interest in the political economy of trade. Research on this topic has contributed to the development of various influential theories of the international political economy, many of which highlight the effects of hegemony, political-military relations, and commercial institutions. Increasingly, quantitative methods are being used to test these theories, and the primary purpose of this essay has been to survey and assess some statistical analyses of the political economy of international trade.

While quantitative research has shed considerable light on many debates in the field of international political economy, it is obvious that scholars remain deeply divided over the political influences on trade. These divisions stem from a number of sources, some of which were discussed earlier. However, one especially important reason why empirical studies of the international political economy have not made more headway is that we lack adequate measures of various central concepts in this field. The study of international political economy is hardly unique in this regard. As Paul Huth and Todd Allee (chap. 9, this vol.) point out, the field of international security faces a similar problem. However, the severity of this problem is particularly striking in the field of international political economy. It is far from obvious how to even begin measuring factors emphasized in certain theories of the international political economy, such as the normative and ideational variables stressed by constructivists. In addition, there is considerable disagreement over the utility of many measures—including those of interdependence, hegemony, economic cooperation, and economic sanctions—that have been used repeatedly in this field. In order to more fully evaluate theories of the international political economy using quantitative (or qualitative) methods, much more attention needs to be focused on improving existing measures of these and other concepts.

Despite the importance of this issue, quantitative studies have done much to improve our understanding of the international political economy. One way they have done so is by showing that, holding constant economic factors, international trade is strongly influenced by international politics. Moreover, these studies have helped to clarify the strength and nature of the relationship between many political factors and commerce. Whereas economic models frequently ignore the political underpinnings of trade, empirical research on the international political economy has demonstrated that this omission risks generating biased results and, hence, arriving at misleading conclusions about the determinants of foreign commerce.

Recommended Readings

Frey, B. S. 1984. *International Political Economics.* Oxford: Basil Blackwell.

Gowa, J. 1994. *Allies, Adversaries, and International Trade.* Princeton: Princeton University Press.

Mansfield, E. D. 1994. *Power, Trade, and War.* Princeton: Princeton University Press.

Mansfield, E. D., and B. M. Pollins, eds. 2003. *Economic Interdependence and International Conflict: New Perspectives on an Enduring Debate.* Ann Arbor: University of Michigan Press.

Martin, L. L. 1992. *Coercive Cooperation: Explaining Multilateral Economic Sanctions.* Princeton: Princeton University Press.

Notes

I am grateful to Patrick McDonald, Beth Simmons, Detlef Sprinz, and Yael Wolinsky-Nahmias for helpful comments on this chapter.

1. I am grateful to Patrick McDonald for collecting the data used to make these calculations.

2. By virtue of my emphasis on systemic analyses, this essay does not address the domestic political influences on trade. It should be noted, however, that there is a large and important literature on this issue, some of which relies heavily on quantitative methods.

3. For a discussion of the differences between these strands of hegemonic stability theory, see Lake (1993).

4. For a more extensive discussion of this issue, see Mansfield (1994, 177–79).

5. This difference may also stem from the different capabilities that McKeown and I used to measure concentration and the somewhat different time periods we analyzed.

6. The gravity model is so named because of the similarity between its underlying logic and the law of gravity in physics. Although economists disagree about this model's precise theoretical basis, it is consistent with various models of international trade (Anderson 1979; Bergstrand 1985; Deardorff 1998). Furthermore, it is widely acknowledged that the gravity model generally provides a very good fit to data on bilateral trade flows. For empirical studies that rely on this model, see Aitken (1973); Frankel (1993); Linnemann (1966); Pelzman (1977); Pollins (1989a); and Tinbergen (1962).

7. It should be noted that a number of minor variations on this model have been proposed. For example, some studies replace the population of each trade partner with per capita income; others estimate the model after taking the logarithm of $GDP_i \times GDP_j$ and $POP_i \times POP_j$ rather than taking the logarithm of GDP_i, GDP_j, POP_i, and POP_j, respectively.

8. Other justifications for the gravity model and its multiplicative form are offered by Anderson (1979) and Bergstrand (1985).

9. The years analyzed were 1905, 1913, 1920, 1930, 1938, 1955, 1965, 1975, and 1985. In the nine regressions, trade was measured in these years and the independent variables were measured one year earlier, since it is generally assumed that most variables in our model have a lagged effect on trade, and also in order to avoid problems of simultaneity.

10. For an exception, see Pollins (1989a).

11. For overviews of these arguments, see Barbieri and Levy (1999); Doyle (1997); Mansfield (1994); and Stein (1993).

12. Although most of the research discussed in this section treats conflict as exogenous, a number of studies have treated both conflict and trade as endogenous. These studies have used a system of simultaneous equations to estimate the relationship between commerce and conflict. For the most part, they have concluded that heightened trade inhibits hostilities, but the effects of conflict on trade are less consistent across these studies. See, for example, Mansfield (1994, 186–90); Polachek (1980); and Pollins and Reuveny (2000).

13. It should be noted that the strength of war's effect on trade continues to be the subject of some debate. For example, Katherine Barbieri and Jack S. Levy (1999) found that war has little effect on trade flows, based on an analysis of seven dyads during the period since 1870.

14. For discussions of why the factors promoting cooperation might dampen the success of sanctions, see Drezner (1999, 124) and Mansfield (1995).

References

Aitken, N. D. 1973. The Effect of the EEC and EFTA on European Trade: A Temporal and Cross-Section Analysis. *American Economic Review* 63:881–92.

Anderson, J. E. 1979. A Theoretical Foundation for the Gravity Equation. *American Economic Review* 69:106–16.

Anderson, K., and R. Blackhurst. 1993. Introduction and Summary. In *Regional Integration and the Global Trading System,* edited by K. Anderson and R. Blackhurst. London: Harvester Wheatsheaf.

Baldwin, D. 1985. *Economic Statecraft.* Princeton: Princeton University Press.

Barbieri, K., and J. S. Levy. 1999. Sleeping with the Enemy: The Impact of War on Trade. *Journal of Peace Research* 36:463–79.

Bergstrand, J. H. 1985. The Gravity Equation in International Trade: Some Microeconomic Foundations and Empirical Evidence. *Review of Economics and Statistics* 67:474–81.

Bhagwati, J. 1993. Regionalism and Multilateralism: An Overview. In *New Dimensions in Regional Integration,* edited by J. de Melo and A. Panagariya. New York: Cambridge University Press.

Conybeare, J. A. C. 1983. Tariff Protection in Developed and Developing Countries: A Cross-Sectional and Longitudinal Analysis. *International Organization* 37:441–67.

Deardorff, A. V. 1998. Determinants of Bilateral Trade: Does Gravity Work in a Neoclassical World? In *The Regionalization of the World Economy,* edited by J. A. Frankel. Chicago: University of Chicago Press.

Doyle, M. W. 1997. *Ways of War and Peace: Realism, Liberalism, and Socialism.* New York: W. W. Norton.

Drezner, D. W. 1999. *The Sanctions Paradox.* New York: Cambridge University Press.

Eichengreen, B., and D. A. Irwin. 1998. The Role of History in Bilateral Trade Flows. In *The Regionalization of the World Economy,* edited by J. A. Frankel. Chicago: University of Chicago Press.

Frankel, J. A. 1993. Is Japan Creating a Yen Bloc in East Asia and the Pacific? In *Regionalism and Rivalry: Japan and the United States in Pacific Asia,* edited by J. A. Frankel and M. Kahler. Chicago: University of Chicago Press.

Gilpin, R. 1987. *The Political Economy of International Relations.* Princeton: Princeton University Press.

Gowa, J. 1994. *Allies, Adversaries, and International Trade.* Princeton: Princeton University Press.

Gowa, J., and E. D. Mansfield. 1993. Power Politics and International Trade. *American Political Science Review* 87:408–20.

Hufbauer, G. C., J. J. Schott, and K. A. Elliott. 1990. *Economic Sanctions Reconsidered: History and Current Policy.* Washington, DC: Institute for International Economics.

Jones, D. M., S. A. Bremer, and J. D. Singer. 1996. Militarized Interstate Disputes, 1816–1992: Rationale, Coding Rules, and Empirical Patterns. *Conflict Management and Peace Science* 15:163–213.

Kindleberger, C. P. 1973. *The World in Depression, 1929–1939.* Berkeley: University of California Press.

Krasner, S. D. 1976. State Power and the Structure of Foreign Trade. *World Politics* 28:317–47.

Lake, D. A. 1993. Leadership, Hegemony, and the International Economy: Naked Emperor or Tattered Monarch with Potential? *International Studies Quarterly* 37:459–89.

Linnemann, H. 1966. *An Economic Study of International Trade Flows.* Amsterdam: North-Holland.

Mansfield, E. D. 1994. *Power, Trade, and War.* Princeton: Princeton University Press.

———. 1995. International Institutions and Economic Sanctions. *World Politics* 47:575–605.

Mansfield, E. D., and R. Bronson. 1997. Alliances, Preferential Trading Arrangements, and International Trade. *American Political Science Review* 91:94–107.

Mansfield, E. D., and H. V. Milner. 1999. The New Wave of Regionalism. *International Organization* 53:589–627.

Mansfield, E. D., and J. C. Pevehouse. 2000. Trade Blocs, Trade Flows, and International Conflict. *International Organization* 54:775–808.

Martin, L. L. 1992. *Coercive Cooperation: Explaining Multilateral Economic Sanctions.* Princeton: Princeton University Press.

McKeown, T. J. 1991. A Liberal Trade Order? The Long-Run Pattern of Imports to the Advanced Capitalist States. *International Studies Quarterly* 35:151–72.

Morgan, T. C., and V. L. Schwebach. 1997. Fools Suffer Gladly: The Use of Economic Sanctions in Economic Crises. *International Studies Quarterly* 41:27–50.

Morrow, J. D., R. M. Siverson, and T. E. Tabares. 1998. The Political Determinants of International Trade: The Major Powers, 1907–90. *American Political Science Review* 92:649–61.

———. 1999. Correction to "The Political Determinants of International Trade." *American Political Science Review* 93:931–33.

Pahre, R. 1999. *Leading Questions: How Hegemony Affects the International Political Economy.* Ann Arbor: University of Michigan Press.

Pelzman, J. 1977. Trade Creation and Trade Diversion in the Council of Mutual Economic Assistance, 1954–1970. *American Economic Review* 67:713–22.

Polachek, S. W. 1980. Conflict and Trade. *Journal of Conflict Resolution* 24:55–78.

Pollins, B. M. 1989a. Conflict, Cooperation, and Commerce: The Effects of International Political Interactions on Bilateral Trade Flows. *American Journal of Political Science* 33:737–61.

———. 1989b. Does Trade Still Follow the Flag? *American Political Science Review* 83:465–80.

Pollins, B. M., and R. Reuveny. 2000. The Liberal Peace: Testing Propositions in a Simultaneous Framework. Paper presented at the Annual Convention of the International Studies Association, Los Angeles.

Stein, A. A. 1993. Governments, Economic Interdependence, and International Cooperation. In *Behavior, Society, and Nuclear War,* vol. 3, edited by P. E. Tetlock, J. L. Husbands, R. Jervis, P. C. Stern, and C. Tilly. New York: Oxford University Press.

Tinbergen, J. 1962. *Shaping the World Economy: Suggestions for an International Economic Policy.* New York: Twentieth Century Fund.

Wallerstein, I. 1983. The Three Instances of Hegemony in the History of the Capitalist World-Economy. *International Journal of Comparative Sociology* 24: 100–108.

Waltz, K. 1979. *Theory of International Politics.* Reading, MA: Addison-Wesley.

Williamson, O. E. 1985. *The Economic Institutions of Capitalism.* New York: Free Press.

World Trade Organization. 1995. *Regionalism and the World Trading System.* Geneva: World Trade Organization.

Yarbrough, B. V., and R. M. Yarbrough. 1992. *Cooperation and Governance in International Trade: The Strategic Organization Approach.* Princeton: Princeton University Press.

8. Environment Meets Statistics: Quantitative Analysis of International Environmental Policy

Detlef F. Sprinz

Until recently, the study of international environmental policy was dominated by case study analysis (Mitchell and Bernauer, chap. 4, this vol.), and few quantitative analyses were undertaken in the comparatively new subfield of international relations (Sprinz 1999). The following assessment of the situation in the mid-1990s referred to international regime research in general, but it was equally applicable to the specific area of international environmental policy.

> For understandable reasons, case selection in most studies [on international regimes] has been driven by practical considerations instead of methodological requirements. Moreover, the choice of both dependent and independent variables for systematic attention in these small-n case studies has failed, in general, to produce a cumulative and consistent set of information on an agreed-upon set of important variables. Each study, in practice, has tended to select idiosyncratic variables, or operationalize common ones in radically different ways. As a result of these limitations, the study of international regimes stands out as somewhat peculiar in its absence of systematic, large-n studies making use of quantitative methods, methods which have advanced the state of the art in almost all other areas of political science. (Breitmeier et al. 1996a, 1)

While more quantitative studies have been published in recent years, they have been concentrated in the subfields of international political economy and international security studies (see Mansfield, chap. 7, and Huth and Allee, chap. 9, this vol.). In this chapter I summarize the quantitative research on international environmental policy, which largely clusters around the themes of ecological modernization, the effect of international trade on the environment, environmental regulation, and environmental security, as well as international regime effectiveness. Subsequently, I cover methodological problems in the field and conclude with a description of recent developments in multimethod research.

Central Themes of Research

Quantitative research on international environmental policy focuses around five themes of inquiry, namely, (1) the effects of economic development, abatement costs, and democracy on pollution patterns, (2) the debate on the effects of growing trade on environmental degradation, (3) regulatory issues, (4) the link between environmental factors and violent conflict, and (5) the formation and effectiveness of international regimes.

First, beginning in the 1980s, several projects led by M. Jänicke at the Research Unit for Environmental Policy at the Free University of Berlin (Germany) studied the effect of increasing wealth (measured as gross domestic product [GDP]) as well as the effects of changed industry structures on the environment. This group of researchers has focused on industrialized countries and has investigated whether increased wealth has led to reduced or increased pressures on the environment (Jänicke et al. 1988, 1993; Jänicke 1996). Their composite hypothesis suggests that as poor countries become richer, they first increase environmental pressures until a turning point in their economic development; beyond this point, countries reduce environmental pressures as they become even richer—a phenomenon that has also become known as the "environmental Kuznets curve." Alternatively, we may wish to dub this hypothesis the "environmental stages of economic development." Jänicke and collaborators conclude that for some indicators, increases in wealth have led to improved environmental performance, while in other cases increasing wealth has led to worsening environmental performance. In few countries, the complete trajectory of the "environmental stages of economic development" hypothesis seems to hold (Jänicke et al. 1993, 48–49; Jänicke, Mönch, and Binder 1996, 129).

Material wealth, measured as per capita gross national product (GNP), also plays a major role in the investigation of a variety of other issues, in particular as a control variable in research on the effect of democracy on environmental performance and also in studies on the effect of trade on the environment. Inspired by the discussion of the "democratic peace,"[1] Midlarsky (1998) hypothesizes that democracy should have a beneficial effect on environmental performance. Midlarsky explores a variety of ways to operationalize democracy, ranging from basic political rights to more complex institutional requirements, and he finds a positive association between democracy and protected land and negative relationships with deforestation, carbon dioxide emissions, and soil erosion by water. The latter three findings are clearly at variance with his guiding hypothesis, and Midlarsky concludes, "there is no uniform relationship between democracy and the environment" (358).[2] The study also shows that per capita GDP has a benign effect on the environment in all but one (out of six) analyses of environmental performance. Furthermore, the study indicates that European location (implying membership in the European Union or the hope to become a member in the foreseeable future) is positively correlated with greater environmental protection in most analyses. By contrast, in a topically related paper, Neumayer, Gates, and Gleditsch (2002) find that democracy—regardless of the operationalization chosen—enhances the environmental commitment of countries even in the presence of controls for GDP per capita and other factors. The difference in dependent variables, environmental outcomes vs. environmental commitments, may account for the difference in findings.

A second cluster of research in international environmental policy surrounds the question of whether international trade is associated with a shift of pollution patterns from industrialized countries to developing countries (see, e.g., Anderson and Blackhurst 1992). Researchers have investigated the possibility that developed countries would witness the export of their most polluting industries to developing countries due to increased environmental regulation (the "industry-flight" hypothesis), whereas select developing countries would offer themselves as "pollution havens." In his empirical qualitative analysis, Leonard (1988) finds that neither hypothesis receives much support. The economist J. A. Tobey, using econometric analysis, concurs "that the stringent environmental regulations imposed on industries in the late 1960s and the early 1970s by most industrialized countries have not measurably affected international trade patterns in the most polluting industries" (1990, 192) and "a reasonable explanation for these empirical results may simply be that the magnitude of environmental expenditures in countries with stringent environmental policies are not sufficiently large to cause a noticeable effect" (206). Other authors felt obliged to challenge these early findings.

Directly testing the impact of trade on the degree of deforestation, Lofdahl shows that "trade-connected GNP" increases deforestation, as does population growth. Per capita GNP is not able to sufficiently offset such adverse effects on deforestation (1998, 351),[3] thereby countering the argument of the benign effect of free trade on the environment.

Building on the premise of an "environmental Kuznets curve" mentioned earlier, Heil and Selden (2001) explore the effect of international trade on the emissions of carbon dioxide during the period 1950 through 1992. By including per capita GDP, the square thereof, and trade, as well as all interactions among the previous three independent variables in their time-series analysis, they are able to demonstrate that the trade variables and the interaction variables including trade are jointly statistically significant. Furthermore, they show that "holding income constant, increased trade intensity is associated with decreased emissions in high-income countries and with increased emissions in low-income countries" (46). The demonstration of these results rests on simulation graphics, as the highly interactive part of the estimation results is otherwise difficult to interpret in substantive terms. Regrettably, the study also relies on indirect evidence regarding the effect of trade on the environment as the trade-related emissions could actually be better accounted for by focusing on the carbon emission associated with consumption (discussed later).[4]

A third track of research has focused on the domestic-international link by relating domestic political variables to national support for international environmental agreements. Sprinz shows how problem pressure[5] and the costs of regulation (relative to GNP) explain why countries were willing to sign stringent international environmental agreements in the context of the United National Economic Commission for Europe during the second half of the 1980s (Sprinz 1992, chap. 7; 1993; Sprinz and Vaahtoranta 1994). Subsequent research by Sprinz inserts a more detailed political process model that intervenes between the two structural variables and domestic approval of international environmental treaties. This expanded explanatory model allows environmental problem pressure to translate into public support for international environmental regulation (individual-level support as well as organized support by environmental movements and green political parties), which in turn is positively related to support for international treaties. Conversely, the costs of regulation translate positively into the net perceived strength of polluting industries over industries that produce abatement technologies. The latter is negatively associated with support for international environmental regulation. The regression results show that this operationalization of the various domestic political pressure components and model specification explain the regulation of sulfur emissions more convincingly than the regulation of nitrogen oxide emissions (Sprinz 1992, chap. 6; 1998). The findings partially rest on removing outlier cases[6] that would otherwise obscure the relationship in this comparatively small-N study.

Fourth, the question of whether environmental degradation could lead to violent conflict within and between countries has been investigated by Homer-Dixon (1990, 1991, 1994), who relied on exploratory case study analysis. While well-designed comparative case studies (see chaps. 2–5, this vol.) have been missing, Hauge and Ellingsen (1998) pioneered the first quantitative study in this domain, and they demonstrate that economic and political institutional factors can easily overwhelm environmental effects in accounting for the onset of civil conflict. Inspired by this line of research, Toset, Gleditsch, and Hegre (2000) find that shared rivers and water scarcity are positively related to the outbreak of militarized interstate disputes. However, the magnitude of such effects is the same as for standard economic and regime type variables. Absent very detailed data sets, the authors suggest that the cause of such conflicts remains unclear, be they "over navigation, pollution, fishing rights, or territorial issues" (992). Subsequent research by Gleditsch and Hamner (2001) conjectures that shared rivers and associated water scarcity may lead to both (1) enhanced armed conflict and militarized disputes and (2) increased levels of cooperation. The former effect is supposed to hold due to resource competition, whereas the latter effect may result from the need to establish informal or formal arrangements for reliable sharing of a scarce resource. In their dyadic analysis of two event data sets, these researchers find modest support for their hypothesis regarding shared rivers, but this result varies both with the particular operationalization and with the data set chosen. A more consistent finding is the positive relationship between water scarcity and levels of cooperation. One potential problem with the study may be that it uses country dyads as the unit of analysis (see also Huth and Allee, chap. 9, this vol.), which may prove inadequate when more than two countries share a river system. This is especially problematic when an international river runs through a larger number of countries and the downstream countries' access to freshwater (or effluents) is largely a function of the decisions taken by all upstream countries. What appears to be a multitude of independent cases in dyadic analysis is more properly one larger case, especially if there are river basin–wide agreements.

Finally, a fifth area of research deals with the rise of international environmental regimes and their effects. The study by Meyer et al. (1997) explains why a world environmental regime emerged during the past century in the absence of a central authority in world politics. The authors argue that both the strong growth of a scientific discourse on environmental problems, measured, inter alia, by the growth in scientific organizations, and the overall rise of nonenvironmental international treaties and nonenvironmental intergovernmental organizations, which reflect a growing degree of organization in world society, positively contributed to the rate of founding relevant environmental associations, signing international environmental treaties, and creating international environmental organizations during the past century. This effect is partially offset by the increase in government-centered organization in environmental matters, including the growth of national environmental ministries, as well as a growing interstate system over the past century. Given strong multicollinearity[7] between the operational variables across the explanatory concepts, the ultimate conclusions rest to a substantial degree on the theoretical specification of the model. The assessment of the degree to which more specific international environmental regimes matter has been explored by a range of other studies.

Several neoliberal institutionalist studies suggest that international (environmental) regimes should matter (Keohane 1984; Keohane, Haas, and Levy 1993; Young 1989a, 1989b). In order to test whether such hopes actually materialize, Helm and Sprinz have developed a systematic measurement method for regime effectiveness (Sprinz and Helm 1999; Helm and Sprinz 2000) that rests on establishing lower and upper bounds of performance, and then relates an actual level of performance to both bounds. This measurement procedure is illustrated in figure 1, where the lower bound is represented by the counterfactual level of emission reductions (no-regime counterfactual, or NR) in the absence of an international regime.[8] Such counterfactuals have often been derived by highly structured expert coding procedures, combined with averaging techniques across expert responses. Simulation techniques may provide alternative methods of delineating counterfactual levels of emission reductions. The upper level of emission reductions is represented by a collective optimum (CO), that is, a level of emission reductions commensurate with environmental problem solving (discussed earlier) or maximizing collective economic welfare in emission reductions efforts. To derive such collective optima, researchers can either use economic calculations to equate marginal abatement costs with the sum of marginal benefits of emission reductions across all countries (Helm and Sprinz 2000), or they can use environmental thresholds as measures of environmental problem solving (Sprinz and Churkina 1999). The actual degree of performance (AP) normally falls between these lower and upper boundaries.[9] By relating the distance AP–NR to the distance CO–NR, a simple coefficient of regime effectiveness (E) has been devised that falls strictly into the interval [0, 1] (Helm and Sprinz 2000) (see fig. 1). The derivation of effectiveness scores necessitates the development of counterfactuals for the no-regime counterfactual (Tetlock and Belkin 1996; see also Sprinz and Wolinsky-Nahmias, chap. 15, this vol.) and also implies causal impact for the difference between actual performance and the no-regime counterfactual (Underdal 2002a). The methodology for regime effectiveness is, however, hardly restricted to international environmental problems; it can also be applied to regimes of international security and in the field of international political economy by adapting the central dimension of intervention (see fig. 1).

A simplified, yet related, way to measure the effects of international regimes has been devised by Underdal (2002a), who relies on a variety of case studies conducted by contributors to his edited volume. The cases assess the effects of international regimes as reflected in behavioral change (changed policies) and distance to a technical optimum (the latter is associated with problem solving) (see previous discussion). Underdal accounts for variation in regime effectiveness, as the dependent variable, by hypothesizing that (1) the type of environmental problem (malign rather than benign) being negatively related to regime effect, whereas (2) problem-solving capacity and (3) the level of collaboration within the international regime are both positively related to regime effectiveness.[10] Subsequently, Underdal conducted statistical analyses of the fourteen regimes[11] under

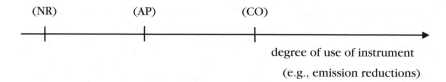

Fig. 1. Measuring regime effectiveness.
Effectiveness score: ES = (AP – NR) / (CO – NR). (NR = no-regime counterfactual, CO = collective optimum, AP = actual performance. Source: Helm and Sprinz 2000.)

investigation. The statistical analysis of the overall model shows that the broader hypotheses largely hold; the comprehensive analysis (as opposed to the analysis of major subcomponents) rests on partial correlation analysis because of the impact of influential outliers on the results (2002b).[12]

The methods of Helm and Sprinz and of Underdal are research intensive and thus far have been applied to smaller-N studies. One way to overcome the problem of an insufficient number of cases has been proposed by Mitchell (2002), who suggests replacing the systemic level of analysis with the analysis of country-level performance variables and adding a time dimension. In particular, he suggests deriving the dependent variable of country-specific "regime effort units" as the product of per annum percentage change of emissions multiplied by per unit effort (in dollars or euros). Subsequently, variation in regime effort units could be explained by variables representing regime properties (e.g., sanctioning systems) as well as other control variables. In effect, Mitchell suggests that measures of covariation (regression coefficients) associated with regime variables would capture the effect of the international regime, while the dependent variable reflects the costs that a country is willing to shoulder per year. This is a substantially different conceptualization of regime effectiveness that has often been associated with problem solving as developed earlier.

Common Methodological Challenges

Because international environmental politics is a relatively new subfield of international relations, it presents a wide range of methodological challenges. Perhaps the most salient challenge is to develop larger and more comprehensive data sets. Most data sets are created for particular studies (e.g., Hauge and Ellingsen 1998; Miles et al. 2002; Sprinz 1992). Fortunately, at least three major projects are under way that may rectify the situation. In addition to Miles et al. (2002), efforts by Breitmeier et al. are in progress to build an international regimes database to code at least sixteen international environmental regimes and a much larger set of associated treaties that fall within these regimes (1996a, 1996b). This will clearly allow for much better comparative case study designs and will permit medium-N quantitative analyses once a unit of analysis "below" the level of a regime (e.g., intergovernmental treaties) is chosen. The data protocol is extremely detailed, yet generic, and allows the protocol also to be used outside the environmental field. As of November 15, 2001, twenty-three regimes with ninety-two subcases have been coded.[13] Once the data are released, systematic comparisons of international regimes across the various subfields of international relations will become possible. As a result, we will be much better prepared to assess the conditions under which international regimes emerge, the effectiveness of these regimes, and the degree of compliance with their rules. Furthermore, we will be better able to study the interaction among regimes, which will permit systematic research into important questions such as whether and how environmental and trade regimes interact, as well as whether metanorms (e.g., major assistance to be given to developing countries) developed in one subfield actually spread to another.

R. Mitchell has initiated a project to analyze the effects of international environmental agreements quantitatively. The project is compiling a unique meta-data set to link existing and new data on a wide range of environmental agreements, the outcomes they target, and the indicators of the legal, economic, political, and social drivers of those outcomes. The project will employ regression models of the outcomes of agreements in order to distinguish the design effects of international agreements from other explanatory factors. In addition, this approach will allow meaningful comparison of the effects of agreements that address quite different environmental problems and help to evaluate how generalizable "successful" design features are. The project's quantitative approach also permits assessment of whether qualitative findings are case-specific or can be generalized to other cases.[14]

While small sample size often impedes the chance to find statistically significant coefficient estimates, the field of international environmental policy also needs more conceptual consolidation. In small-N studies, it routinely is difficult to find statistically significant results. Furthermore, outliers have a substantial effect on outcomes, as witnessed by the studies

of Sprinz (1993) and Miles et al. (2002). The removal of outliers or the use
of estimation methods that do not require demanding metrics for the measurement of variables may be practical responses to such problems, but this
also entails a loss of information. Furthermore, much of the study of international environmental policy is characterized by the omission of proper
control groups, such as issue areas where no regime has yet come into existence. This has led Underdal to caution scholars in the field of international
environmental policy that "there is a real possibility that *the entire field of
regime analysis may be biased in favor of positive findings*" (2002b, 447, emphasis in original), as only cases of successful regime formation are included in
the analysis. While this omission of nonregime cases is also characteristic
of other subfields of international relations, it may be most pronounced in
international environmental policy (see also Sprinz and Wolinsky-Nahmias, chap. 15, this vol., on selection bias). Only the systematic inclusion
of "nonregime" cases will shed light on the validity of the findings of much
research on international regimes.

Besides small sample size, lack of conceptual consolidation is an additional problem in the field of international environmental policy. As the
study by Midlarsky (1998) shows, three different ways of measuring
democracy yield partially different results on the effect of democracy on
environmental protection, and although it is a mature concept, democracy
fails in directional hypothesis testing.[15] While Mitchell's suggestion of
how to analyze international regime effectiveness is likely to reduce estimation problems (2002), it appears to involve a different substantive concept of regime effect. The problem does not lie with replacing the systemic
with the national level of analysis. The conceptualization by Helm and
Sprinz (2000) of regime effectiveness works simultaneously on both levels
of analysis. It is reliance on explaining variation in resource expenditures
rather than variables representing environmental problem solving that
constitutes a change of concept. By using the coefficient estimates associated with regime-related explanatory variables, Mitchell employs indirect
techniques where more direct measurement is both conceptually preferable
and practically feasible—although at higher cost to the researcher. The
same problem of indirect measurement can be found, for example, in the
study of Heil and Selden (2001) on trade-related effects on national carbon
emissions. In order to corroborate their findings of carbon emissions shifting from industrialized to developing countries due to international trade,
they should augment their statistical inference with direct measurement of

the carbon intensity of commodities produced and commodities consumed in a country. After all, income influences not only production patterns but especially consumption patterns. As Braumoeller and Sartori insist (chap. 6, this vol.), attention to theory and subsequent model specification are of major importance for statistical findings.

In conclusion, the most pressing problems for quantitative analyses of international environmental policies lie with the difficulties involved in efforts to create sufficiently large data sets. Furthermore, consolidation in measuring major concepts is needed (see also Huth and Allee, chap. 9, this vol.), and whenever possible, direct ways of measurement is preferable to indirect inference.

Multimethod Research

While the field of international environmental policy is still characterized by dominance of single or comparative case studies, there has been an increase in statistical and formal analyses (see Kilgour and Wolinsky-Nahmias, chap. 13, this vol.). We find a discernible rise in multimethod research in international relations over the past quarter century, and the concluding chapter here gives examples from all three subfields (see Sprinz and Wolinsky-Nahmias, chaps. 1, 15, this vol.). The field of international environmental policy may become a good candidate for multimethod research, such as that suggested by Ness (1985), who advocates combining statistical techniques with case studies on prominent outliers for the analysis of medium-N studies.

Because we lack a long-established body of theoretical development in international environmental policy, formal models can be of particular help in generating sufficiently precise hypotheses that subsequently can be subjected to quantitative analysis. (This combination of methods has typically been found in economics [e.g., Murdoch and Sandler 1997a, 1997b]). Furthermore, case studies could help to explain why some statistical studies of international environmental policy are inconclusive (see Midlarsky 1998, 359).

Perhaps the best demonstration of multimethod research on environmental policy-making is the study by Miles et al. (2002). The theory developed is grounded in a soft rational choice approach (Wæver 1998), augmented by an array of intensive case studies that are later drawn together by statistical analysis and the use of Ragin's qualitative case analysis method (see Bennett, chap. 2, this vol.). Thus, Miles et al. appropriately guard themselves against methods-induced findings. It would not be surprising to see future studies influenced by these pioneers.

The quantitative study of international environmental policy is new in comparison with developments in the subfields of international security and international political economy, and as a consequence, it largely is organized around substantive concerns rather than methodologically oriented groupings. But we can expect this subfield to grow. Efforts at building larger databases will facilitate a fruitful discussion on central concepts of international environmental policy and provide the basis for cumulative growth of knowledge in the field. Furthermore, the field may be particularly well suited for multimethod research as we saw earlier.

Recommended Readings

Hauge, W., and T. Ellingsen. 1998. Beyond Environmental Scarcity: Causal Pathways to Conflict. *Journal of Peace Research* 35 (3): 299–317.

Helm, C., and D. F. Sprinz. 2000. Measuring the Effectiveness of International Environmental Regimes. *Journal of Conflict Resolution* 45 (5): 630–52.

Miles, E. L., A. Underdal, S. Andresen, J. Wettestad, J. B. Skjærseth, and E. M. Carlin. 2002. *Environmental Regime Effectiveness: Confronting Theory with Evidence.* Cambridge: MIT Press.

Notes

The author is indebted to Harold Jacobson, Ronald Mitchell, Marco Overhaus, Arild Underdal, and Yael Wolinsky-Nahmias for comments on an earlier version.

1. Theories and tests of the democratic peace refer to the finding that democracies normally do not fight each other. See Kacowicz (chap. 5), Huth and Allee (chap. 9), and Kydd (chap. 14) in this volume for details.

2. The problems encountered by Midlarsky in operationalizing democracy are further elaborated in the "Common Methodological Problems" section of this chapter.

3. The concept of "trade-connected GNP"—its major explanatory variable— is not described well in this study.

4. This point is a perennial problem of statistical estimations of environmental Kuznets curves. I am grateful to Doris Fuchs for a discussion of this issue.

5. In the most narrow interpretation, environmental problem pressure refers to "ecological vulnerability" in terms of purely natural science measures, whereas

a wider interpretation includes political mobilization as a response to environmental degradation.

6. Outliers are the (few) observations that both do not fit the otherwise existing pattern of association and have a substantial effect on the estimated results.

7. Multicollinearity among independent variables implies strong statistical association among the variables involved and, inter alia, does not allow for the precise separation of the effect of the independent variables on the dependent variable—precisely because the independent variables are not independent of each other.

8. See also Bennett (chap. 2) and Odell (chap. 3) in this volume for the use of counterfactuals in case study analyses.

9. All three levels of emission reductions (NR, AP, and CO) take levels of environmental problem solving into account. See Helm and Sprinz (2000) for details.

10. The model is actually much more detailed in terms of the subcomponents of problem malignancy and problem-solving capacity. The interested reader is referred to Underdal (2002a).

11. The study used regime phases as the actual unit of analysis, which increases the number of usable cases to thirty-seven for comparative analysis.

12. Partial correlations account for the degree of correlation between two variables while holding all other variables constant. For the effect of outliers, see note 6.

13. See http://www.ifs.tu-darmstadt.de/pg/ird_case.htm (July 18, 2003).

14. The database is available at http://www.uoregon.edu/~rmitchel/iea/. A description of the data set can be found in Mitchell (2003).

15. Alternative explanations of these results may be problems with data, incorrect model specification, or insufficient theory development.

References

Anderson, K., and R. Blackhurst, eds. 1992. *The Greening of World Trade Issues.* New York and London: Harvester Wheatsheaf.

Breitmeier, H., M. A. Levy, O. R. Young, and M. Zürn. 1996a. *The International Regimes Database as a Tool for the Study of International Cooperation.* Laxenburg, Austria: International Institute for Applied Systems Analysis.

———. 1996b. *International Regimes Database (IRD): Data Protocol.* Laxenburg, Austria: International Institute for Applied Systems Analysis.

Gleditsch, N. P., and J. H. Hamner. 2001. Shared Rivers, Conflict, and Cooperation. Paper presented at the Fourth Pan-European International Relations Conference, University of Kent, Canterbury.

Hauge, W., and T. Ellingsen. 1998. Beyond Environmental Scarcity: Causal Pathways to Conflict. *Journal of Peace Research* 35 (3): 299–317.

Heil, M. T., and T. M. Selden. 2001. International Trade Intensity and Carbon Emissions: A Cross-Country Econometric Analysis. *Journal of Environment and Development* 10 (1): 35–49.

Helm, C., and D. Sprinz. 2000. Measuring the Effectiveness of International Environmental Regimes. *Journal of Conflict Resolution* 45 (5): 630–52.

Homer-Dixon, T. F. 1990. *Environmental Change and Violent Conflict.* Cambridge, MA: International Security Program, American Academy of Arts and Science.

———. 1991. On the Threshold: Environmental Changes as Causes of Acute Conflict. *International Security* 16 (2): 76–116.

———. 1994. Environmental Scarcities and Violent Conflict. *International Security* 19 (1): 5–40.

Jänicke, M., ed. 1996. *Umweltpolitik der Industrieländer* (The environmental policy of industrialized countries). Berlin: Edition Sigma.

Jänicke, M., H. Mönch, and M. Binder. 1996. Umweltindikatorenprofile im Industrieländervergleich: Wohlstandniveau und Problemstruktur (Comparison of the environmental indicator profiles of industrialized countries: Wealth and problem structure). In *Umweltpolitik der Industrieländer* (The environmental policy of industrialized countries), edited by M. Jänicke. Berlin: Edition Sigma.

Jänicke, M., H. Mönch, M. Binder, A. Carius, G. Foltjanty-Jost, N. Götz, T. Ranneberg, and M. Schneller. 1993. *Umweltentlastung durch industriellen Strukturwandel? Eine explorative Studie über 32 Industrieländer (1970 bis 1990)* (Improvement of the environment as a result of the structural change of the economy? An exploratory study of thirty-two industrialized countries, 1970–1990). Berlin: Edition Sigma.

Jänicke, M., H. Mönch, T. Ranneberg, and U. E. Simonis. 1988. *Structural Change and Environmental Impact.* Berlin: Wissenschaftszentrum Berlin für Sozialforschung (Social Science Center Berlin).

Keohane, R. O. 1984. *After Hegemony: Cooperation and Discord in the World Political Economy.* Princeton: Princeton University Press.

Keohane, R. O., P. M. Haas, and M. A. Levy. 1993. The Effectiveness of International Environmental Institutions. In *Institutions for the Earth: Sources of Effective International Environmental Protection,* edited by P. M. Haas, R. O. Keohane, and M. A. Levy. Cambridge: MIT Press.

Leonard, H. J. 1988. *Pollution and the Struggle for the World Product: Multinational Corporations, Environment, and International Comparative Advantage.* Cambridge: Cambridge University Press.

Lofdahl, C. L. 1998. On the Environmental Externalities of Global Trade. *International Political Science Review* 19 (4): 339–55.

Meyer, J., D. J. Frank, A. Hironaka, E. Schofer, and N. B. Tuma. 1997. The Structuring of a World Environmental Regime, 1870–1990. *International Organization* 51 (4): 623–51.

Midlarsky, M. I. 1998. Democracy and the Environment: An Empirical Assessment. *Journal of Peace Research* 35 (3): 341–61.

Miles, E. L., A. Underdal, S. Andresen, J. Wettestad, J. B. Skjærseth, and E. M. Carlin. 2002. *Environmental Regime Effectiveness: Confronting Theory with Evidence.* Cambridge: MIT Press.

Mitchell, R. B. 2002. A Quantitative Approach to Evaluating International Environmental Regimes. *Global Environmental Politics* 2 (4): 58–63.

———. 2003. International Environmental Agreements: A Survey of Their Features, Formation, and Effects. In *Annual Review of Environment and Resosurces* 28:429–61.

Murdoch, J. C., and T. Sandler. 1997a. Voluntary Cutback and Pretreaty Behavior: The Helsinki Protocol and Sulfur Emissions. *Public Finance Review* 25 (2): 139–62.

———. 1997b. The Voluntary Provision of a Pure Public Good: The Case of Reduced CFC Emissions and the Montreal Protocol. *Journal of Public Economics* 63:331–49.

Ness, G. D. 1985. Managing Not-So-Small Numbers: Between Comparative and Statistical Methods. *International Journal of Comparative Sociology* 26:1–13.

Neumayer, E., S. Gates, and N. P. Gleditsch. 2002. *Environmental Commitment, Democracy, and Inequality: A Background Paper to the World Development Report 2003.* London: London School of Economics and Political Science.

Sprinz, D. F. 1992. Why Countries Support International Environmental Agreements: The Regulation of Acid Rain in Europe. Ann Arbor: Department of Political Science, University of Michigan. http://www.sprinz.org.

———. 1993. The Impact of International and Domestic Factors on the Regulation of Acid Rain in Europe: Preliminary Findings. *Journal of Environment and Development* 2 (1): 37–61.

———. 1998. Domestic Politics and European Acid Rain Regulation. In *The Politics of International Environmental Management,* edited by A. Underdal. Dordrecht: Kluwer Academic Publishers.

———. 1999. Empirical-Quantitative Approaches to the Study of International Environmental Policy. In *Policy Analysis Methods,* edited by S. S. Nagel. Commack, NY: Nova Science Publishers.

Sprinz, D. F., and G. E. Churkina. 1999. The Analysis of Environmental Thresholds. Presented at the international conference "Caspian Sea: A Quest for Environmental Security." Venice International University, Venice, Italy: NATO Advanced Research Workshop. http://www.sprinz.org.

Sprinz, D. F., and C. Helm. 1999. The Effect of Global Environmental Regimes: A Measurement Concept. *International Political Science Review* 20 (4): 359–69.

Sprinz, D., and T. Vaahtoranta. 1994. The Interest-Based Explanation of International Environmental Policy. *International Organization* 48 (1): 77–105.

Tetlock, P. E., and A. Belkin, eds. 1996. *Counterfactual Thought Experiments in World Politics: Logical, Methodological, and Psychological Perspectives.* Princeton: Princeton University Press.

Tobey, J. A. 1990. The Effects of Domestic Environmental Policies on Patterns of World Trade: An Empirical Test. *Kyklos* 43: 191–209.

Toset, H. P. W., N. P. Gleditsch, and H. Hegre. 2000. Shared Rivers and Interstate Conflict. *Political Geography* 19:971–96.

Underdal, A. 2002a. One Question, Two Answers. In *Environmental Regime Effectiveness: Confronting Theory with Evidence,* edited by E. L. Miles, A. Underdal, S. Andresen, J. Wettestad, J. B. Skjærseth, and E. M. Carlin. Cambridge: MIT Press.

———. 2002b. Conclusions: Patterns of Regime Effectiveness. In *Environmental Regime Effectiveness: Confronting Theory with Evidence,* edited by E. L. Miles, A. Underdal, S. Andresen, J. Wettestad, J. B. Skjærseth, and E. M. Carlin. Cambridge: MIT Press.

Wæver, O. 1998. The Sociology of a Not So International Discipline: American and European Developments in International Relations. *International Organization* 52 (4): 687–727.

Young, O. R. 1989a. *International Cooperation: Building Regimes for Natural Resources and the Environment.* Ithaca: Cornell University Press.

———. 1989b. The Politics of International Regime Formation: Managing Natural Resources and the Environment. *International Organization* 43 (3): 349–75.

9. Research Design in Testing Theories of International Conflict

Paul Huth and Todd Allee

Scholars studying the causes of international conflict confront a number of lingering questions. Under what conditions are disputes between states likely to escalate to war? What impact do alliances have on the outbreak of militarized conflict? When will a deterrent threat be credible? How do domestic political institutions affect a state's propensity to settle disputes nonviolently? One of the most important social scientific methods for investigating these ongoing questions is statistical analysis.

In this chapter we detail a number of issues regarding research design and estimation that researchers must consider when using statistical analysis to address important questions within the study of international conflict and security. We do not engage in a straightforward review of past statistical research on international conflict, but rather put forward a series of suggestions for ongoing and future statistical research on this important topic. However, during the course of our discussion we identify and discuss several statistical studies that converge with our suggestions and exemplify some of the most promising current work by political scientists.

Our central argument is that statistical tests of the causes of international conflict can be improved if researchers would incorporate into their research designs for empirical analysis a number of insights that have been emphasized in recent formal and game-theoretic approaches to the study of international conflict. We believe that greater attention to the implications of the formal and deductive theoretical literatures for statistical analyses can improve research designs in four areas.

1. Selecting theoretically appropriate units of analysis for building data sets
2. Understanding how to better address problems of selection effects in the construction of data sets and estimation of models
3. Accounting for nonindependent observations
4. Reducing the amount of measurement error in the construction of variables for testing hypotheses

We focus on these four aspects of research design because they address a set of important problems that empirical analysts need to address if compelling findings are to be produced by statistical tests. If researchers do not address these issues of research design effectively, weak empirical results can be expected despite the use of sophisticated statistical methods to test rigorously derived theoretical propositions. Even worse, the failure to give careful attention to problems of research design can result in the use of data sets that (1) are actually ill-suited for testing the theories that scholars claim to be evaluating or (2) severely limit our ability to draw accurate conclusions about causal effects based on the empirical findings produced by statistical analyses.

In this chapter we first describe four phases or stages that are associated with international disputes. These stages provide a useful depiction of how international disputes can evolve over time, and they illuminate a number of central research design issues faced by statistical researchers. Second, we discuss four particular research design questions and suggest possible answers. We conclude with a few brief observations about the implications of our analysis for future quantitative work.

Alternative Paths to Conflict and Cooperation in International Disputes

Broadly conceived, the theoretical study of international conflict involves four different stages.

1. Dispute Initiation
2. Challenge the Status Quo
3. Negotiations
4. Military Escalation

Existing quantitative tests of international conflict generally focus on one of these stages, although an increasing number of recent studies focus on more than one stage. We believe that statistical researchers need to think carefully about each of the four stages as part of a unified depiction of the evolution of international conflict. An initial theoretical description of the four stages and the linkages between the stages will help to identify the practical challenges facing the quantitative researcher. These different stages are presented in figure 1, along with some of the principal paths leading to various diplomatic and military outcomes.[1]

In the Dispute Initiation stage, the analysis centers on whether a dispute or disagreement emerges between countries in which one state (the challenger) seeks to alter the prevailing status quo over some issue(s) in its relations with a target state (see fig. 2). An example would be a decision by the leaders of a state to claim the bordering territory of their neighbor. If the leaders of the target state reject the claim, then a territorial dispute has emerged between the two states (e.g., Huth 1996). Other common reasons for the emergence of disputes include economic conflicts over the tariff and nontariff barriers to trade between countries (e.g., see Lincoln 1999, 1990 on U.S.-Japanese trade disputes), or the intervention by one country into the domestic political affairs of another (e.g., Daalder and O'Hanlon 2000 for an analysis of NATO policy in Kosovo). Theoretical analyses of this stage focus on explaining what issues and broader domestic and international conditions are likely to give rise to disputes and why it is that some state leaders are deterred from raising claims and disputing the prevailing status quo.

Once a state has voiced its disagreement with the existing status quo and a dispute has emerged, in the next stage, the Challenge the Status Quo stage, leaders of the challenger state consider both when to press their claims in a dispute and whether they wish to use diplomatic or military pressure to advance their claims. Statistical analyses of this stage, then, attempt to explain when and how states attempt to press or resolve existing disputes. As shown in figure 3, foreign policy decision makers can choose among options such as not actively pressing claims, reliance on negotiations and diplomatic efforts to change the status quo, or more coercive pressure involving military threats. The outcomes to this stage include: (1) the status quo, if the challenger remains quiescent, (2) the opening or resumption of negotiations due to diplomatic initiatives undertaken by the challenger, or (3) a military confrontation when the chal-

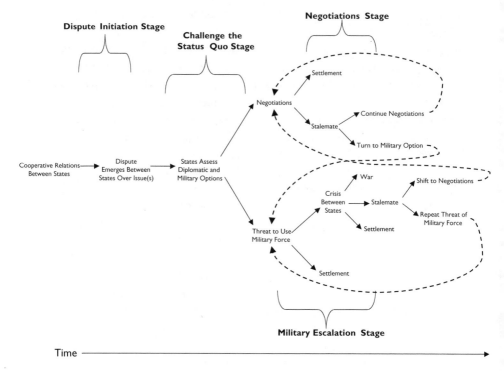

Fig. 1. The evolution of international disputes

lenger resorts to verbal warnings and threatening the deployment of its military forces. The theoretical analysis of this stage would typically focus on explaining what policy choices would be selected by leaders among the various diplomatic and military options available and how domestic and international conditions influence such choices (e.g., Bueno de Mesquita and Lalman 1992; Powell 1999; Huth and Allee 2002).

In the Negotiations stage the challenger and target have entered into talks, and empirical tests attempt to explain the outcome of such rounds of talks (see fig. 4). In this stage, the focus shifts to questions such as which party has more bargaining leverage and is willing to withhold making concessions, whether the terms of a negotiated agreement would be accepted back home by powerful domestic political actors, and whether problems of monitoring and enforcing compliance with the terms of a potential agreement would prevent a settlement from being reached (e.g., Fearon 1998;

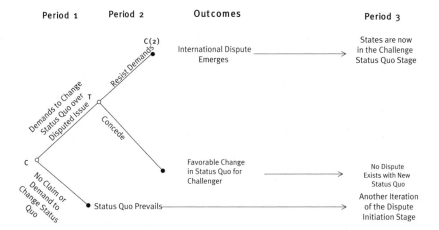

Fig. 2. The Dispute Initiation stage
(Note: C = Challenger State; T = Target State)

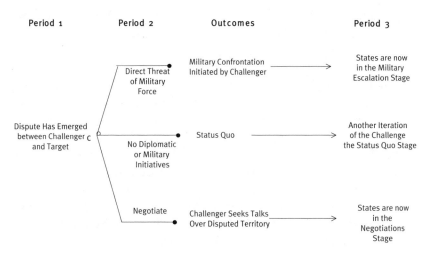

Fig. 3. The Challenge the Status Quo stage
(Note: C = Challenger State; T = Target State)

Powell 1999; Putnam 1988; Downs and Rocke 1990; Schoppa 1997; Milner 1997). The possible outcomes to the Negotiations stage might include a settlement through mutual concessions or capitulation by one side. Furthermore, a stalemate can ensue if neither party is willing to compromise, while limited progress toward a resolution of the dispute can occur if one or both sides offer partial concessions. In the case of stalemate or partial concessions, the dispute continues, and the leaders of the challenger state reassess their policy options in another iteration of the Challenge the Status Quo stage.

In the Military Escalation stage the challenger state has issued a threat of force (see fig. 1). If the target state responds with a counterthreat, a crisis emerges in which the leaders of both states must decide whether to resort to the large-scale use of force (see fig. 5). Statistical tests of this stage generally investigate whether the military standoff escalates to the large-scale use of force or the outbreak of war, or is resolved through some type of less violent channel. This stage of international conflict has drawn considerable attention from international conflict scholars for obvious reasons, yet it remains the most infrequently observed stage of international conflict. Some of the more interesting theoretical puzzles posed at this stage center around questions of how credible the threats to use force are, what actions by states effectively communicate their resolve, and what the risks of war are as assessed by the leaders of each state (Fearon 1994a; Huth 1988; Schultz 1998; Smith 1998; Wagner 2000). The outcome to the international crisis determines whether the dispute continues, and if so, which foreign policy choices need to be reconsidered. For example, if war breaks out, a decisive victory by one side is likely to bring an end to the dispute; whereas a stalemate on the battlefield will lead to the persistence of the dispute in the postwar period. Conversely, the avoidance of war may bring about the end of the dispute by means of a negotiated agreement, while a standoff in the crisis will result in the continuation of the dispute. In either case where the dispute persists, the focus shifts back to the challenger's options in another iteration of the Challenge the Status Quo stage.

Over the duration of a dispute, decision makers pass through the various stages numerous times; that is, they make repeated choices regarding the threat or use of force, negotiations, and dispute settlement. These choices of action (or inaction) become the cases that comprise the data sets used in quantitative studies of international conflict. Interestingly, the sequence of policy choices over time produces common diplomatic and military outcomes that may be arrived at through very different pathways

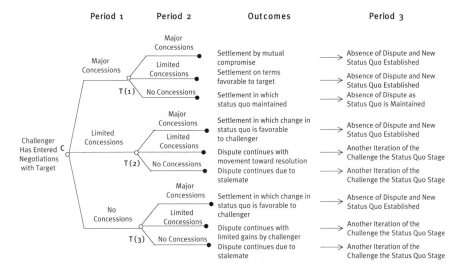

Fig. 4. The Negotiations stage
(Note: C = Challenger State; T = Target State)

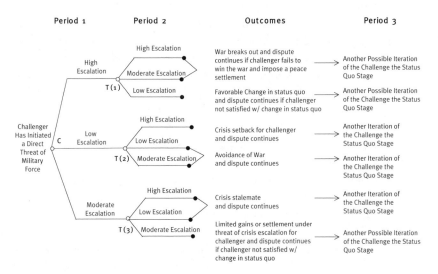

Fig. 5. The Military Escalation stage
(Note: C = Challenger State; T = Target State)

(see fig. 1). For example, consider the outcome of a negotiated settlement reached through mutual concessions. In one dispute, this could be achieved by peaceful talks and mutual compromise in a short period of time, whereas, in another dispute, repeated military conflicts and then difficult and protracted negotiations eventually produce a settlement.

Several important implications for quantitative studies of international conflict may be drawn from our discussion of figure 1 and the various stages of international conflict.

1.   The outbreak of war and the use of large-scale military force are almost always preceded by a preexisting international dispute in which diplomatic efforts at negotiations and talks had been attempted. As a result, very few military confrontations take place without a prior history of failed diplomacy and negotiations between states over disputed issues. Furthermore, most international disputes do not evolve into military confrontations. Since the threat and use of military force is a rare and often final option, empirical studies need to investigate the conditions under which disputes will become militarized. In particular, statistical tests need to account for potential selection effects due to the fact that leaders might turn to military force under specific circumstances, such as when they are risk-acceptant or highly resolved.

2.   Similarly, state leaders often engage in repeated efforts at negotiations before deciding to make substantial concessions. As a result, international disputes are rarely settled without states probing and seeking to shift the burden of concession making onto their adversary. For this reason it is important for theoretical models of international conflict and the empirical tests of such models to account for the process of dispute resolution in which leaders will often shift from an initial hard-line stance that seeks unilateral concessions by their adversary to a more accommodative bargaining position in which they accept the need to offer at least some concessions themselves.

3.   In addition, a state's behavior in one dispute is often affected by its involvement in other disputes. Statistical tests need to consider the larger strategic context of a state's foreign policy in which the state's leaders must manage their country's simultaneous involvement in multiple international disputes. In other words, quantitative studies of international conflict need to consider the fact that a state's behavior in one dispute might be correlated with its behavior in another international dispute.

4.   The impact of history and time may also be important. Empirical tests need to account for the fact that new information might be revealed to states over the course of an international dispute. The past history of diplomatic or military exchanges in the dispute might shape the current diplomatic and military behavior of states. For example, states are likely to shift away from conflict resolution strategies that have proven unsuccessful in previous interactions with an adversary. Not only may previous negotiations, stalemates, or military interactions be important, but short-term actions and more recent changes in prevailing conditions can lead decision makers to update their beliefs and change the policy options during a particular encounter with an adversary. Militarized disputes and crises can unfold over many months, and during that time domestic political conditions can change, other international disputes can arise, third parties can intervene, and the target state's own behavior can signal new information about its resolve and military strength. New information may therefore be revealed in the transition from one stage to the next stage. For example, a decision by a challenger state to issue a threat of force in the Challenge the Status Quo stage (see fig. 3) should not be treated necessarily as reflecting a firm decision to escalate and resort to the large-scale use of force in the subsequent Military Escalation stage (see fig. 5). A threat of force may be designed to probe the intentions and resolve of a target state, to induce the target to resume talks by signaling the dangers of a continued stalemate, or to pressure the target into making concessions in a new round of upcoming talks. As a result, a theoretical distinction should be drawn between the initiation and escalation of militarized conflicts.

Questions of Research Design

In this section we address a number of issues of research design that have significant implications for statistical tests of theories of international conflict. We use the four stages described previously (see fig. 1) to guide our discussion of these issues. We focus on four particular research design questions.

1. What are the units of analysis for building data sets?
2. How can problems of selection effects be addressed in empirical tests?
3. In what ways can problems of nonindependent observations arise in statistical analyses?

4. What are common problems of measurement error in statistical analyses of international conflict theories?

Before discussing these questions, it is useful to touch upon a few general features of the framework we use when thinking about the evolution of international disputes. Typically, our conceptualization is of a situation in which two states interact over an issue of (potential) disagreement, although in principle there is nothing to preclude one or both of the parties from being a nonstate actor. Also, we maintain that the primary decision makers (who would typically be state leaders) can be influenced by factors from a variety of levels of analysis. They could be subject to various domestic political impulses and constraints, for example. Furthermore, one could also examine individual-level traits of decision makers, if necessary, or aspects of the decision-making process. Therefore, we consider our framework to be quite general and flexible. Our basic structure is of a two-player game, but third parties can affect the calculus of either or both actors. The actors might, for example, consider whether an ally is likely to intervene in a certain scenario or how an international legal body would be likely to rule if referred a disputed issue. Our framework, however, is not designed to explain long-term, dynamic processes that involve multiple independent actors. In such a situation, simulations based on agent-based modeling might be quite useful (e.g., Cederman 1997). Nevertheless, we feel that our conceptualization of international conflict is one that can accommodate many types of international interactions, as well as a wide variety of explanations for different types of behavior.

Selecting the Units of Analysis

We have argued that the theoretical study of international conflict centers on four generic types of stages in which state leaders select different policy options. Empirical tests will need to be designed for each of these four stages. Our general argument is that in building data sets for statistical analyses of theories about the causes of international conflict the appropriate unit of analysis in most empirical studies should be *the individual state in a given international dispute with another state.* Put slightly differently, one might say that we advocate looking at the behavior of each individual state in a directed dyad. The reasons for this are twofold.

1. Compelling theoretical explanations for conflict behavior must be grounded in the actions of individual states, which are based on the choices of their political and military leaders.[2] Rational choice models based on game-theoretic analyses do follow this approach, and we believe any powerful theoretical approach ultimately rests on understanding how the choices of state leaders and their strategic interactions with other states lead to various international conflict outcomes.

2.   As previously argued, war and international crises rarely, if ever, occur in the absence of preexisting disputes over issues and prior periods of negotiations and diplomatic interactions. In fact, war and crises threatening war are quite infrequent forms of interstate interactions. It is important to understand why state leaders in some disputes at particular points in time are unable to resolve the issues in contention and why they are willing to escalate the dispute to the highest levels of military conflict. As a result, a full explanation of the causes of international conflict should be based on the recognition that there are multiple stages through which international disputes may evolve.

If we consider the four stages in figure 1, we can see that the units of analysis in the Dispute Initiation stage would be "potential challenger and target" states. For the challenger state the dependent variable in a statistical test would center on the decision of its foreign policy leadership whether to contest the policies of another government in some selected issue area(s). Examples might include compliance with arms control or cease-fire agreements, disputes over one country's suppression of internal political opposition, or charges that one country is permitting rebel forces to operate on its territory. For this unit of analysis, theoretical models would explain when the potential challenger actually presses its claims and demands that the target state change its policies.

Once the demands and claims are clearly articulated, the target state would then have to decide whether to resist the policy changes called for by the challenger (see fig. 2). Thus, the dependent variable when the target state is the unit of analysis focuses on how firmly the leaders of the target state respond to demands for changing their policies. In the Challenge the Status Quo stage we know that an international dispute already exists. Thus, the observations in this stage would consist of all challenger states and the potentially repeated opportunities that their leaders had to initiate diplomatic or military policies in an attempt to achieve a favorable change in the prevailing status quo (see fig. 3).

For these first two stages the temporal definition of what we might term a "play of the dispute" needs to be given careful attention by researchers. One might initially define this as an annual observation and code what initiatives, if any, were pursued by the challenger in a given year. Theoretically, however, there is no compelling reason to believe that a single foreign policy decision occurs once every twelve months. For example, in some international disputes leaders of the challenger state might move through several stages in a single year. For example, efforts to rely on negotiations early in the year might end quickly in stalemate, yet by the end of the year the leaders might decide to turn to military pressure and threats of force in an attempt to break the diplomatic deadlock.

In contrast, in a different international dispute the issues at stake for the challenger state might be not that salient, and, as a result, it makes no effort to escalate or settle the dispute in a given year. The lack of attention given to the dispute raises questions about whether any policy options were even considered within a given year and whether that year of observation should be included in the data set. A research design setup that was grounded in a game-theoretic approach would shift away from relying on the convenient annual time period for each observation and instead would develop a more flexible set of coding rules to establish the temporal bounds of each iteration of a stage. With these more adaptable rules it would be possible to identify multiple iterations of a stage within a given year and to extend a single iteration of one stage beyond a year when theoretically appropriate.

In both the Negotiations and Military Escalation stages the units of analysis are *the challenger and target states involved in a given round of talks or military confrontation.* Once again, this is analogous to an examination of the negotiation or escalation behavior of each state in a directed dyad. The duration of the round of talks or military confrontation would determine the time period of each state-level observation. In these two stages the dependent variables would typically focus on outcomes such as the extent of concessions by a state in negotiations, each state's level of military escalation, or how responsive one state's policies were to the short-term actions of the other.

One important implication of our discussion about the units of analysis in statistical analyses is that we do not generally favor or advocate the use of nondirected dyads (see Bennett and Stam 2000). While the use of directed dyads is desirable because it allows the researcher to capture individual state decisions in a particular strategic environment, much of the existing work utilizes nondirected dyads—and focuses only on the joint outcome resulting from the interaction of pair of states. Dyadic analyses have become increasingly common in statistical studies of international conflict, particularly in the democratic peace research program. For example, a number of statistical studies of the democratic peace have analyzed data sets consisting of pairs of states in which the occurrence of a war or militarized dispute short of war is coded on an annual basis over some specified time period. In some tests the population of dyads consists of all possible pairings of states, while other scholars rely on a smaller set of "politically relevant" dyads (e.g., Bremer 1992, 1993; Maoz 1997, 1998; Maoz and Russett 1992, 1993; Oneal and Ray 1997; Oneal and Russett 1997, 1999a, 1999b, 1999c; Ray 1995, chap. 1; Gowa 1999; Russett 1993). Politically relevant dyads are typically composed of states that are contiguous or pairs of states in which at least one party is a great power. These studies have produced many useful and important findings; nevertheless, we think there are reasons to question research designs that rely upon nondirected dyads as the basic unit of analysis. In particular, there are at least three limitations to such dyadic studies that can be nicely illustrated by considering empirical studies of the democratic peace.

First, in dyadic studies of the democratic peace the dependent variable takes the form of conflict *involvement* for the countries in the dyad, without identifying patterns of military initiation and response, or conflict resolution, by each state. This is an important drawback, since hypotheses about democratic institutions and norms of conflict resolution logically predict which states in a dyad should be most likely to initiate militarized disputes and escalate disputes to the brink of war as well as seek diplomatic settlements of disputes. Data on initiation and escalation are particularly important in testing the monadic version[3] of the democratic peace. A nondirected dyadic democratic peace study, however, would simply note the occurrence of war or the existence of large-scale military action between two states in a mixed dyad for a given time period. This coding of the dependent variable would not distinguish between two very different scenarios in which democratic and nondemocratic states would resort to the large-scale use of force. In the first case, the nondemocratic state initiates the large-scale use of force after rejecting compromise proposals, and the democratic state responds by defending itself against the attack. In the second case, the reverse is true, as the democratic state initiates the large-scale use of force after rejecting compromise proposals, and the nondemocratic state responds by defending itself against the attack.

These two cases represent very different pathways to war and therefore suggest quite different conclusions about the monadic approach to the democratic peace. The second pathway is seemingly quite at odds with a monadic democratic peace argument, whereas the first pathway is not. The same general point is applicable regarding different pathways to conflict resolution. In one case the dispute is settled by a nondemocratic state initiating concessions or withdrawing claims, while in a second case a democratic state takes the initiative to propose concessions, which are then accepted by a nondemocratic adversary. The first case runs counter to prevailing monadic arguments about democratic norms, while the second seems consistent. The findings of many existing quantitative studies, however, do not provide a solid foundation upon which to draw conclusions about the monadic version of the democratic peace (Rousseau et al. 1996). It seems very desirable then to disaggregate conflict behavior within a dyad into a more sequential analysis of each state's behavior over the course of a dispute between states. Thus, Huth and Allee (2002), in their study of the democratic peace, examine 348 territorial disputes from 1919 through 1995 in which each state's behavior for cases of the Challenge the Status Quo, Negotiation, and Military Escalation stages is analyzed. The result is that hypotheses about democratic patterns of initiation and response regarding negotiations and military conflicts can be clearly posited and then empirically tested.

A related problem with dyad-based data sets is that hypotheses regarding the impact of important independent variables, such as democratic norms and structures, on conflict outcomes cannot be tested directly. Instead, the researcher is forced to make inferences about the causal process that might have produced patterns of observed dyadic conflict outcomes. Consider the case in which one of the two states in a dispute is led by a minority government. This minority government might be unlikely to offer concessions to its adversary because of the difficulties in securing legislative or parliamentary support for such concessions. However, its adversary, knowing it is bargaining with a highly constrained opponent, might be more likely to offer concessions. However, the existence of a minority government could have the opposite impact on each of the states in the dyad. By splitting the dyad into two state-level, directional observations, the researcher is able to more directly test the causal impact of minority government on conflict or bargaining behavior for democratic states (e.g., Huth and Allee 2002). The use of nondirected dyads, however, would obscure the true causal impact of domestic institutional arrangements such as minority government.

The final, related limitation of these dyadic studies, especially those using the popular nondirected dyad-year format, is that they test hypotheses about international conflict without grounding the empirical analysis in the development and progression of international disputes between states (fig. 1). When analyzing whether states become involved in a militarized dispute or war, the causal pathway necessarily includes a first stage of a dispute emerging. We do not think dyad-year arguments, such as those for the democratic peace, explain why disputes arise, but rather, only how disputes will be managed. The problem with the typical dyad-year-based data set is that the observed behavior of no militarized dispute or no war for certain dyad-years could be explained by two general processes, one of which is distinct from arguments in the democratic peace literature. That is, no military conflict occurs because (1) states were able to prevent a dispute from escalating, which the democratic peace literature addresses; and (2) states were not involved in a dispute, and thus there was no reason for leaders to consider using force. This second pathway suggests that democratic peace explanations are not that relevant. As a result, dyads that do not even get into disputes for reasons that are not related to democratic institutions or norms may appear to be cases in support of the democratic peace.

The use of politically relevant dyads helps to reduce this problem of irrelevant nondispute observations, but many relevant dyads are not parties to an international dispute that has the potential to escalate to military conflict. If one has the typical data set that contains observations in which states never even considered using force, then potential problems of overstated standard errors and biased estimates of coefficients for the democratic peace variables can arise. For example, the negative coefficient on a democratic dyad variable in a study of military conflict could reflect the ability of democratic leaders to manage disputes in a nonviolent way, but it might also capture the fact that some democratic dyads were not involved in any disputes for many of the dyad-year observations in the data set. As a result, it is difficult to draw strong and clear causal inferences about the impact of joint democracy on conflict behavior (see Braumoeller and Sartori, chap. 6, this vol.). In the first scenario, it would not be worrisome to witness a conflict between two democratic states, since they should be able to manage the dispute without resorting to violence. However, if the second claim is true, then the occurrence of military confrontations is cause for concern, since the democracies are only pacific insofar as they are able to avoid getting into militarized disputes in the first place.

In sum, the nondirected dyad-year as the unit of analysis aggregates multiple stages in the development of an international dispute into a single observation that renders it difficult for researchers in empirical tests to assess the causal processes operating at different stages in the escalation or resolution of international disputes.

Accounting for Selection Effects

Selection effects are a potential problem for any empirical test that fails to understand that states do not enter into negotiations or become involved in a violent military clash randomly, but rather state leaders choose to go down a particular path during the evolution of a dispute. For the relatively few cases making it to either the Negotiations or Military Escalation stages, the story of how and why state leaders selected their countries into these samples is of utmost importance. Similarly, the related idea of strategic interaction tells us that state leaders consider the anticipated response of opponents to various policy options. Even though some factors may affect the decisions of leaders in a potential conflict situation, this impact is not captured by standard statistical techniques because leaders avoid taking these potentially undesirable courses of action. This idea is particularly salient when analyzing the Dispute Initiation and the Challenge the Status Quo stages.

One way to think about selection effects hinges on the idea of sample selection bias (see Achen 1986; Geddes 1990; King, Keohane, and Verba 1994). In the simplest terms, using a nonrandom sample of cases to test causal relationships will often result in biased estimation of coefficients in statistical tests. Not only might the causal relationships suggested by the results of such statistical analyses be inaccurate for the limited sample examined, but they also cannot be used to draw inferences about the generalizable relationship that might exist between the independent variables and dependent variable outside of that sample. The logic is straightforward: cases that advance to some particular phase in the evolution of conflict may not be typical of relations between states (Morrow 1989).

There may be some systematic reason or explanation for why these cases reach a certain stage, and the failure to account for this can produce misleading statistical results.

Unobserved factors, such as beliefs, resolve, risk attitudes, and credibility, might exert a selection effect (Morrow 1989; Fearon 1994b; Smith 1995, 1996). States may select themselves into certain stages of conflict or down certain paths of dispute resolution based upon the private information they possess about these unobserved factors. The ideas of alliance reliability and extended deterrence illustrate this idea. Reliable alliances and credible deterrent threats should rarely be challenged, so the large number of cases where alliance ties and general deterrence prevent challenges to the status quo are often excluded from data sets of militarized crises (Fearon 1994b; Smith 1995). During the Challenge the Status Quo stage, only highly resolved challengers would challenge strong alliances and credible deterrent threats. The failure to account for a challenger's resolve to carry out its military threat might lead the empirical researcher to mistakenly conclude that alliances increase the risk of military escalation in crises and to fail to appreciate that alliances might act as powerful deterrents to states initiating military confrontations (Smith 1995). Once again, statistical analyses of a single stage can be biased if they do not consider how state leaders selected themselves into the data set that is being tested for that stage.

Put slightly differently, sample selection bias is likely to exist when the variables that explain the ultimate outcome of the cases also explain why those cases got into the sample in the first place. If the factors explaining the outcome of the Military Escalation stage also help explain the decision to get into the Military Escalation stage (the choice made during the Challenge the Status Quo stage), then the estimated coefficients produced by statistical tests of cases that only appear in the Military Escalation stage are likely to be biased. Variables such as wealth, regime type, and satisfaction with the status quo may affect the decisions made during the Challenge the Status Quo stage and the Military Escalation stage in similar or different ways (see Hart and Reed 1999; Huth 1996; Reed 2000). For example, Huth (1996) reports that the military balance does not systematically influence challenger decisions to initiate territorial claims against neighboring states, but among cases of existing territorial disputes, challengers are much more likely to threaten and use force if they enjoy a military advantage. In a study of the democratic peace, Reed (2000) explicitly models the decisions to initiate and then escalate military confrontations, and he finds that the impact of democratic dyads is far stronger in preventing the emergence of military confrontations compared to the escalation of such conflicts.

Incorporating strategic interaction in research designs on international conflict is also a desirable goal (see Signorino 1999; Smith 1999). In our framework, accounting for sample selection bias generally requires looking backward to explain where cases come from, whereas the idea of strategic interaction requires looking forward to see where cases would have gone if they had reached later stages in the evolution of conflict. The key idea is that the decisions within and across different stages are interdependent; actors take into account the likely behavior of other states at present, as well as possible future decisions during the escalation of international conflict (Signorino 1999). Strategic interaction may also be thought of as "the explicit study of counterfactuals" (Smith 1999, 1256). Actors anticipate how potential adversaries will behave under certain circumstances, such as at any of the decision-making nodes in our four stages, and avoid making decisions that may ultimately lead to undesirable outcomes. In our multiphase model of disputes (fig. 1), a challenger state may refrain from choosing the path leading to the military escalation stage because they anticipate a swift, strong military reaction from the defender in the event of a military threat. Or they may shun the decision to enter into negotiations because they anticipate no concessions being made by the leader on the other side. Once again, factors that truly affect the calculus of state leaders to make certain decisions or enter into certain phases or stages— such as the credibility of a defender's swift response, or the domestic constraints placed on a foreign leader—are not captured by standard statistical techniques because they are unobserved.

The most widely used statistical estimators fail to capture the concerns we raise about selection issues, and such techniques produce biased results when a nonrandom sample is used (Achen 1986). In many cases, the effects of some independent variables may become weakened or rendered insignificant. In fact, some claim that selection bias may produce coefficients with reversed signs (Achen 1986). For example, Huth (1988) finds in his statistical tests that alliance ties between defender and protégé are surprisingly associated with an increased risk of extended-immediate deterrence failure. Fearon (1994b), however, argues that the reason for this finding is due to selection effects in which an unmeasured variable (the challenger's resolve to initiate a threat against the protégé) is correlated with the observed variable of alliance ties. The result is that the estimated coefficient for the alliance variable is actually picking up the impact of the unmeasured challenger-resolve variable, and this helps to explain the unexpected negative sign on the alliance variable. In general, scholars incorporating the ideas of strategic interaction and selection bias into their models have discovered significant differences between coefficients produced by these "corrected" models and those produced by "biased" models (see Signorino 1999; Smith 1999; Reed 2000). These changed estimates even affect some of our most important propositions in world politics, such as the impact of joint democracy on conflict escalation as noted earlier (Hart and Reed 1999; Reed 2000).

Our general conclusion is that quantitative studies of military conflict should incorporate some type of correction for selection effects. In our opinion, the best suggestion is to model the multiple stages in the escalation of international conflict simultaneously. This is generally done by estimating both a selection equation (to explain which cases get into a particular sample) as well as an outcome equation (to explain how the cases in this sample are played out). A good example of this is Huth and Allee's (2002) analysis of dispute resolution efforts by democratic states that are involved in territorial disputes. In estimating the probability that a democratic challenger will offer concessions in a round of talks (the outcome equation), they include a selection equation that accounts for the initial decision of the democratic challenger to propose talks. Given the prevalence of categorical variables in studies of international conflict, probit and logit selection models seem most promising, although other models may be appropriate for different types of dependent variables. When thinking about how particular cases get where they are, one should compile data on those cases that had some legitimate probability of making it to some stage, but did not. In other words, if analyzing the Negotiation stage, one should also have some information about cases that went to the Military Escalation stage, or in which the status quo was accepted.

It is often cumbersome and difficult to acquire data on relevant non-events, such as instances in which leaders considered threatening force but did not do so, or where a state had the ability to press a claim concerning the treatment of ethnic minorities abroad and decided to accept the status quo. Yet we feel that acquiring and incorporating this information into quantitative analyses should be a high priority for scholars. In other words, we advocate greater attention to the Dispute Initiation and Challenge the Status Quo stages—to the identification of those situations that could plausibly become international disputes—and then tracking which disputes might proceed through various Negotiations and Military Escalation stages. When this is not possible, and therefore no selection equation is specified, a different approach would be to include in the outcome equation those independent variables that would have been in a selection equation. In other words, researchers studying the outcomes of crises or militarized disputes should try to include independent variables that explain why those disputes and crises might have arisen in the first place.

In sum, the problems of selection bias and strategic choice are illustrated nicely by game-theoretic models of military conflict, which capture the real-life choices faced by state leaders. Our primary point is that quantitative analyses of international conflict need to account for the variety of choices that states have at different stages in the evolution of a dispute. Focusing narrowly on one phase of an interstate dispute without accounting for past and potential future choices can lead to biased statistical results and therefore limit our ability to draw accurate conclusions concerning the factors that contribute to military conflict.

Problems of Nonindependent Observations

Researchers conducting statistical analyses of data sets on international conflict need to consider potential problems of nonindependent observations. There are a number of ways in which the dependence of observations can occur in international conflict data sets. We focus on two types that are likely to be present in many data sets in which the basic units of analysis are states that are involved in international disputes. In the first case, the dependence of observations is due to the time-series nature of the data in which the same state appears multiple times in the data set since the international dispute spans many years. With this data set the analyst is testing models that seek to explain variation in a state's dispute behavior over time. In the second case, cross-sectional or spatial dependence is present because in a given time period (e.g., a year) the same state is a party to several different international disputes or is influenced by the behavior of neighboring states. The empirical analysis in this second study centers on testing models that might account for variation in a state's behavior across the different international disputes in which it is involved.

In the time-series example, the statistical problem is that values on the dependent variable for a state-dispute observation in time period t are systematically related to the behavior and actions of that same state in preceding time periods. Put differently, the prior history of the dispute is important in understanding the current behavior of the disputants. In the cross-sectional example, the problem is a bit different in that the actions of a single state in one dispute are influenced by the behavior of that same state or other states in a second dispute. In either of these two cases of dependent observations, the statistical implications are that the assembled data sets do not contain as much independent information as is assumed by the standard statistical models utilized by researchers. As a result, the standard errors associated with the estimated coefficients are likely to be inaccurate. In particular, they are likely to be underestimated and, as a result, researchers run the risk of overstating the statistical significance of coefficients and the findings they report (see Greene 1997, chap. 13).

If we refer back to figure 1, problems of both time-series and cross-sectional dependence of observations are likely to be present in data sets that are used to test models for the Dispute Initiation and Challenge the Status Quo stages. The reason is that a common research design for each of these stages is to assemble what are termed pooled cross-sectional time-series data sets. Researchers might build a data set that includes many different states that are involved in many different disputes (or potential disputes) over some extended period of time.

One such illustrative example comes from Huth's (1996) study of territorial disputes, in which he conducted a two-stage analysis in which the first stage was very similar to what we have termed the Dispute Initiation stage. In this initial analysis he included all states from 1950 through 1990 that issued territorial claims against another state as well as a random sample of states that did not dispute their borders. He then tested models that sought to explain which "challenger" states did in fact dispute territory. In the second stage of analysis, he focused on all of the territorial dispute cases from 1950 through 1990, and he analyzed the varying levels of diplomatic and military conflict initiated by challenger states. In this two-stage analysis Huth found evidence of both temporal and cross-sectional relationships between cases. For example, challenger states that had signed formal agreements settling border disputes with a particular country prior to 1950 were very unlikely to repudiate those agreements and initiate a new territorial dispute in the post-1950 period. Challenger states in a territorial dispute were also less likely to resort to military threats in an attempt to change the status quo if they were involved simultaneously in multiple territorial disputes (chaps. 4–5).

In the Military Escalation and Negotiations stages in figure 1 the data sets that would be relied upon for statistical tests would not be standard pooled cross-sectional time-series in nature, but rather would be pooled cross-sectional designs. For example, a data set for testing the Military Escalation stage would typically consist of all military confrontations initiated by a challenger state over some disputed issue. Similarly, in the Negotiations stage the data set would include all rounds of talks held by states over disputed issues. For each type of data set, cross-sectional dependence of observations could be a problem, as could temporal dependence of observations due to the potential for repeated rounds of talks or military confrontations. For example, in the military escalation data set the decision by a state's leadership to resort to the large-scale use of force in a particular case could be influenced by whether their adversary was already engaged in a military confrontation with another state (see Huth, Gelpi, and Bennett 1993) or whether they had suffered a military defeat at the hands of their current adversary in a prior military confrontation (see Huth 1996).

A common problem for many quantitative researchers who are working with probit and logit models is that standard corrections for time-series or spatial dependence in data are not well-developed in the statistical literature. Political methodologists, however, have devised a number of potentially useful corrections that can be employed to deal with nonindependent observations due to time series effects (e.g., Beck, Katz, and Tucker 1998), and such corrections are often desirable in estimating equations. Nevertheless, we want to express a note of caution because researchers may too readily turn to these statistical corrections and only rely upon them to deal with the important problem of dependent observations. We strongly recommend that researchers also devote considerable effort to accounting for problems of nonindependent observations through better specification of the theoretical models that are empirically tested. This would entail researchers developing hypotheses that capture the influences of time-series and cross-sectional factors and then including such factors as explanatory variables in the equations that are tested. An excellent example of this approach is the work of Michael Ward and Kristian Gleditsch that includes explanatory variables in their models that reflect spatial clustering of conflict, trade, and democratization among states (see Gleditsch

214

and Ward 2000; Gleditsch 2002). The primary advantage of this is that any estimated coefficients that are intended to pick up the effects of dependent observations can be interpreted in a more direct manner given that a theoretically grounded and more specific causal argument has already been provided.

Another recommendation is to switch from standard logit and probit models to event history or duration models that do explicitly account for time-series effects (for a general discussion of such models see Zorn 2001). Event history models focus on explaining the transition from an initial condition (or status quo) to a new one as a function of time. For example, drawing on the democratic peace literature, researchers might hypothesize that given a territorial dispute between two states, the time to settlement of the dispute by means of a negotiated agreement would be shorter if both states were democratic. Good examples of IR scholars using event history models include Werner's (1999) study of the durability of peace agreements in the aftermath of wars and Bennett and Stam's work (1998) on the duration of interstate wars.

The Measurement of Variables

Measurement error is a ubiquitous concern in all sciences, especially the social sciences. Imprecise measurement of explanatory variables, especially if systematic, casts doubt on our ability to draw accurate causal inferences. We feel concerns about measurement should be strongly emphasized in research designs of international military conflict. Our four-stage model of international conflict illustrates some specific issues faced by quantitative researchers of international conflict, such as the need to incorporate variables and measures that may be uniquely relevant to certain stages in the evolution of international conflict. In addition, all studies of military conflict are saddled with certain unique data and measurement concerns, such as the use of large data sets with large numbers of variables, the ambiguity of many key concepts, a lack of creativity in measurement, and disincentives to devote resources to better measurement.

Since the actions taken by leaders over the course of an international dispute may provide additional useful information, researchers may need to modify preexisting measures at later phases of conflict. Some important underlying concepts, such as the military balance between two states, could be measured differently depending on which stage in figure 1 is being analyzed. For example, a general indicator of standing military capabilities might be used to measure the "military balance" in a test of the Challenge the Status Quo stage. However, once both sides have made threats to use military force or have mobilized troops, adding information on the local balance of forces in this dispute would improve the measurement of the military balance in the Military Escalation stage. For example, measures of the local balance of forces have been reported to have strong effects on the success or failure of extended-immediate deterrence or whether territorial disputes escalate to war (e.g., Huth 1988; Huth and Allee 2002).

In addition, as mentioned earlier, the decisions made by political and military leaders during the evolution of a dispute may convey new information. This information should then be incorporated into empirical tests of later phases of a dispute. For example, leaders may generate audience costs or use costly signals at the beginning of the Military Escalation stage to make their threat of military force appear credible to an adversary (Fearon 1994a). Therefore, this new information about the added credibility of a state's threat of force should be used to modify preexisting measures of credibility or added to any test of the Military Escalation stage. An example of this is Huth and Allee's (2002) study of state behavior in military crises in which they code a variable for whether democratic leaders send a strong public signal of the resolve to use force at the outset of the crisis. In their statistical analyses they find that such democratic signals of resolve are strongly associated with deterring escalation by the adversary state. Another interesting example is the finding reported by Schultz (2001) that the deterrent threats of democratic states are more likely to succeed if the leaders of opposition parties signal their support for the government's deterrent policy during the confrontation with a potential attacker. The overriding idea is that variables reflecting additional information can be added to analyses of the Military Escalation stage or the Negotiations stage. One should not always rely on the same measure of credibility, resolve, or military balance in empirical tests of the different stages of an international dispute.

A more general measurement concern for quantitatively minded scholars of military conflict is that the quality of data is often poor. The recent turn to dyad-years as the unit of analysis in many studies of military conflict typically results in tens of thousands, if not hundreds of thousands, of cases in data sets. Trying to find data on all variables for so many dyads is a daunting task. With limited time and limited resources, there is a trade-off between the quantity of data collected and the quality of this data. So researchers are forced to settle for imprecise or suspect data, or to drop observations with missing data.[4] In addition, the increasing acceptance of the idea that domestic politics variables should be included in studies of international conflict adds to the data collection burden.

One promising solution to the cumbersome task of collecting quality data lies with sampling. The strategy of what can be termed retrospective random sampling has rarely been used in large-n studies of international military conflict, yet the use of retrospective sampling designs would allow scholars to devote more energy toward the collection of better data. In such sampling designs the researcher combines the population of observed military conflicts (crises or wars, for example) with a random sample of cases in which no military conflict occurred.[5] Logit models can then be used to estimate equations in which the coefficients are unbiased and the degree of inefficiency associated with standard errors is quite small. Taking a random sample from the large population of noncases of conflict could be a valuable tool for addressing concerns about selection bias (Achen 1999; King and Zeng 2001).

Furthermore, studies of international conflict and crisis behavior often employ concepts that are difficult to measure. Game-theoretic models often generate hypotheses about the "beliefs" of actors, yet it is nearly impossible to get inside the minds of decision makers to understand how they interpret a situation. As a result, researchers have to develop imperfect operational measures for key concepts such as the "credibility" of a threat, the "political constraints" on leaders, or the "resolve" of state leaders. In addition, scholars have reached little consensus on how to measure such central concepts, and there has been too little critical debate on how to measure certain difficult or important concepts.[6] The pursuit of ways to creatively measure theoretical concepts should be a high priority. Hard-to-measure concepts are typically measured by single proxy variables intended to capture the concept of interest. Yet these concepts could also be measured by employing techniques, such as confirmatory factor analysis, that allow one to combine related, observable variables into a single underlying factor that captures this hard-to-measure concept in a theoretically informed manner. Substituting alternative measures for purposes of robustness checks could also be done more often.

It is important that more of an effort be made to collect data and assemble new data sets. Unfortunately, the cost and time required to collect new data can be substantial, and, as a result, the incentives to rely upon existing data sets are quite strong. Yet the key principle of measurement in the social sciences is that an empirical researcher should make every attempt to use, collect, or obtain data that best fits the theoretical propositions. Widely used measures for concepts like military capabilities or democracy may be appropriate for testing certain hypotheses, yet less desirable for testing other propositions. Scholars should be as careful as possible to capture the precise logic of their hypotheses. For example, the hypothesis that democratic institutions restrict the use of force should be tested with data on institutional arrangements, not with a general measure of democracy such as the widely used net democracy measure from the Polity data set. Once again, while existing data sets often provide a valuable function, more of an effort should be made to put together new data sets and compile new measures whenever such measures do not exist, or when available variables are insufficient for the task at hand.

Conclusion

We have argued that the theoretical and empirical analysis of international conflict should be broken down into four generic stages. By thinking about the causes of international conflict in terms of these stages, we believe researchers are more likely to develop research designs for statistical tests that

1. focus on state leaders and their choices in international disputes as the unit of analysis for building data sets,
2. recognize that selection effects and strategic behavior are central concepts for understanding how international disputes evolve into stages where higher levels of conflict occur,
3. better account for how policy choices in international disputes are linked across time and space, and
4. include explanatory variables that better capture and measure the impact of domestic and international conditions during periods of more intense diplomatic and military interactions.

In our judgment, such research designs will greatly improve statistical tests of theories of international conflict by better addressing problems of selection bias, nonindependent observations, and measurement error. One of the central implications of our analysis is that there should be a tighter connection between the formal game-theoretic literature and the design of statistical analyses and tests. Another implication is that empirical researchers will need to devote more time, effort, and resources to developing more microlevel data sets of international disputes across different issue areas as well as developing data on dispute behavior that does not involve military threats and the use of force.

Recommended Readings

Achen, C. 1986. *The Statistical Analysis of Quasi-Experiments.* Berkeley: University of California Press.

Fearon, J. 1994. Domestic Political Audiences and the Escalation of International Disputes. *American Political Science Review* 88 (3): 577–92.

Hart, R., and W. Reed. 1999. Selection Effects and Dispute Escalation. *International Interactions* 25 (3): 243–64.

Huth, P. 1996. *Standing Your Ground.* Ann Arbor: University of Michigan Press.

Huth, P., and T. Allee. 2002. *The Democratic Peace and Territorial Conflict in the Twentieth Century.* New York: Cambridge University Press.

Signorino, C. 1999. Strategic Interaction and the Statistical Analysis of International Conflict. *American Political Science Review* 93 (2): 279–98.

Smith, A. 1999. Testing Theories of Strategic Choice: The Example of Crisis Escalation. *American Journal of Political Science* 43 (4): 1254–83.

Notes

1. We present each stage in its most simplified form to highlight only a few basic points. For example, we focus on only two actors but certainly third parties could be included as actors. In addition, we make no effort to model these stages rigorously. We simply map the choices available to states in a dispute and the outcomes of the various paths to illustrate the questions and concerns statistical researchers need to address.

2. Of course, if the researcher's focus is on explaining nonstate conflict behavior then we would argue that the unit of analysis is the individual political actor or the leader of some organization that adopts and carries out particular policies.

3. By *monadic* we mean that democratic states are less likely to initiate military threats and the use of force against all other states, not just other democratic states.

4. The idea of dropping cases from statistical analyses of international conflict is especially problematic, since the cases dropped often exhibit systematic similarities. Data on military expenditures, military capabilities, and GNP are often hardest to obtain for certain types of countries, such as developing countries or countries with closed political systems. Dropping such cases eliminates certain types of meaningful cases and results in truncated values of some independent variables.

5. This idea is logically similar to the use of control group designs in quasi-experimental research (see Cook and Campbell 1979).

6. Recent debates on how to measure joint democracy and the similarity of security interests constitute a welcome advance (see Thompson and Tucker 1997; Signorino and Ritter 1999).

References

Achen, C. 1986. *The Statistical Analysis of Quasi-Experiments.* Berkeley: University of California Press.

———. 1999. Retrospective Sampling in International Relations. Annual Meeting of the Midwest Political Science Association, Chicago.

Beck, N., J. Katz, and R. Tucker. 1998. Taking Time Seriously. *American Journal of Political Science* 42 (4): 1260–88.

Bennett, D. S., and A. C. Stam. 1998. The Declining Advantages of Democracy. *Journal of Conflict Resolution* 42 (3): 344–66.

———. 2000. Research Design and Estimator Choices in the Analysis of Interstate Dyads: When Decisions Matter. *Journal of Conflict Resolution* 44 (5): 653–85.

Bremer, S. 1992. Dangerous Dyads. *Journal of Conflict Resolution* 36 (2): 309–41.

———. 1993. Democracy and Militarized Interstate Conflict, 1816–1965. *International Interactions* 18 (3): 231–49.

Bueno de Mesquita, B., and D. Lalman. 1992. *War and Reason: Domestic and International Imperatives.* New Haven: Yale University Press.

Cederman, L. 1997. *Emergent Actors in World Politics.* Princeton: Princeton University Press.

Cook, T., and D. Campbell. 1979. *Quasi-Experimentation.* Boston: Houghton Mifflin.

Daalder, I., and M. O'Hanlon. 2000. *Winning Ugly.* Washington, DC: Brookings Institution.

Downs, G. W., and D. M. Rocke. 1990. *Tacit Bargaining, Arms Races, and Arms Control.* Ann Arbor: University of Michigan Press.

Fearon, J. 1994a. Domestic Political Audiences and the Escalation of International Disputes. *American Political Science Review* 88 (3): 577–92.

———. 1994b. Signaling versus the Balance of Power and Interests. *Journal of Conflict Resolution* 38 (2): 236–69.

———. 1998. Bargaining, Enforcement, and International Cooperation. *International Organization* 52 (2): 269–306.

Geddes, B. 1990. How the Cases You Choose Affect the Answers You Get: Selection Bias in Comparative Politics. *Political Analysis* 2:31–50.

Gleditsch, K. 2002. *All International Politics Is Local: The Diffusion of Conflict, Integration, and Democratization.* Ann Arbor: University of Michigan Press.

Gleditsch, K., and M. Ward. 2000. War and Peace in Space and Time. *International Studies Quarterly* 44 (1): 1–30.

Gowa, J. 1999. *Ballots and Bullets.* Princeton: Princeton University Press.

Greene, W. H. 1997. *Econometric Analysis.* Upper Saddle River, NJ: Prentice-Hall.

Hart, R., and W. Reed. 1999. Selection Effects and Dispute Escalation. *International Interactions* 25 (3): 243–64.

Huth, P. 1988. *Extended Deterrence and the Prevention of War.* New Haven: Yale University Press.

———. 1996. *Standing Your Ground.* Ann Arbor: University of Michigan Press.

Huth, P., and T. Allee. 2002. *The Democratic Peace and Territorial Conflict in the Twentieth Century.* New York: Cambridge University Press.

Huth, P., C. Gelpi, and D. S. Bennett. 1993. The Escalation of Great Power Militarized Disputes: Testing Rational Deterrence Theory and Structural Realism. *American Political Science Review* 87 (3): 609–23.

King, G., R. O. Keohane, and S. Verba. 1994. *Designing Social Inquiry: Scientific Inference in Qualitative Research.* Princeton: Princeton University Press.

King, G., and L. Zeng. 2001. Explaining Rare Events in IR. *International Organization* 55 (3): 693–716.

Lincoln, E. 1990. *Japan's Unequal Trade.* Washington, DC: Brookings Institution.

———. 1999. *Troubled Times.* Washington, DC: Brookings Institution.

Maoz, Z. 1997. The Controversy over the Democratic Peace. *International Security* 22 (1): 162–98.

———. 1998. Realist and Cultural Critiques of the Democratic Peace. *International Interactions* 24 (1): 3–89.

Maoz, Z., and B. Russett. 1992. Alliance, Contiguity, Wealth, and Political Equality. *International Interactions* 17 (3): 245–67.

———. 1993. Normative and Structural Causes of Democratic Peace, 1946–86. *American Political Science Review* 87 (3): 624–38.

Milner, H. V. 1997. *Interests, Institutions, and Information: Domestic Politics and International Relations.* Princeton: Princeton University Press.

Morrow, J. D. 1989. Capabilities, Uncertainty, and Resolve: A Limited Information Model of Crisis Bargaining. *American Journal of Political Science* 33 (4): 941–72.

Oneal, J., and J. L. Ray. 1997. New Tests of the Democratic Peace Controlling for Economic Interdependence, 1950–1985. *Political Research Quarterly* 50 (3): 751–75.

Oneal, J., and B. Russett. 1997. The Classical Liberals Were Right. *International Studies Quarterly* 41 (2): 267–94.

———. 1999a. Assessing the Liberal Peace with Alternative Specifications. *Journal of Peace Research* 36 (4): 423–42.

———. 1999b. Is the Liberal Peace Just an Artifact of the Cold War? *International Interactions* 25 (3): 213–41.

———. 1999c. The Kantian Peace. *World Politics* 52 (1): 1–37.

Powell, R. 1999. *In the Shadow of Power.* Princeton: Princeton University Press.

Putnam, R. D. 1988. Diplomacy and Domestic Politics. *International Organization* 42 (3): 427–60.

Ray, J. L. 1995. *Democracy and International Conflict: An Evaluation of the Democratic Peace Proposition.* Columbia: University of South Carolina Press.

Reed, W. 2000. A Unified Statistical Model of Conflict Onset and Escalation. *American Journal of Political Science* 44 (1): 84–93.

Rousseau, D., C. Gelpi, D. Reiter, and P. Huth. 1996. Assessing the Dyadic Nature of the Democratic Peace. *American Political Science Review* 90 (3): 512–33.

Russett, B. 1993. *Grasping the Democratic Peace.* Princeton: Princeton University Press.

Schoppa, L. 1997. *Bargaining with Japan.* New York: Columbia University Press.

Schultz, K. A. 1998. Domestic Opposition and Signaling in International Crises. *American Political Science Review* 92:829–44.

———. 2001. *Democracy and Coercive Diplomacy.* New York: Cambridge University Press.

Signorino, C. S. 1999. Strategic Interaction and the Statistical Analysis of International Conflict. *American Political Science Review* 93 (2): 279–98.

Signorino, C. S., and J. Ritter. 1999. Tau-B or Not Tau-B: Measuring the Similarity of Foreign Policy Positions. *International Studies Quarterly* 43 (1): 115–44.

Smith, A. 1995. Alliance Formation and War. *International Studies Quarterly* 39 (4): 405–26.

———. 1996. To Intervene or Not to Intervene: A Biased Decision. *Journal of Conflict Resolution* 40 (1): 16–40.

———. 1998. International Crises and Domestic Politics. *American Political Science Review* 92 (3): 623–38.

———. 1999. Testing Theories of Strategic Choice: The Example of Crisis Escalation. *American Journal of Political Science* 43 (4): 1254–83.

Thompson, W., and R. Tucker. 1997. A Tale of Two Democratic Peace Critiques. *Journal of Conflict Resolution* 41 (3): 428–54.

Wagner, R. H. 2000. Bargaining and War. *American Journal of Political Science* 44 (3): 469–84.

Werner, S. 1999. The Precarious Nature of Peace. *American Journal of Political Science* 43 (3): 912–34.

Zorn, C. 2001. Generalized Estimating Equation Models for Correlated Data. *American Journal of Political Science* 45 (2): 470–90.

Part III. Formal Methods

10. Formal Models of International Politics

Duncan Snidal

Why use formal mathematical models to study international politics? The reason is that mathematics provides a precise language to describe the key elements of a problem, a powerful deductive machinery that extends the logical power of our theories, and an important means to expand our understanding and interpretation of the world. Used properly, which means never in isolation from less formal theory or empirical analysis, mathematical models can greatly enrich our analysis of international politics.

We use models all the time. A map is a model that reduces geography to a piece of paper. In doing so, it distorts our spherical world by projecting it onto a flat surface: the U.S.-Canada border along the 49th parallel is no longer an arc but a straight line. Moreover, good maps leave out many details—since including every hummock and ridge would obscure the more important details that we care about. But a good map also leaves out details that are important in other applications. For example, some maps leave out geography almost entirely and instead display economic or demographic data about (say) the relative wealth or health of different states. Other maps deliberately distort geography by scaling the size of countries to population so that Indonesia appears roughly eight times as big as Australia. In short, maps are descriptively incomplete and even inaccurate, yet they are tremendously valuable. Indeed, maps are valuable only insofar as they offer (useful) distortions. As Lewis Carroll once observed, a descriptively accurate map would have to be as big as the kingdom—but then it would not be of much use since when you opened it up it would obscure the very kingdom of interest.

A model is nothing more than a "simplified picture of a part of the real world" (March and Lave 1975). Some models like maps are valuable primarily because of the description they provide. As in the case of maps, however, the value of the description depends not on including all possible facts but on careful selection of the most important elements of a situation. Indeed, a good model, like a good map or a good description, requires setting aside most of the "facts" of the case. What facts to retain depends on the intended use of the model: topographical maps are more useful for canoeists, and subway maps are more useful for tourists.

Like maps, models come in many different forms. Many are "verbal" descriptions of the relations between key elements of a situation and are often based on comparisons to seemingly similar situations. A description of a state as a democracy invokes an implicit model of the properties of democratic states, while "balance of power" among states invokes an analogy to physical balances among weights. Other models are presented graphically with arrows running between various concepts to indicate causal effects from one variable to another.[1] Formal models provide a more precise statement of the relations among various concepts in a mathematical form.

Models become most useful, however, when they allow us to make logical inferences. A series of close, parallel contour lines tells the canoeist to portage around a waterfall, while the arrangement of subway lines tells the tourist how to get from one station to another. Many models in international relations make deductions through analogies such as the "balance of power" to describe military relations or "the tragedy of the commons" to describe environmental issues. The formal models we are concerned with here are distinguished by drawing on some form of mathematics to make logical deductions. Their ability to help us make such deductions is why formal models are of special value.

My argument is that models are essential for understanding international politics and that formal models have special advantages over less formal models, as well as notable disadvantages. In particular, mathematical models push research toward tightly specified descriptions and arguments, and then provide a valuable apparatus for theoretical inquiry. In some areas, formal models have substantially advanced international relations theory. In other areas, they have made a useful contribution to improving the precision of our theoretical language, but they are not close to replacing verbal theory. Finally, although all models have major limitations, the greatest virtue of a good model is that it makes its own limitations apparent. It thereby enhances our understanding of what we do not know and, sometimes, offers guidance to how we can know more.

This essay proceeds in several stages. The first section introduces an example of different ways to model the same environmental problem. I use a physical model to illustrate the point that models may take a diverse range of forms even while sharing roughly the same logic. The second section uses comparisons among the different environmental models to discuss the advantages of models. I focus on three broad categories—description, deduction, and testing—to consider the circumstances under which mathematical models are (or are not) more useful than less formal models. The third section uses a progression of formal mathematical models to illustrate both their advantages and their limitations in analyzing international politics. This progression shows the important role that models have played in the development of our understanding of international politics and introduces some of the most widely used game-theoretic models. I make this case not so much by pointing out the successes of models, however, as by emphasizing how their limitations and failures led to successor models that did represent advances.

The essay presumes no familiarity with formal models and does not try to teach about specific models or modeling techniques. I do illustrate my points with simple models and provide bare-bones explanations of how they work.

The Diversity of Models

Suppose we are interested in understanding an international environmental problem. Marc Kilgour and Yael Wolinsky-Nahmias (chap. 13, this vol.) provide an overview of the use of game-theoretic models to study such problems, but here I want to focus on a simple example of pollution in the Great Lakes system of North America to illustrate the variety of modeling approaches. Before we can understand what political arrangements are appropriate for governing this ecosystem—who should be allowed to release what sort of effluent at what point? or who should be forced to clean up at what point?—we first need to understand the technology of the lakes. How, for example, does pollution of an upstream lake such as Superior affect a downstream lake like Ontario? How might we investigate this?

One strategy would be empirical. For example, we might trace the diffusion of mercury pollution from northwestern Ontario paper mills, or sewage effluent from northwestern Indiana, through the lake system. While valuable, this information is likely to be difficult to obtain and probably incomplete with respect to important questions we might want to investigate, such as the long-term course of the pollution. Also, by itself, the empirical analysis might not be able to tell us whether results from mercury or sewage apply to iron ore tailings and DDT. Indeed, there may be no data at all available on some prospective pollutants, so while empirical analysis is essential, it cannot offer a complete analysis of the problem.

A second possibility would be to develop a verbal theory. Here we might canvass various factors that potentially affect the course of pollution in the lakes. We would draw on images like the ones introduced later in this essay to think about the different ways that pollution enters and leaves the various lakes. Informal theory like this provides an essential guide to empirical research. Moreover, none of the more formal models discussed later could have been developed without being preceded by this sort of reasoning process. Verbal theory has the advantage of being very open-ended and allowing for certain types of creativity that can be lost when arguments are overly constrained by methodological dictates. The advantages of more formal approaches to theorizing come from using them in concert with, not in opposition to, traditional theorizing. Everything that can be done formally can (in principle) be done verbally, and formal work must build on verbal theory for its creation, its interpretation, and its future development.

An alternative strategy would be to create a physical model of the Great Lakes to explore the consequences of pollution. Consider a rudimentary model where each lake is represented by a container proportionate to its size: Lake Superior by a large wash bucket, Lake Huron by a bucket, Lake Erie by a quart bottle, and so on. Each container is filled halfway with water, and the lake system is simulated as follows: Add water to each lake to represent its annual inflow from surrounding rivers, and pour water from higher lakes (buckets) to lower lakes (buckets) to represent the flow of water from Lake Superior through the other lakes to the St. Lawrence. Each repetition of the process represents a year of the lake system's operation. Finally, the impact of pollution is simulated by adding red dye to a particular lake and observing its diffusion through the system.

Since pouring water is messy—and since most international problems cannot be analogized in such straightforward physical terms—it is fortunate that there are alternative ways to model such phenomena. One is computer simulation where the computer replaces the containers as an accounting machine that keeps track of the inflows to, outflows from, and resulting pollution level of each lake. Another alternative is to represent water flows into and out of the Great Lakes by a set of differential equations[2] that track how the level of pollution in each lake changes over time in response to various inflows and outflows. Here the solution to the differential equations provides an analytic description of the path of pollution in the lakes over time.

The computer simulation and differential equations are only two of many possible formal representations. Different formal approaches have different advantages for studying particular problems, especially according to how well they can capture the most salient aspects of a substantive problem. Later in the essay, I will focus on game-theoretic models, which have become the dominant approach to IR modeling because of how well they capture many important aspects of international politics.

The Advantages and Limitations of Models

With this expansive view of models, the relevant question is not so much "Why use a model?" as "Why use a particular type of model?" While the focus here is on more formal models, their virtues and defects are best seen in comparison with alternative types of models. I argue that formal models have important advantages in certain cases, but in other cases verbal theory might be more effective. Combining the different approaches at different stages of research offers the best prospect for improving our understanding of international politics.

Models as a Guide to Description

A model provides a description of a phenomenon—but it is never a comprehensive representation of the problem. Instead, a good model is a radically simplified description that isolates the most important considerations for the purpose at hand, as the differences between subway and topographical maps illustrate. Thus a model is always a partial representation of some aspect of a problem rather than of its entirety, and different models may illuminate different elements of the same problem.

The process of abstraction necessary for representing a complicated real-world phenomenon in a simple model requires us to identify the most important elements of a problem, and to define them and their interrelations clearly. For example, we abstract from "Lake Superior" and represent it simply by its "size"—or more precisely, its volume, since size might also refer to surface area, which is not the relevant concept for our problem—as the key aspect of interest. We deliberately ignore other possibly interesting factors as its shape, temperature, currents, or color. While formalization is not necessary for achieving such parsimony and precision, mathematical approaches promote the move in this direction by requiring clear specification.

The process of identifying key elements of a problem may also force us back to our substantive analysis. For example, volume is the correct notion of size given our current analysis; but if evaporation is an important consideration, then surface area must also be taken into account. Such judgments depend on detailed knowledge of the problem combined with considerations of which and how much detail the model can accommodate.

The simplicity and abstract character of a model promote comparisons to other situations and generalizations across them. For example, the buckets could potentially represent not only the Great Lakes but—with appropriate substitution of different-sized buckets—any other set of interconnected lakes, or even the tributaries of a large river system. As always, the generalization is likely to be imperfect—for example, the flow and currents in rivers may lead to different mixing properties than we observe in lakes—but may nevertheless provide a satisfactory first model that can then be adapted to fit particular circumstances. In the case of the formal models, the possibility of generalization is implicit in the replacement of specific features of the model by parameters and coefficients that can be varied to fit alternative systems. For example, the volume of Lake Superior might be represented by a variable v that can be varied to make the model fit some other setting. In this way, the model moves us beyond a description or model of a particular system and toward a more general analysis of a category of pollution problems (e.g., with certain flow patterns).

The process of model construction is an important way to build theory and often poses questions that suggest further elements that might be included in the description. Pouring water between buckets, for example, forces us to consider the mixing properties of the lakes (e.g., does the pollution mix perfectly, or does sedimentation occur?). The formal model addresses the same question in terms of how it specifies the relation between pollution entering a lake and becoming a part of its outflow. Now the description goes beyond the elements of the model to address the relations among them.

Often the best way to build a model is to set aside such complications and begin with the simplest descriptive assumptions (e.g., perfect and instantaneous mixing). Later we can come back to include more descriptively realistic conditions and investigate their consequences. Because it is possible to overwhelm the model with details, it is typically more effective to first pin down the most significant aspects of the problem and then add complications gradually.

It is important to stress once again that good verbal theory works in a similar way. Theorizing of whatever stripe begins by simplifying descriptions, developing precise concepts, and seeking generalizations. If the process of modeling stopped here, we would surely use rudimentary models as instructive analogies, but translation into more complicated formal models with sometimes difficult technical language would not be worth the effort. The reason for making this translation is that, in some circumstances, formal models allow us to do much more.

Models as a Guide to Deduction

The logical structure of a model is valuable for checking the internal consistency of our assumptions and the inferences made from them. It offers an accounting device to keep track of all the important elements of a problem and the relations among them. A simple example is that the inflows to and outflows from each lake must balance in each time period, or else the water level of the lake must change. If this identity does not hold, then our model is wrong or incomplete. This might lead us to consider whether other factors—rainfall on the lake or evaporation from it—are the source of the discrepancy. Of course, just as we could in principle keep our own personal accounts in our head, verbal theory can provide a similar check on the consistency of our arguments. But just as double-entry bookkeeping helps us keep better track of complicated accounts, more formal models can help us avoid internal mistakes in our theories.

The greatest advantage of models emerges when their deductive power moves us beyond description to inferences from the assumptions. Consider what we might learn from our physical model by varying inputs of pollution and clean water to investigate the different consequences of pollution.

We would quickly discover that Lake Superior is so large that it would take an enormous amount of dye to pollute the entire lake. Conversely, Lake Erie is small and becomes polluted very easily. Because its stock of water (here, the size of the wash bucket) is so great relative to the flow of fresh water into it, should Lake Superior ever becomes polluted it will remain so long after the pollution source is stopped completely. Happily, water flows through Erie quickly and flushes it clean remarkably quickly. By using "pollutants" with different properties (e.g., ones that dissolve less well and sediment out), or changing the water inflows to reflect different levels of precipitation, we could analyze the impact of a wide range of different pollution scenarios.

While these deductions could be derived from purely verbal theory (I have just done so), other forms of the model offer alternative ways to make deductions that may have additional advantages. For example, a physical or computer simulation provides a means to check deductions that seem to be supported by verbal argument by, in effect, running an experiment. They may point out implicit assumptions that are not apparent without working through the argument in greater detail. The more precise specification of the computer simulation and formal model can further increase precision regarding the relative size of effects. And the running of the model forces us to be careful about our assumptions (e.g., how much fresh water and pollution we add at each point, and how much water we pour between lakes), and it keeps track of an increasingly complicated set of calculations about the various stocks and levels. But the physical, computer, and formal models do nothing that we could not, in principle, accomplish with verbal models. The only question is whether they do so in a way that is more precise, more efficient, more generalizable, and easier to convey to others.

At a sufficiently general level, all these models—verbal, physical, computer simulation, mathematical—have the same logical structure since they are models of the same interrelated system. In practice, the implementation of each model requires choices and decisions that differentiate them. More important, each has different advantages and limitations as an engine of theoretical analysis. For example, the physical model has the advantage of immediacy—we can see the color of the water changing as we pour it back and forth—and its deductive logic is transparent even to those with no technical sophistication. For some purposes—including teaching, advocacy, or handling problems that we cannot specify in formal terms—it might offer the best way to analyze the problem.[3]

By contrast, a computer simulation is more difficult to set up and explain. But, once established, it is much easier to change the assumptions of the model (e.g., increase the pollution in one lake, or decrease the inflow in another due to drought by changing a line in the computer program) and trace their implications. Simulations are particularly useful for handling complex problems—for example, many inflows and outflows that follow erratic or random patterns and that would be difficult or tedious to implement physically—as well as problems that do not lend themselves to direct mathematical solution.

A mathematical model makes even stronger demands on our ability to represent the problem in analytic terms. It cannot handle as much detail about the lake system as the other models and is typically expressed in a more general form. Its offsetting advantage is its generality, and that it opens up a mathematical deductive machinery which allows us to express outcomes precisely in terms of the parameters and coefficients of the model. In turn, this provides a systematic way to see the consequences of altering our assumptions (as will be illustrated later). Taking advantage of this power sometimes requires casting the model in certain ways (e.g., mathematical forms that we know how to manipulate). This raises important questions as to whether the model has sufficient fidelity to the original problem so that the resulting implications are meaningful for the problem at hand.

Whatever its form, the deductive power of a model is most compelling when its conclusions pack surprise. Famous examples include the Prisoners' Dilemma (discussed later) and collective action problems, which show that when each does what is best for him- or herself, all may be worse off. Once we understand the logic of the underlying models, however, their conclusions are no longer surprising in the sense that they follow logically, if not straightforwardly, from their assumptions. Moreover, as these results become familiar, they seem less surprising even as the models are applied to new circumstances. Nevertheless, without the model we would be back at square one and would need to derive the conclusions again each time that we encountered the problem. Thus while the results of models are sometimes dismissed as "obvious," the obviousness is often due to the model's success in making clear a point that had previously been only immanent and perhaps misunderstood.[4]

In this way, models provide a rich addition to our conceptual and theoretical repertoire. Models allow us to characterize situations not only in terms of their descriptive properties but also in terms of logical interconnections among those properties. By describing something as a *collective action problem,* we are not only describing the interests of the actors; we are offering an implicit deductive account of their inability to achieve joint gains. By respecifying the problem as one of public good provision with one large actor, we create a description that corresponds to hegemonic stability theory and entails a new prediction about the likelihood of a successful solution to the problem.[5] In short, models create a shorthand language that brings together description and deduction to advance our discussion of international politics. They also promote generalization insofar as they show that the same deductive arguments apply in seemingly different circumstances.

The surprise of a model lies equally in the conclusions that it does *not* support. Too frequently, in a contentious field like international politics, one argument leads to a certain conclusion, while another argument leads to roughly the opposite conclusion. Tighter reasoning—which may be verbal but is often facilitated by formalization—resolves this inconsistency either by locating the error in one of the arguments or by specifying the conditions under which each argument holds. Again, once these differences are resolved, the results are no longer surprising, but they are no less important.[6]

The deductions of models can also be surprising because they predict things that we cannot observe, or perhaps hope not to observe. Our models of the Great Lakes, for example, provide a way to predict the consequences of an environmental catastrophe if massive pollution were to enter the system at some point. Less dramatically, they provide guidance as to the likely consequences of allowing cities to increase the amounts of water they draw off for industrial purposes. In effect, a model provides a means for (thought) experimentation. Another situation is when an observable outcome depends on an unobserved cause. For example, the credibility of nuclear deterrence rests on our willingness to retaliate (perhaps massively) against anyone who uses nuclear weapons against us. We hope never to observe our credibility put to the test, but models of deterrence provide ways to understand its importance in promoting nuclear weapon stability. Finally, we may observe only one of many outcomes that *could* have occurred. Here models can be useful in describing these "multiple equilibria" and perhaps in identifying the factors that determined a particular outcome. These factors may be surprisingly subtle—as when different expec-

236

tations serve as self-fulfilling prophecies that lead to different outcomes in otherwise identical situations. Simulation models, in particular, are useful for understanding the sensitivity of outcomes to perturbations in the initial circumstances. In all these cases, our analysis hinges heavily on understanding counterfactual "other worlds" that might have been. More formalized models often provide a systematic way to do so; the tighter logic of the model constrains the conclusions we can draw and guides our interpretation of them.[7]

Finally, models pack surprise because they suggest different ways to think about problems or different aspects to consider. Just as the process of pouring water between lakes might direct our attention to different possible mixing properties, so writing the computer or mathematical statement to represent the "average" pollution level of a lake leads us to ask whether that average is an appropriate characterization of the overall quality of the lake. More formalized models sometimes have the advantage that they link the discovery of such questions to specific deductive approaches for tracing the consequences of different answers.

Models as Guides to Testing

Models and modelers are sometimes insufficiently attentive to the empirical validity of their arguments and, especially, to the testing of their models. This shortcoming can be understood partly in terms of the success of the deductive side of the modeling enterprise, partly in terms of a division of labor due to the different and difficult skills required for both modeling and empirical work, and partly because models are fun so that their practitioners have enjoyed sticking with them rather than doing sometimes more arduous empirical work. The power and elegance of the verbal argument or mathematical proof and its logical "truth" may mislead the theorist to act as if the conclusions need no testing. But the internal validity of an argument is no guarantee that it provides an accurate model of the external world. The only way to ensure this is by paying careful attention to the empirical referents of the model.

Models do not aspire to descriptive detail, but applied models of international relations are strongly empirical in a more general sense. While a purely abstract model need not have any empirical content, a "model of something" is necessarily empirical. Empirical content is built into a model through its specific assumptions—the size of the buckets, the rate of the inflow, the procedures for mixing water, and so forth. In more abstract models where variables and coefficients replace physical entities, the empirical referents become more general but no less important. Crucially, the meaning of the model hinges on the empirical referents of its terms. Without such an interpretation, for example, differential equations are nothing more than mathematical expressions. Only through an interpretation such as that discussed previously do these equations become a model of the Great Lakes. With another interpretation the same equations might constitute a problem in thermodynamics or a model of an arms race (shown later). And, of course, the reason we care about the model is because of what it tells us about the world. Thus the empirical referents of a model are essential to its usefulness.

Because models are concerned with general things, their empirical content is based not on facts per se but on what are often called stylized facts. A *stylized fact* is an empirical generalization—something that is true in general though not in every specific instance—captured either in the assumptions of the model or in what the model seeks to explain or predict. For example, we often assume in international relations models that states maximize their security and that they are reluctant to surrender sovereignty to supranational institutions. Similarly, there has been considerable effort to develop models to explain observed regularities such as why democracies do not fight against each other. Such stylized assumptions and predictions are always imperfect (e.g., some states might maximize economic performance instead, or perhaps democracies fight on rare occasions), but models rely on them for empirical guidance and as points of testing.

A model that is not logically sound will be rejected on deductive grounds. Thus, when we test a model empirically we are not testing the correctness of the model itself but rather we are testing the applicability of the model to a given empirical situation. One place to start is through evaluating the fit of a model's assumptions—and hence the applicability of the model—to an issue. While never strictly accurate, the stylized assumptions of a model must be reasonably good approximations to warrant using them as the basis for logical deductions. Logical inferences from unsound assumptions are likely to be valid only by chance.[8] Unfortunately, our ability to test certain assumptions (especially those regarding actors' motivations or beliefs) may be limited because they cannot be observed directly. This problem is not unique to formal models, of course, which at least should make their assumptions clear. Nevertheless, a minimal test is that the assumptions accord with our intuitions and that the model works well in different but similar problems. Where stronger supporting evidence is available, modelers need to make the empirical relevance and testability of assumptions a priority in order to improve the grounds for accepting (or rejecting) the model's conclusions.

Sometimes an assumption can be tested logically in terms of the robustness of the model to different specifications. For example, an argument based on the assumption that states care about relative gains (that is, about doing better than others regardless of how well they do absolutely) will be more persuasive if it holds even if states care about both relative and absolute gains. When the results are not robust to plausible variations in the assumptions, the model needs to be reformulated. A model that assumes states seek security rather than power, for example, may be very sensitive to even a low probability that even one state is a power maximizer whose behavior forces security-seeking states to behave the same way or be eliminated. The model will have to be changed to allow for this possibility (e.g., by incorporating uncertainty about motivations) if it is to provide an accurate analysis and prediction about international politics in this setting.

The more standard way to test a model, of course, is by evaluating its predictions. Sometimes this is as easy as checking the face validity of model implications as a basis for rejecting models that fly in the face of observed outcomes. We know that something is wrong, for example, with models that predict that states always cooperate, or that they never do. Such intuitive testing is an ongoing part of the process of model construction, and more finished models should have already passed such tests and be subjected to stronger tests. This typically requires connecting the model to more rigorous empirical techniques (see Braumoeller and Sartori, chap. 6, this vol.).

Unfortunately, models sometimes generate so many predictions that they are indeterminate, and testing is less conclusive. Before blaming this completely on the model, however, it is worth remembering that the model may be illuminating an indeterminacy that is a fundamental feature of the world. In this case, the model does a service by illuminating a difficulty that may not be as apparent without it. Regardless, the difficulty can only be overcome by developing a stronger theoretical understanding of the problem.

A better testing alternative in these cases may be through case studies that focus less heavily on single predictions and focus more heavily on associated mechanisms and processes. Models have often been viewed as producing fairly "thin" predictions so that they are not as useful for understanding the rich and detailed empirical analysis that represents the best of the historical and case study tradition. The developing literature on analytic narratives shows how models can be used more broadly as interpretive guides to understand the details of cases.[9] Andrew Bennett (chap. 2, this vol.) provides an analysis of how case study, statistical, and formal methods are complementary in IR research.

Ultimately, the test of a model is a joint test of its predictions and assumptions together. When predictions are wrong, something is missing from or incorrect in its underlying assumptions. If the model is not going to be rejected, it must be altered to produce more reasonable predictions. Of course, this leads to the concern that with enough cleverness, a sophisticated modeler can produce a model that can predict anything (and therefore that really predicts nothing). This claim is misleading on several counts. The tightly constrained deductive structure of a formal argument will be less open to such chicanery than is verbal theory, which typically allows for greater play between assumptions and conclusions. The formal character of a model helps limit trickery by requiring that assumptions be made explicit. This allows others to more readily scrutinize the suspicious result and challenge the presumably unbelievable assumptions that are necessary to generate it.[10] The revised model may also generate additional predictions that serve to invalidate it if it is false. Finally, the original claim that it is easy to create a model to show any result you want is usually not correct. The process of trying to make different assumptions fit together to obtain particular conclusions is arduous; it usually requires modifying and adapting assumptions, and this process often changes and alters the argument. While reasonable scholars will disagree, any tightly articulated model based on plausible assumptions and with supporting evidence deserves serious scrutiny and consideration.

A Progression of Models in the Study of International Politics

Next we look at some specific applications of formal models in IR theory using an overview of the progression from Richardson arms race models through a series of different game-theoretic models. The actual progression was neither as smooth as it might look here, nor generated solely by processes internal to the field. The abandonment of the Richardson model was due to its theoretical and empirical limitations, but the shift to game theory depended heavily on the importation of key results from outside the field. Further developments of IR game models also depended on the availability of techniques borrowed from the outside, and the intellectual progression has evolved together with substantive debates within international politics.

The fundamental point is that the development of models in international politics has been closely linked—both as cause and effect—to the development of our thinking about international politics more generally. As models have been found wanting—on both analytic and substantive grounds—they have been abandoned or reformulated to deal with their shortcomings. Conversely, the results of models have influenced and shifted the course of IR theoretical debates. Throughout, there has been a strong interaction with verbal theory that has furthered the development of both. The advantage of models has shown up partly through their successes but also partly through their failures, which have led to useful reformulation in both the model and, especially, in our substantive understanding.

The Richardson Arms Race Model

It is of more than historical interest to start with the first significant formal model of international politics. Lewis Frye Richardson (1960), a Quaker physicist, brought the tools of his discipline to bear on the problems of conflict. His simplest model proposed that an arms race can be understood as an interaction between two states conditioned by three motivations. First, *grievances* between states cause them to acquire arms to use against one another. Second, states are *fearful* of one another and so acquire arms to defend themselves against each other's weapons. Finally, the costs of acquiring weapons create *fatigue* that decreases future purchases. These assumptions can be summarized thus.

> *Verbal theory:* States increase armaments because of *grievances* against and *fear* of other states, but these increases are inhibited by the *fatigue* of maintaining greater armament levels.

Richardson wanted to predict the circumstances that create an arms race (as in the pre–World War I Anglo-German naval arms race): when will two states rapidly increase armaments against each other?[11] A plausible verbal deduction is that arms races will result among fearful states and among states that have grievances but will be less likely among states that are sensitive to the fatigue induced by the costs of the arms race. While this prediction is in the generally right direction, the mathematical model is able to refine it considerably and make clearer inferences. (You might want to check this claim seeing if you can refine the predictions further with verbal theorizing before going on. For example, can you predict when an arms "race" will be characterized by accelerating, stable, or declining expenditures?)

Richardson's novel technique was to transform these assumptions into a simple expression describing each state's behavior.

$$\text{Rate of weapons acquisition = grievance + fear − fatigue} \tag{1}$$

which can be translated into mathematical symbols as a differential equation:

$$dx/dt = g + by - cx \tag{2}$$

where dx/dt is calculus notation for "the rate at which nation X changes its level of armaments (x) over time (t)," g stands for grievance, y is the other state's level of arms that induce the fear, b is a coefficient that indexes how strong the fear is, and c is an index of the cost of maintaining each unit of the current level of armaments (x). A parallel equation describes state Y's arms acquisition:

$$dy/dt = h + fx - ey \tag{3}$$

where h, f, and e are the grievance, fear, and fatigue coefficient that characterize state Y, and x and y are the armament levels of the two states, respectively.

Together, equations (2) and (3) provide a simple model of the arms interaction between X and Y. The equations are merely translations of the verbal argument and, as such, can be praised or criticized on the same grounds. The mathematical statement is more precise than the verbal one since it presents the relationship between the various factors in very specific terms. The parameters b, c, f, and e are greater than zero for substantive reasons offered in the verbal theory; g and h are positive for rivals but might be negative for friends or allies. I next develop how relations among these parameters are central to understanding the model and its implications. Indeed, once we know the values of the coefficients (g, b, c, h, f, e), we can trace out the entire history of weapons acquisition by the two sides from any initial levels of armaments. This sort of precision is a strong feature of the model but only, of course, provided that the underlying assumptions are accurate. I will focus on one particular criticism, but first let us consider the advantages of bringing together the two descriptive statements in mathematical form.

Figure 1a does this graphically. Each line represents combinations of armaments levels along which one state is neither increasing nor decreasing its armaments (e.g., $dx/dt = 0$ along one line; $dy/dt = 0$ along the other line). The reason is that at a point on its own line (e.g., point M on X's line), the fatigue that a state experiences from its level of armaments ($-cx$) exactly balances the combination of its fear of the other's armaments (by) and its grievances (g) toward the other. Anywhere to the right (left) of its line, X will decrease (increase) armaments because fatigue outweighs (is outweighed by) the other two factors. These changes are reflected by the horizontal arrows representing X's decisions to decrease (i.e., move to the left) or increase (i.e., move to the right) its armaments in different quadrants of the diagram. Similarly, Y does not change its armaments along its line ($dy/dt = 0$) but decreases armaments above its line and increases them below its line, as reflected by the vertical arrows. The overall direction of change in armaments is different in each of the four quadrants (I–IV) of figure 1, as indicated by the arrows.

While this translation of our verbal model into mathematical form is useful in clarifying our arguments, its real value lies in going the next step to draw some conclusions from it. Several are quite readily evident. First, the intersection of these curves at point E corresponds to an "equilibrium" level of armaments for each side that would persist over time. Only at this unique combination of arms are both states satisfied so that neither will change its level of armaments. Although the "qualitative" result shown by point E is sufficient for present purposes, it is straightforward to solve equations (2) and (3) for $dx/dt = dy/dt = 0$ to obtain an algebraic solution for the equilibrium: equilibrium occurs at the intersection of the two lines when $x = (eg + bh)/(ec - bf)$ and $y = (hc + fg)/(ec - bf)$, corresponding to point E. In turn, this quantitative solution allows us to see how the equilibrium

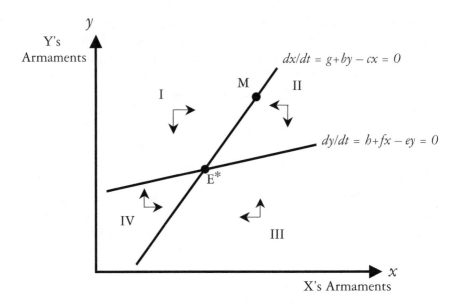

$$dx/dt = g + by - cx = 0$$

$$dy/dt = h + fx - ey = 0$$

Fig. 1a.   Stable Richardson arms race

shifts with changes in the values of various parameters. For example, equilibrium military spending is higher when either state is more fearful (i.e., higher b or f) or has greater grievances (i.e., g or h). These results are fairly obvious, but the model also shows that Y's spending increases as X is more fearful (i.e., with higher b), which is not so obvious. The reason is that X's increased fear increases X's spending which increases Y's spending—which in turn feeds X's fear to increase its spending. But how (and when) does this process stop? We'll see shortly that the model answers this sort of question as well.

Second, the arrows in the diagram show what happens when we are not at equilibrium E. In quadrant I, for example, state Y's fatigue factor dominates its fear-grievance considerations and leads it to reduce its armaments; state X finds the opposite and increases its armaments. By examining the direction of change in armaments in all four quadrants, the arrows suggest that, whatever the initial level of armaments, there is a tendency to move back toward the equilibrium. However, the nature of this approach can be complicated in ways that cannot necessarily be seen in the graphical

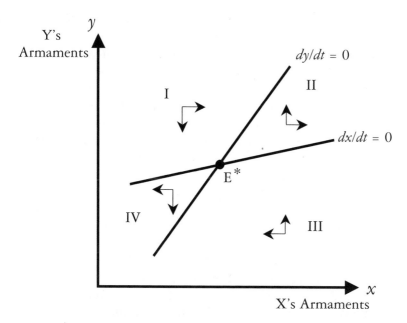

Fig. 1b.   Unstable Richardson arms race

analysis. Different specifications of the dynamics—for example, how strongly and quickly the rivals react to each other or the inclusion of lags in their responses—could result in a direct approach to equilibrium that occurs totally within one quadrant or movement through multiple quadrants leading to an oscillating pattern of weapons expenditures that might never reach the equilibrium point.

This way of thinking about arms races forces careful consideration of what we mean by an arms race—for example, that it might entail not "racing" but stable or fluctuating levels of military spending. However, figure 1a contains an important and nonobvious assumption: The line for state X is steeper than that for state Y. Substantively, this choice of slopes for the two lines implicitly assumes that the fatigue factors for the two states are relatively larger than the fear factors, which is what induces the stability of the system. By changing the assumption, so that fear matters more than fatigue—in which case the curve for Y is steeper than that for X—we get a quite different situation in figure 1b. While there is still an equilibrium at E where the lines cross, it is now not stable but very fragile. If the countries spend only a little more on armaments—or suppose each side found an extra gun in a basement—then we move to quadrant II where armament levels increase without bound for both sides. This is the stylized arms race that originally motivated Richardson. Conversely, if both sides spend less than the equilibrium level then they will fully eliminate military spending. Now we get either an arms race with no upper bound or else an equally peculiar "race" to disarm!

Here the algebraic solution is more revealing than purely verbal or graphical analysis. Solving for the condition under which the X curve is steeper than the Y curve, we obtain $ce > bf$ as the condition for arms race stability. This is a more precise statement than our verbal intuition and also makes clear that whether or not we have an arms race depends not simply on the individual evaluations of the two states but centrally on their interaction. If one state has a very high fear coefficient relative to its fatigue coefficient—for example, if b is very much bigger than c in equation (2)—an arms race may result even if the other state has a closer balance of considerations. Finally, note that grievance factors do not affect the likelihood of an arms spiral, although they do affect the equilibrium levels of spending.

The Richardson model spawned a cottage industry trying to understand and empirically evaluate arms interactions between the Soviets and Americans, the Israelis and Arabs, and so forth. While the insight regarding an interactive competition between states was valuable, and it organized research for a decade, the model garnered only limited empirical support. One reason is that the model has significant flaws that lead to clearly untenable conclusions—especially the possibility that arms spending might alternately go to zero or to infinity. But the fundamental problem with the model is revealed in Richardson's (1960, 12) own observation that "the equations are merely a description of what people would do if they did not stop to think." Thus the interaction modeled was purely mechanical and not strategic in the sense that it is not based on the reasons for or consequences of acquiring weapons. Since military strategy is very much about thinking, a model that leaves that out is surely doomed. And despite valiant efforts to solve the problem by throwing more mathematics at it, the research tradition was doomed because it was based on a flawed intuition. The problem, however, lies not in the mathematics but in the substantive argument.[12]

From Richardson Reflex to Game Theory Choice

Rational choice models provide a considerable advance on the Richardson model by allowing the actors to think rather than to react reflexively to each other's behavior.[13] The rationality assumption holds that actors pursue their goals efficiently with the options available to them. In the case of armaments, that means choosing the best level of military forces given security objectives and the costs of weapons. In other substantive issue areas, the goals could be as different as achieving material self-interest in trade negotiations or maximizing normative concerns in human rights issues.[14] The distinctive feature of game models (as opposed to models of individual rationality) is that actors are interdependent so that each actor's outcome depends in part on the other's behavior. Whereas Richardson's actors reacted reflexively to each other, game-theoretic actors act strategically by choosing their best policy in anticipation of each other's behavior. This leads to a range of possible outcomes according to the exact nature of their interrelationship.

It is worth stressing that rationality is a substantive assumption about states or whatever other actors are in our models. Indeed, taking states as actors (whether in a game-theoretic or Richardsonian model) already assumes that a state-centric perspective is a useful way to analyze international politics. Rationality applied to states further assumes that their decision making can reasonably be approximated as a coherent and consistent decision-making arrangement. If domestic politics mean that the goals being sought at the international level are not consistent but erratic, or if state leaders or bureaucrats cannot be characterized as capable of such decisions, then rational models will be of limited value. While there has been some success in including domestic processes in the analysis (noted later), and there are ongoing efforts to extend game-theoretic approaches to different settings (e.g., bounded rationality and evolutionary games), these assumptions remain important for interpreting the models and for understanding their limitations.

Figure 2 presents the armaments interaction as a Prisoners' Dilemma (PD) game where each state has a choice either to Cooperate (by building no new arms) or to Not Cooperate (by increasing arms). The first number in each cell of the matrix is the payoff to state X; the second number is the payoff to state Y. Each state's best outcome {payoff = 4} results when it

State Y

Cooperate Not Cooperate

No New Arms Increase Arms

	Cooperate No New Arms	Not Cooperate Increase Arms
Cooperate No New Arms	*3, 3*	*1, 4*
Not Cooperate Increase Arms	*4, 1*	*2, 2**

State X

Fig. 2. Arms race as a Prisoners' Dilemma

alone increases arms, since the additional benefits of military superiority outweigh its costs; second best {3} results when neither side increases arms, so that each state avoids the costs of arms and the military balance is unaltered; third best {2} results when both increase arms, so that each incurs the costs of additional arms but neither gains a military advantage; and the worst outcome {1} results when the other unilaterally increases arms and gains a military advantage. Given these preference rankings, each side will increase its armaments because that choice provides a higher payoff regardless of the other's armament decision. (That is, X receives 2 instead of 1 by arming when Y arms, and 4 instead of 3 by arming when Y does not arm. A parallel analysis applies to Y's choice.) The {2, 2} payoff has an asterisk to indicate that it is a Nash equilibrium outcome—the solution to the game—where neither state has any incentive to change its behavior. The surprise of the model—and the dilemma in Prisoners' Dilemma—lies in the conclusion that when each side follows its individual self-interest by not cooperating, both sides end up worse off (getting 2, 2) than if they had both cooperated (getting 3, 3). Individual and collective rationality clash.

The Prisoners' Dilemma has been a central model in the study of international relations. At its most general, PD has been taken as *the* representation of the Hobbesian anarchy that characterizes the international setting and of the presumed impossibility of cooperating without an overarching sovereign or government. It provides a logical explanation for the difficulty of cooperation in many international issues, including not only arms spending but, by changing the substantive interpretation of Cooperate and Not Cooperate, also decisions to impose trade barriers or failures to reduce global pollution. (Note that the dilemma dissolves if an agreement to cooperate could be enforced in the same way that domestic contracts are enforced by the state.) As such, PD was the workhorse for the first wave of game-theoretic analysis of international relations and continues to provide a background setting for much theoretical work on international politics.

Of course, such a simple model is far too thin to capture all of the important elements of international politics. A number of shortcomings are immediately apparent by examining the assumptions of the model. It includes only two actors; it assumes actors have only a single dichotomous choice; it considers only one of a large number of possible arrangements of the payoffs; it treats only a single issue, thus implicitly ignoring possible linkages to other issues; it assumes that actors have complete knowledge of all choices and preferences; and it looks at only a single point in time without considering the dynamics of the interaction that Richardson focused on. One of the powerful attractions of models, however, is that identification of such limitations points the way to subsequent extensions of the model. The deductive machinery of the model provides a way to investigate such questions and expand our theoretical knowledge of the model and the circumstances to which it applies. In short, the critique of a model can be as important and informative as the model itself, as illustrated later.

A model should also be critiqued in terms of its substantive shortcomings. A glaring one is that simple PD only predicts noncooperation among actors, whereas we observe states cooperating in at least some settings. This immediately raises questions as to whether a richer model might identify characteristics of the issues (e.g., What is it about economic issues that makes cooperation easier than on security issues?) or the actors (e.g., Are they friends or enemies? The same size or different sizes?) that affect the likelihood of cooperation. Another shortcoming is that treating aggregate state actors as if they were like individual decision makers ignores the role of domestic politics in determining foreign policy. Domestic divisions— the executive versus the legislative branches in the United States, or exporters versus importers on trade issues—are surely important factors explaining how states interact with each other on certain issues. A third shortcoming is that the institutional environment of the Prisoners' Dilemma is very thin compared to what we observe at the international level. While useful for depicting the absence of strong centralized enforcement that would enable states to "contract out" of the problems posed by anarchy, such a simplification ignores many other features of international institutions—ranging from traditional practices of diplomacy, through customary to formal legalization, to highly articulated international organizations with quasi-legislative and quasi-judicial capacities—that make them effective in mediating international interactions.

These three examples hardly exhaust the substantive shortcomings of such a simple model. Each of them has been the subject of extensive work to increase the realism of the model. Some of this is formal, but much of it relies on verbal theory built around the simple formal results. Here I focus on some of the efforts to address the first problem regarding the possibility of cooperation. My goal is to briefly illustrate the value of formal approaches in advancing our understanding of such problems and, more important, the new questions that are raised.

As noted, the failure of single-play PD to allow for cooperation is unsatisfactory from a substantive point of view since cooperation often does occur in international relations. This shortcoming can be overcome by addressing the unrealistic assumption that the game is only played once. In fact, states are enduring actors and interact frequently and over long periods of time. A central result of game theory known as the folk theorem demonstrates that when games repeat and actors care sufficiently about the future, then cooperation is possible on a decentralized basis.[15] The reason is that by making future cooperation contingent on each other's current cooperation—for example, by adopting a strategy of the form "I'll cooperate as long as you cooperate but I'll stop cooperating if you stop cooperating"—actors can create an equilibrium where the long-run advantages of participating in a mutually beneficial cooperative scheme outweigh the short-run temptation of not cooperating. Once applied to international affairs, this finding immediately opened up the possibility of "cooperation in anarchy" and fundamentally changed the terms of the debate as to whether international cooperation was possible. Moreover, it also suggested why cooperation might be less likely in security than economic affairs. The disastrous consequences of being taken advantage of in the short term on security affairs makes it much more difficult to pursue cooperative strategies based on a willingness to take short-run risks for the prospect of long-run cooperative gains.

The folk theorem has been influential, however, not so much because it resolved the question of cooperation but because it opened up a new set of questions—many of which originated in other limitations of the simple model. One example is that cooperation in the iterated PD is supported by reciprocity where an actor cooperates if the other does, but retaliates if the other does not cooperate. Such strategies are significantly degraded if actors do not have good information about each other's behavior or if accidents, mistakes, or misperceptions cloud events. The reason is that, although actors want to retaliate against intentional noncooperation, they may want to "forgive" unintentional noncooperation in order to sustain their ongoing cooperation. This problem is further complicated because the possibility of forgiveness gives actors an incentive to not cooperate and then to disguise their noncooperation by claiming it was in error even though it was intentional. This has led to important work about how cooperative arrangements need to balance a willingness to retaliate with a recognition that mistakes happen. The result is cooperation that is less deep but also less brittle.

A seemingly troublesome implication of the folk theorem is that not only is cooperation possible but, indeed, the number of possible equilibrium outcomes with at least some cooperation is infinite. Different levels of cooperation and different distributions of cooperative gains can be supported by the long-run incentives of reciprocity. This *multiple equilibria* problem is disturbing because it means the model cannot predict which particular cooperative outcome will occur. Economists sometimes restrict the set to the efficient outcomes (i.e., where no one can be made better off without harming someone else). Such restrictions are less than satisfactory in international affairs where there is no obvious mechanism (like the economic market) to ensure we move to efficiency and, especially, where the fundamental problem has been to explain the inefficiency observed in noncooperation. Alternatively, more psychological or cultural explanations rely on concepts like "focal points" to suggest that certain outcomes are more likely to emerge because they possess other properties.

If the inconclusiveness of the folk theorem is unsettling, it fits nicely with an important substantive critique that the PD model focuses too heavily on efficiency and has largely ignored the issues of distribution that are central in international politics. The distribution problem with multiple equilibria is illustrated in figure 3. Here there are three alternative equilibria defined by the pure strategies of each state. Both states prefer cooperation at any one of these points over noncooperation off the diagonal, but they have exactly opposed interests as to where they should cooperate. Each wants the other to bear the burden of greater cooperation while it bears relatively less of that burden. Recent work has begun to explore how these distributive incentives may impede the ability of states to attain cooperation in the first place.

This provides only a glimpse into the analyses that have opened up through investigation of the repeated-play PD model. This line of research has produced some important answers about the possibility of cooperation and the circumstances under which it is (or is not) likely. Other extensions have included the introduction of different preferences and hence strategic problems among the actors, consideration of the impact of imperfect information about other actors and their behavior, and the role of institutional arrangements. Again, some of these analyses have been conducted through highly mathematized models, but other contributions have been based on softer theorizing informed by formal models (Snidal 2002).

From Structure to Process: Extensive Form Games

Simple games like PD capture the overall structure of a strategic interaction, but they do not portray the underlying contextual details that can be crucial in the actual course of events. For this reason, game theory applications to international politics have increasingly emphasized extensive form (or tree-form) games that depict interactions among actors in greater detail. In part, this change in emphasis was driven by exciting developments in game theory itself, but its success in international relations theory was due to its ability to represent many of the important issues being discussed. The significance of looking at the processes underlying the overall structure of the payoffs can be illustrated with a simple extension of the preceding analysis that takes the sequence of actions into account.

Suppose we modify our single-play PD problem by allowing one actor to take the lead in initiating cooperation by unilaterally reducing armaments. The extensive-form version of the game in figure 4 shows the first mover (X) with a choice whether or not to initiate cooperation at decision node X. If she chooses not to cooperate by taking the lower branch, then

State Y

	Low	Medium	High
High	3, 6 *	4, 4	2, 2
State X Medium	1, 2	5, 5 *	4, 4
Low	0, 0	1, 2	6, 3 *

Fig. 3. Multiple cooperative equilibria

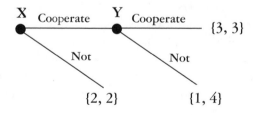

Fig. 4. Extensive form of Trust Game

the noncooperative equilibrium of the PD game {2, 2*} obtains. If X cooperates along the upper branch, then Y must choose (at decision node Y) either to reciprocate cooperation along the upper branch to {3, 3} or not cooperate by choosing the lower branch to {1, 4}. Because Y receives a higher payoff by not cooperating (i.e., {4} instead of {3}), he will choose the latter course of action if X cooperates. This makes X worse off than if she had not cooperated in the first place. Therefore, X will not initiate cooperation. The outcome remains at the {2, 2*} PD equilibrium, which again is inferior to {3, 3}. This game is sometimes called the Trust Game because it revolves around whether X can "trust" Y to reciprocate cooperation—because she cannot, X will not initiate cooperation. The normal form representation of this game in figure 5 shows this same equilibrium outcome.

The first state might try to improve the situation with the following proposal: "I will cooperate. But if you don't reciprocate my cooperation, then I will punish you [e.g., on some otherwise unrelated issue] so that you are worse off than if you had cooperated." With this threat as an additional alternative, X now has three strategies—not cooperate, cooperate and not implement the threat, or cooperate and implement the threat—that can be represented in the normal form game of figure 6. The variables c and p represent the cost to X of implementing the threat and the impact of the punishment on Y, respectively.

There are potentially two (asterisked) Nash equilibria in this game. One is at the {2, 2*} payoff where neither cooperates, as in the original Trust Game. The other Nash equilibrium occurs at the {3, 3*} payoff provided X's threatened punishment is sufficiently large so that Y's payoff from cooperation {3} exceeds its payoff from not cooperating {4 − p}. In this case, the threat of retaliation—it is only a threat since it leads Y to cooperate so that X never has to carry through on it—makes *both* states better off than at the other equilibrium.

While this unilateral route to cooperation looks promising, closer examination reveals it is seriously flawed. The flaw is that whereas the normal form game in figure 6 treats the interaction as if the actors were choosing at the same time, the threat depends on observing what the other has already done, and so implementing it (or not) must entail a subsequent choice. Figure 7 presents the underlying extensive form game depicting the sequence of choices faced by the actors as their interaction proceeds. X's threat is represented as a move whereby X can decide whether to punish Y after observing whether or not he cooperated. Note that punishment is

Y

	Cooperate	Not Cooperate
Not Cooperate	2, 2	2, 2*
Cooperate	3, 3	1, 4

X

Fig. 5.   Normal form of Trust Game

Y

	Cooperate	Not Cooperate
Not Cooperate	2, 2	2, 2*
Cooperate	3, 3	1, 4
Cooperate with Threat	3, 3*	1-c, 4-p

X

Fig. 6.   Normal form of Threat Game

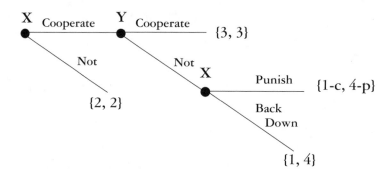

Fig. 7. Extensive form of Threat Game

not automatic but is represented as a choice since X might be bluffing and not truly be prepared to punish Y's noncooperation. Indeed, if $c > 0$—for example, if X threatened to impose trade sanctions against Y, but those would hurt her own economy as well—then X harms herself by carrying through the threat and so will not rationally do so (since $\{2\} > \{2 - c\}$). In this case, X's threat is not credible—the game theory terminology is that this equilibrium is not "subgame perfect" since it depends on the false assumption that X would choose Punish in the "punishment" subgame, whereas X would actually choose Back Down if given that choice. Knowing this, Y has no incentive to reciprocate cooperation since he won't be punished. In turn, X will not cooperate in the first place, since her cooperation will not be reciprocated because her threat to punish is not credible. Cooperation will not happen.

This illustrates how working through a model more precisely (here, by incorporating the sequence of moves) can give us a better understanding of the problem (here, that cooperation cannot be supported unless a threat is credible). The extensive form provides a further guide to circumstances under which the threat will be credible. One possibility is that an actor actually enjoys punishing the other (i.e., $c < 0$), perhaps for reasons of vengeance, so that credibility is not an issue.[16] But in the probably more typical case that punishment is costly, other tactics are warranted. Since the problem arose because X had a choice whether or not to carry out the threat, one way to make a threat credible is by removing the choice in the punishment subgame. Thus irrevocably committing oneself to carrying out the punishment when warranted would solve the problem. Unlike the mythical general who can burn a bridge behind his troops so they cannot retreat, however, international actors rarely can literally deprive themselves of the possibility of backing down later. Instead, they must rearrange their own incentives to ensure that they will want to carry through the punishment if necessary. A government might publicly pledge retaliation so that its domestic political costs of backing down outweigh the international costs of imposing the punishment. Staking one's international reputation could have a similar effect if the cost of backing down today is increased by the loss of credibility in the future. Surprisingly, lowering its payoff for one outcome (i.e., backing down) makes X better off by increasing the credibility of her threat and thereby inducing cooperation from Y. Finally, note that Y has an interest in X having an effective threat since they are *both* better off with it.

The comparison of the normal and extensive forms shows how different modeling approaches, even within the game-theoretic tradition, illuminate different aspects of the "same" problem. While the more structural normal form game could identify equilibria, the more detailed analysis of the extensive form eliminated one of them on the grounds that it entailed a noncredible threat. However, the extensive form accomplishes this at the cost of imposing more structure and detail on the analysis and so may not be possible or feasible for every problem. Marc Kilgour and Yael Wolinsky-Nahmias (chap. 13, this vol.) show how a third form of game model—the cooperative game where the parties can make binding agreements—is useful for studying problems of joint management of international environmental resources. Cooperative games include even less institutional detail than the normal form games but have the compensating advantage of facilitating the analysis of distributional questions. The choice between models, as with the earlier choice between maps, will depend on the substantive problems we are investigating.

This is only one example of the rich analysis that can be developed by specifying and formalizing the problem. It shows how seemingly minor details—in this case, the consequences of an action that will never occur—can have a major impact on events. While this particular analysis could be developed without formalization (Schelling 1960), the framework of game theory is invaluable in developing and clarifying the argument. More complicated problems often require more extensive formalization and cannot be handled by purely verbal theory. I close this section with three examples.

Consider the impact of different levels of information on interactions. In the preceding analysis, we assumed that actors were completely informed about their circumstances. John Conybeare's discussion (chap. 12, this vol.) of rational expectations shows how the assumption of perfect information can have far-ranging consequences. For example, war will not occur unless information is incomplete in the sense that actors are uncertain about each other's preferences. Andrew Kydd (chap. 14, this vol.) builds on the importance of uncertainty in explaining both the outbreak of war as well as the bargaining and signaling that surround it to explore the implications of democracy for war. Marc Kilgour and Yael Wolinsky-Nahmias (chap. 13, this vol.) discuss how a similar informational logic is essential to understanding environmental conflicts such as that over the Jordan River. While these chapters present the results of game-theoretic analysis in clear verbal terms, the underlying models being discussed are complicated and include results that could not have been readily arrived at without careful formal development. One of the major contributions of formal models has been to trace out the consequences of different informational conditions for interactions among actors.

A second complication occurs when we relax the assumption that states are unitary actors. Many international issues are deeply contested domestically so that understanding them requires careful attention to domestic considerations. Helen Milner (chap. 11, this vol.) discusses models that explain the preferences of states on trade issues in terms of the economic positions of underlying domestic groups. For example, import-competing sectors and owners of domestically scarce factors of production will support protection whereas export-oriented sectors and owners of domestically abundant factors will support free trade. Kilgour and Wolinsky-Nahmias (chap. 13, this vol.) show how the related literature on two-level games brings together domestic and international political considerations in environmental agreements. Here the foreign policy decision maker is seen as operating with a dual constraint: She must strike a bargain that gains both international and domestic acceptance. Models are invaluable in capturing the full logic of these interactions.

Finally, an even more complicated problem arises when the actors themselves change over time. Standard game theory models of international relations take the definition of the actors (usually states) as given and cannot incorporate this type of agent change. Robert Axelrod (1984) uses computer simulations of game interactions to incorporate changes in the relative frequency of different types of states in the system. This can have surprising implications. If states that received low payoffs in the past tend to emulate more successful strategies that have been used by other states, for example, then widespread cooperation is often likely to emerge in the system. An example would be protectionist states that lower their trade barriers after observing the superior economic performance of free-trading states. Lars-Erik Cederman (1997) has used the related simulation logic of complex adaptive systems to model the emergence of nations and states themselves. His simulation runs create "data" that allow him to inductively determine the analytic conditions under which anarchy leads to the emergence of power politics among a small group of states. The results contravene traditional wisdom by showing, for example, that balance of power politics are more likely to emerge when the military offense dominates the defense rather than vice versa.

While they are highly complementary, the choice between simulation and "regular" mathematical methods is driven by different substantive perspectives on the complexity of human interaction combined with different methodological views as to the best way to analyze that complexity. Cederman's analysis makes another important point in this regard. Because he is concerned with the emergence and character of the actors themselves, he frames his analysis as a sociological or "constructivist" approach. But whereas many constructivists have equated the substantive limits of rational choice analysis with its use of models, Cederman points out that constructivists' "advocacy of theoretical complexity actually increases the need for models, albeit of a different kind" (1997, 219). This brings us full circle to the point that models in international relations are not tied to any particular research program but rather provide an important means to investigate all of our substantive theories and the differences among them.

Conclusion

I hope this chapter has conveyed a sense of the importance of models for the study of international relations and of the special advantages of formal models in this enterprise. Mathematical approaches provide powerful tools because they promote conceptual precision, logical consistency, generality, and, especially, deductive inference. Verbal approaches can and should aspire to these same properties, but sometimes formal approaches are better in achieving them. Yet just as models are only part of the broader enterprise of theory building, formalization should not be separated from verbal theorizing. Formalization depends on good verbal theory as a place to start, and its final results are only as good as the verbal interpretation and extensions that it generates.

Model building is a process, not a goal. It is a way of engaging problems, of channeling creativity and improving our analysis by exploring the implications of different assumptions. Even the best models are just a way station to an improved understanding. By their nature, models are never right. They are, if things go well, progressively better approximations to the problem being studied. Furthermore, failures and shortcomings of models are important ways to learn. While sometimes it makes sense to abandon a whole tradition, as happened with Richardson models, often the defects provide key insights to the problem and can be remedied within the particular modeling tradition. The dominant example in international relations is game theory, which has progressed far in its study of such problems as deterrence and cooperation. It is no exaggeration to say that contemporary IR theory has been and continues to be heavily shaped by theoretical results from formal models.

Finally, like most academic research, formal model building carries with it a mix of both pain and pleasure. Developing models is hard work. In addition to the extra set of mathematical tools that must be learned, the actual process of constructing a model is rarely straightforward. Behind the finished result—assuming things work out, and they usually don't—lie many dead ends and algebraic slipups that brought the researcher grief along the way. But model building is also fun. Nothing beats refining an intuition about how the world works into a tight and systematic theoretical argument.

Recommended Readings

Cederman, L.-E. 1997. *Emergent Actors in World Politics.* Princeton: Princeton University Press. Cederman introduces computer simulation techniques to explain the emergence of international actors and discusses the relation between different modeling techniques and different substantive approaches to international politics.

Kreps, D. M. 1990. *Game Theory and Economic Modelling.* Oxford: Clarendon. This is an accessible introduction to key concepts of game theory that also offers a thoughtful analysis of strengths and weaknesses in the approach.

Lake, D., and R. Powell, eds. 1999. *Strategic Choice and International Relations.* Princeton: Princeton University Press. A set of essays that discuss the use of the strategic approach in international relations and its connection to a set of broad theoretical concerns.

Morrow, J. 1994. *Game Theory for Political Scientists.* Princeton: Princeton University Press. An introductory text that covers the key topics of the most important modeling approach with many examples drawn from international relations.

Schelling, T. 1960. *The Strategy of Conflict.* Cambridge: Harvard University Press. One of the early classics in the game theory tradition shows how the power of the approach can be realized in verbal theory.

Snidal, D. 2002. Rational Choice and International Relations. In *Handbook of International Relations,* edited by W. Carlsnaes, T. Risse, and B. Simmons. London: Sage. A discussion of critiques and limitations in rational choice applications to international relations and directions for addressing them.

Notes

I thank Sven Feldman, Sean Gailmard, Detlef Sprinz, Lora Viola, Yael Wolinsky-Nahmias, and an anonymous referee for comments useful in revising this chapter.

1. Such causal arrows are often used to set up statistical analyses and then translated into more precise mathematical statements for estimating purposes (e.g., regression equations). Moreover, most statistical methods (e.g., the general linear model of regression analysis) are themselves models of data. I do not discuss those important interconnections here.

2. Bender (1978) offers such a model. A differential equation is a formula that shows how one variable changes with respect to another variable as a consequence of other variables. In this case, it would show how the pollution level in a lake varied over time with the inflows and outflows of waters of differing qualities plus other factors. A more detailed example offered later in the essay uses differential equations to model an arms race.

3. Physical models are used to simulate complex environmental problems like this one but are less relevant for more political problems that are typically of interest to students of international politics. Simulation models based on participant role-playing are the analogue for such problems (e.g., different students "play" different countries in a global warming conference) and are useful for teaching purposes and exploring the nature of the problem.

4. The question of obviousness goes to the criticism that formal analysis merely restates "what we already know." In international security studies this is

often expressed as "but didn't Thomas Schelling [an important innovator in strategic analysis] already say that?" However, Schelling (1960) was writing in response to what he labeled the "retarded science of international strategy" and used (formal) bargaining and game theory to greatly improve the existing verbal theory. The power of his work lies in combining very simple mathematics with substantive analyses. Subsequent developments in both empirical and formal work—some of it very technical in nature—have greatly expanded our understanding of the operation of deterrence.

5. Hegemonic stability theory is an international relations theory that predicts cooperative outcomes when there is a dominant state in the system (e.g., Britain in the nineteenth century; the United States after World War II) that is able and willing to provide stability and other benefits to all states. This conclusion follows from the "privileged group" case of public good provision. See Milner (chap. 11, this vol.) for a discussion.

6. An example is the relative gains debate. See Grieco, Powell, and Snidal (1993).

7. On the analysis of counterfactuals see Tetlock and Belkin (1996), especially the articles by Fearon, Bueno de Mesquita, Weingast, and Cederman that discuss models of different types.

8. Here I differ sharply with claims that the accuracy of a model's assumptions is irrelevant and that all that matters is the accuracy of its predictions (Friedman 1953). The two factors are inextricably linked since grossly inaccurate assumptions (as opposed to somewhat inaccurate assumptions that provide reasonable approximations) will not lead to accurate predictions. Of course, as a practical matter it may be difficult to test assumptions, and so the burden of evaluation often falls on the predictions. The related "as if" argument—which says that assumptions don't have to be true provided they mimic the "true" assumption (e.g., actors need not actually be rational provided they act *as if* they were rational)—meets the approximation standard in the limited sense that they presumably will offer correct predictions. But they miss in a far more important sense. The failure of "as if" assumptions to provide a correct understanding of the underlying mechanisms at work means that they cannot provide a proper explanation or interpretation of the problem. They may provide a useful simplification that allows research into other questions to proceed—but they leave important considerations still to be explained.

9. See Bates et al. (1998) and, for a critique, Elster (2000).

10. It is possible, of course, that the "trick" is hidden in the mathematics itself, or is the result of a mistake in the derivations. Here, as in the case of similar mistakes in verbal theorizing or empirical work, we rely on the academic division of labor whereby others scrutinize and challenge results—which is facilitated by the clear standards for assessing formal deductive inferences.

11. In fact, this is only one definition of an arms race—as a spiral. Another type of arms race, defined as high but constant levels of arms, as witnessed through the Cold War, can also be represented in the model developed later. While such distinctions can be made verbally (Huntington 1958), mathematics provides a language that both facilitates and necessitates such precision.

12. See Glaser (2000) for a general review of the arms race literature. Kydd (2000) develops a single framework that brings together arms racing, bargaining, and war.

13. Anatol Rapoport (1960) provides a more detailed analysis of the Richardson model and critiques it as an overly deterministic form of "social physics." He develops a similar case for the value of game-theoretic models, which the present analysis elaborates in terms of some of the many subsequent and significant advances in game-theoretic analysis that can be connected directly to contemporary theoretical and empirical issues of international relations.

14. A common misconception is that rational models are about material things or self-interest in the sense of selfishness. A good example of international relations actors who are rational and strategic in the service of other-regarding normative goals is Keck and Sikkink's (1998) analysis of the human rights activists.

15. This illustrates our earlier point regarding what it means for a model's conclusion to be understood with or without the model. It is called the folk theorem because it was widely believed to be true (at least among economic theorists) before it was actually demonstrated. Moreover, the terminology of the tit-for-tat strategies that are often discussed as exemplary cooperative strategies in iterated games originated in English pubs in the sixteenth century, and the comparable eye-for-an-eye strategy is biblical. So the intuition behind the iterated model had been in the air for a very long time. However, neither the conditions under which the result applies nor the extensions discussed later can be fully understood without a fairly detailed, and sometimes technical, understanding of the underlying iterated game model.

16. Comparisons across different models are also instructive. Why isn't credibility an issue in the repeated Prisoners' Dilemma discussed earlier? The reason is that "punishment"—noncooperation on future plays—is in the aggrieved party's interests if the other is not adhering to the cooperative equilibrium.

References

Axelrod, R. 1984. *The Evolution of Cooperation*. New York: Basic Books.

Bates, R., A. Greif, J. Rosenthal, and B. Weingast. 1998. *Analytic Narratives*. Princeton: Princeton University Press.

Bender, E. A. 1978. *An Introduction to Mathematical Modeling.* New York: John Wiley.

Cederman, L. 1997. *Emergent Actors in World Politics.* Princeton: Princeton University Press.

Elster, J. 2000. Book Reviews—Rational Choice History: A Case of Excessive Ambition. *American Political Science Review* 94 (3): 696–702.

Friedman, M. 1953. The Methodology of Positive Economics. In *Essays in Positive Economics,* edited by M. Friedman. Chicago: University of Chicago Press.

Glaser, C. L. 2000. The Causes and Consequences of Arms Races. *Annual Review of Political Science* 3:251–76.

Grieco, J., R. Powell, and D. Snidal. 1993. The Relative Gains Problem for International Cooperation. *American Political Science Review* 87 (3): 729–43.

Huntington, S. P. 1958. Arms Races: Prerequisites and Results. *Public Policy* 8:41–86.

Keck, M. E., and K. Sikkink. 1998. *Activists Beyond Borders: Advocacy Networks in International Politics.* Ithaca: Cornell University Press.

Kydd, A. 2000. Arms Races and Arms Control: Modeling the Hawk Perspective. *American Journal of Political Science* 44 (2): 222–38.

March, J. G., and C. A. Lave. 1975. *An Introduction to Models in the Social Sciences.* New York: Harper and Row.

Rapoport, Anatol. 1960. *Fights, Games, and Debates.* Ann Arbor: University of Michigan Press.

Richardson, L. F. 1960. *Arms and Insecurity.* Pittsburgh: Boxwood Press.

Schelling, T. 1960. *The Strategy of Conflict.* Cambridge: Harvard University Press.

Snidal, D. 2002. Rational Choice and International Relations. In *Handbook of International Relations,* edited by W. Carlsnaes, T. Risse, and B. Simmons. London: Sage.

Tetlock, P. E., and A. Belkin, eds. 1996. *Counterfactual Thought Experiments in World Politics: Logical, Methodological, and Psychological Perspectives.* Princeton: Princeton University Press.

11. Formal Methods and International Political Economy

Helen V. Milner

Rational choice approaches to international political economy (IPE) have been a long-standing part of the field, beginning with Hirschman's early work (1945) on the structure of international trade and dependence. A central reason for this has been the field's close links to economics. This article surveys such approaches in IPE and argues that they can be fruitful under certain conditions.

I first discuss the definition of the field of IPE and examine how it has evolved over time and why changing definitions are important. I argue that the definition of the field is important for it allows us to identify the core questions of the field. The second section discusses rational choice theory, and in particular the advantages and disadvantages of formal modeling. In the third section, I trace how rational choice theory has been used in three different IPE areas and argue that its use has been fruitful in the sense that it has led to progress in the development of theory and testable hypotheses in these areas. Hegemonic stability theory (HST) has employed rational choice models to understand the hegemon's and followers' likely behavior. In the areas of trade and monetary policy, scholars have used various economic models, all based on the rationality assumption, to predict actors' policy preferences. Finally, in the area of international institutions and cooperation, rational choice theory has been widely used to explore the conditions under which international institutions might matter and those under which economic cooperation is most likely to emerge.

The last section addresses the comparison between security studies and IPE in the use of rational choice models. Its central question involves the issue of formalization of such models, a topic of much debate (e.g., Walt 1999). Much research using rational choice in IPE has been employed in informal or soft approaches. Models are rarely formalized in this field, in sharp contrast to the security field where almost all topics have an extensive formal literature (e.g., deterrence, crisis bargaining, war, balance of power, democratic peace, alliance formation, etc.; also see Kydd, chap. 14, this vol.). Why has IPE been less formal, especially given its links to economics? Is this lack of formalism an advantage or hindrance to theory building and testing? The conclusion addresses the strengths and weaknesses of formal model building in IPE and looks at future directions for research in the field.

What Is IPE?

The field of international political economy (IPE) is a rather young one in some ways. As an established part of IR, it seems to have appeared in the late 1960s and early 1970s. This means that it is only about thirty years old. The oil shocks beginning in the early 1970s provided a strong impetus to research in the field. Since then, the area has grown greatly, and the field has become well established within American and European political science departments.[1]

What is the subject matter of IPE? This is less clear than ever. Defining the field is often done in at least two very different ways. Either it is implicitly defined as everything that is not part of security studies in IR, or it is more narrowly defined (as at its inception) as dealing with the interaction of economic and political variables in the international system. When used in this latter sense it involves using economic variables as either the independent or dependent variables. That is, it sees economic factors as causes (usually of political outcomes), or it explains economic policy choices or outcomes (usually as a result of political causes).

In this narrower sense IPE is defined as only those issues related to the interaction of politics and economics.[2] In this tradition, research in IPE must have either an independent or dependent economic variable(s). That is, the variable being explained or the variable doing the explaining must have an economic component. Thus defined, the field focuses on the interaction of markets and states. It includes research on how states and their policy choices affect markets and other economic players. In this area, studies of foreign economic policy-making have been most important. Analyses of trade, industrial, exchange rate, monetary, and financial policy have been prominent; see, for example, the seminal volumes by Katzenstein (1978) and Krasner (1978), which set the agenda for research about the role of states in economic policy-making for many years. In addition, the impact of markets and other economic forces on states has been a well-researched area. From dependency theory in the 1970s and 1980s to globalization in the 1990s, the constraints that markets, especially global capitalist ones, exert on states have been at the research frontier in IPE.

Finally, in this narrower definition studies that emphasize the relationship between power and plenty are of importance. Indeed, the first volume of *World Politics* (1948) contains the founding article in this tradition; Jacob Viner's study of the interaction between power and plenty added a new twist to the old mercantilist ideas about this relationship. Further research on "economic statecraft" has continued in this tradition; see, for instance, Baldwin (1985), Martin (1992), Kirschner (1995), and Drezner (1999). The hard core of IPE then comprises these areas that emphasize the interaction between states and economic factors, like markets.

I prefer the narrower definition of IPE, which assumes that economic factors are an inseparable part of the field. It is the interaction of markets and states that is key in this approach. It involves showing how political factors like government policy choices influence economic ones, especially the operation of markets; and conversely, it entails showing how economic phenomena may alter the way politics—especially states and governments—operates. The mutual interaction of these two then is the central distinguishing feature of the field.

In the more expansive definition, IPE includes basically all issues except those in security studies.[3] Fundamentally, this seems to mean any issue where the use of military force is not a likely event or a central preoccupation. IPE then becomes the study of a huge range of phenomena that may have very little to do with economic factors, either as causes or outcomes. These include the study of international institutions—whether or not they involve economic issues—environmental issues, human rights, and international cooperation of any sort.

Is this a useful expansion of the field? Since many of these topics belong more to the debates in IR than to those in political economy, one may wonder if such an expansion of the field is progressive. Issues like the possibility of cooperation in international politics or the utility of international institutions belong firmly within the larger IR research tradition. Furthermore, IPE is not just about cooperation or about international institutions. It may include these if they relate to economic factors or issues, but not all institutions or forms of cooperation have economic causes or consequences of salience. Studying the UN does not necessarily make one an IPE scholar; studying the IMF probably does. IPE also involves conflict, sometimes involving the military and sometimes not. The economic causes of war or the economic consequences of military conflict, for example, certainly fall within the realm of IPE. On the other hand, research on cooperation or on conflict reduction need not fall within IPE; for instance, studies of third-party intermediation in conflicts, while about cooperation, are not necessarily part of IPE. IPE and the study of international institutions and/or cooperation are different subjects, although they do overlap when both involve economic issues.

Why does the definition of the field matter? Defining the field is important because it focuses attention on a common set of critical questions and issues. The narrower definition has the advantage that it draws researchers to concentrate on a well-defined series of topics. In the field of security studies, for example, most researchers agree that the central topic is war—its causes, consequences, and prevention (see Huth and Allee, chap. 9, and Kydd, chap. 14, this vol.). In IPE, there is probably no such single topic of attention. But there are two or three topics that dominate the field's agenda. First, the issue of economic growth and development has been a central one. Why some countries (or regions) grow faster than others has been a motivating research question for many studies. Political scientists have focused on the political determinants of economic growth and development. This is not just limited to studies of current developing countries (e.g., Haggard 1990; Haggard and Kaufman 1995; Shafer 1994), but also applies to studies of how the West became the center of the industrial revolution and the consequences of its economic superiority (e.g., North and Thomas 1973; Gilpin 1987; Wallerstein 1974; Tilly 1990) and extends to studies of the political prerequisites of economic growth for developing and transition countries (e.g., Przeworski 1991; Hellman 1998). In addition, many studies of economic policy-making by political scientists have sought to understand policy choices largely because of their impact—often indirect and untested—on the differential economic growth rates of countries (e.g., Katzenstein 1985; Simmons 1994; Wade 1990).

A second issue that defines the field is the impact of the international economy on domestic politics. The older literature on interdependence and the more recent work on globalization are examples (e.g., Keohane and Nye 1977; Morse 1976; Keohane and Milner 1996; Garrett 1998). Dependency theory also examined this question as well as the former one about economic growth (e.g., Caporaso 1978; Wallerstein 1974; Cardoso and Faletto 1979).

A third topic that has defined the field's range of interests has been the examination of how states use their economic capabilities and policies to achieve political goals, domestically and internationally. This includes not just the literature on economic sanctions and statecraft (e.g., Hirschman 1945; Baldwin 1985; Martin 1992; Drezner 1999; Kirschner 1995), but also studies of the ways in which economic assets can help countries to achieve their political goals (e.g., Gilpin 1975, 1987; Papayoanou 1999; Gruber 2000). The central questions all relate to the interaction of politics and economics among states in the international system. The causes and consequences of differential economic growth rates for nations is the central focus when the field of IPE is more narrowly defined.

What Are Formal Models and Rational Choice?

Not all of international political economy employs rational choice theory, but a significant part of it does. What is rational choice theory? There is a very extensive literature on this topic (e.g., Elster 1986; Coleman and Fararo 1992; Snidal, chap.10, this vol.) written by social scientists over the years, which I do not want to repeat. But a few comments on its core assumptions are necessary to understand its strengths and weaknesses. The central assumption is that individuals are rational; they have preferences that they pursue in a consistent manner, and they do not act primarily in an expressive, random, or habitual way. As Conybeare (chap. 12, this vol.) notes, rationality implies that individuals are assumed to have transitive preferences and to make consistent choices given those preferences. That individual behavior is purposive in this sense is the bedrock of rational choice. Rational choice theory also assumes that an individual's preferences are exogenous; that is, they are givens with which the theory must work. It does not comment on the rationality of these goals. Moreover, rational choice theory does not make any assumptions about the actor's information beyond the very deep claims about common knowledge. Most rational choice models initially assume that players have complete and perfect information, but many go on to relax this assumption and see how it changes the outcomes. On the other hand, the assumption of common knowledge is central to almost all rational choice models. As Morrow says: "Any information that all players know, that all players know that all players know, and so on, is common knowledge" (1994, 55).

In a more restrictive definition, the theory further assumes that actors try to pursue their preferences in order to maximize their utility. Rational choice theory then shows what are the most efficient ways for actors to accomplish their goals. This entails a comparison of the costs and benefits of alternative actions that could be taken in pursuit of one's goals. A rational actor is one who picks the most efficient action, or the one that maximizes her net (expected) benefits, whatever her goals are. One of the major criticisms of rational choice theory is that actors cannot possibly process all of this information; instead they at best act boundedly rational (Simon 1976).

In the simplest case, where each actor is independent of the other, rational choice theory employs utility maximization to show how the actors should behave. Each actor scans the options available to her and then picks the one having the highest net benefits, given her goals and other constraints. The gains of others—relative or absolute—are usually not a consideration. Utility maximization often has one actor (the "representative agent") faced with a constrained maximization problem. It seeks to show that in different environments where the constraints vary, different strategies will be maximal.

In more complex cases where each actor's pursuit of her goals depends on the behavior of others, such simple utility-maximizing models do not work. In this case, one must employ game theory that models such strategic interaction explicitly, such as those discussed by Kilgour and Wolinsky-Nahmias (chap. 13, this vol.). Utility-maximizing choices now depend on the likely behavior of others. Game theory implies at least two agents interacting in ways such that each one's behavior affects the other's. The Prisoners' Dilemma is one of the simplest depictions of this type of game. In such strategic environments the concept used most often to determine rational behavior is the Nash equilibrium. In a Nash equilibrium, each player's choice is the best reply to the other's choice; no player wants to change her strategy given what the other is doing.

In more complicated environments when there are many stages to the interaction between actors, the rational player uses backward induction to figure out her optimal strategy for pursuing her goals. These dynamic environments entail thinking about the last step of the interaction and reasoning backward from there, using the Nash equilibrium in each step to figure out what is the optimal play at the start of the interaction. In even more complex environments of strategic interaction where the actors do not possess complete information about the others or about their environments, game theory has developed techniques for analyzing rational strategies for players using the Nash equilibrium and Bayesian updating.[4] In these Bayesian equilibria one can again show each player's best strategy, given the other players' strategies and their beliefs. Rational choice theory thus has evolved into being able to examine rational behavior in ever more complex contexts.

As noted earlier, the preferences that actors have are exogenous in rational choice theory. Nonetheless, the players must be assumed to have certain preferences. For economics, the usual assumption is that the main actors are firms who are profit-maximizing; while debated, this assumption is not without some semblance to reality. For political science, the assumptions about the actors and their preferences are much more contested. Many in international relations simply assume that states are unitary actors who want to maximize their power or security. Others object, suggesting that the real actors are governments who desire to ensure that they remain in power. In IPE the actors range over a wide gamut: states, governments, firms, international institutions, and legislatures have all served as actors in models. Which actors to pick and what preferences to ascribe them are thorny issues. Indeed, one of the biggest challenges to rational choice theory has been from constructivists and others who argue that understanding actors' preferences is a vital, prior step to undertaking rational choice analysis.

Rational choice theory has been used mostly in an informal way in IPE. However, increasingly more formal treatments of topics in the field are emerging. These should be seen as supplementing, not substituting for, softer rational choice models. What do such formal models involve? Formalization means the explicit transformation of actors' decision problems into a deductive, mathematical framework. Formal models include an explicit statement of the assumptions underlying the analysis, the actors' utility functions and payoffs, the moves available to actors at each stage, and their information and beliefs. These are usually stated in the language of mathematics or logic so that the deductions made can be easily reproduced.

The use of mathematics is important because it allows the modeler to deduce propositions that must follow from the premises stated. It operates as a check on whether the propositions flow logically from the assumptions made. Formalization also helps to derive a series of comparative statics results. That is, once one has derived an equilibrium one can see how changes in various factors (ceteris paribus) lead to changes in the game. These comparative statics are often the basis for the testable hypotheses that are drawn from such models. Hence formalization adds explicitness, enhances confidence in the logic of the argument, and allows the derivation of testable hypotheses that follow ineluctably from the model.

This modeling strategy has a number of benefits, as Snidal (chap. 10, this vol.) also points out. The assumptions are generally made clear. One knows who the main actors are, what their preferences are, what strategies are available to them, when each of the players can make a move, and what information (and beliefs) they possess at each point in time. These provide an understanding of the microfoundations of behavior in complex situations. That is, we can connect the outcome to the behavior of each actor when interacting with the others. Having clearly stated assumptions is very important because all of the model's results follow ineluctably from these. Furthermore, the assumptions are of vital importance in making progress in research. If the assumptions used are known, then others can change those assumptions one-by-one and see how they change the results. Such a process enhances the cumulative growth of our understanding about a topic. Relaxing the assumptions of simple models is a way of creating ever more complex ones, which may better explain the behavior of actors.

If rational choice theory has numerous critics, formalization of such models probably has even more. In a series of exchanges between Stephen Walt (1999) and others ("Formal Methods, Formal Complaints") in *International Security* (1999), the issues raised by formal modeling in international relations were clearly evidenced. What are the main drawbacks to such modeling? Formalism as a word connotes the problem. The implication is that formalization makes analysis harder without adding any content. It cuts off those who do not speak the language of mathematics or logic from the analysis, even when, it is claimed, such a result is not necessary. The argument is that the exact same claims could be made without formalization. This is undoubtedly true—all mathematics can be translated into ordinary language—but one does face at least two problems in doing so: increasing imprecision and loss of deductive power.

Formalization in rational choice theory means providing an exact statement of who the actors are, what their preferences and payoffs are, what moves are available to them, and what information and beliefs they possess at each stage of the game. Moving away from this explicit formulation allows for a great deal of slippage in the definition of these attributes of the actors. Of course, such exact knowledge is uncommon in everyday life, but it is useful to theorists since it allows them to deduce specifically how (small) changes in these attributes affect each actor's behavior and the outcome. Furthermore, the use of words instead of formal models means that the analyst has lost an important check on the deductive rigor of the claims made. It is much harder to check independently the logical consistency of the claims, and one is left more at the mercy of the analyst to ensure that all propositions flow logically from the implicit assumptions. If, as Bueno de Mesquita and Morrow argue (1999, 56), logical consistency must be prior to originality and empirical accuracy, then formalization is of obvious benefit.

The other main criticism of formalization in rational choice is that it produces unoriginal as well as untestable results. It is hard to understand why formalization in this area necessarily must produce unoriginal claims. Whether the knowledge gained from rational choice models is novel or not has little to do with the technique and more to do with the theorists using it. And of course originality is a very hard claim to make; most ideas can be found to have originated elsewhere if one looks hard enough. As for the lack of testability, this is sometimes claimed to be inherent to the method. Green and Shapiro come closest to making this position: "The weaknesses of rational choice scholarship are rooted in the characteristic aspiration of rational choice theorists to come up with universal theories of politics. This aspiration leads many rational choice theorists to pursue even more subtle forms of theory elaboration, with little attention to how these theories might be operationalized and tested. . . . Collectively, the methodological defects of rational choice theorizing . . . generate and reinforce a debilitating syndrome in which theories are elaborated and modified in order to save their universal character, rather than by reference to the requirements of viable empirical testing" (1994, 6).

Later, however, the authors are more sanguine when they note that there is nothing inherent in rational choice theory that makes it victim to these defects; rather they seem to imply that they are the fault of the political science practitioners of the theory (196). Given that economics is the primary domain using rational choice theory and that it does much empirical research, it seems difficult to conclude that any lack of testable results derive from the method itself. In any case, in the following pages I survey several research areas in IPE that use rational choice theory—especially formal models—and examine whether this research has produced anything useful or whether it has fallen prey to the defects of incomprehensibility, unoriginality, and/or untestability that its critics aver.

Formal Modeling in IPE: Three Prominent Areas of Research

To make this task manageable, I have chosen three areas in IPE that have been prominent in the use of rational choice theory and formal models. These three areas, hegemonic stability theory, foreign economic policy-making, and international economic cooperation, have contributed importantly to the field as well. Most of the work in these areas, however, has been informal rational choice; only recently has the research in any of them been presented in formal models. The question I ask of each of them is whether they have contributed to IPE and what strengths and weaknesses they display given the methods used.

1. Hegemonic stability theory (HST) has employed rational choice models to show why the most powerful country in the world, the so-called hegemon, and other less powerful states, its "followers," might indeed construct an open trading system. Kindleberger's (1973) early insight was that an open and stable international trading system was a public good that required a single actor to play the role of stabilizer. This argument was developed further by Krasner (1976), who proposed an informal rational choice account of the hegemon's role. Krasner deduced the hegemon's preferences for free trade from its international position and showed why other states might support it in creating an open trading system.

Hegemonic stability theory was vigorously attacked throughout the 1980s and early 1990s. These attacks were both theoretical and empirical. Theoretically, the logic of the theory seemed questionable on at least three points. First, it was unclear whether the hegemon should prefer free trade; optimal tariff theory suggested that the hegemon should actually prefer some level of closure (e.g., Conybeare 1984). The second point challenged the role of the other states. It was unclear both why other states would go along with the hegemon if free trade was not in their interest and why the hegemon would bother to sanction them if they didn't follow its lead (e.g., Stein 1984). That is, the logic of why countries other than the hegemon pursued openness was not clear. Finally, the logic connecting the necessity for one stabilizer, instead of a small group ("k group"), was challenged (e.g., Snidal 1985). Failure to formalize the arguments in HST was part of the problem. No clear, consistent logic was ever established connecting the states' preferences and behavior to the creation and maintenance of an open international trading system. The use of formal models to criticize the theory was important for making progress in the field.

More recent research has tried to be more conscious of these issues and more systematic. Lake (1988) focused greatly on the hegemon's preferences and on the behavior of the other states. He wanted to show the conditions under which openness would result given different distributions of international capabilities. His research, although never formalized, showed that hegemons were not necessary for openness, but it never resolved the other issues. Gowa's response (1994) to the criticisms of HST was to move closer to formalization, using various game-theoretic ideas from the economics of industrial organization. While providing some support for the theory, her research ultimately undermined it. She showed that hegemons were not really hegemonic but actually part of the larger balance of power and that polarity in this larger balance was more important than hegemony for openness.

Finally, Pahre (1999) has produced the most formal model of HST. He shows that leadership by one country does matter, but depending on whether the leader is malevolent or benevolent it will have different effects. Yet in the end many of the same issues as in earlier studies of HST remain open. The one result that seems to stand up well is that a hegemon is neither necessary nor sufficient for an open trading system. The other major issues remain unresolved. The hegemon's preferences for free trade have never been completely established; the definition of the hegemon has never been clarified; and the hegemon's strategic interaction with the other states, except in Pahre's Stackleberg leadership model, has never been rigorously deduced in a formal model.

While some of the issues in this debate—especially the conceptual ones, like defining hegemony—would not be any clearer with the use of formal models, a number of the issues could have been clarified long ago if formalization had been employed. As Gowa (1994) has hinted, models could have been produced to show under what conditions the hegemon would prefer free trade. Moreover, as Lake and Pahre have adumbrated, modeling the strategic interaction among the major states to show when an open trading system would have been in all their interests is an important result. Thus, although some issues in this debate could not be advanced by the use of formal models, a number of them could be and were, as Snidal's research on k groups demonstrated. By and large such models remain to be devised, but seem unlikely to be, given the loss of interest in the theory (Keohane 1998). Interestingly, research in the security studies area on power transition theory, which shares much common ground with HST in asserting that stability results from hegemonic dominance of the system, has produced more formal rational choice research and seems more vibrant these days (e.g., DiCicco and Levy 2003).

2.   Attempts to explain foreign economic policy have also turned to rational choice models. In the areas of trade and monetary policy especially, scholars have used various economic models, all based on the rationality assumption, to predict actors' policy preferences. Most of these models, however, have been informal rational choice ones; they have not systematically formalized the logic behind the claims made. But since many of these claims rest on well-known economic theories, which have been extensively formalized, the results seem more robust. Unlike HST, a clear and consistent logic connecting the actors to the policies has been developed for many of these arguments. A chain of logic links actors' incomes to their policy preferences. Policies that lead to a gain in income are favored; ones that lead to a loss are opposed. Economic theory in the trade and monetary areas sets out which types of actors gain from which types of policies.

The clearest example of this is in the trade area. Here the classic results of international trade theory, by Heckscher and Ohlin, Stolper and Samuelson, and Ricardo and Viner, provide the logical underpinnings for the deduction of actors' policy preferences. The way in which a trade policy (re)distributes income is the central factor used to predict which groups should favor or oppose a policy. These deductive economic models tell us how political divisions over the political economy of trade policy will be structured.

The key point of contention between these models has been between so-called factoral models based on the Stolper-Samuelson theorem versus the sectoral or firm-based theories of preferences resting on the Ricardo-Viner model. In both cases, preferences are deduced as a result of the changes in income that accrue to different actors when policy changes from free trade to protection or vice versa. The main difference between these two sets of models is in the character of the groups that they identify as the central actors. Models based on Heckscher-Ohlin and Stolper-Samuelson theorems, so-called factoral models, predict that the main groups vying over trade policy are determined by their economic endowments of labor (skilled or unskilled), land, and capital. Actors possessing mainly labor, for example, will form a group demanding particular trade policies; similarities in factor endowments lead to similar trade preferences. Models based on Ricardo-Viner, so-called sectoral models, identify different groups. Here it is the industry in which a factor is employed that determines its preferences over trade. Agents with capital or labor who are employed in the same industry will have similar trade preferences, even though their endowments differ.

Factoral theories rely on the Stolper-Samuelson theorem, which shows that when factors of production, like labor and capital, can move freely among sectors, a change from free trade to protection will raise the income of factors in which a country is relatively scarce and lower it for factors that are relatively abundant. Thus scarce factors will support protection, while abundant ones will oppose it. Rogowski (1989) has developed one of the most interesting political extensions of this, claiming that increasing exposure to trade sets off either increasing class conflict or urban-rural conflict according to the factor endowments of different countries.

In contrast, sectoral and firm-based theories of trade preferences follow from the Ricardo-Viner (specific factors) model of trade. In that model, at least one factor is immobile, so factors attached to import-competing sectors lose from trade liberalization, while those in export-oriented sectors gain. Conflict over trade policy thus pits labor, capital, and landowners in particular sectors besieged by imports against those sectors who export their production (e.g., Milner 1988; Frieden 1990). How tied factors are to their sectors—that is, their degree of factor specificity—is the key difference between these two models (Alt et al. 1996).

The arguments behind these two theories have been well-developed, in large part because of the formalization of the central theorems they are based on. Each has a slightly different, yet clear set of microfoundations. The theories have been shown to produce distinct testable hypotheses (e.g., Magee, Brock, and Young 1989). A number of studies have tested these two models, sometimes singly and sometimes simultaneously. Irwin

(1996), Magee, Brock, and Young (1989), Milner (1988), and Frieden (1990) have found evidence in support of the specific factors model; in contrast, Beaulieu (1996), Balestreri (1997), Rogowski (1989), and Scheve and Slaughter (1998) find support for the Stolper-Samuelson factoral models. Because these arguments about trade preferences rest on formal deductive models, researchers have been able to develop clear models of the political economy of trade and to devise and test hypotheses about them. Thus while scholars have not solved the problem of the political economy of trade, they have made progress in defining the theories and developing testable implications.

In the monetary area, research on preferences and policy choices has been less strong because the models here are less formal. In part, the economic models used provide less clear deductive predictions about the effects of monetary policy (Gowa 1988; Giovannini 1993). Frieden (1991), Simmons (1994), and Leblang (1999) have produced some of the most rigorous informal rational choice models of the political economy of monetary and exchange rate policy. Their theories have tried to show which groups and governments would prefer what types of exchange rate regimes and what levels of exchange rates. Each of the models focuses on a different factor, however, making competing tests difficult. Nonetheless, Frieden's attention to interest groups, Simmons's focus on government partisanship and stability, and Leblang's concern with electoral and party systems all provide clear hypotheses about the political economy of monetary policy. This is an area again where most research by political scientists is informal rational choice, and where some of the debates could be advanced by the use of more formal models.

3. Finally, research on international economic institutions and cooperation has employed rational choice theory widely to explore the conditions under which institutions might matter and those under which economic cooperation is most likely to emerge. A number of the seminal works here have either depended upon or used formal models to develop their central insights. Scholars have turned to many different sources to establish the microfoundations of their arguments in this area; hence it is not as unified as in trade, but it offers a number of clear and consistent arguments that make it more progressive than in hegemonic stability theory.

Axelrod's *The Evolution of Cooperation* (1984) expanded upon formal and experimental models showing the utility of tit-for-tat strategies in strategic games. Keohane's *After Hegemony* (1984) relied upon formal models in economics (e.g., the Coase theorem which argues that when transaction costs are high, efficient exchanges are less likely to occur) to show why international institutions that help lower transaction costs might be in states' interests to create and obey. Downs and Rocke (1995) show in a formal model why institutions for promoting trade cooperation may well need to be weak if they are to be effective; Rosendorff and Milner (2000) similarly argue that building escape clauses into international trade agreements may make them more durable over time and hence better at promoting cooperation.

Milner (1997) and Milner and Rosendorff (1996, 1997) have used formal models to demonstrate the conditions under which international cooperation is likely to emerge if domestic politics is important. Their formal two-level games show the precise way in which strategic interaction at the domestic level may affect bargaining at the international one. In the highly complex two-level game area, early formalization has led to a deepening understanding (e.g., Iida 1993b, 1993a; Mo 1994, 1995). Informally deducing the optimal behavior of players in two-level games with incomplete information is a very difficult task; only by breaking down the complicated games into manageable and simplified formal models has progress in pinning down testable hypotheses been made. For instance, the circumstances under which one might expect the Schelling conjecture, which argues that domestic divisions provide international bargaining influence, to hold have been slowly identified.

In all of these cases and others, reliance on the findings of deductive models or use of deductive modeling has produced clear and consistent microfoundations for claims about the sources of international institutions and economic cooperation. In some instances they have also produced testable claims. For instance, Axelrod's work (1984) suggests that reciprocity strategies should produce more durable cooperation than other strategies. Keohane (1984) suggests that areas rich (poor) in information should have less (more) need of international institutions. And Milner and Rosendorff (1996, 1997) suggest that more divisions in domestic politics should make cooperation harder to achieve, but incomplete information need not always impede cooperation. Whether any of these claims are novel is always debatable, but they are empirically testable. In many ways formalization of the arguments in the area of international economic cooperation seems to have proceeded the furthest.

This survey of three important areas of research in IPE seems to suggest that (1) most rational choice research in IPE is informal, (2) formalization can at times help clarify the logic and establish firm microfoundations for arguments, and (3) rational choice theory in IPE has produced testable hypotheses that seem original to some scholars.

Rational Choice in IPE and Security Studies

From a cursory examination of the two fields, it seems that security studies has generally been more ready to use formal rational choice models than has IPE (e.g., Kydd, chap. 14, this vol.). For example, among the leading journals in security studies, the *Journal of Conflict Resolution* has long been a major outlet for formal work in the field. In IPE none of the leading journals publishes much formal research; only recently have *World Politics* and *International Organization* begun publishing such research.[5] This is surprising given the close links of IPE to economics. Why has the field of IPE been less likely to employ formal modeling than security studies?

One argument that has been advanced is that the subfield of security studies has an easier time doing formal work because it can focus on two-player games, which are well known and easier to solve. Many security issues can be broken down into contests between two states, who are conceived of as unitary rational actors (or at least the claim is that this is how relations among states in the security field have been treated generally). In the field both the assumption that the state can be conceived as unitary (and hence that domestic politics can be ignored) and that bilateral relations are most important have been commonly accepted. The contrast is made with IPE in which modeling interaction among states as a two-player game is more problematic. This is probably also true of at least two of the areas surveyed earlier where the system involves more than two states. In HST and in models of economic policy-making, rarely can the game be simplified to a two-player one; HST demands that interaction between the hegemon and its followers as well as among the followers themselves be incorporated so that collective action problems can be studied, and economic policy-making studies usually also find that multiple interest groups as well as state actors matter. In contrast, a number of IPE studies of the role of economic statecraft are framed in terms of two states interacting (e.g., Drezner 1999; of course, as Martin 1992 shows, such games may be incomplete). In sum, the multiplicity of states and greater importance of domestic political actors besides the state in the IPE area make modeling less likely since they make it much harder. However, whether security studies benefit from the use of such simple, two-player models remains to be seen. Whether robust and valid testable hypotheses can be deduced from such models is questionable; when multiple actors are added to such models the results often change (e.g., Bueno de Mesquita and Lalman 1992; Niou, Ordeshook, and Rose 1989).

A more fundamental difference between the two fields, I argue, has been the much greater acknowledgment of the importance of strategic interaction in the security field. Much research in this area begins with the idea that the ability of states to realize their goals depends on the behavior of other states. From the earliest work on deterrence theory in the 1950s onward, many scholars in security studies have accepted this central premise. Of course, it implies that for any state to calculate its best strategy or policy choice it must first try to understand other states' likely behavior. Improving one's security, for example, depends not just on one's own strategy but also on the behavior of other states. Deterring conflict also means that each state has to take into account other states' behavior if it wants to be successful. Such attention to strategic interaction has been less apparent in IPE.

This neglect seems to result from at least two factors. First, much of IPE rested on neoclassical economics, which assumed perfect markets and hence avoided issues of strategic interaction. No firm was large enough to exert any influence on prices within the market. In this framework, for instance, free trade was the best policy choice no matter what others chose. With the move of economics away from such perfect competition models, strategic interaction has become far more important in economics, as the debate over strategic trade policy makes evident. Perhaps IPE will follow this evolution.

Second, research in parts of IPE has roots in comparative politics, where strategic interaction—especially among states—has not been central. The research, in particular on foreign economic policy-making, has avoided concerns about strategic interaction because of its comparative focus. The view of policy-making was often one that privileged either the state or interest groups but never the strategic interaction between them, or between them and players in other states, as Milner (1998) argues. However, as strategic interaction models have become more important in comparative politics (e.g., Tsebelis 1990, 1995; Baron and Ferejohn 1989;

Huber 1997), one might expect more attention to this in IPE as well. Thus the tight links between IPE and both economics and comparative politics have contributed to the inattention paid in the past to strategic situations.

This inattention to strategic interaction is apparent in the three areas of IPE research previously discussed. As noted, one of HST's worst problems has been how to deal with the interaction between the hegemon and other states. Why and when states would follow the hegemon are questions that plague the theory. Moreover, conceiving of the hegemon as a state with such power that it alone can shape the system once again turns attention away from strategic interaction. In the trade and monetary policy areas, there has been a notable lack of attention to strategic interaction as well. Theories about the preferences of domestic groups rarely, if ever, discuss how interactions among these groups or among these groups and the government might matter (Milner 1998).[6] But clearly in other areas where interest groups interact scholars have modeled their behavior strategically (e.g., Austen-Smith and Wright 1992, 1994). Research on the state as an actor in policy-making has also not tended to see it as a strategic player either domestically or internationally. The strong-weak state argument was not at all strategic, for instance. More recent work has added a greater strategic angle to the field (e.g., domestically, see Lohmann and O'Halloran 1994; internationally, see Gawande and Hansen 1999). In the international economic cooperation area the lack of strategic interaction has been less of an issue. The greater use of game theory here has been accompanied by more attention to strategic issues, notably in Axelrod (1984) and Downs and Rocke (1995). Nevertheless, much research in international economic cooperation and institutions often fails to adopt a strategic perspective (see, for example, the regime volume of *International Organization* from 1982).

In addition to the lack of attention to strategic interaction, the IPE field has focused less on problems of incomplete information and the credibility issues thus raised. In security studies these issues have been at the center of the field's attention for many years (e.g., Schelling 1960; Jervis 1989). The credibility of threats (and promises) has been a critical issue, as was the concern about defection or reneging in the future due to time inconsistency problems. Indeed, as Fearon (1995) recently showed for rationalist theories of war, the problem of incomplete information is the central one. When states are involved in strategic interaction and they face incomplete information about the other states or about the environment, the situation becomes highly complex and ripe for war.

Under these circumstances, figuring out a state's optimal strategy requires careful attention to the possible actions and beliefs of the other states. As the security field has shown, these complex situations can be handled well through rigorous formalization. When strategic interaction is combined with incomplete information, especially in dynamic situations, it can be very helpful to formalize the game being played, because otherwise it is difficult to unravel the logic behind the players' moves. Formalization allows one to untangle these complex situations and deduce the best strategies for the players in a clear and precise way. Since IPE scholars rarely try to understand the field in terms of such complexity, they may feel less need for formalization. But it is likely that strategic interaction and incomplete information are as important in the field of political economy as in security. IPE scholarship has begun to take these issues more seriously, and future research may thus be more drawn to formal modeling as it becomes increasingly attentive to these complex environments.

Conclusion: The Strengths and Weaknesses of Formal Modeling in IPE

Rational choice theory is a prominent form of analysis in IPE. One reason for this is the field's close relationship to economics. But rational choice models in the field have tended to be informal ones. This has had both costs and benefits for the field. The benefits are that much of the research has remained very accessible and that divisions around epistemological issues have been less vitriolic than in security studies. The costs have included a lack of tightly reasoned logical arguments and an inattention to behavior in complex situations of strategic interaction and incomplete information. Do these costs outweigh the benefits of an informal rational choice approach? It is certainly not necessary that formalization lead to inaccessibility. Formal models should be combined with verbal explanations that are as easily readable as informal rational choice approaches. On the other hand, it seems likely that gaining a better understanding of actors' behavior in increasingly complex environments will propel scholars to formalize their claims. IPE in particular could benefit from greater attention to these complex situations.

Must the use of rational choice theory and formalization render research unoriginal and untestable? If the formal research in IPE is any guide to this, then the initial answer is no. HST, the importance of reciprocity, and two-level bargaining games all suggest that interesting ideas can be produced with rational choice models and that testable hypotheses can be devised. Beth Simmons's award-winning book (1994) *Who Adjusts?* is also a testament to the way that informal rational choice theory in the field has generated very interesting and testable ideas.

A failure to develop formal rational choice models may also hamper the integration of IPE with international economics. Indeed, many economists are now working on topics that once were the domain of political scientists. The work of Grossman and Helpman (1994, 1995) on the politics of trade policy is one example; others are the studies by Bagwell and Staiger (1999) on the role of international institutions in trade and the impact of domestic politics. If scholars in IPE who use rational choice desire to communicate with or have an impact upon the expanding work by economists, then formalization of their models will certainly help.

The field of IPE has always been a broad field. Many methodological approaches will be part of the field. But for those scholars who employ rationalist models the move to formalization is an important one. It will provide much greater integration with economists who are now working on very similar issues. This move should not be done in a way that cuts off this part of the field from other approaches. The use of mathematical models does not obviate the need for scholars to treat interesting and important questions, to write clearly in words, and to devise hypotheses and ultimately test their claims.

Suggested Readings

Downs, G., and D. Rocke. 1995. *Optimal Imperfection: Domestic Uncertainty and Institutions in International Relations.* Princeton: Princeton University Press.

Martin, L. L. 1992. *Coercive Cooperation: Explaining Multilateral Economic Sanctions.* Princeton: Princeton University Press.

Milner, H. V. 1997. *Interests, Institutions, and Information: Domestic Politics and International Relations.* Princeton: Princeton University Press.

Rogowski, R. 1989. *Commerce and Coalitions.* Princeton: Princeton University Press.

Simmons, B. 1994. *Who Adjusts?* Princeton: Princeton University Press.

Notes

I wish to thank David Baldwin, James Fearon, Detlef Sprinz, and Yael Wolin-sky-Nahmias for their helpful comments.

1. Whether political science departments in other areas of the world, such as Asia or Russia, have established IPE positions and research centers would be an interesting question to address.

2. I would also not define the field in such a way that the research methodology used determines whether it is IPE. That is, just because a study employs rational choice (formal or not) or quantitative analysis does not mean it is automatically IPE.

3. The initial issues of the *Review of International Political Economy* (1994) lay this spectrum out forthrightly. A more recent article seems to open up the field even more; Amoore et al. (2000) desire to not only include history but also large epistemological concerns as part of IPE.

4. This involves using the Harsanyi doctrine about common prior beliefs as well.

5. *International Organization* recently reported that about 8 percent of its published articles (or 6 of 73) from winter 1997 until summer 2000 involved formal models. Of these none were in IPE and 4 (of 22) were in security studies.

6. Grossman and Helpman (1994) do show how group interactions affect outcomes. If all groups are organized to lobby for protection, there will be none!

References

Alt, J., J. Freiden, M. Gilligan, D. Rodrik, and R. Rogowski. 1996. The Political Economy of International Trade. *Comparative Political Studies* 29:689–717.

Amoore, L., R. Dodgson, R. Germain, B. Gills, P. Langley, and I. Watson. 2000. Paths to a Historicized International Political Economy. *Review of International Political Economy* 7 (1): 53–71.

Austen-Smith, D., and J. Wright. 1992. Competitive Lobbying for a Legislator's Vote. *Social Choice and Welfare* 9:229–57.

———. 1994. Counteractive Lobbying. *American Journal of Political Science* 38:25–44.

Axelrod, R. 1984. *The Evolution of Cooperation.* New York: Basic Books.

Bagwell, K., and R. Staiger. 1999. Domestic Policies, National Sovereignty, and International Economic Institutions. NBER Working Paper #7293.

Baldwin, D. 1985. *Economic Statecraft.* Princeton: Princeton University Press.

Models, Numbers, and Cases

Balestreri, E. 1997. The Performance of the Heckscher-Ohlin-Vanek Model in Predicting Endogenous Policy Forces at the Individual Level. *Canadian Journal of Economics* 30:1–17.

Baron, D., and J. Ferejohn. 1989. Bargaining in Legislatures. *American Political Science Review* 83:1181–1206.

Beaulieu, E. 1996. Who Supported the Canada-US Free Trade Agreement? Manuscript, Columbia University.

Bueno de Mesquita, B., and D. Lalman. 1992. *War and Reason: Domestic and International Imperatives.* New Haven: Yale University Press.

Bueno de Mesquita, B., and J. D. Morrow. 1999. Sorting through the Wealth of Nations. *International Security* 24:56–73.

Caporaso, J. E. 1978. Dependence and Dependency in the Global System. *International Studies Quarterly* 32 (1). Special issue.

Cardoso, F. H., and E. Faletto. 1979. *Dependency and Development in Latin America.* Berkeley: University of California Press.

Coleman, J., and T. Fararo, eds. 1992. *Rational Choice Theory: Advocacy and Critique.* Newbury Park, CA: Sage.

Conybeare, J. 1984. Public Goods, Prisoners' Dilemma, and the International Political Economy. *International Studies Quarterly* 28:5–22.

DiCicco, J., and J. Levy. 2003. The Power Transition Research Program. In *Progress in International Relations Theory,* edited by C. Elman and M. F. Elman. Cambridge: MIT Press.

Downs, G., and D. Rocke. 1995. *Optimal Imperfection: Domestic Uncertainty and Institutions in International Relations.* Princeton: Princeton University Press.

Drezner, D. 1999. *The Sanctions Paradox.* New York: Cambridge University Press.

Elster, J., ed. 1986. *Rational Choice.* New York: New York University Press.

Fearon, J. D. 1995. Rationalist Explanations for War. *International Organization* 49:379–414.

Frieden, J. A. 1990. *Debt, Development, and Democracy.* Princeton: Princeton University Press.

———. 1991. Invested Interests: The Politics of National Economic Policies in a World of Global Finance. *International Organization* 45:425–51.

Garrett, G. 1998. *Partisan Politics in the Global Economy.* New York: Cambridge University Press.

Gawande, K., and W. Hansen. 1999. Retaliation, Bargaining, and the Pursuit of "Free and Fair" Trade. *International Organization* 53 (1): 117–60.

Gilpin, R. 1975. *US Power and the Multinational Corporation.* New York: Basic Books.

———. 1987. *The Political Economy of International Relations.* Princeton: Princeton University Press.

Giovannini, A. 1993. Economic and Monetary Union: What Happened? Exploring the Political Dimensions of Optimal Currency Areas. In *The Monetary Future of Europe,* edited by G. de la Dehesa, A. Giovannini, M. Guitián, and R. Portes. London: C.E.P.R.

Gowa, J. 1988. Public Goods and Political Institutions. *International Organization* 42 (winter): 15–32.

———. 1994. *Allies, Adversaries, and International Trade.* Princeton: Princeton University Press.

Green, D. P., and I. Shapiro. 1994. *Pathologies of Rational Choice Theory: A Critique of Applications in Political Science.* New Haven: Yale University Press.

Grossman, G., and E. Helpman. 1994. Protection for Sale. *American Economic Review* 84:833–50.

———. 1995. The Politics of Free Trade Agreements. *American Economic Review* 85:667–90.

Gruber, L. 2000. *Ruling the World: Power Politics and the Rise of Supranational Institutions.* Princeton: Princeton University Press.

Haggard, S. 1990. *Pathways from the Periphery.* Ithaca: Cornell University Press.

Haggard, S., and R. Kaufman. 1995. *The Political Economy of Democratic Transitions.* Princeton: Princeton University Press.

Hellman, J. 1998. Winners Take All: The Politics of Partial Reform in Postcommunist Transitions. *World Politics* 50 (2): 203–34.

Hirschman, A. 1945. *National Power and the Structure of Foreign Trade.* Berkeley: University of California Press.

Huber, J. 1997. *Rationalizing Parliament.* Cambridge: Cambridge University Press.

Iida, K. 1993a. Analytic Uncertainty and International Cooperation: Theory and Application to International Economic Coordination. *International Studies Quarterly* 37:431–57.

———. 1993b. When and How Do Domestic Constraints Matter? Uncertainty in International Relations. *Journal of Conflict Resolution* 37 (3): 403–26.

Irwin, D. A. 1996. Industry or Class Cleavages over Trade Policy? In *The Political Economy of Trade Policy,* edited by R. C. Feenstra, G. M. Grossman, and D.A. Irwin. Cambridge: MIT Press.

Jervis, R. 1989 [1970]. *The Logic of Images.* New York: Columbia University Press.

Katzenstein, P., ed. 1978. *Between Power and Plenty.* Madison: University of Wisconsin Press.

Katzenstein, P. 1985. *Small States in World Markets.* Ithaca: Cornell University Press.

Keohane, R. O. 1984. *After Hegemony: Cooperation and Discord in the World Political Economy.* Princeton: Princeton University Press.

———. 1998. Problem Lucidity: Stephen Krasner's "State Power and the Structure of International Trade." *World Politics* 50:150–70.

Keohane, R. O., and H. V. Milner, eds. 1996. *Internationalization and Domestic Politics.* Cambridge: Cambridge University Press.

Keohane, R., and J. Nye. 1977. *Power and Interdependence.* Boston: Little, Brown.

Kindleberger, C. P. 1973. *The World in Depression, 1929–1939.* Berkeley: University of California Press.

Kirschner, J. 1995. *Currency and Coercion.* Princeton: Princeton University Press.

Krasner, S. D. 1976. State Power and the Structure of Foreign Trade. *World Politics* 28:317–47.

———. 1978. *Defending the National Interest.* Princeton: Princeton University Press.

Lake, D. 1988. *Power, Protection, and Free Trade.* Ithaca: Cornell University Press.

Leblang, D. 1999. Domestic Political Institutions and Exchange Rate Commitments in the Developing World. *International Studies Quarterly* 43:599–620.

Lohmann, S., and S. O'Halloran. 1994. Divided Government and US Trade Policy. *International Organization* 48:595–632.

Magee, S., W. Brock, and L. Young. 1989. *Black Hole Tariffs and Endogenous Policy Theory.* New York: Cambridge University Press.

Martin, L. L. 1992. *Coercive Cooperation: Explaining Multilateral Economic Sanctions.* Princeton: Princeton University Press.

Milner, H. V. 1988. *Resisting Protectionism.* Princeton: Princeton University Press.

———. 1997. *Interests, Institutions, and Information: Domestic Politics and International Relations.* Princeton: Princeton University Press.

———. 1998. Rationalizing Politics: The Emerging Synthesis of International, American, and Comparative Politics. *International Organization* 52 (4): 759–86.

Milner, H. V., and B. P. Rosendorff. 1996. Trade Negotiations, Information, and Domestic Politics. *Economics and Politics* 8:145–89.

———. 1997. Democratic Politics and International Trade Negotiations: Elections and Divided Government as Constraints on Trade Liberalization. *Journal of Conflict Resolution* 41:117–46.

Mo, J. 1994. The Logic of Two Level Games with Endogenous Domestic Coalitions. *Journal of Conflict Resolution* 38:402–22.

———. 1995. Domestic Institutions and International Bargaining: The Role of Agent Veto in Two-Level Games. *American Political Science Review* 89:914–24.

Morrow, J. D. 1994. *Game Theory for Political Scientists.* Princeton: Princeton University Press.

Morse, E. 1976. *Modernization and the Transformation of International Relations.* New York: Free Press.

Niou, E. M. S., P. C. Ordeshook, and G. F. Rose. 1989. *The Balance of Power: Stability in International Systems.* Cambridge: Cambridge University Press.

North, D., and R. Thomas. 1973. *The Rise of the Western World.* New York: Cambridge University Press.

Pahre, R. 1999. *Leading Questions: How Hegemony Affects the International Political Economy.* Ann Arbor: University of Michigan Press.

Papayoanou, P. 1999. *Power Ties: Economic Interdependence, Balancing, and War.* Ann Arbor: University of Michigan Press.

Przeworski, A. 1991. *Democracy and the Market: Political and Economic Reforms in Eastern Europe and Latin America.* New York: Cambridge University Press.

Rogowski, R. 1989. *Commerce and Coalitions.* Princeton: Princeton University Press.

Rosendorff, B. P., and H. V. Milner. 2001. The Optimal Design of International Trade Institutions: Uncertainty and Escape. *International Organization* 55: 829–58.

Schelling, T. 1960. *The Strategy of Conflict.* Cambridge: Harvard University Press.

Scheve, K., and M. Slaughter. 1998. What Determines Individual Trade Policy Preferences? National Bureau of Economic Research working paper no. 6531.

Shafer, M. 1994. *Winners and Losers.* Ithaca: Cornell University Press.

Simmons, B. 1994. *Who Adjusts?* Princeton: Princeton University Press.

Simon, H. 1976. *Administrative Behavior.* New York: Free Press.

Snidal, D. 1985. The Limits of Hegemonic Stability Theory. *International Organization* 39:579–614.

Stein, A. 1984. The Hegemon's Dilemma. *International Organization* 38:355–86.

Tilly, C. 1990. *Coercion, Capital, and European States.* Cambridge: Blackwell.

Tsebelis, G. 1990. *Nested Games.* Berkeley: University of California Press.

———. 1995. Decision Making in Political Systems: Veto Players in Presidentialism, Parliamentarianism, Multicameralism, and Multipartyism. *British Journal of Political Science* 25:289–325.

Wade, R. 1990. *Governing the Market.* Princeton: Princeton University Press.

Wallerstein, I. M. 1974. *The Modern World System.* Vol. 1. New York: Academic Press.

Walt, S. M. 1999. Rigor or Rigor Mortis? Rational Choice and Security Studies. *International Security* 23:5–48; see also the responses, Formal Methods, Formal Complaints. 24 (2): 56–130.

12. Consumption, Production, and Markets: Applications of Microeconomics to International Politics

John A. C. Conybeare

Deriving from the Greek word *mikros* (small), microeconomics explains the decisions of individuals and organizations to produce, consume, and exchange goods, services, and factors of production (i.e., resources or inputs). The general goal is to yield a prediction of how supply and demand interact to yield a price and quantity that are in equilibrium, or have no endogenous tendency to change. Microeconomics covers the most basic choices (e.g., whether an individual prefers apples or oranges) and more complex aggregations of behaviors (such as how OPEC attempts to set oil production so as to maximize its profits). Macroeconomics examines variables at the level of the nation, including unemployment, inflation, and the balance of payments. In recent decades microeconomics has extended into less tangible areas of human behavior, partly in response to a questioning of the common assumptions of simple microeconomics (for example, issues of how much information people will seek to acquire and what incentives they have to act in ways that are productive and efficient).

Apart from explaining how individuals, groups, and firms behave, microeconomics may be used for prescribing behaviors for individuals and organizations (e.g., cost-benefit calculations) and for society as a whole, the latter constituting the field of "welfare economics." Microeconomics also extends into the role of government in taxing, spending, and regulating the behavior of individual economic units. In recent years game theory has sometimes been considered part of microeconomics (Kreps 1990), though I will not do so here. Readers interested in an accessible introduction to microeconomics are referred to Pindyck and Rubinfeld (1989) and Varian (1987).

Before moving to applications of microeconomic reasoning to international politics, it would be prudent to note some of the often unstated assumptions of microeconomics, which are problematic even within the confines of purely economic activity, but especially so when extended to international politics. Microeconomics assumes that people make rational choices, though not necessarily with perfect information. This is usually not objectionable, since it implies little more than that people have transitive preferences and do not make perverse selections (e.g., say they prefer A over B and then pick B). Rational choices are normally conducive to increasing technical efficiency (e.g., a firm will combine labor and capital to get a given output at lowest cost), but may well reduce allocative efficiency, the latter being the overall welfare of the relevant group (e.g., free riding on a public good, discussed later, reduces social efficiency but is quite rational for the individual). A more extensive discussion of the value of formal models with assumptions about rational behavior may be found in chapter 10.[1]

More needful of examination are the assumptions about perfectly competitive markets (i.e., many agents, all of whom have complete information) that infuse some areas of microeconomics and have been subject to critical reassessment in recent decades. Transferring metaphors or models of microeconomics to politics often entails some more arguable assumptions not usually examined by economists: the freedom to make contracts, the enforceability of contracts, and the absence of violence as a primary mechanism for allocating resources. Care needs to be taken to ask whether and when we are implicitly and possibly inappropriately transferring those assumptions to applications of the models to international politics.

What types of questions may microeconomic models answer about international politics? Many examples cited here are drawn from international political economy, but microeconomic reasoning may be applied more generally to the entire field of international politics. Most important, microeconomics may help answer explanatory questions. To what extent, for example, might we explain decisions to go to war as being the result of a calculation of the marginal costs and benefits of war? Is the stability of an international political system analogous to a market, and is it a function of the number of major players in that system? The tools of microeconomics are also well suited to prescription. What rules should states have for sharing payoffs of uncertain value when they have differing degrees of risk aversion (such as, for example, OPEC ministers allocating output quotas or states contributing to a joint war effort)? What is the optimal amount of territorial expansion? Can we prescribe international redistributions that all states will regard as fair? Finally, microeconomics may also help with the simpler descriptive task of organizing and classifying information in ways that are helpful for suggesting and testing theories. States may be risk averse or risk acceptant, free riding or net contributors to international cooperation, protectionist or free trading, expansionist or status quo oriented.

Microeconomics encompasses an enormous body of knowledge, and in a survey such as the present essay, I cannot offer more than illustrative examples of how insights from the field may be applied to international relations. Some of its basic concepts, such as utility maximization, are widely used in other formal approaches to social science, such as game theory. The strategy here is that of an introductory text in microeconomics, beginning with the preferences and decisions of individuals and proceeding upward to larger aggregations of units, analogous to firms, industries, and nations. Individuals make decisions about production, consumption, and exchange, and it is often useful to examine the behavior of states as if they were such individuals making choices in markets. Aggregations of states in the international system are analogous to firms in markets, subjected to different types of distributions of market power and strategic (or opportunistic) behavior. Prescriptions for optimal behavior for individuals and firms in markets may be transferable to states in their interactions with each other. Like individuals, states make choices in situations of uncertainty; they possess varying amounts of information and have differing attitudes to risk. Varying our conjectures about such constraints has important implications for predicting the choices made by individuals, firms, and states. Finally, this essay will examine some issues of justice and fairness, not typically the subject of microeconomics, but an area where microeconomics may have useful criteria to offer, particularly as to which distributions of goods may be acceptable to all and which distributions may be welfare enhancing for the group as a whole.

Building Blocks: Utility, Consumption, Production, and Input

Utility and Consumption

Microeconomics starts with the notion of utility: individuals seek to maximize their subjective enjoyment of a good or service, subject to cost constraints. Consider a state that derives utility from territory, perhaps because of the tax value of land. In a two-dimensional space we would measure the payoff value of land on the x axis and utility on the y axis, the utility function represented by a curve, concave to represent diminishing utility from each successive unit of land. If used as an instrument of choice, the model must specify the probability that the payoff will be acquired (and hence the expected utility of the action) and the alternative courses of action with their associated utilities and probabilities.

It was with such a simple representation of state action that Bueno de Mesquita constructed and tested his famous utility-maximizing explanation of why nations go to war. It is possible to make the model quite complex, but its basic form is simple and tautological: a state will go to war if the expected utility (EU)—the product of a probability (pr) and a utility (U)—of going to war is greater than the expected utility of not going to war (presumably the status quo).

EU(war) > U(status quo)

Where EU(war) = pr(win) × U(win) + pr(lose) × U(lose)

The specification poses measurement issues. Bueno de Mesquita computes utility from the similarity of policies with a potential opponent (utility of winning increases with the dissimilarity of policies), and probabilities are assumed to be a function of resources (i.e., more resources increases the probability of winning). A further difficulty with trying to operationalize an expected utility model is that one must specify a utility function in order to transform the quantity or monetary value of the good in question into a measure of cardinal utility. Only when this has been done can one make behavioral predictions. Consider figure 1 below. Expected outcomes are derived from the products of the payoffs from winning (W) or losing (L) and the probabilities of those events. Even though the expected value of the payoff from war, EV(war), is greater than the value of

293

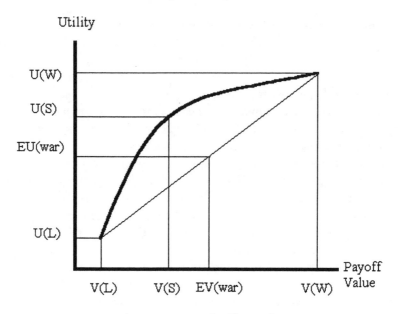

Fig. 1. Expected utility and war

the payoff from the status quo, V(S), the expected utility of war, EU(war), is less than the utility of the status quo, U(S). Hence the state will presumably not initiate this particular war. This apparent paradox is a result of the state being risk averse, manifested in the form of a utility function that is concave to the origin, so that the state prefers a fixed payoff to one that has a greater expected yield but is uncertain. However, in order to make such a prediction one must be able to specify the exact shape of the utility function (fig. 1) and measure the value of the payoffs (in, for example, monetary units) on the x axis and also the probabilities of winning or losing.

Economists rarely attempt to test expected utility models outside of an experimental laboratory setting, but instead use the model to derive testable propositions. Utility functions form the basis for demand curves, which are measurable and testable. We cannot easily measure how much utility a person derives from an orange, but we can easily measure how many oranges people will buy at a given price. Given these problems, Bueno de Mesquita is appropriately cautious in offering his finding that the model explains 85 percent of the decisions of states to initiate war between 1815 and 1980 (1980, 129).[2]

Production

The building blocks of microeconomics are supply and demand. Utility functions allow us to derive demand curves. Predicting equilibrium market prices and quantities requires the specification of supply conditions. Bueno de Mesquita's expected utility theory of war specifies demand conditions but omits supply. The opposite problem occurs in the work of some writers who apply themselves to the supply side. Gilpin (1981) asks why hegemons inevitably decline, and he provides an answer in terms of hypothesized supply conditions: hypothesized because, unlike Bueno de Mesquita, he provides no empirical test for his assertions.

The supply side of microeconomics starts with the question of how producers will combine inputs in order to produce a given output at the lowest cost. A supply curve may then be derived that tells us how much the producer will offer to the market at any price. Supply curves typically slope upward because of the assumption of decreasing returns to scale, or increasing marginal costs (each successive unit costs more to produce), though there may be increasing returns (economics of scale), up to a point. Gilpin (1981) argues that hegemons decline because they expand their control over other states past the point of increasing returns, into the realm of decreasing returns, and so fritter away their national resources with continued expansion for decreasing benefits.

The idea that nations may expand beyond the point of zero net marginal gains is interesting and certainly quite possible, but how does Gilpin know this is true? The fact that some empires have short life spans is hardly evidence of overexpansion. The reasons he gives (e.g., diffusion of technology to other countries, increasing consumption in the home country) are speculative. Furthermore, he assumes a unitary rational actor model, so one might wonder why this unitary actor cannot stop expanding once it reaches the point of optimal size. According to Luttwak (1976), the Romans curtailed expansion when marginal tax revenues exceeded the marginal military cost of holding the territory.

Input

Supply is partly determined (as noted earlier) by the cost of inputs, or factors of production. It is empirically much easier to specify and test models in this area than with, say, utility or returns to scale in production because one does not have to make any assumptions about returns to scale or the shape of utility functions, or the measurement of utility. Two examples may make this clear, both of which focus simply on the supply and demand of factors, such as labor, land, and capital.

North and Thomas (1973) achieve a considerable degree of explanatory power with a simple model of the market for labor. Without making any unsupportable assumptions about market conditions, they provide a persuasive explanation of the rise of the modern world market system. The feudal system was characterized by a shortage of labor, making serfdom a cost-effective way of organizing a labor market. Assuming that the users of labor had the physical power to enforce the system, the costs of serfdom were outweighed by the benefits of holding down the cost of labor in a factor market that would otherwise have bid up free-market wages. Hence the manorial system, with relatively self-contained economic units and little labor mobility, was an efficient economic system for the owners of land, though obviously not to the advantage of labor and not necessarily efficiency-improving for the economy as a whole.

As the population of Europe increased rapidly from the tenth century on, serfdom became less cost effective as free-market wages fell until at some point (impossible but unnecessary to calculate) they would have been below the costs of enforcing serfdom.[3] Rational landowners would then free their serfs and hire them back as wage labor. Former serfs were free to leave the manor, and there were subsequently large population movements, particularly to eastern Europe. Production and trade diversified and increased in value, as did the national incomes of European nations. The ability of free markets to promote growth did depend on the willingness of rulers to arrange property rights in such a way as to allow economic agents to capture a competitive rate of return. This was not always the case, an observation North and Thomas use to explain faster growth in England (parliament breaking down the predatory taxing power of the monarchy) over France (a centralized monarchy retaining inefficient property rights for the venal benefit of the Crown but to the detriment of the nation). By the same logic, serfdom did not disappear in eastern Europe or Russia (1867) until the land/labor ratio decreased to the point that the burdens of enforcing serfdom were not cost effective for the owners of land.

North and Thomas offer a microeconomic explanation for the rise of the modern international system that may provide a more satisfying explanation than that offered by more qualitative arguments, such as that of Wallerstein (1974). The latter works from the opposite end of the level of analysis, explaining the emergence of the modern system as a result of a systemic historical accident: Britain and Holland just happened to diversify out of agriculture into textiles before other nations. These two states then pursued polices designed to marshal national power (e.g., efficient administration, ethnic homogeneity) in a way that allowed them to militarily and economically dominate "peripheral" regions, such as eastern Europe, and use those areas as suppliers of raw materials. Wallerstein's argument leaves more holes than the tight microeconomic explanation of North and Thomas. Aside from the "accidental" diversification of the "core" nations, Wallerstein's theory requires that military strength be associated with diversifying out of agriculture. He has had a hard time explaining why some purely agricultural countries around the sixteenth century were also powerful (e.g., Sweden he describes as a "mild deviant case"!). The contrast between the explanations of North and Thomas (1973) and Wallerstein (1974) is instructive, showing the advantage of the greater theoretical specificity or clarity of microeconomics over a discursive "structural" explanation that dismisses anomalous cases.

Other models based on a characterization of factor markets explain aspects of a country's national policies, also based on the relative scarcity of factors. Consider the famous Heckscher-Ohlin model of trade. International trade is based on differences of costs of production, and Heckscher and Ohlin argued that these differences are based on the comparative advantage conferred by the abundance of specific factors. The United States in the nineteenth century, for example, was a land-abundant country. Hence land was cheap, and the United States had a comparative cost advantage in making products that required large amounts of land (e.g., wheat, tobacco, cotton) and specialized in and exported those products. Western Europe today, on the other hand, has a scarcity of land and labor but an abundance of capital and therefore exports capital-intensive goods.

However, what is good for the abundant factor is bad for the scarce factor, and that factor will be expected to lobby against free trade.

Consider the example of NAFTA. Assume for the sake of simplicity that the United States is capital abundant, Mexico is labor abundant, and two goods may be produced: steel (capital intensive) and textiles (labor intensive). Once trade is opened up, the United States will begin to specialize more in steel, and Mexico in textiles. Labor and capital in the United States will move out of textiles and into steel. Given the capital intensity of steel production, the textile industry will be releasing capital at a lower rate than the steel industry wants to take up capital, and releasing labor at a faster rate than steel wants to hire labor. The factor markets must adjust to equate supply and demand, so the rate of return on capital must rise and wages must fall. Hence one would expect labor in the United States and capital in Mexico to lobby against NAFTA, which is exactly what happened. The Heckscher-Ohlin theorem often provides remarkably accurate predictions about long-term interest group politics in cases where a policy changes the composition of national output.

Rogowski (1989) takes the logic of this argument further, contrasting the effects of expanding and contracting trade on the macropolitics of nations. He argues, for example, that since expanding world trade in the nineteenth century increased the income of the abundant factor in the United States (land), it also enhanced the political power of the free-trade groups, reflected partly in the rise of the populist movement. Conversely, declining trade in the 1930s benefited the scarce factor, providing labor with the resources to lobby for the benefits manifested in the New Deal. Milner (chap. 11, this vol.) further discusses the Heckscher-Ohlin model.

Factor scarcity models have also been used, especially in the past two decades, to predict what kinds of policies politicians will "supply" to the electorate. If, for example, a certain factor gains from free trade, then the owners of this factor will vote for free-trading politicians. These types of models attempt to predict the preferences of the median voter and which policies vote-seeking politicians will offer in order to be elected. One of the earliest and most complete elaborations of this type of model may be found in Magee, Brock, and Young (1989). Factor scarcity explanations were not unknown to more mainstream IR theory; the older "lateral pressure" theories of war (e.g., Choucri and North 1975) include increasing population as one of the factors leading to the geographic expansion of a nation's boundaries.

Markets and Industrial Organization

The applications of microeconomic reasoning discussed thus far have little to say about the structure of markets, with the exception of North and Thomas, who explain the incentives to create a monopsonistic market for labor.[4] Implicit in much of this approach is the assumption that markets are competitive. The Heckscher-Ohlin theory, for example, assumes that factors exist in perfectly competitive markets and are also perfectly mobile (so that, in the NAFTA example, factors in the United States can easily move from textiles into the steel industry). Assumptions about the markets being competitive are not always appropriate.

The familiar concepts of unipolarity, bipolarity, and balance of power implicitly invoke models of industrial organization: monopoly, duopoly, and oligopoly. Hegemonic stability theory (i.e., the argument that hegemony creates free trade, or at least a stable international economic system) assumes that a hegemon has some monopoly of power to unilaterally impose conditions on world markets. Early versions emphasized the belief that free trade would be imposed, and its costs largely paid, by a hegemon. This argument was based on the erroneous belief that free trade is a public good from which the hegemon gets enough benefit that it is willing to maintain it for all. Yet free trade is not a public good (gains from trade are rival in consumption and are easily excludable by, for example, multitiered tariff rates). Even if there are some elements of publicness in free trade, it is far from clear that free trade benefits a hegemon more than predatory trade-taxing policies (see Pahre 1999), such as those employed by OPEC in exercising its hegemonic powers in world oil markets. Snidal (chap. 10, this vol.) notes that one of the most useful outcomes of formal theory is that it can produce predictions that are "surprising." Unfortunately, surprising predictions may also be wrong, and in the case of hegemonic stability theory, the mostly erroneous predictions came from an insufficiently formal elaboration of the theory and its assumptions, a lacuna rectified most recently by Pahre (1999).

The two main examples of hegemons supporting free trade are rare and short-lived (e.g., Britain from the 1840s to World War I, and the United States during the 1950s and 1960s).[5] The proponents of the theory have focused on what Odell (chap. 3, this vol.) gently calls "theory-confirming" cases. Considering a longer sweep of history, it is far more common for hegemons to behave in a predatory fashion when they have control over international markets or military force, as may be seen from a casual observation of the policies of classical Athens, imperial Rome, or Elizabethan England. However, it is possible to suggest conjectures that justify a hegemon preferring an open world economy (see Mansfield, chap. 7, this vol.).

Balance of power models invoke one form of oligopoly model, that in which each firm is primarily concerned with maintaining market share (and its share of the pool of profits) and reducing uncertainty. Hence classical balance of power theory emphasizes flexible alliances, collective action against aggressors, and rehabilitation of defeated players. Yet economics tells us that oligopoly markets are not always stable, and there may sometimes be massive market changes, such as those occurring presently in the international automobile-manufacturing industry.[6] Scholars who apply the oligopoly metaphor to the international balance of power have chosen to focus on the incentives for collusion and the stability-enhancing imperatives of a multiplayer world.

Waltz (1979) argued that a bipolar system is not only analogous to a duopoly, where there are two firms in a market, but that such systems will be very stable because two large powers will, like two collusive firms, divide up the world into spheres of influence and agree not to fight. This may well be the case, and two firms may, like the United States and the Soviet Union during the Cold War, agree that direct conflict would be far too destructive to yield any net benefits for either party. Whether that lack of a direct war between the superpowers was due to political duopoly or to nuclear weapons, a qualitative characteristic of the system emphasized by Waltz, is open to debate. Nevertheless, Waltz neglects the equally likely prediction for a duopoly model: two duopolists may decide to engage in a price war and try to put each other out of business. Economists have offered few criteria for predicting whether duopoly markets will be cooperative or competitive, though most agree that it is more likely to be competitive during depressions, as firms become desperate to preserve profits.[7]

Time horizons and possibilities for exit may also be relevant. Consider the difference between the dynamic Prisoners' Dilemma and the "chain store paradox." The latter is a parable about how a chain store should react to a new market entrant: collude and divide the market, or engage in a costly price war to put the new entrant out of business? A short-term perspective might lead to collusive joint profit maximization, but a longer-term view could lead managers to accept short-term losses to drive the other firm off the market. The Prisoners' Dilemma is usually interpreted as suggesting that cooperation is the better strategy insofar as one is looking for long-term gains. A key difference between the two conjectures is that the chain store parable allows exit; most presentations of the Prisoners' Dilemma do not. An example of the exit option in international politics might be a state deciding to abandon a conflict situation, as the United States did in Vietnam, rather than negotiating a compromise solution or continuing to fight.

Information, Incentives, and Bargaining

Strategic Behavior: Public Goods and the Tragedy of the Commons

Public goods are a familiar bargaining problem in international political economy and international politics generally. A public good exhibits nonexcludability (those who do not contribute cannot be prevented from consuming the good) and nonrivalry (consumption by one beneficiary does not reduce the amount available to others). Clean air and some military alliances are examples. Public goods produce free riding, more so as the number of consumers increases. Each beneficiary thinks he may as well not contribute because it makes no difference, irrespective of whether anyone else cooperates, and as a result very little of the public good may be provided. The thought process of the free rider is simple: if everyone else contributes, the good will be provided; if no one else contributes, my efforts would be too small to make a difference.[8] Public goods are an example of a much broader category of situations known as externalities: one (or in this case, each) actor imposes an unintended and uncompensated side effect on others.

Free-riding problems may be found throughout the history of international politics. Pericles urged his fellow Athenians to war with Sparta by claiming that the Spartans had a public good problem in their alliance (among other reasons).

> They cannot fight a war . . . so long as they have no central deliberative authority. . . . It never occurs to any of them that the apathy of one will damage the interests of all. Instead each state thinks that the responsibility for its future belongs to someone else, and so, while

everyone has the same idea privately, no one notices that from a general point of view things are going downhill. (Thucydides 1970, 93)

Adam Smith complained bitterly that the American colonists were unwilling to pay their fair share of the costs of defending the colonies:

> The last war [the Seven Years' War, 1756–63], which was undertaken altogether on account of the colonies, cost Great Britain . . . upwards of ninety millions. . . . If any of the provinces of the British Empire cannot be made to contribute towards the support of the whole Empire, it is surely time that Great Britain should free herself from defending those provinces in time of war. (1976 [1776], 2:486–87)

Davis and Huttenback (1987) note that this problem continued throughout the nineteenth century, Britain being chronically exploited by colonies unwilling to contribute to their own defense costs. Perhaps the British policy of sacrificing commonwealth soldiers in high casualty operations (e.g., Gallipoli, Dieppe) was partial recompense.

One solution is the hegemon, who gains enough from the public good to provide it for all and possibly supplies coercive incentives for others to contribute.[9] Following Olson and Zeckhauser's (1966) famous test of free riding in NATO (viz., the largest member contributes a greater share of its national income than others because, as the dominant beneficiary, it derives enough gain to be willing to provide a disproportionate share of the output, despite being exploited by the smaller allies), the public good prediction has been applied to many international political issues.

Closely related is the "tragedy of the commons" (a term coined by Hardin [1968]), a quasi–public good problem where there is nonexcludability but rivalry in consumption (e.g., fishing grounds). Both of these problems, at least when there is a large number of beneficiaries, create an incentive issue similar to that of the single-play Prisoners' Dilemma, where each has a dominant strategy of refusing to contribute or to cooperate by restraining one's use of the common resource. If the number of agents involved in the issue is small, cooperation is more likely because there may evolve norms of cooperation from their ability to observe each other's actions (Ostrom 1990). The popularity of the "tragedy of the commons" as a metaphor has led to its misuse. Porter, Brown, and Chasek (2001), for example, imply that the European practice of paying African countries to take toxic waste is such a tragedy. It is not, and does not meet the basic requirements for the existence of an externality. The exchange of toxic waste for money is both intended and compensated, and the transaction would not take place unless Pareto optimal.[10]

Risky Business: The Portfolio Problem

Finance is a subfield of microeconomics. One of the most well-known financial problems is that of constructing an investment portfolio incorporating the investor's preferred combination of risk and return. The more risk averse the investor, the more that investor will prefer a portfolio with lower risk but lower return. Portfolio theory is one branch of decision theory, where an agent is making choices subject to states of nature that have different probabilities associated with them. Hence the microeconomics of portfolio models are different from those of public good or game theory models generally, because in the latter cases there is bilateral or multilateral strategic behavior. Aspects of portfolio theory may be operationalized in international politics. One empirical example is that risk-averse countries may choose to enter military alliances that have low risk and low return, which in one study were measured as the mean and variance of states' military outputs over the relevant time periods (Conybeare 1992).

Optimal Sharing: The Syndicate

Recent developments in the theory of intragroup bargaining have drawn attention to factors other than free riding. The theory of the syndicate postulates a group that must work as a team to achieve a goal of uncertain value. If the agents differ in their attitude to risk, an optimal sharing arrangement will entail the less risk-averse agents taking a payoff that is larger but more variable, and the more risk-averse ones taking a share that is smaller but less variable. A simple way to conceptualize this is to think of the less risk-averse agent as selling an insurance policy to the more risk-averse partner. OPEC's output sharing may be an example. Members that have a high share of oil exports in their GNP can be expected to be more averse to risk, and OPEC's optimal-sharing rule would entail these members receiving a lower but less varying share of the total oil exports of OPEC. It is empirically the case that members with a high ratio of oil exports to GNP are permitted less fluctuation in their oil exports (Cony-beare 1997).

The Diffusion of Information: Rational Expectations

Assuming that actors have perfect information, or otherwise, has led to major changes in many pieces of conventional wisdom in economics and related fields. *Rational expectations* is a term that gained currency in the 1960s (Sheffrin 1983). It is the assumption that actors' expectations about the value of a random variable are normally distributed around the actual value of that variable or, more colloquially, that actors can make good predictions about the outcomes of specific actions or events. The idea led to some stunning insights into how markets work and why government policies may fail.

Under rational expectations, stock price movements are random: if the price tomorrow is different from the price today, it is because new information comes on the market tomorrow, and since we cannot predict this new information (if we could, the price would already reflect that information), any price change between today and tomorrow must be random and unpredictable.[11] Government policies (according to monetarists who have adopted the tenets of rational expectations) may fail because people anticipate the consequences and act so as to nullify the policy. If, for example, the government prints money and offers to hire the unemployed, the tactic may not work because the objects of the policy will realize that once the increased money supply causes inflation, they may be no better off than if they had remained unemployed. Gartzke (1999) argues that wars are random, and the logic of his argument is the same as that which argues that stock prices are random. If all potential belligerents had perfect information, all would correctly predict who would lose a war, the loser would back down, and no war would occur. Since wars do occur, it must be because of some random, unpredictable factors; hence war is "the error term."[12]

Another area where rational expectations may be useful in the study of international relations is in issues of "time inconsistency." This concept refers to the problem that an optimal policy may be self-defeating once the objects of that policy know what the policy is and strategically incorporate those expectations into their own behavior. An announced policy of retaliating against terrorism may be ineffective because the terrorist, who has already discounted the retaliation, will be influenced only by unexpected retaliations (Brophy-Baermann and Conybeare 1994). One implication of this argument is that governments might be better off tying their hands to a specific retaliatory policy, since if they announced an optimal rate of retaliation, it would not be believed by the terrorist, since it would leave them open to being "surprised." The situation is like that of a government announcing a specific monetary target in order to induce people to hold government financial instruments (including currency) and then surprising them with a higher-than-announced rate of inflation in order to extract more resources from the population—hence the monetarist call for predetermined and fixed rates of monetary expansion.

The diffusion of rational expectations ideas into social science has also led to the opposite question: what are the consequences of imperfect information? The classic example is Akerlof's (1984) "market for lemons": bad used cars drive good used cars off the market because those who are selling a good used car will not accept the discount demanded by buyers to protect themselves against the positive probability that they will be stuck with a lemon. The usual term for this problem is "adverse selection," a problem where one side of the transaction has more information than the other.

The enormous literature on signaling often makes implicit use of selection issues. A recent example from Simon (1999) may suffice: states that could develop nuclear weapons, but chose not to do so, experienced more severe dyadic conflict escalation. This evidence is consistent with the conjecture that potential enemies took nonacquisition of nuclear weapons as an indication that the nonacquirers were weak or lacked resolve. Fearon (1994) invokes the same logic in suggesting why classical deterrence predictions (i.e., strong countries' deterrence threats will be successful) may be empirically falsified: "when the observable balance of interests favors the defender, only relatively resolved challengers will choose to threaten, implying that the defender's effort at immediate deterrence will be relatively unlikely to succeed" (238). Huth and Allee (chap. 9, this vol.) note that selection issues are problematic in much of the literature on international conflict, and particularly in studies of deterrence.

A similar problem, but one due more to monitoring costs than asymmetric information, is "moral hazard." The archetypical moral hazard problem is insurance: people who insure their houses are more likely to play with matches, and the insurance company cannot monitor this behavior. Moral hazard problems abound in international relations. Countries like Argentina may engage in profligate economic policies in the expectation of being bailed out with loans from the International Monetary Fund. Having an implicit or de facto defense alliance with the United States (and U.S. treasury guarantees on their defense bonds), Israel may behave more assertively than we would wish. In 1914, Austria's insurance policy (the German alliance) may have induced it to play with matches (attack Serbia). The standard solution to moral hazard is to force the party engaging in undesirable behavior to bear some of the costs associated with consequences of its behavior. Hence the deductibles and exclusions in insurance policies. Seen from this perspective, many international agreements have the equivalent of deductibles. Alliances, for example, are often qualified, at least before the age of collective security alliances like NATO. The German-Italian alliance of 1882, for example, obliged each to come to the aid of the other only if the partner were to be attacked first by France. When states wish to borrow from the IMF, they must first borrow the capital they themselves have contributed to the institution. Lipson's (1986) explanation of the function of cross-default clauses in sovereign debt agreements suggests that they too are meant to constrain opportunistic behavior that may arise when monitoring is costly.[13]

International Policies and National Welfare

The three functions of government are effecting an efficient allocation of resources, maintaining order, and redistributing resources. These functions may be identified in both the domestic and international activities of states and in the goals of international organizations. Maintaining order is a sufficiently self-evident function that the following discussion will focus on examples of efficiency and redistribution.

Efficiency

One issue in foreign policy is the efficiency of war and imperialism. Do they yield net gains for the country? The microeconomic approach to the study of international politics suggests that we should be able to see evidence that states have at least expected to see net gains. I emphasize expectations because states, like individual investors, can make mistakes. Hence Fieldhouse's (1961) critique of the economic theory of imperialism (some colonies were unprofitable in the aggregate) does not disprove the possibility of an economic motive for imperialism. Furthermore, imperialism may benefit some parts of society and not others, so that there may be a net national loss even though some make large gains. Davis and Huttenback (1987) provide evidence that British imperialism entailed the heavy subsidization of investors and merchants involved in empire expansion. Had British voters been aware of this, they might still have regarded it as an appropriate sunk cost for future net national gains. Luttwak (1976) asserted that the Romans were careful to require provinces to generate net gains or else they would pull back the boundaries. This is not as unrealistic as it may appear. Provincial consuls were the administrative and military heads of their districts. They would see both the military costs of controlling the territory and the revenues going back to Rome and would be in an ideal position to make rough inferences as to the point at which marginal gains equaled marginal costs. More recently, Liberman (1996) has argued that the invasion and occupation of some modern industrial societies produced net gains.

International organizations are also fertile areas for observing microeconomics at work in guiding policy. Since Coase's famous theorem, it has become conventional wisdom that externalities need not necessarily require government intervention. If transaction costs are low, it matters not how rights and responsibilities are assessed; the parties will simply bargain until the optimal level of control over the externality is attained. For example, the United States produces acid rain that damages Canada. Who should have responsibility to correct the externality: should Canada pay the United States to control emissions, or should the United States pay Canada compensation? The Coase theorem says that if bargaining costs are low, it does not matter; either rule will cause bargaining to proceed up to the point where the marginal gains of controlling acid rain equal the marginal costs (see Conybeare 1980). Scholars who understand the Coase theorem will then be better able to explain why, for example, the Kyoto conference of 1997 adopted a scheme for tradable international pollution permits. Each country is granted an initial allocation of greenhouse gas emission permits, and countries then are allowed to trade. The efficiency of the scheme is that countries that can cheaply and easily control greenhouse gases can sell the permits to countries that cannot or do not wish to do so, reducing the total cost of attaining any given level of global pollution abatement.

Redistribution

It is tempting to think that microeconomics has nothing to say about redistribution (apart from endorsing redistributions that yield allocative efficiency or Pareto-optimal gains), since redistribution entails making an arbitrary judgment that one person is more deserving than another. The following are two examples of how microeconomics may offer solutions to questions of redistribution.

Voluntary Redistributions

The argument made famous by Rawls (1975), then extrapolated into international relations by Beitz (1979) and others, is that the simple microeconomics of individual choice suggests that we would all wish to live in a society that redistributes resources so as to favor the least well-off and raise them to a minimal floor of resource endowment. The microeconomic basis of the assertion is both the strength and weakness of the argument. If people are risk averse (i.e., they have utility functions that are concave to the origin), they will prefer a lower guaranteed allocation than an allocation that is on average higher but has variation. The utility of a smaller but certain allocation is greater than the expected utility of an allocation with the same expected value. Rawls himself did not think the argument applicable to international relations because the international system is anarchic, governed only by the principle of self-help. Redistribution via a social contract required a stronger sense of community or, as he put it, a "cooperative venture for mutual advantage." Nonetheless, Beitz (1979) argued that Rawls's contract was applicable to international relations because no nation should automatically have a right to the wealth that lies within its borders, and the existence of international trade implies that the world is an enterprise for mutual gain.

Involuntary Redistributions

It is possible to present a microeconomic argument that involuntary redistributions may be efficient (yielding a net gain to society), though not necessarily Pareto optimal (which requires that no one be made worse off), if one assumes that the transfer is from an actor with a low marginal utility for income to one with a high marginal utility for income. Put simply, an extra dollar is worth more to a poor person than to a rich person, so that taking a dollar from a rich person and giving to someone less wealthy will not only improve the welfare of the poor person but also be efficiency enhancing for society as a whole, because the gain to the poor person is greater than the loss to the rich one. There are at least two difficulties with such an argument. One is that it assumes interpersonal comparability of utilities (i.e., a utility unit lost to the rich person is comparable to a utility unit gained by the poor person). It also raises that practical problem of deciding which involuntary transfers are efficient. If we were to legalize robbery, on the grounds that it typically transfers money from a richer person to a poorer person, we would still be left with the problem of deciding on a case-by-case basis which robberies satisfied that efficiency criterion. Criminal law and, to a lesser extent, international norms frown upon involuntary transfers because it is difficult to determine in advance, even within narrow classifications of events (e.g., thefts of Ford Escorts, whose legal owners are unlikely to be rich, versus thefts of Porsches, whose owners are very likely to be richer than the thief), which transfers would be socially efficient (Calabressi and Melamed 1972).

Nozick (1977) has offered one justification for involuntary redistributions that does not guarantee efficiency, but does ensure that some possibly inefficient transfers will not be allowed to stand. This is the "rectification principle": involuntary redistributions are permissible when the purpose is to redress a past involuntary redistribution. This principle does not ensure efficient transfers, since some efficient redistributions may be reversed, but it does obviate the transaction costs of determining which redistributions are efficient and which are not. Unfortunately, by offering a solution to one microeconomic aspect of redistribution, Nozick introduces another: how far back can one go in making claims for restitution? In the case of individuals under municipal law, the answer is fairly simple: claims die when individuals die. Even then it is not that simple. The postcommunist Hungarian parliament debated the hypothetical case of the Jew whose property was seized by the Iron Guard in 1938, given to an ethnic German, confiscated and given to a Hungarian in 1946, and finally nationalized by the state in 1948. To whom should the property be returned? To the owner in 1948, it was arbitrarily decided.

At the international level, states (and corporations) are not like individuals. The state that is the England of today is the same as the England of the fifteenth century. Hence Nozick's argument should endorse France claiming reparations for the Hundred Years' War. Such a claim is not as absurd, or at least not as unlikely to be made, as it may seem. President Mugabe of Zimbabwe claims that expropriating white farms and killing white farmers is justified because Britain owes Zimbabwe reparations for imperialism.

This debate now extends to corporations. Should Daimler pay reparations to its former slave laborers from the 1940s? A rabbi has suggested not, citing Deuteronomy's admonition not to punish the son for the sins of the father. Again, however, corporations are more like states than individuals: the Daimler of today is the same corporation that existed in 1944, so the fact that the current employees and shareholders are different people is irrelevant (Landsburg 1999).

Regardless of where one stands on these issues, the important point to note is that the debate is grounded in the microeconomic principle that possibly inefficient redistributions (or redistributions where it would be too costly to determine on a case-by-case basis which are efficient and which are not) should be discouraged.

Summary and Conclusions

The principal contribution of microeconomic reasoning to the study of politics is analytic rigor, though it is obviously not the only formal approach to make such a claim. More specifically, microeconomics focuses our attention on how actors choose to allocate resources and on whether in doing so they attain efficient outcomes in a variety of situations, including such problems as the decision to produce guns or butter and how to solve free-riding problems in alliances. This essay has cited only a few of the ways in which microeconomics may shed light on international politics, but does provide a basis for some general conclusions about the benefits of such a perspective.

First, microeconomics can help explain anomalous puzzles that seem inconsistent with existing explanations. An example cited earlier is the ineffectiveness of Israeli retaliation against terrorism, evidence that is inconsistent with most of the conventional bargaining ideas about Tit-for-Tat and deterrence theory.

Second, microeconomics may provide explanations for observations not addressed by existing theories. Why, for example, are members of OPEC with higher ratios of oil exports to GNP granted output quotas with less variation over time? Why do risk-averse countries gravitate toward alliances with less variation in the alliance's military output?

Third, microeconomics may shed new light on phenomena already addressed by existing theories, adding explanations that are complementary or independent of existing explanations. Why, for example, do some empires last longer than others? Is it because some empire managers are better at equating marginal costs and marginal benefits? How did an increase in the labor supply help to topple the feudal political system? Why was the United States chronically unhappy with the contributions of its NATO allies?

Fourth, microeconomics theories may replace existing explanations. Why did the American Revolution occur? Adam Smith's public good perspective suggests that it may have been partly because the colonists wanted to evade paying their fair share of the costs of defending the empire. Hegemonic stability is a good example of an explanation that has gradually crumbled to dust when examined with the tools of microeconomics. Beginning with the claim that hegemons necessarily benefit from free trade, an assertion easily questioned with the microeconomic tools of trade theory, proponents of the theory have progressively retreated until they were left only with the argument that big countries may impose their will on small countries, an observation already made by Thucydides' Athenian delegates to the Spartan assembly: "It has always been a rule that the weak should be subject to the strong" (1970, 55).

Microeconomics does not explain everything, and I am mindful that some (notably the constructivists) feel that the field needs to turn away from economic rationality as a theoretical guide and examine epistemological issues. Yet it is important to note that the microeconomics perspective does not deny the relevance of other types of variables, such as ideology in all its various manifestations. Properly used, the microeconomic perspective must always allow that there are factors outside the explanatory scope of the approach.[14]

What core questions for future research are suggested by the microeconomic approach to international politics?

1. It is time to bring together the microeconomic approach to domestic politics with that of international politics. Typically they are kept separate, primarily for the sake of simplicity. Some effort has been made to integrate them, in explaining trade policy (the literature known as endogenous tariff theory) and two-level games. To use the phraseology of microeconomics, we need to look for simultaneous equilibria in domestic and international political markets, rather than examining them separately.

2. Some of the most interesting problems in applying microeconomics to international politics are those where the theory leaves the issue underdetermined (i.e., the theory could be used to explain many of the possible outcomes). The example cited previously is that of understanding when two duopolists will cooperate and jointly manipulate the market and when they will engage in economic warfare and try to put each other out of business. We have no shortage of possible intervening variables (e.g., income levels, discount rates over time), but little progress beyond the Waltzian assumption that two global duopolists will cooperate to create a system more stable than a multipolar one, the latter being vulnerable to "chain gang" and buck-passing alliances that may lead to war.

3. Though there is little disagreement about the usefulness of rational choice theory in explaining aspects of international politics in which payoffs are measurable, particularly as monetary amounts, there is little serious exploration (especially by rational choice proponents themselves) of what areas of international politics might not be very well explained in such terms. North and Thomas, for example, would appear to be suggesting that "ideology" might be best left to qualitative scholars, and constructivists would surely agree. Exploring the limits of any research technique is usually enlightening, as Karl Popper reminded us in his admonition to look for evidence that is inconsistent with our ideas.

Suggested Readings

Bueno de Mesquita, B. 2000. *Principles of International Politics.* Washington, DC: CQ Press. The first general international politics textbook based explicitly in microeconomic principles and rational choice theory generally. Admirably clear and accessible.

Drazen, A. 2000. *Political Economy in Macroeconomics.* Princeton: Princeton University Press. Though the title refers to macroeconomics, much of it is about applications of microeconomic reasoning to politics, including such topics as decision making, time consistency, institutional incentives, credible commitments, and public goods.

Frey, B. 1984. *International Political Economics.* Oxford: Blackwell. An older but interesting collection of essays by a European economist interested in international politics.

Pahre, R. 1999. *Leading Questions: How Hegemony Affects the International Political Economy.* Ann Arbor: University of Michigan Press. A recent example of the best kind of rational choice theory using the microeconomics of public goods applied to hegemony and the incentives to act in a predatory or benevolent manner. Rigorously deductive, yet empirically grounded; this is the way it should be done.

Sandler, T., and K. Hartley. 1999. *The Political Economy of NATO.* New York: Cambridge University Press. The culmination of a long stream of research on the microeconomics of military alliances, inspired by the theory of public goods; both theoretical and empirical.

Notes

1. The basic postulates of rational choice may be found in Frohlich and Oppenheimer (1978).

2. This line of reasoning is continued in subsequent works; see Bueno de Mesquita and Lalman (1992) and the recent textbook, Bueno de Mesquita (2000).

3. A similar argument may be made for the end of slavery in the United States: originally a response to a relative shortage of labor, it would have become increasingly inefficient with the large population movement into the United States during the latter part of the nineteenth century. Fogel and Engerman (1995) doubt this argument, finding that slavery was still highly profitable on the eve of the Civil War.

4. A monopsony market is one where there is collusion on the buyer side, the extreme form being a single buyer from multiple sellers.

5. The postwar U.S. commitment to free trade was eroding by the 1970s, manifested in congressional action (protectionist bills, restrictions on the trade-negotiating authority granted to the executive, and belligerent slogans about "level playing fields"), a proliferation of nontariff barriers to trade, and conflict with major trade partners, principally the EU and Japan.

6. The number of major world auto manufacturers has shrunk from several dozen in 1970 to about five today: General Motors, Ford, Toyota, Volkswagen, and Peugeot account for more than 50 percent of the world market, a state of industrial organization very close to a classical balance of power situation. It is reasonable to surmise that any of these companies would be delighted to put the others out of business, contrary to the predictions of those political scientists who invoke the oligopoly analogy in their balance of power theories. See Conybeare (2003).

7. Note that this prediction is consistent with the conventional assumption in microeconomics that income is subject to diminishing marginal utility, so that firms will fight harder for profits when incomes are declining.

8. Yossarian, the antihero of *Catch-22,* provides a clever example. Asked why he did not want to fight, he replied that the Germans always shot at him. Told that if everyone thought like that there would be no one to fight the Germans, he replied that if everyone took the same view, he would be a fool to fight the Germans by himself.

9. Annoyed by free riding during the Persian Wars, the Delian League of classical Greece inflicted severe punishments on free riders.

10. A Pareto-optimal exchange is a subset of efficient allocations (those yielding net gains to the group) where at least one agent is better off than before and no one is worse off.

11. The same argument was made in the 1930s (though not published until 1944, in the journal *Economica*) by Karl Popper (1957), in his critique of the Marxist belief in predicting the future: history is partly a function of knowledge; we cannot predict future knowledge; therefore we cannot predict future history.

12. Dogs rarely fight. Barking and fur standing on end is a signaling process that almost invariably leads to one dog concluding that, if the confrontation came to biting, he or she would lose, and that dog backs down. Interstate signaling is subject to more distortion and hence a greater chance of random disturbances leading to war.

13. Cross-default clauses require that the entire loan be declared in default if the borrower defaults on payments to one or more members of the lending syndicate.

14. North (1981) is careful to note that the microeconomics of property rights and transaction costs does not deny the relevance of ideology, though he does pass over it quickly and returns to the approach with which he is most comfortable.

References

Akerlof, G. 1984. *An Economic Theorist's Book of Tales.* Cambridge: Cambridge University Press.

Beitz, C. 1979. *Political Theory and International Relations.* Princeton: Princeton University Press.

Brophy-Baermann, B., and J. Conybeare. 1994. Retaliating against Terrorism: Rational Expectations and the Optimality of Rules versus Discretion. *American Journal of Political Science* 38:196–210.

Bueno de Mesquita, B. 1980. *The War Trap.* New Haven: Yale University Press.

———. 2000. *Principles of International Politics.* Washington, DC: CQ Press.

Bueno de Mesquita, B., and D. Lalman. 1992. *War and Reason: Domestic and International Imperatives.* New Haven: Yale University Press.

Calabressi, G., and A. Melamed. 1972. Property Rules, Liability Rules, and Inalienability. *Harvard Law Review* 85:1089–1129.

Choucri, N., and R. North. 1975. *Nations in Conflict*. San Francisco: Freeman.

Conybeare, J. 1980. International Organization and the Theory of Property Rights. *International Organization* 34:307–34.

———. 1992. A Portfolio Diversification Model of Alliances: The Triple Alliance and the Triple Entente, 1879–1914. *Journal of Conflict Resolution* 36:53–85.

———. 1997. Financial Models of the Risky State. In *Enforcing Cooperation: Risky States and the Intergovernmental Management of Conflict*, edited by G. Schneider and P. Weitsman. London: Macmillan.

———. 2003. *Merging Traffic: The Consolidation of the International Automobile Industry*. Lanham, MD: Rowman and Littlefield.

Davis, L., and R. Huttenback. 1987. *Mammon and the Pursuit of Empire*. Cambridge: Cambridge University Press.

Fearon, J. 1994. Signaling versus the Balance of Power and Interests. *Journal of Conflict Resolution* 38 (2): 236–69.

Fieldhouse, D. 1961. Imperialism: An Historiographical Revision. *Economic History Review*, 2d s., (14): 187–209.

Fogel, R., and S. Engerman. 1995. *Time on the Cross*. New York: Norton.

Frohlich, N., and J. Oppenheimer. 1978. *Modern Political Economy*. Englewood Cliffs: Prentice-Hall.

Gartzke, E. 1999. War Is in the Error Term. *International Organization* 53:567–87.

Gilpin, R. 1981. *War and Change in World Politics*. Cambridge: Cambridge University Press.

Hardin, G. 1968. The Tragedy of the Commons. *Science* 162:1243–48.

Kreps, D. 1990. *Microeconomic Theory*. Princeton: Princeton University Press.

Landsburg, S. 1999. Guilt by Acquisition. *Slate* [online magazine]. Available from http://slate.msn.com/?id=12950 (accessed January 13, 1999).

Liberman, P. 1996. *Does Conquest Pay?* Princeton: Princeton University Press.

Lipson, C. 1986. Bankers' Dilemmas. In *Cooperation under Anarchy*, edited by K. Oye. Princeton: Princeton University Press.

Luttwak, E. 1976. *The Grand Strategy of the Roman Empire*. Baltimore: Johns Hopkins University Press.

Magee, S., W. Brock, and L. Young. 1989. *Black Hole Tariffs and Endogenous Policy Theory*. New York: Cambridge University Press.

North, D. 1981. *Structure and Change in Economic History*. New York: Norton.

North, D., and R. Thomas. 1973. *The Rise of the Western World*. New York: Cambridge University Press.

Nozick, R. 1977. *Anarchy, State, and Utopia*. New York: Basic Books.

Olson, M., and R. Zeckhauser. 1966. An Economic Theory of Alliances. *Review of Economics and Statistics* 48:266–79.

Ostrom, E. 1990. *Governing the Commons.* Cambridge: Cambridge University Press.

Pahre, R. 1999. *Leading Questions: How Hegemony Affects the International Political Economy.* Ann Arbor: University of Michigan Press.

Pindyck, R., and D. Rubinfeld. 1989. *Microeconomics.* New York: Macmillan.

Popper, K. 1957. *The Poverty of Historicism.* London: Routledge.

Porter, G., J. Brown, and P. Chasek. 2001. *Global Environmental Politics.* 3d ed. Boulder: Westview.

Rawls, J. 1975. *A Theory of Justice.* Cambridge: Harvard University Press.

Rogowski, R. 1989. *Commerce and Coalitions.* Princeton: Princeton University Press.

Sheffrin, S. 1983. *Rational Expectations.* Cambridge: Cambridge University Press.

Simon, M. 1999. Asymmetric Nuclear Acquisition and International Conflict. Ph.D. diss., Iowa City, University of Iowa.

Smith, A. 1976 [1776]. *The Wealth of Nations.* Vol. 2. Chicago: University of Chicago Press.

Thucydides. 1970. *The Peloponnesian War.* Harmondsworth: Penguin.

Varian, H. 1987. *Intermediate Microeconomics.* New York: Norton.

Wallerstein, I. M. 1974. *The Modern World System.* Vol. 1. New York: Academic Press.

Waltz, K. 1979. *Theory of International Politics.* Reading, MA: Addison-Wesley.

13. Game Theory and International Environmental Policy

D. Marc Kilgour and Yael Wolinsky-Nahmias

Environmental issues have been a significant component of international politics since the 1970s. Concern over pollution, the depletion of the atmospheric ozone layer, the threatened extinction of plants and animals, and climate change has grown in step with scientific research on the consequences of human intervention in natural systems. Although many governments were slow to respond, public pressure and growing scientific evidence eventually motivated political leaders to address environmental problems, in part through international negotiation and cooperation. Now hundreds of international environmental treaties and dozens of international environmental regimes have been established. International Relations (IR) scholars have sought to explain how sovereign states solve—or fail—to overcome the collective action problems associated with international environmental management. Many environmental issues, such as climate change and biodiversity, involve complicated problems of externalities, shared resources, and undefined property rights.

In addition to exploring how governments address these problems, another research issue is to account for the high level of compliance with environmental treaties and regimes, most of which lack enforcement mechanisms. Two very different explanations have emerged: some students of international law and environmental politics view the high level of compliance as an indication of a coincidence of national and international interests in the solution of environmental problems. According to this view, the enforceability of an agreement may not be important, since governments respond better to cooperative initiatives than to threats of sanctions.

On the other hand, the idea that enforcement has little importance for international environmental treaties has led rational choice advocates to the conclusion that research on compliance suffers from significant problems of selection bias and endogeneity. In an article in *International Organization,* Downs, Rocke, and Barsoom (1996) suggest that the relatively high level of compliance with environmental regimes is easily explained by their shallowness—many agreements prescribe minimal changes in behavior. Indeed, countries sometimes negotiate and sign international environmental agreements, like the Long-Range Transboundary Air Pollution Convention of 1979 (LRTAP), with which they are already mostly in compliance.

The enforceability question may not be central, however. Increasingly, governments are called upon to make tough decisions about costly changes in their economic policies in order to prevent future harm or to correct and remediate environmentally reckless behavior. Shallow agreements may no longer be an option. Political leaders now face more difficult choices in forming environmental policies.

The goal of this chapter is to explain how game theory can contribute to the study of environmental policy-making within the discipline of international relations. We show that if decision making is presumed rational, then game theory can help generate important insights without regard to the role of enforcement. Although game theory's application to international environmental politics is relatively recent, we argue that it has great potential to advance the analysis of central problems in this field, such as management of common resources, environmental negotiation, enforcement of environmental agreements, and the balance of domestic and international incentives.

Game theory can help explore these issues because its mathematical form means that it is based on precise definitions, makes clear assumptions, and relies on logical structures. Game theory presumes a rational decision process in which decision makers know their range of possible choices, understand how these choices develop into outcomes, and know their preferences over these outcomes. But unlike other formal approaches, game theory posits that decision makers act strategically in that they take account not only of the existence and capabilities of other decision makers but also of their interests. This is feasible because game models always specify a player's information, which may be complete or incomplete, about the preferences of other players. It is a fundamental principle of game theory that decision makers consider the implications of their knowledge of others in making their own choices. In this context, game theory constitutes a valuable methodology for analyzing the decision processes of state leaders as they interact over international environmental policies.

After briefly introducing the branches of game theory, we discuss their relevance to international environmental politics, focusing on international negotiation over environmental issues, environmental management, and international environmental conflict. We then illustrate the kinds of insights that can be derived from game modeling and analysis of environmental problems. We conclude with a summary of our view of the prospects for game-theoretic contributions to the understanding of environmental issues within international relations.

A Very Brief Introduction to Cooperative and Noncooperative Game Theory

The birth of game theory is universally acknowledged to have taken place in 1944 with the publication of *Theory of Games and Economic Behavior* by John von Neumann, a mathematician, and Oskar Morgenstern, an economist. Von Neumann and Morgenstern divided game theory into two branches, noncooperative and cooperative. To understand the distinction, assume that in an interactive decision problem, all decision makers, or players, know

- their own, and all others', possible choices;
- how those choices (possibly in combination with random events with known probabilities) determine an outcome; and
- their own, and all others', preferences over all possible outcomes.

Noncooperative game theory addresses each player's decisions in such a situation, asking what choices would be "rational" for a player and what combinations of choices by all players would be "stable." General references include Aumann (1987), Aumann and Hart (1992, 1994, 2002), and Rubinstein (1991). (A more recent viewpoint is that these conditions define a game of *complete information.* In a game of *incomplete information,* each player has a probability distribution over the possible games it might be playing. Typically, a player would know its own preferences for certain but would have only probabilistic knowledge of its opponents' preferences.)

Note that each player is assumed to be in total control of his or her own choice but to have no influence whatsoever over any other player's choice, except what is implicit in the "rules of the game." In other words, players may influence each other's choices only through their common knowledge of all players' available choices, of how an outcome is determined, and of all players' preferences. In some formulations, players are not even allowed to communicate; in others, they may do so but only to coordinate their choices. Note another fundamental principle of game theory: everything there is to know about the interaction of the players, except the choices they make, is spelled out in the rules.

Cooperative game theory adds another dimension to this interaction, postulating that players can make agreements that are binding in the sense of being enforceable at no cost. This fundamental change motivates cooperative game theory's preoccupation with how the players should distribute the joint gains of cooperation, based on the outcomes they can achieve on their own, that is, on how essential each one is to the welfare of the group. In cooperative game theory, a player can threaten or promise anything and be believed. In noncooperative game theory, only commitments that are in a player's interest can possibly affect the outcome. (The relevance of communication in a noncooperative game can sometimes be assessed by determining whether the outcome is different when "speech acts" are introduced into the model.)

Von Neumann and Morgenstern's formulation of cooperative game theory went so far as to allow side payments ("transferable utility") from one player to another, though now there are other approaches based on weaker assumptions about the comparability of value (Aumann and Hart 1992, chap. 13). In general, cooperative game theory places no emphasis on the mechanics of achieving particular total values or distributions, focusing instead on whether stable and equitable distributions of value are possible if binding agreements are available and on how each decision maker's contribution to group welfare can be measured.

Noncooperative Games and International Negotiation over the Environment

Understanding how governments negotiate over environmental issues is critical to understanding international environmental policy-making. Current environmental negotiations concern a broad range of issues from the relatively local (the sharing of fishing and water rights) to the global (strategies to address climate change). Since the 1980s environmental issues have also played a role in major trade agreements, such as NAFTA. The characteristic feature of bargaining on environmental issues—in comparison, for example, to trade and security issues—is that environmental negotiation almost invariably involves problems of commons, shared natural resources, and transboundary externalities.[1]

Noncooperative game models can provide important insights into the many environmental problems rooted in humanity's ever-increasing demands on natural systems. In particular, they can model bargaining over the division of shared environmental assets, responsibility for pollution reduction and cleanup, or global action on issues such as biodiversity or ozone depletion. Moreover, because they analyze behavior not so much in terms of outcomes as in terms of sides' values for all possible outcomes on all issues, game models constitute a tool that can be applied to issue linkage, a bargaining strategy that can turn a specific environmental problem into one component of a constellation of international issues.[2]

Noncooperative game theory is the more basic of the two main branches of game theory and has been more widely applied in international relations (see Brams 1975; O'Neill 1994; Snidal 1986). Game models with an environmental focus are still relatively uncommon in the IR literature, but students of both political science and economics are working to fill this gap. Explorations of significant environmental issues using game theory include the work of Ecchia and Mariotti (1998) and Payne (2000), which address the role of institutions in international environmental politics. Grundig, Ward, and Zorick (2001) present four models describing the bargaining behavior of governments and nongovernmental actors in negotiations over climate change, both within an international regime (which the authors argue tends to constrain opportunistic behavior) and outside any institutional arrangements.

Environmental issues involving contiguous states are very common, as simple physical proximity often implies the sharing of watersheds, airsheds, offshore resources, mineral deposits, and so forth. But environmental issues have now become an important component of relations among geographically separated states; for example, widely dispersed coalitions of countries now support bans on chlorofluorocarbons to protect the ozone layer, and preservation of tropical rain forests to reduce the greenhouse effect.

The diffusion of interests through issues is another important aspect of international environmental policy-making. International agreements typically commit a government to policy changes that impact domestic constituencies. It is hardly surprising that governments are sensitive to the domestic implications of possible international agreements, particularly those that affect the environment.

The question of exactly how domestic constraints impinge on international bargaining behavior was first raised in Robert D. Putnam's (1988) article on "the logic of two-level games." Putnam argued that domestic politics shapes the outcomes of international bargaining because negotiators think not only about reaching agreement with their foreign counterparts but also about ratification by their domestic jurisdictions. Thus, the anticipated ratification process rationally shapes the prior bargaining strategy. Putnam claimed that domestic politics narrows the win-set[3] of decision makers, improving their bargaining power but doing so only by putting the agreement at risk.[4]

Two-level game modeling has developed into a very useful method of analyzing the interaction of domestic and international incentives. Noncooperative game models that relax the assumption that states are "unitary actors" have been used to explore the consequences of leaders' attempts to balance domestic (inside) and international (outside) motivations, predicting and explaining the interaction of domestic and international constraints in rational policy-making (Morrow 1991; Iida 1993; Mo 1994; Wolinsky 1997).

Formal analysis aims not just to produce empirically testable hypotheses but also to suggest when those hypotheses are most likely to be corroborated. For two-level game modeling, predictions depend on two major institutional factors: the domestic decision-making process and the structure of the international negotiation (Ishida and Wolinsky 1996).

A two-level analysis of bargaining must clearly delineate three features:[5] domestic politics, the preference structure of the focal government, and the international bargaining process. Domestic politics must be specified in order to generate empirically falsifiable hypotheses about how internal issues shape negotiation strategies. Two-level games often specify a democratic system with a parliamentary ratification procedure for international agreements (Iida 1993; Mo 1994), though the domestic component could be any well-defined selectorate.

The second essential component of a two-level bargaining model is a

322

description of decision makers' preferences. Political leaders' electoral incentives are the most intensively studied, and two-level game models often portray decision makers as concerned about the effects on reelection probabilities of their international interactions.

Finally, two-level bargaining games must clearly define the bargaining process. One way to operationalize strategic interaction during an international negotiation is to apply Rubinstein's alternating-offer bargaining model (Iida 1993). Another possibility is an ultimatum ("take it or leave it") model, which can be justified by the assumption that negotiations will reach this stage eventually (Wolinsky 1997).

The implications of domestic incentives on foreign policy have been explored using two-level game models mainly in the contexts of U.S. security and trade (Knopf 1993; Milner and Rosendorff 1997; Morrow 1991). Wolinsky (1997) illustrates that two-level games are also relevant to international environmental negotiation. She argues that although international environmental agreements may not determine election outcomes, they do affect voters' perceptions of their government and consequently influence votes. For this reason, governments weigh international bargaining strategies in terms of potential electoral effects.

In her analysis, Wolinsky (1997) models voters as uncertain about the quality of the incumbent government. Performance in international environmental bargaining is then a signal to the electorate about the government's effectiveness.[6] She shows that when an incumbent government is uncertain about the reservation level[7] of its negotiation partner, it tends to make high concessions in equilibrium, even when the issue under negotiation is salient—provided the costs to the electorate of replacing the government are high. But when the costs of replacing it are low, the same government may make low concessions on a salient issue, even at the risk of negotiation failure.

Wolinsky's conclusions are clearly illustrated by Germany's behavior in the negotiations on the 1985 Sulfur Protocol to the 1979 Long-Range Transboundary Air Pollution Convention. In the early 1980s, the public in West Germany learned that acid rain had caused substantial damage to the Black Forest. Transboundary air pollution was an important contributor to this problem, and public opinion polls in Germany showed high saliency for the pollution issue and weak support for the incumbent government. Germany became a leader in the negotiations over the Sulfur Protocol, making very strong demands: a 30 percent reduction of sulfur relative to

1980 as a base year. Wolinsky's findings explain Germany's risky low-concession strategy as a way to avoid sending a "weak government" signal at a crucial time.

As two-level game models illustrate, noncooperative game models can capture the logic of interactions in the international arena because they constitute a natural model for states' tendencies to act on the basis of self-interest, taking into account not only immediate outcomes but also the consequences of choices made by other actors. Up to now, many noncooperative game models have been simple in structure, have relied on complete information, and have made heroic assumptions about the rationality of decision makers. But, to an increasing degree, these characteristics can now be avoided.

Game models with incomplete information are now fairly common, as illustrated in the international crisis example discussed later in the chapter (see also Morrow 1989; Powell 1990; Fearon 1995). Of course, incomplete information games must also account for players' beliefs about the types of their opponents, which adds another layer of complexity. Nonetheless, it is often possible, albeit difficult, to solve these models. Wolinsky's two-level game analysis is another example of an incomplete information game: the electorate is uncertain about the quality of the government, and the government is uncertain about the preferences of its (foreign) negotiation partner.[8] Bounded rationality models are now available and are used increasingly in some game theory applications; the rationality requirement of game theory is now viewed simply as the requirement that individuals' actions be consistent with their preferences and beliefs (on the rationality assumption, see also chaps. 10, 11, and 12, this vol.).

Noncooperative game modeling has its costs. One unavoidable problem is that formulation of noncooperative game models requires information, such as the players' utilities, that may in practice be difficult to obtain reliably (for this reason, some decision support systems simplify the game structure in order to reduce the information requirements; see Fang, Hipel, and Kilgour 1993). The usual formulation of games of incomplete information requires that the probabilities representing each player's beliefs be specified; again, these may be especially difficult to obtain credibly, particularly in retrospect. Finally, conclusions from noncooperative games are notoriously dependent on details: seemingly small changes in a model can lead to radically different conclusions. One way to cope with this problem is to model only "generic" problems—an approach adopted, for example, in some of the later deterrence models (Brams and Kilgour 1988; Zagare and Kilgour 1995, 2000). Another influential generic model is Hardin's analysis (1968) of "The Tragedy of the Commons" and its relation to the n-person Prisoner's Dilemma. Hardin showed the clash of incentives inherent in the collective management of any commonly held resource; if access is unrestricted and utilization is subtractive (i.e., reduces the amount available to others), individuals are strongly motivated to behave selfishly, to the detriment of the group (see also Ostrom 1990; Ostrom, Gardner, and Walker 1994). Unfortunately, the generic modeling strategy is not readily adapted, as empirically oriented researchers usually focus more on the distinctive features of a problem, rather than on those it shares with other problems.

Nonetheless, there are good reasons to expect that in the future noncooperative game models will make a significant contribution to our understanding of environmental issues in international relations. For example, repeated-game models are now a well-developed part of noncooperative theory, and can be applied to international environmental problems. One important contribution of game-theoretic analysis may be, quite simply, to foster a clear and precise expression of ideas. For interacting decisions made in the context of a poorly understood scientific base, noncooperative game models seem particularly appropriate. Another important area in which game theory may be able to contribute is fairness, but that requires a different branch of game theory. We now turn to the characteristics and uses of cooperative game theory models.

Cooperative Game Theory and International Environmental Management

Among the first problems explored by social scientists in the realm of environmental politics was management of environmental commons (such as the high seas) and of shared natural resources (such as waterways). An early conclusion was that the main roadblock preventing cooperative environmental management is that environmental commons have the characteristics of public goods; in particular, free riding could be in the self-interest of each participant.

In his "Tragedy of the Commons" article, Garrett Hardin (1968) argues that the commitment of democratic governments to improve the welfare of citizens, combined with the human temptation to reproduce and free ride, may lead to dire consequences for the earth and all species it supports, including humanity. Arguing noncooperatively, he concludes that a top-down autocratic approach to environmental management is justified to protect the earth for future generations. Elinor Ostrom offers a contrasting perspective in her 1990 book *Governing the Commons*. She advocates a bottom-up approach to the management of common-pool resources, focusing on voluntary local solutions. Like Hardin, Ostrom accepts that individuals are motivated by self-interest, yet her approach is to study patterns of cooperation that might emerge when interactions are repeated and actions are transparent (for another view, see Ward 1993, 1996).

Alternatively, international environmental management may be seen as an issue to be resolved by the creation of appropriate international regulatory regimes. Indeed, much of the current literature on international environmental management is devoted to the emergence and effectiveness of such regimes (Haas, Keohane, and Levy 1993; Brown Weiss and Jacobson 1998; Young and Osherenko 1993; Miles et al. 2001). According to Young and Osherenko (1993), the emergence of international environmental regimes may have power-based explanations, interest-based explanations, knowledge-based explanations, and contextual explanations. Their analysis seems to cover all the bases, but it is not always clear what resolution they see to the problems inherent in the public good structure of many environmental problems.

More recent research on international environmental management introduces a different approach that is nicely captured by cooperative game theory, which up to now has rarely been applied to international bargaining in any forum, perhaps because researchers in political science have been inclined toward models that emphasize the inherent anarchy of the international system. (An exception is the use of power indices to measure voting power in international bodies with complex voting rules, such as the United Nations [Kerby and Göbeler 1996] or the European Union [Brams and Affuso 1985; Hosli 1996].) To use cooperative game theory to model bargaining or sharing may be seen as imposing unrealistic assumptions on international enforcement mechanisms in that a fundamental feature of cooperative game theory is its assumption that players can make agreements that are enforceable at no cost. While this assumption is dubious in the international context, it is unfortunate that cooperative game theory has not been applied more frequently, as cooperative game models can provide much useful information, such as which divisions of joint wealth can be justified by the underlying strategic structure and how much efficiency can be achieved.

The assumption that players can enter into binding agreements makes cooperative game theory very different from noncooperative game theory.[9] In cooperative games, one can generally assume that all players will cooperate eventually—the only question is how to distribute the total surplus that their cooperation will generate. Many of the greatest successes of cooperative game theory can be characterized as allocation procedures satisfying particular sets of axioms (required properties that may be normatively justified), such as anonymity [the allocation to a player should depend only on that player's role in the game, so that if two players' roles are reversed, then so are their allocations] and Pareto efficiency [it should not be possible to make one player better off without making another worse off]. Different combinations of axioms give rise to bargaining solutions, values, and power indices[10] (see Owen 1995 for details).

Like virtually all other international accords, environmental agreements require administrative councils to oversee monitoring and verification operations; adjudicate disputes; assess evidence; and undertake enforcement functions, including sanctions. Countries with a greater stake in an environmental management problem may demand more central decision roles, increasing the complexity of the decision process. The information provided by power indices and related analyses may someday be recognized as essential to the design of complex and sophisticated decision structures.

An important new area of application for cooperative game theory is arising in the context of a fundamental international environmental problem, the joint management and joint utilization of shared environmental assets. Internationally shared assets include air, the ozone layer, and international water bodies. The latter may be the most difficult of all to manage—water is an irreplaceable input to many vital processes; in arid regions, it is often said that water is life.

Both the quantity and the quality of water in international water basins have often been the focus of international tensions and conflicts, and arrangements for the shared management of international water bodies now preoccupy many governments. The most severe problems seem to arise for international rivers and river basins, perhaps due to the asymmetry inherent in the directionality of flow. The Nile basin, shared by ten countries, may be the most extreme case. In the following, we will discuss water quantity problems, ignoring water quality. This is not to imply that quality is unimportant; however, allocation questions in themselves are an excellent area of application for cooperative game theory.

According to Sofer (1992), the principles that have been proposed to prevent or resolve disputes within an international river basin include the following.

- The Harmon Doctrine, that a state has absolute sovereignty over the area of the basin within it.
- The Territorial Integration Principle, that all states in a basin have a right to "equal" use of all waters within it.
- The Equitable Utilization Principle, that all states can use river water unless this use negatively affects other riparians.
- The Mutual Use Doctrine, that any state in a basin can demand compensation for any other state's use of water from the basin.
- The Principle of Linkage, that, as a condition for agreeing to a particular water allocation, a state can demand compensation in a nonrelated area.

Taken together, these principles are mutually contradictory. Nonetheless it is possible to see them as axioms, or statements of norms of fairness. Thus, adopting some combinations of these statements will constrain or determine allocation of water within a river basin. In some cases, it may be useful simply to understand whether a particular allocation is consistent with a norm of fairness. The careful selection of sets of precisely formulated axioms may lead to acceptable principles for sharing international river waters. If acceptable norms are selected first, then mutually satisfactory allocations may be easier to identify and implement.

Recently, satellite data on snow depth and stream flow have become publicly available for many river basins, making accurate predictions of river flows available to all riparians up to a year in advance. This development is very significant for international water sharing: in the past, many water-sharing agreements have been undermined by uncertainty about flow volumes and by the ability of upstream riparians to conceal information.

Kilgour and Dinar (2001) argue that these new information conditions make it possible to replace agreements that provide for fixed annual volumes with agreements that determine a water schedule detailing how much each riparian receives as a function of river flow. They show that, in simple cases, a few basic axioms are sufficient to determine a schedule that is Pareto optimal, provided riparians' water-demand functions are known. Their methods are cooperative, so of course they do not consider enforceability of agreements. Nonetheless, they give an optimal allocation for policymakers to aim at, and they also provide a way of rating suboptimal allocations according to their distance from the optimum.

Unlike in the noncooperative case, it is not possible to state with confidence what is required for a cooperative game model. In general terms, the information requirements are the same in the two branches of game theory—the difference is in the assumption in the cooperative theory, that enforcement costs are negligible. Modeling requirements, however, seem to depend on the specific model, and it is difficult to draw a general conclusion about them. The procedures of Kilgour and Dinar (2001), for example, require riparian states' demand functions for water, which can be estimated using econometric methods.

A very appealing observation about cooperative game theory is that it is robust in a way that noncooperative game theory is not. In cooperative game theory, small changes in the input data (i.e., the model) generally produce small changes in the results. What plagues cooperative game theory is, instead, an existence and uniqueness problem—it is difficult to assess in advance whether a particular set of axioms is so weak that there are many solutions or so demanding that it cannot be satisfied by any allocation. Again, it can only be hoped that experience will teach us when the benefits of the answers that cooperative game theory can provide will justify the effort required to apply it.

International Environmental Conflict and Game-Theoretic Modeling

Modeling can be thought of as a sequence of choices by the modeler (Ishida and Wolinsky 1996). First, what is being endogenized (i.e., the observed regularities that the theory is trying to explain) must be distinguished from what is exogenous (i.e., assumed). The level of specificity of the hypotheses must also be decided. For example, the model can attempt to explain a particular phenomenon, such as the concessions made by a developed democratic country in an international environmental negotiation under a particular set of constraints, or a general phenomenon, such as the success or failure of threats to deter an aggressor in the context of an environmental conflict. The choice of assumptions is guided by the question of interest and the characteristics and explanatory power of the methodology being applied.

To describe a noncooperative game (of complete information), one must specify five elements.

- The players
- The choices available to each player whenever it must make a decision
- The information about previous choices in the game that is available to a player at the time it makes a decision
- The possible outcomes and how they are determined by the decisions made (and, possibly, by chance events) during the course of the game
- The players' preferences over the possible outcomes (usually in the form of utilities)

Noncooperative games in which choices are simultaneous and complete are generally modeled in matrix (strategic) form; if decisions fall in a sequence, the game is usually modeled graphically in extensive (tree) form to display both the choices and the flow of information.

To describe a noncooperative game of incomplete information, one must specify for each player each of the possible games that the player may be playing and a (subjective) probability associated with each of these possible games. In principle, a player may be uncertain exactly who the opponents are or what moves they have available. In practice, however, most incomplete information games—like the one to be described next—involve uncertainty only about players' values. To model a player who has one of several possible payoffs, several versions, or *types,* of the player must be specified. The game usually begins with a chance move that determines players' actual (realized) types with common-knowledge probabilities; each player is then informed of his or her own type, but not of the types of the opponents.

Next we illustrate the use of an incomplete information game to model a generic deterrence problem relating to possible conflict over the sharing of a natural resource such as river water. Problems like this one are typical of international politics in many regions of the world. For instance, most of the freshwater available to Israel and Jordan comes from the Jordan River, which receives all of its water from tributaries in Syria (the Yarmouk and Banias Rivers) and Lebanon (the Hasbani River). These simple geographical facts have been major determinants of relations among Israel, Jordan, Syria, and Lebanon for some time.

The problem was not always serious. During the 1950s, U.S. officials mediated a series of negotiations among Israel, Jordan, Syria, and Lebanon over sharing the waters of the Jordan River and its tributaries. In 1955, Israel accepted the Unified Plan, later known as the Johnston Plan, for the allocation of these waters. Although the Arab League formally rejected the Johnston Plan, Jordan unofficially followed it (Wolf 1994, 19–23), producing a more-or-less stable arrangement that endured until 1964. But then, faced with a growing need for water for agricultural development, Israel began to divert water from the Jordan River to its newly built National Water Carrier (Ha'Movil Ha'Arzi).

In Israel's view, this diversion was consistent with the Johnston Plan, but Syria and Egypt saw it as an unacceptable challenge to the status quo. A 1964 Arab League summit authorized Jordan, Syria, and Lebanon to divert the Hasbani and the Banias so as to reduce the flow into Israel's Lake Tiberias and increase the flow of the Yarmouk River to Jordan. Jordan's consequent construction of a dam on the Yarmouk prompted Israeli military action. The Arab League counterdiversion plan was halted, and Jordan has not subsequently challenged Israel over water.

We illustrate game modeling by showing how a simple game model throws some light on conflicts such as the one over the diversion of the Jordan. This model was developed in another context by Zagare and Kilgour (1993; see also 2000) but is readily adaptable to environmental conflicts. Indeed, past or potential conflicts over many rivers in the world, including the Euphrates, the Nile, the Indus, and the Columbia, may follow a similar pattern.

The Asymmetric Deterrence model[11] is shown as a game in extensive form in figure 1. This game has two players, Challenger (Ch) and Defender (Def). The decision tree grows from left to right, so the game begins with Challenger's decision whether or not to Initiate a crisis. If there is no initiation, the game ends at the outcome "Status Quo." But if Challenger chooses to Initiate, the next move belongs to Defender, who must choose whether or not to Resist. If Defender does not Resist, the game ends at an

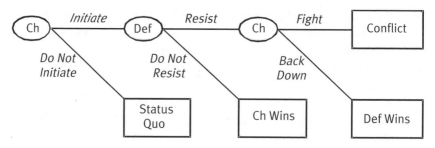

Fig. 1. Asymmetric Deterrence Game
(Adapted from Zagare and Kilgour 2000.)

outcome called "Ch Wins," but if Defender Resists, the game continues to a second decision by Challenger. At its second decision point, Challenger must decide whether to Back Down or Fight. If Challenger Backs Down, the outcome is "Def Wins," whereas if Challenger Fights, the outcome is "Conflict."

Of course, the Asymmetric Deterrence model is too simple to represent the detail of real-world events such as the Jordan River diversion conflict. All models are! Our intention is to show how a very simple model can capture some of the most important considerations of decision makers, who may, under certain conditions, risk unwanted war in order to obtain more of a vital resource.

The game analysis of the Asymmetric Deterrence model hinges on the players' preferences over the four outcomes. It is only natural to assume that each player prefers its winning to the status quo, and the status quo to giving in to the opponent. The crucial variable is whether the player prefers conflict to the opponent's winning (without a fight). Zagare and Kilgour define a player as Hard if it prefers conflict to capitulation and as Soft if it prefers the reverse. Thus, they define the preference orderings of the two types of Challenger as

> Hard Challenger: Ch Wins > Status Quo > Conflict > Def Wins
> Soft Challenger: Ch Wins > Status Quo > Def Wins > Conflict

while the preference orderings of the two types of Defender are

332

Hard Defender: Def Wins > Status Quo > Conflict > Ch Wins
Soft Defender: Def Wins > Status Quo > Ch Wins > Conflict

Zagare and Kilgour (1993) determine that, provided both players know their own and their opponent's type, the outcome of the Asymmetric Deterrence model cannot be Conflict. According to a very fundamental principle of noncooperative game theory (subgame perfect equilibrium), the outcome must be either Status Quo or Ch Wins. Specifically, if Ch is Hard and Def is Soft, then Ch will choose Initiate and Def will follow with Do Not Resist, producing the outcome Ch Wins. In every other case (i.e., if Def is Hard or if Ch is Soft) Ch rationally chooses Do Not Initiate, and the outcome is Status Quo.

But this is not the end of the story. The parties to a conflict do not normally advertise their preferences, especially over less desirable alternatives, so that each antagonist may doubt whether its opponent is Hard or Soft. Thus, in applications of the Asymmetric Deterrence model in the real world, we can assume that each player will know its own type, but we must allow for uncertainty over the type of the opponent.

Game theory provides a framework that can include these uncertainties—incomplete information games. As applied by Zagare and Kilgour (1993), each player has a "credibility," the probability that its opponent assigns to its being Hard. Thus, Challenger's credibility, p_{Ch}, is the probability that Defender assigns to the possibility that Challenger is Hard; it follows that Defender assigns a probability of $1 - p_{Ch}$ to the possibility that Challenger is Soft. For instance, a very credible Challenger (p_{Ch} near 1) is one believed by Defender to be very likely Hard. Note that Challenger knows for certain whether it is Hard or Soft and also knows the probabilities, p_{Ch} and $1 - p_{Ch}$, that Defender assigns to these two events. Analogously, Defender's credibility, p_{Def}, is the probability that Challenger assigns to the possibility that Defender is Hard. Defender knows whether it is Hard and knows the value of p_{Def}. Notice that, in this formulation, information is incomplete because each player has private information about itself that its opponent is uncertain about.

The incomplete information version of the Asymmetric Deterrence model can be solved using the concept of perfect Bayesian equilibrium (see Fudenberg and Tirole 1991). A solution is now a complete specification of what each player would do, depending on its actual type and the prior actions of the opponent. Zagare and Kilgour (1993, 2000) find that there are actually four perfect Bayesian equilibria.

Certain Deterrence Equilibrium
Behavior: Challenger: Do Not Initiate (regardless of type).
Outcome: Status Quo.

Separating Equilibrium
Behavior: Soft Challenger: Do Not Initiate.
            Hard Challenger: Initiate. Fight if Defender Resists.
            Soft Defender: Do Not Resist.
            Hard Defender: Resist.
Outcome: Status Quo (if Challenger Soft), Ch Wins (if Challenger Hard and Defender Soft), or Conflict (otherwise).

Attack Equilibrium
Behavior: Soft Challenger: Initiate. Back Down if Defender Resists.
            Hard Challenger: Initiate. Fight if Defender Resists.
            Soft Defender: Do Not Resist.
            Hard Defender: Resist.
Outcome: Ch Wins (if Defender Soft), Def Wins (if Challenger Soft and Defender Hard), or Conflict (otherwise).

Bluff Equilibrium
Behavior: Soft Challenger: Initiate sometimes. Back Down if Defender Resists.
            Hard Challenger: Initiate. Fight if Defender Resists.
            Soft Defender: Resist sometimes.
            Hard Defender: Resist.
Outcome: All four outcomes are possible.

Which of these perfect Bayesian equilibria is in play depends on the values of Ch's credibility p_{Ch} and Def's credibility p_{Def}, as shown in figure 2. Note that the four corners of the square represent the four possible complete information games discussed earlier. The locations of the boundaries between the different equilibria, and the probabilities for "bluffing" at a Bluff Equilibrium, depend on the von Neumann–Morgenstern utilities of the four possible outcomes (see Zagare and Kilgour 1993, 2000 for details).

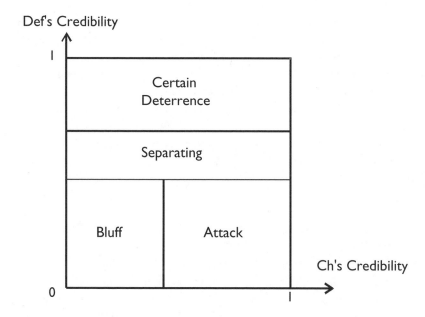

Fig. 2.   Perfect Bayesian equilibria of Asymmetric Deterrence Game
(Adapted from Zagare and Kilgour 2000.)

We now review some conclusions that can be drawn from the analysis. If Defender is credible enough, the Certain Deterrence Equilibrium applies, the Status Quo is secure, and Defender's threat to Resist is sufficient to deter Challenger from Initiating. If Challenger's credibility is high and Defender's is low, the Attack Equilibrium applies: Challenger goes ahead and Initiates; a Soft Challenger plans to Back Down if Defender Resists, but a Hard Challenger will press on. The Bluff Equilibrium is perhaps the most disquieting. Both players are likely Soft. If they happen to be Hard, they act aggressively by Initiating or Resisting. But if they are Soft, they may act Hard, according to probabilities that can be calculated. Under a Bluff Equilibrium an "unwanted" or unexpected conflict can occur—when a side that really does not want conflict nonetheless tries to face down the opponent.

We described the Asymmetric Deterrence model as a generic model for environmental conflicts and suggested that it might apply to crises such as the Jordan River diversion conflict of 1964. We believe that the model gives a rough picture of the interacting decisions that created this crisis. A partial explanation is that both sides were (at least initially) willing to risk war and each thought that it was more committed to the issue than its opponent. Although this model is too simple to account for some aspects of the crisis, such as relations between Jordan and Syria, and although it cannot be said to "explain" the crisis until independent evidence is produced about both sides' actual preferences and beliefs, it does show how two sides may end up in an unwanted conflict because they are uncertain about the credibility of each other's threat. In any case, the consistency of the 1964 events with the Bluff Equilibrium of the model suggests that war was narrowly averted at that time.

Conclusions: The Benefits of Game-Theoretic Modeling

Many questions of international environmental management might be resolved, or at least clarified, by game-theoretic modeling and analysis; a few of them have been suggested here. But rather than simply list possible future applications, we will step back and review the benefits and shortcomings of game-theoretic models in general, and we will comment on how game theory is developing and assess its overall potential to improve international environmental management.

To begin with, game-theoretic models are models; they intentionally simplify reality. The objective of modeling is to explain how a phenomenon of interest is related to other features. It is not reasonable to expect game-theoretic models, or any other models, to provide complete explanations—to say all there is to say. The best one can hope for is to identify and measure the features and relationships that are most relevant to the phenomenon under investigation.

Game-theoretic models are formal models, and formal models can contribute to analysis in many ways. First, they require that premises be formulated precisely, which is often a valuable step because it focuses on the essential similarities and differences of real-world instantiations. Second, the fact that the conclusions follow logically from the premises provides a credible test of the model; a model that passes the test permits us to economize on information—we can concentrate on the determining features of a situation, rather than on those that are derivative. Third, a model that can be analyzed formally may lead in unexpected directions, providing new information, suggesting something unexpected to look for, or uncovering a connection with other problems that was not apparent in advance.

Moreover, game-theoretic models are decision models. To examine an event using game theory, one must represent it as being determined by the choices of individual decision makers. These decision makers, aware of the constraints under which they labor and the values they place on the possible outcomes, are assumed to make deliberate decisions that are consistent with their preferences, at least insofar as they are able.

The growth of game-theoretic modeling within international relations demonstrates that many specialists find it effective. Yet game-theoretic models have been criticized for making "unrealistic" assumptions about decision makers. For instance, the original formulation of game theory required that all players have complete knowledge of all possible choices by any player, of all possible outcomes, and of all players' preferences over all outcomes. In addition, players were endowed with the capacity for unlimited, costless, and instantaneous calculation. It is surely obvious that the knowledge and capabilities of real-world decision makers fall far short of these ideals.

In fact, game theory has evolved, and now some approaches do not impose these demanding requirements. Incomplete information models, like the one described earlier, are now standard and have been applied extensively in international relations. There is now an increasing technical literature on the behavior of boundedly rational players, although to date it seems not to have been applied in political science. Of course, game theory is a continuing project, and it is impossible to predict how it will develop. One can guess based on past experience that at core it will remain a normative theory of interacting decisions, each made consistent with the interests of the decision maker but within the decision maker's capabilities and knowledge.

In particular, those who develop game theory, like those who apply it, consider many of its methods and principles ripe for change. For instance, one problem for empirical application of game models is multiple equilibria, particularly in incomplete information models. Indeed, proposals have been made to reduce or eliminate the problem of nonuniqueness of noncooperative equilibria by strengthening the definition of equilibrium, producing what are called Nash equilibrium refinements (in fact, the simplest refinement is the perfect Bayesian equilibrium applied earlier in the Asymmetric Deterrence example). Unfortunately, many of the proposed definitions are inconsistent, and—as with bargaining solutions and values in cooperative game theory—there is no consensus on how to select among them.

It is therefore prudent to refer only to the most central features of game theory when assessing whether and how game-theoretic models may be applied to questions of environmental management. In fact, this restriction makes it easy to argue that game theory is a natural tool for this purpose. First, problems of international environmental management involve the interactions of sovereign states, which can usually be thought of as independent, self-interested decision makers. Alternatively, two-level game models can be adopted to study decision making in a sovereign state that is more complex than implied by the "unitary actor" assumption. Second, as with other international interactions, stability, relative power, fairness, and efficiency are of central importance; game theory has made, and is making, great strides in accounting for these aspects. Third, national opportunities and central objectives are often straightforward and therefore easy to formulate in a game model. Fourth, environmental knowledge— how decisions affect environmental outcomes—can be incorporated directly into game models. Moreover, where this knowledge is lacking, models can reflect the possibilities and can be updated, and grow in usefulness, as underlying environmental knowledge increases. Finally, game theory, especially on the cooperative side, provides many useful procedures to find allocations that satisfy appropriate standards of fairness, and both fairness and the perception of fairness are essential to successful international management of shared resources.

Recommended Readings

Güner, S. 1998. Signaling in the Turkish-Syrian Water Conflict. *Conflict Management and Peace Science* 16:185–206.

Kilgour, D. M., and A. Dinar. 2001. Flexible Water Sharing within an International River Basin. *Environmental and Resource Economics* 18:43–60.

Morrow, J. D. 1994. *Game Theory for Political Scientists.* Princeton: Princeton University Press.

Ostrom, E. 1990. *Governing the Commons: The Evolution of Institutions for Collective Action.* New York: Cambridge University Press.

Zagare, F. C., and D. M. Kilgour. 2000. *Perfect Deterrence.* Cambridge: Cambridge University Press.

Notes

1. For example, climate change negotiations involve both commons (global climate) issues and transboundary externalities (such as CO_2 emissions from one country affecting the climate of others).

2. For instance, as Güner (1997, 1998) suggests, one very plausible interpretation of events in southeast Turkey is that Syria sees Turkey as threatening Syria's water supply and is responding to this environmental problem by supporting PKK (Kurdish Workers' Party) activities in Turkey.

3. Putnam defines *win-set* as the set of all possible agreements that will gain the support of all essential domestic constituencies. Shepsle and Weingast (1987) also introduce the concept but with a different interpretation.

4. Iida (1993) formalizes Putnam's conjectures, showing that under complete information, greater domestic constraints are indeed a bargaining advantage.

5. This discussion is based on Ishida and Wolinsky (1996).

6. The idea of an international agreement as a signal of competence also appears in Morrow (1991).

7. A bargainer's "reservation level," or walk-away price, is the level of benefits that would make the bargainer indifferent between accepting and rejecting an agreement. Unless each bargainer receives at least its reservation level, there will be no agreement.

8. Wolinsky (1997) identifies several sequential equilibria that are of interest in the context of the model. The analysis of the relatively simple international crisis example identifies all perfect Bayesian equilibria. For details of these and other equilibrium definitions, see Fudenberg and Tirole (1991), Myerson (1991), Gibbons (1992), or Morrow (1994).

9. Many noncooperative models of the enforcement of agreements and the development of cooperation have been proposed. For example, Folk theorems (see Morrow 1994, chap. 9) identify which outcomes can be stabilized in an indefinitely repeated noncooperative game.

10. When all possible final distributions of utility have been specified, as well as the utilities for failing to agree, a *bargaining solution* recommends a specific distribution of utility that satisfies particular axioms. Well-known bargaining solutions are due to Nash and Kalai-Smorodinsky. A *value* is a utility distribution that is justified only by the total achievable utility for each possible coalition of players. The best-known values are due to Shapley and Banzhaf. A bargaining solution

may make sense even if utility is not transferable; in contrast, a value assumes transferable utility. A *power index* is a value applied to a model that contains only information about which coalitions win and which ones lose. The Shapley value produces the Shapley-Shubik index, and the Banzhaf value produces the Banzhaf-Coleman index. See Owen (1995) for details.

11. For other illustrations of deterrence models see Huth and Allee, chapter 9, and Kydd, chapter 14, in this volume.

References

Aumann, R. J. 1987. What Is Game Theory Trying to Accomplish? In *Frontiers of Economics,* edited by K. J. Arrow and S. Honkapohja. Oxford: Blackwell.

Aumann, R. J., and S. Hart. 1992, 1994, 2002. *Handbook of Game Theory with Economic Applications.* 3 vols. Amsterdam: North-Holland.

Barrett, S. 1994. Self Enforcing International Agreements. *Oxford Economic Papers* 46:878–94.

Brams, S. J. 1975. *Game Theory and Politics.* New York: Free Press.

Brams, S. J., and P. J. Affuso. 1985. New Paradoxes of Voting Power on the EC Council of Ministers. *Electoral Studies* 4:187–91.

Brams, S. J., and D. M. Kilgour. 1988. *Game Theory and National Security.* New York: Basil Blackwell.

Brown Weiss, E., and H. K. Jacobson. 1998. *Engaging Countries: Strengthening Compliance with International Environmental Accords.* Cambridge: MIT Press.

Carraro, C., and D. Siniscalco. 1998. International Environment Agreements: Incentives and Political Economy. *European Economic Review* 42:561–72.

Downs, G. W., D. M. Rocke, and P. N. Barsoom. 1996. Is the Good News about Compliance Good News about Cooperation? *International Organization* 50 (3): 379–406.

Ecchia, G., and M. Mariotti. 1998. Coalition Formation in International Environmental Agreements and the Role of Institutions. *European Economic Review* 42:573–83.

Evans, P. B., H. K. Jacobson, and R. D. Putnam, eds. 1993. *Double-Edged Diplomacy: International Bargaining and Domestic Politics.* Berkeley: University of California Press.

Fang, L., K. W. Hipel, and D. M. Kilgour. 1993. *Interactive Decision Analysis: The Graph Model for Conflict Resolution.* New York: Wiley.

Fearon, J. D. 1994. Domestic Political Audiences and the Escalation of International Disputes. *American Political Science Review* 88 (3): 577–92.

———. 1995. Rationalist Explanations for War. *International Organization* 49:379–414.

————. 1997. Signaling Foreign Policy Interests. *Journal of Conflict Resolution* 41:68–90.

Fudenberg, D., and J. Tirole. 1991. *Game Theory.* Cambridge: MIT Press.

Gibbons, R. 1992. *Game Theory for Applied Economists.* Princeton: Princeton University Press.

Grundig, F., H. Ward, and E. R. Zorick. 2001. Modeling Global Climate Negotiations. In *International Relations and Global Climate Change,* edited by U. Luterbacher and D. Sprinz. Cambridge: MIT Press.

Güner, S. 1997. The Turkish-Syrian War of Attrition: The Water Dispute. *Studies in Conflict and Terrorism* 20:105–16.

————. 1998. Signaling in the Turkish-Syrian Water Conflict. *Conflict Management and Peace Science* 16:185–206.

Haas, P. M., R. O. Keohane, and M. A. Levy, eds. 1993. *Institutions for the Earth: Sources of Effective International Environmental Protection.* Cambridge: MIT Press.

Hardin, G. 1968. The Tragedy of the Commons. *Science* 162:1243–48.

Hoel, M. 1992. International Environmental Conventions: The Case of Uniform Reductions of Emissions. *Environmental and Resource Economics* 2:141–59.

Hosli, M. 1996. Coalitions and Power: Effects of Qualified Majority Voting in the Council of the European Union. *Journal of Common Market Studies* 34 (2): 255–73.

Iida, K. 1993. When and How Do Domestic Constraints Matter? Uncertainty in International Relations. *Journal of Conflict Resolution* 37 (3): 403–26.

Ishida, A., and Y. Wolinsky. 1996. Double-Edged Theories: Rationality, Domestic Institutions, and Foreign Policy. Mimeo, University of Chicago.

Kerby, W., and F. Göbeler. 1996. The Distribution of Voting Power in the United Nations. In *Models for Security Policy in the Post-Cold War Era,* edited by R. K. Huber and R. Avenhaus. Baden-Baden: Nomos Verlagsgesellschaft.

Kilgour, D. M. 1994. The Use of Costless Inspection in Enforcement. *Theory and Decision* 36:207–32.

Kilgour, D. M., and A. Dinar. 2001. Flexible Water Sharing within an International River Basin. *Environmental and Resource Economics* 18:43–60.

Kilgour, D. M., and F. C. Zagare. 1994. Uncertainty and the Role of the Pawn in Extended Deterrence. *Synthèse* 100:379–412.

————. 1997. Preamble on Discrete Models. Manuscript, Wilfrid Laurier University.

Knopf, R. W. 1993. Beyond Two-Level Games: Domestic International Interaction in the Intermediate-Range Nuclear Forces Negotiation. *International Organization* 47 (4): 599–628.

Loehmann, E., and D. M. Kilgour. 1997. *Designing Institutions for Environmental and Resource Management.* Cheltenham, UK: Edward Elgar.

Miles, E. L., A. Underdal, S. Andresen, J. Wettestad, J. B. Skjaerseth, and E. M.

Carlin, eds. 2001. *Environmental Regime Effectiveness: Confronting Theory with Evidence.* Cambridge: MIT Press.

Milner, H. V., and B. P. Rosendorff. 1997. Democratic Politics and International Trade Negotiations: Elections and Divided Government as Constraints on Trade Liberalization. *Journal of Conflict Resolution* 41 (1): 117–46.

Mo, J. 1994. The Logic of Two Level Games with Endogenous Domestic Coalitions. *Journal of Conflict Resolution* 38:402–22.

Moravcsik, A. 1993. Introduction: Integrating International and Domestic Theories of International Bargaining. In *Double Edged Diplomacy,* edited by P. Evans, H. K. Jacobson, and R. Putnam. Berkeley: University of California Press.

Morrow, J. D. 1989. Capabilities, Uncertainty, and Resolve: A Limited Information Model of Crisis Bargaining. *American Journal of Political Science* 33 (4): 941–72.

———. 1991. Electoral and Congressional Incentives and Arms Control. *Journal of Conflict Resolution* 35 (2): 245–65.

———. 1994. *Game Theory for Political Scientists.* Princeton: Princeton University Press.

Myerson, R. 1991. *Game Theory: Analysis of Conflict.* Cambridge: Harvard University Press.

O'Neill, B. 1994. Sources in Game Theory for International Relations Specialists. In *Cooperative Models in International Relations Research,* edited by M. D. Intrilligator and U. Luterbacher. Boston: Kluwer Academic Publishers.

Ostrom, E. 1990. *Governing the Commons.* Cambridge: Cambridge University Press.

Ostrom, E., R. N. Gardner, and J. Walker. 1994. *Rules Games and Common-Pool Resources.* Ann Arbor: University of Michigan Press.

Owen, G. 1995. *Game Theory.* New York: Academic Press.

Pahre, R., and P. Papayoanou. 1997. Using Game Theory to Link Domestic and International Politics. *Journal of Conflict Resolution* 41 (1): 4–11.

Payne, D. C. 2000. Policy-Making in Nested Institutions: Explaining the Conservation Failure of the EU's Common Fisheries Policy. *Journal of Common Market Studies* 38 (2): 303–24.

Powell, R. 1990. *Nuclear Deterrence Theory: The Problem of Credibility.* Cambridge: Cambridge University Press.

Rubinstein, A. 1991. Comments on the Interpretation of Game Theory. *Econometrica* 59 (4): 909–29.

Shepsle, K. A., and B. R. Weingast. 1987. The Institutional Foundations of Committee Power. *American Political Science Review* 81:85–104.

Snidal, D. 1986. The Game Theory of International Politics. In *Cooperation under Anarchy,* edited by K. Oye. Princeton: Princeton University Press.

Sofer, A. 1992. *Rivers of Fire.* Tel Aviv: Am Oved Publishers.

Sprinz, D. 1994. Editorial Overview: Strategies of Inquiry into International Environmental Policy. *International Studies Notes* 19 (4): 32–34.

Von Neumann, J., and O. Morgenstern. 1944. *Theory of Games and Economic Behavior.* Princeton: Princeton University Press.

Ward, H. 1993. Game Theory and the Politics of Global Commons. *Journal of Conflict Resolution* 37 (2): 203–35.

———. 1996. Game Theory and the Politics of Global Warming: The State of Play and Beyond. *Political Studies* 44 (5): 850–71.

Ward, H., F. Grundig, and E. R. Zorick. 2001. Marching at the Pace of the Slowest: A Model of International Climate-Change Negotiations. *Political Studies* 49 (3): 438–61.

Wettestad, J., and S. Andresen. 1994. The Effectiveness of International Resource and Environmental Regimes. *International Studies Notes* 19 (4): 49–52.

Wolf, A. J. 1994. A Hydropolitical History of the Nile, Jordan, and Euphrates River Basins. In *International Waters of the Middle East,* edited by A. K. Biswas. New York: Oxford University Press.

Wolinsky, Y. 1997. Two-Level Game Analysis of International Environmental Politics. Paper presented at the Convention of the International Studies Association, Toronto.

Young, O. R. 1989. *International Cooperation: Building Regimes for Natural Resources and the Environment.* Ithaca: Cornell University Press.

Young, O. R., and G. Osherenko, eds. 1993. *Polar Politics: Creating International Environmental Regimes.* Ithaca: Cornell University Press.

Zagare, F. C., and D. M. Kilgour. 1993. Asymmetric Deterrence. *International Studies Quarterly* 37:1–27.

———. 1995. Assessing Competing Defence Postures: The Strategic Implications of "Flexible Response." *World Politics* 37 (3): 373–417.

———. 2000. *Perfect Deterrence.* Cambridge: Cambridge University Press.

14. The Art of Shaker Modeling: Game Theory and Security Studies

Andrew Kydd

Shaker chairs are famous in the world of design for their minimalist aesthetic. Constructed of dowels, slats, and woven cloth tape, they are light and strong, and fulfill their function beautifully. They seem like physical embodiments of the abstract idea of a chair, as simple as a chair can be and still be useful as a chair. Formal models share a similar aesthetic. As Duncan Snidal points out (chap. 10, this vol.), models strip away extraneous details to arrive at the underlying essence of strategic problems. The best models are often those that capture the core of a strategic situation in the simplest possible framework. Of course, the tradeoff is that one analyst's extraneous detail is another's primary interest, so the simplicity of any one formal model prevents it from meeting all needs. Shaker chairs have no cup holders, extending footrests, or magic finger massage capabilities.[1]

The field of international security studies seems to have a curious love-hate relationship with the Shaker style of theorizing embodied in formal modeling and game theory. On the one hand, there is a long tradition of formal modeling in the study of international security dating back to the differential equation models of arms races created by Lewis F. Richardson at the time of World War I (as discussed by Snidal).[2] In the 1960s, the new science of game theory began to be applied to international relations and the U.S.-Soviet confrontation (Schelling 1960). The 1970s saw the growth of interest in simple two-player normal form games as models of international conflict (Jervis 1978; Snyder and Diesing 1977), while the 1980s saw the widespread application of the repeated Prisoners' Dilemma model to a variety of international security and economic issues (Axelrod 1984;

Oye 1986). Starting in the 1980s and gathering momentum in the 1990s, incomplete information game theory has become a pervasive tool in the analysis of the origins of war (Bueno de Mesquita and Lalman 1992; Fearon 1995), deterrence (Powell 1990), alliance politics (Morrow 1994), arms racing (Downs and Rocke 1990), and the democratic peace thesis (Bueno de Mesquita and Lalman 1992; Schultz 1999), among other issues. On the other hand, perhaps in reaction to its increasing prominence, formal modeling in security studies has also generated something of a backlash. Critics of "rational deterrence theory" argued that abstract theorizing did not produce useful knowledge (George and Smoke 1989), while defenders highlighted the limitations of the case study method (Achen and Snidal 1989). Stephen Walt warned against the increasing salience of the rational choice perspective and the imperial ambitions of its practitioners while claiming that formal work in the field suffers from a lack of originality and has contributed little in the way of important, empirically verifiable insights (1999). Another critique, by Pierre Allan and Cedric Dupont, claims that formal modeling in international relations has strayed from its Shaker roots and has become too baroque to have robust empirical implications (1999).

This chapter will review the strengths and weaknesses of rational choice in security studies. I will argue first that if game theory is useful anywhere in political science, it should be useful in security studies, because of three properties that distinguish the field. First, it focuses on interactions between small numbers of actors, often just two, so the strategic nature of the interaction is crucial, unlike in market situations in which each actor can take the behavior of the rest of the market as given. Second, the actors care strongly about the issues at stake in the interactions, so they are less likely to act reflexively without thinking about what they do. Third, the actors often have considerable experience with their partners and with the issues at stake, so they are not coming new to the problem, which lessens the likelihood of simple mistakes from lack of familiarity with the situation.

Then I will examine two issue areas in which I argue that our understanding of international affairs has been significantly improved by formal theory. First, I will focus on the origins of war, comparing the insights generated by the game-theoretic literature with that which went before. I argue that the advent of game-theoretic work has greatly improved our understanding of the conditions under which rational agents will fight. Second, I will look at the intersection of domestic and international politics, and in particular at the democratic peace. Quantitative studies of war have shown that democracies are unlikely to fight each other. Nonformal explanations of this regularity focus on norms and institutions (Russett 1993). Game-theoretical work has produced a third explanation, the informational approach, which is not only original and unanticipated in the nonformal literature, but has been shown to be empirically valid as well. To illustrate these arguments I will present a bargaining model based on Fearon (1995) and Schultz (1999). This model analyzes the link between bargaining and war in the simplest possible framework, exemplifying the Shaker approach to modeling. Finally, I will discuss some of the limitations of formal work in the field, two problems in particular. First, models of interactions involving more than three players have been difficult to execute in a convincing fashion, and this problem has especially plagued the balance of power literature. Second, in some cases the most important part of the explanation may lie in the preferences of the states concerned, or in pervasive misperceptions they may have, not in their strategic situation. If a state simply has a strong aversion to casualties, it may not take a game theorist to figure out that it will be less likely to initiate wars. Conversely, if a state's perception of the strategic environment is dominated by myths, a change in the strategic environment may produce no change in behavior, while a change in who makes the myths may indeed produce a change in policy. While these problems place some limitations on the applicability of game theory in strategic studies, I argue that it has a very important role to play in the field.

Game Theory and Security Studies: If Not Here . . .

The field of security studies is especially well suited for game theory for three reasons, as mentioned earlier. First, the number of actors in many security issues is relatively small. The two most significant arms races of the twentieth century, for example, were the Anglo-German naval race and the Cold War, both bilateral contests. Even multilateral arms races can often be reduced to two sides (e.g., the land arms race involving Germany against France and Russia before World War I). War initiation is another example. Since Thucydides' account of the Peloponnesian War between Athens and Sparta, most theories of war have implicitly or explicitly focused on two actors. Preventive war theory focuses on the rising and the declining power, deterrence theory deals with the challenger and the defender, and so on. Many wars are bilateral, and almost all are two-sided.

Two-actor situations are especially appropriate for game-theoretic techniques. First, two-actor games are simpler to set up and easier to solve. This tractability advantage is important; as will be discussed later, models with larger numbers of actors can become difficult to solve and interpret. More substantively, in two-actor situations, the strategic interdependence of the actors is maximized, and game theory is the study of strategic interdependence. In a competitive market with many actors, each individual actor can more or less take the behavior of others as fixed. If you are a farmer selling a corn crop, it is foolish to worry about what your neighbor is thinking of charging; commodity prices are determined by thousands of buyers and sellers in national and global markets. Your choice by itself makes little difference to the price. The opposite pole from the competitive market is the duopoly or two-actor case, where the other actor's behavior is very important to one's welfare. If you are one of two plumbers in town, the prices charged by your competitor are very important to how much business you will do, and vice versa. Game theory was created to analyze precisely these situations where strategic interdependence is maximized. Hence, as Helen Milner argues (chap. 11, this vol.), game theory is more appropriate in security studies than in international political economy, where there are often multiple actors, and the strategic element is thought to be less salient.

A second reason why game theory is appropriate for security studies is that the participants involved often care quite a bit about the outcomes, that is, the stakes are high. It typically matters a great deal to statesmen whether they win or lose wars, as their tenure in office and their very lives may depend on it (Bueno de Mesquita and Siverson 1995). Rational choice theory is sometimes argued to be a better predictor of behavior in situations in which people have strong interests, as opposed to situations in which they do not care so much about the issues at stake (Aldrich 1993).[3] Where the stakes are low, people are much more likely to make decisions rapidly, without much thought, using habit, rules of thumb, or other nonrational decision-making procedures. It is where the stakes are high that people are more likely to think carefully about their options, consider what others might do in response to their actions, and weigh the relative likelihood of the different outcomes. Of course, if stakes are high and time is short, decision makers may suffer from stress and act irrationally (Lebow 1981). But at least with significant stakes they have a reason to try to act rationally, whereas trivial issues provide no such incentive.

A third reason why formal theory is especially appropriate in security studies is that the practitioners of world politics often have extensive experience with the relevant issues. They are not coming to these issues for the first time. In experimental studies of rational choice theories it is common to throw out the first few trials of a model because the subjects are encountering it for the first time and their behavior tends to have a large random component. After a few trials the subjects gain familiarity with the situation and behave more systematically. Many world leaders have years of experience in international affairs before they come to top decision-making positions, and they subsequently have tenures of several years' duration, enough time to become familiar with the issues and actors on the world scene. Furthermore they are advised by ministries staffed by career bureaucrats who have dealt with international relations professionally for their entire lives. Unfortunately, familiarity can lead to habitual, routinized behavior as well, especially on the part of large bureaucratic organizations (Allison 1971). Such behavior can be irrational, especially from the perspective of the state as a whole. However, the major issues of war and peace are usually decided by top decision makers, not bureaucracies. Leaders may be better equipped to handle such issues than randomly selected individuals with no knowledge of international affairs on the one hand, or routine-driven organizations on the other.

Summing up, I would argue that security studies makes about as good a field of application for game theory as could be hoped for. The two-actor strategic problems commonly found in international relations are the easiest to analyze with game theory: they maximize strategic interdependence, leaders care strongly about the issues at stake in these interactions, and they have developed some familiarity with the problems they face. If game theory is applicable anywhere, then, it should be applicable to security studies.

Game Theory and the Origins of War

One issue that game theory has been most frequently used to investigate is the origins of war, without doubt the most important issue in security studies. Many works are devoted explicitly to war initiation, and much else in security studies derives its interest from its connection to this central topic. Yet I would argue that the discipline had a weak grasp of even the central questions to be asked, let alone the answers, before the advent of game-theoretic applications to security studies. This new approach has greatly revised our understanding of the field. This episode illustrates some of the most important benefits of using formal theory in political science: clarifying ideas and testing the logical coherence of theories.

The most influential scholar on the origins of war of the pre–game-theoretic era was surely Kenneth Waltz. His magnum opus, *Theory of International Politics,* was required reading from the date of its publication in 1979, and his theories shaped the debate for a generation. Waltz's analysis of the origins of war is simple and compelling. He starts with the indisputable fact that the international world is anarchic, or lacking a centralized governance that makes life in at least some states relatively safe. Because of this anarchic environment, states are unrestrained; they can do what they like within the limits of their power. In particular, they can attack, conquer, enslave, and destroy each other. This possibility renders states insecure, and the consequent search for security serves as the principal motivation behind state action. Because states are insecure, they seek to build up their military capabilities, which makes other states less secure—the familiar "security dilemma" (Herz 1950; Jervis 1978). States may also attack each other as they see favorable opportunities to destroy competitors, or they may fear imminent attack from competitors in the harsh struggle for survival that is international politics.[4] As Waltz puts it, "Competition and conflict among states stem directly from the twin facts of life under conditions of anarchy: States in an anarchic order must provide for their own security, and threats or seeming threats to their security abound" (1988, 43). Thus war, according to Waltz, is an inevitable consequence of anarchy and the consequent insecurity of states, and this accounts for the constant recurrence of war throughout history, even as other factors, such as the domestic constitutions of states, change.

This simple, powerful account of war had a tremendous impact on the field. Much of the early criticism leveled against it from a non–game-theoretic perspective had very little effect in diminishing its appeal.[5] However, it was soon appreciated that the conclusions Waltz reached about war might not actually follow from his assumptions about the structure of the international system, and that game theory might be able to show this. As Robert Keohane put it: "Rational-choice theory enables us to demonstrate that the pessimistic conclusions about cooperation often associated with

Realism are not necessarily valid, even if we accept the assumption of rational egoism" (1984, 13).

This was the agenda of cooperation theory, based on the repeated Prisoners' Dilemma model (RPD) (Axelrod 1984; Oye 1986). In the repeated Prisoners' Dilemma, cooperation can be sustained in anarchy by threats of future retaliation for current defections. This was a powerful critique, and it raised questions about the logical coherence of Waltz's theory. However, as applied to the core questions of security studies, at least, the RPD model has a crucial flaw, which was pointed out by Joseph Grieco (1988). Useful as it is in many contexts, the RPD is a questionable model of international security affairs because it does not directly model the possibility of war.[6] In particular, it does not allow for the possibility that one state could conquer another and hence render itself immune to the future punishment that enforces cooperation in the RPD. When Germany overran France in 1940, future retaliation from France was no longer possible and hence could not serve to deter German defection.[7]

What was needed, then, was a model that dealt directly with the decision to initiate war in the context of a strategic interaction in which the loser would be eliminated from the game. This was provided by the crisis-bargaining literature, and it is the link between war and bargaining theory that is perhaps the greatest contribution of modern game theory to the study of international security. Robert Powell (1990) and James Morrow (1989) pioneered the application of incomplete information game theory to the problem of international crises between states, and their models adapted the insights of bargaining models in economics to the international realm. James Fearon drew out the implications of this literature for structural realism (1995). He starts from the premise that states have genuine conflicts of interest that are irreducible to security concerns.[8] The Waltzian logic should apply a fortiori to such states; even more than security seekers, they should find themselves in war inevitably because of anarchy. In fact, as Fearon demonstrates with an extremely simple bargaining model that perfectly exemplifies the Shaker approach to modeling, this is not the case.

A Model of Bargaining and War

Consider two countries who are bargaining over a disputed province, for instance, Pakistan and India bargaining over Kashmir. The disputed border is modeled conceptually by a zero to one interval, x, illustrated in figure 1. Pakistan is to the west, India to the east, and between them is Kashmir, with the status quo division of the territory (the "line of control") marked as a dotted line at x^0. Pakistan wants as much of the province as possible, so it wants the border pushed to the right, while India wants the border pushed all the way to the left and is happiest if $x = 0$. Pakistan's share of the territory is x, while India has a share equal to $1 - x$.

Now consider how these two countries might bargain over the province. A simple bargaining game is illustrated in figure 2.[9] Pakistan first has the option either to make a demand to revise the border to x^1 or to make no demand. If Pakistan makes no demand, then the two countries live with the status quo and receive payoffs of x^0 and $1 - x^0$. If Pakistan makes a demand, India can accept or reject it. If India accepts the demand, then the deal is implemented and Pakistan gets x^1 while India gets $1 - x^1$. If India rejects the demand, then Pakistan has the option of going to war. If Pakistan attacks, a war takes place and the two parties receive their war payoffs, which are derived as follows. War is considered a simple lottery, in which there is a certain probability, p, that Pakistan will win and a corresponding probability, $1 - p$, that India will win. If a player wins, it receives all of Kashmir, worth 1, while if the player loses, the province goes to the other side, and the player receives nothing. Both sides pay the costs of war, c_p and c_I, for Pakistan and India, respectively. Thus the payoff for Pakistan for war is $p(1) + (1 - p)0 - c_p$ or just $p - c_p$ and the payoff for India is $p(0) + (1 - p)1 - c_I$ or $1 - p - c_I$. Finally, if India rejects Pakistan's offer, but Pakistan fails to attack, then the status quo remains in place.

The Complete Information Case

Simple "extensive form" games of this kind are easily solved by backward induction. Backward induction involves starting at the end of the game and working toward the beginning of the decision tree. Starting at the end of the game, Pakistan will not attack if its payoff for war is less than the payoff for backing down, or if $p - c_p < x^0$, which is the case in the example illustrated in figure 1. Thus in this example, Pakistan has no credible threat to attack India if its demand is not met. Working forward, this means that Pakistan cannot hope to extract a concession from India on the Kashmiri border. If Pakistan demands any revision of the border to the east of (greater than) x^0, India can simply reject this demand safe in the knowl-

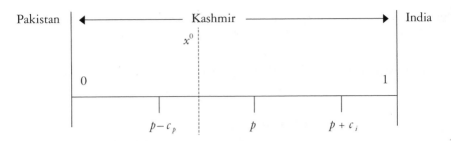

Fig. 1. The bargaining range

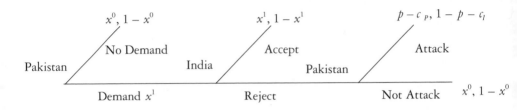

Fig. 2. The game tree (complete information)

edge that Pakistan will back down if its demand is not met. Hence Pakistan should make no demand and accept the status quo, because if it makes a demand, India will reject it and Pakistan will then have to back down.

Now imagine that a new regime comes to power in Pakistan that is considerably more committed to the goal of liberating Kashmir. So committed are they that they put much less value on the loss of life involved in warfare than the previous regime. That is, their costs of war decline. This new situation is illustrated in figure 3. Note that because of the decline in the costs of war, $p - c_p$ is now greater than x^0. Now when we solve the game with backward induction, things are different. Pakistan now has a credible threat to fight because its war payoff, $p - c_p$, is greater than its payoff for backing down, x^0. The bargaining round is altered by the fact that Pakistan will fight rather than accept the status quo. Now India knows that if it rejects Pakistan's demand, the result will be war. This means that India will accept any offer from Pakistan that makes India better off than it is at

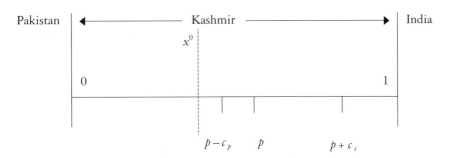

Fig. 3.   The new bargaining range

war, or any value of x less than or equal to $p + c_I$.[10] This means that if the demand x^1 is between x^0 and $p + c_I$, India will accept the revision rather than face war.

These two possibilities illustrate the range of outcomes in the simple bargaining game. If Pakistan cannot credibly threaten to attack if India rejects its demand, then there will be no revision. If Pakistan can make such a threat, then there will be a bargain to shift the status quo in its favor. However, crucially, in no case does war actually occur. The *threat* of war may give Pakistan bargaining leverage that it can use to attain a better outcome, but war never occurs. This is because the existence of costs of war on both sides renders war *inefficient;* it is always to the advantage of the countries to come to some agreement that avoids the terrible costs of war. The existence of costs of war means that there is always a range of agreements that both sides prefer to war, the range between $p - c_p$ and $p + c_I$.

The Incomplete Information Case

Fearon goes on to identify the conditions that do suffice to explain war in a rationalist framework. One of these is uncertainty about relative power or resolve.[11] The model considered so far is one of "complete information" in that there is no uncertainty on the part of the states about each other's motivations or capabilities. If the model is modified by adding such uncertainty, then war can result. For instance, India might be uncertain about the size of Pakistan's cost of war, whether it is high, as in figure 1, or low as in figure 3. This can be captured in a model of incomplete information, as shown in figure 4 (which is just two figure 2s stacked on top of each other). In the top tree, Pakistan has high costs for war, c_{PH}, as indicated in its payoff for the war outcome. In the bottom tree, Pakistan has low costs, c_{PL}. The game starts off with a coin toss determining whether Pakistan has high or low costs, with the probability of Pakistan having high costs being h.[12] Then, as before, Pakistan can make a demand. India must then decide whether to accept or reject the demand, but, crucially, India does not know whether Pakistan has high costs or low costs. This is represented by the dotted line linking India's decision nodes in the top and bottom game; India is uncertain which game it is playing, the top one against a high-cost Pakistan or the bottom one against a low-cost Pakistan.

In this incomplete information bargaining game, war can occur. In one equilibrium of this game, both the high-cost and the low-cost Pakistan make a demand to shift the status quo to x^1, India rejects this demand, and then the high-cost Pakistan backs down while the low-cost Pakistan attacks.[13] Why does war occur here? Essentially because India cannot tell for sure if Pakistan has a credible threat and decides to bet that it does not. India's payoff for rejecting the demand depends on the chance, h, that Pakistan has high costs. There is an h chance that Pakistan has high costs and will back down, so that India receives the status quo payoff of $1 - x^0$, and there is a $1 - h$ chance that Pakistan has low costs, will fight, and India will receive its war payoff, $1 - p - c_I$, yielding a total payoff for rejecting the demand of $h(1 - x^0) + (1 - h)(1 - p - c_I)$. This will be better than the payoff for yielding to the demand, $1 - x^1$, if the likelihood that Pakistan has high costs exceeds a certain threshold, defined in the following equation.

$$h > h* \equiv (p + c_I - x^1)/(p + c_I - x^0)$$

The occurrence of war in the incomplete information bargaining game is illustrated in figure 5. The horizontal axis is h, the likelihood that Pakistan has high costs. For low values of h, where Pakistan is likely to have low costs and be willing to fight, India does not resist the demand, and the status quo is adjusted peacefully in favor of Pakistan. For h above the critical value, however, India resists because Pakistan is likely to be bluffing, so if Pakistan actually does have high costs, it will have to fight to prove it. The likelihood of war here is just $1 - h$, the likelihood that Pakistan has low costs and will fight when the demand is rejected. The war, however, is

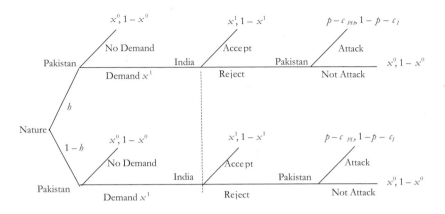

Fig. 4. The game tree (incomplete information)

not simply a product of anarchy and security concerns, but of conflicts of interest complicated by uncertainty about the costs of war.

The centrality of uncertainty to the explanation of war has led to a burgeoning game-theoretic literature on how uncertainty can be reduced and managed. One of the core concepts here is "signaling," especially the use of "costly signals" to communicate resolve (Fearon 1993). Costly signals are actions that speak louder than words because they entail some cost to the sender. In a crisis bargaining context, a costly signal might be to mobilize troops on the border. The mobilization serves to increase the risk of war, thereby demonstrating a willingness to fight over the issue at stake. In our example, Pakistan might engage in some signaling activity, such as supplying rebel forces in Kashmir, to persuade the Indian government that they have low costs and will be willing to fight eventually if Kashmir is not turned over to them.

Game Theory and Structural Realism

Returning to structural realism, then, the Waltzian explanation of the origins of war begins to look inadequate. The existence of anarchy, conflicts of

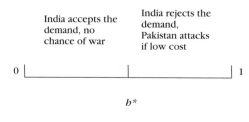

b: the likelihood that Pakistan has
high costs for fighting

Fig. 5. War in the incomplete information bargaining game

interest, and an ever-present possibility of war does not suffice to explain war; with these assumptions alone—as the complete information case makes clear—war is irrational. Even states with serious conflicts of interest will not fight each other simply because the world is anarchic and war is possible. Instead, the game-theoretic literature has reoriented the study of war around a new set of issues—especially bargaining, uncertainty, beliefs, and signaling—while clarifying our understanding of old variables such as power and interests. While these issues were discussed in the pre–game-theoretic era (Jervis 1976; Blainey 1988), the predominant intellectual framework of the time, Waltzian structural realism, assigned them a peripheral status in the explanation of war. The Waltzian argument that anarchy unproblematically produces war between security seekers rendered these issues marginal, and it took the development of game-theoretic models to demonstrate their true importance. This evolution of thought is a clear example of two of the primary uses of formal theory: to clarify and test the deductive links in our theorizing and to generate new avenues of theoretical research.

Game Theory, the Domestic-International Nexus, and the Democratic Peace

A second issue in security studies to which game theory has contributed is the connection between domestic and international politics. Sometimes generically called two-level games (Putnam 1988; Iida 1993), models that combine domestic and foreign actors in one strategic framework are becoming increasingly common. An important subset of these models focuses on the democratic peace.

The democratic peace thesis is one of the most interesting developments in international security studies. The core empirical proposition is that democracies do not fight each other, and it has received substantial empirical support (Doyle 1983a, 1983b; Rummel 1983; Bueno de Mesquita and Lalman 1992; Russett 1993; Chan 1997). Debate continues over whether democracies are demonstrably more pacifistic in general. The explanation for the phenomenon is also still in contention. Bruce Russett divided the possible explanations into two groups, normative and structural (1993). Normative explanations focus on the norms specific to democratic polities and argue that these norms delegitimate war against other democratic regimes as a violation of their right to self-determination and of the rule of law. Structural-based explanations point to the fact that democratic institutions constrain the leader from acting impulsively and force it to be more responsive to the interests of the public at large, which are presumably less belligerent than the military and aristocratic interests that dominated predemocratic regimes.

A third type of explanation has arisen recently in the game-theoretic crisis-bargaining literature. This "informational" perspective argues that democracies are better at signaling their resolve in crises than nondemocracies, in part because of the transparency of democratic societies. For instance, it is easier to tell what the United States will do than what North Korea will do because the policy process is much more open in the U.S. than in the North Korean regime. The transparency of a democratic regime may make it easier for other states to know their costs of war, and as was shown previously, when there is complete information about costs of war and relative power, war is avoided.

With several explanations of the democratic peace available, the question arises which one is correct, if any. Kenneth Schultz (1999) set himself the task of distinguishing between the structural explanation and the informational perspective. To do this one must first draw out conflicting implications from the two theories. Both predict no war between democracies, so they cannot be differentiated on the basis of this primary prediction. To get conflicting predictions, Schultz employs a simple bargaining model of war much like the India-Pakistan game considered here.

Consider the structural perspective in the light of the India-Pakistan game. One implication of the structural perspective is that democracies should have a higher cost for war. Since the democracy is responsive to the interests of the electorate that bears the burdens of war, democracies should be more sensitive to these costs than authoritarian states, which have leaders who are more immune to the costs of war. Thus for a democratic Pakistan, say, c_p will be higher than if Pakistan were authoritarian. What effect would this have on the bargaining? Because its cost of war is higher, Pakistan is less likely to have a credible threat to fight, because its payoff for war is less likely to exceed its payoff for backing down. Therefore, India is more likely to resist a challenge, because Pakistan is more likely to be bluffing.[14] Thus the structural explanation of the democratic peace implies that states receiving a challenge from a democratic state are less likely to acquiesce in the demand made and are more likely to resist the challenge because they will think that the challenger is more likely to have high costs for war and is bluffing.

Now consider the informational perspective. This perspective argues that democracies' motivations are more transparent than nondemocracies'. Transparency can be considered by contrasting the incomplete information version of the game with the complete information version. With uncertainty about Pakistan's costs for war, as discussed earlier, India will sometimes resist Pakistan's demands, leading to either a humiliating retreat for Pakistan if it backs down or war if it does not. This is because India does not know for sure whether Pakistan is bluffing or not, so India sometimes takes a chance and resists. Transparency, however, can be thought of as improving India's knowledge of Pakistan's preferences, including its costs for war. If India has complete information about Pakistan's costs for war, then India will never resist a demand from Pakistan. Pakistan will know that it cannot get away with bluffing because its costs for war are known. Therefore Pakistan will only make a demand when it is in fact willing to back it up. India will therefore never resist a demand. Thus, the informational perspective suggests that India is less likely to resist a demand from Pakistan if Pakistan is a democracy.

The structural and informational perspectives therefore offer different predictions on the question of how likely a country is to resist a demand from a democratic state versus an authoritarian one. The structural perspective suggests that states will be *more* likely to resist a democracy, while the informational perspective suggests that targets will be *less* likely to resist a democratic state than an authoritarian one. Thus the simple bargaining model allows us to deduce contrasting empirical predictions from the two explanations for the democratic peace. Schultz goes on to test these implications with quantitative data on crisis bargaining and finds support for the informational perspective; democratic states are indeed less likely to be resisted in international crises. This illustrates another important use for game theory in security studies: generating more fine-grained contrasting implications of similar theories as a guide for empirical work that seeks to differentiate between them.

Schultz's model does not explicitly include a third actor representing the electorate, and so it is not technically a two-level game, but other models of the democratic peace puzzle and the influence of democracy on foreign policy do so with interesting results. Bruce Bueno de Mesquita, James Morrow, Randolph Siverson, and Alastair Smith (1999) examine the institutional explanation of the democratic peace using a model in which leaders decide whether and how hard to fight, and after the war is over the "selectorate," or the politically important fraction of the population, decides to retain them or replace them with a challenger. The size of the selectorate, large in democracies, small in oligarchies, has implications for when and how hard states fight. Democratic leaders facing large selectorates cannot buy enough of them off to assure reelection, so public policy successes like victory in war are crucial. Hence they fight only when likely to win, and they fight hard to ensure success. Authoritarian leaders, with small selectorates, can buy a winning coalition without public policy success, and hence they put less effort into war. George Downs and David Rocke (1994) use a principal-agent model (in which the leader is the agent and the population is the principal) to examine the problem of gambling for resurrection in war. Sometimes if a leader thinks he will lose a war, he has an incentive to keep fighting rather than negotiate because only a victory will lead to reelection. Thus even if it would make sense for the country as a whole to settle the conflict, the leader will keep fighting, hoping against hope for a reversal of fortune. Alastair Smith (1998) examines how domestic audiences can influence a state's behavior in international crisis negotiations and enable them to signal resolve to other states.

Limitations of Formal Theory in Security Studies

Studies on the origins of war and the democratic peace are by no means the only applications of game theory to security studies. It would be difficult to think of an important issue that has not been modeled. Despite its widespread applicability, however, two factors limit the scope of game theory in security studies. These are the problem of larger numbers of actors and situations in which the preferences or misperceptions of the actors really tell you what you need to know.

While many situations in international relations are bilateral, some are inescapably multilateral. Alliances involve at least three players and often many more. Balance of power politics can involve three, four, five, or more states, all interacting strategically in a single system. These "middling-n" situations are notoriously hard to model. They are much more complicated than the two- or three-actor games we have examined so far, but they do not contain so many actors that strategic interaction can be assumed away, as in a competitive market setting.

One tactic employed in the alliance literature is to radically simplify the strategic structure of the game. For instance, in the enormous literature on burden sharing in alliances, the workhorse model is a basic public good provision game (Sandler 1993). In these games all the players simply decide how much of the public good they will contribute simultaneously, so there is no complicated sequence of events to model. This strategy has proven very fruitful in the context of military-spending decisions in alliance politics, especially concerning NATO.

Difficulties arise when more than three players are involved and the strategic environment cannot plausibly be simplified into a simultaneous-move game. The balance of power literature has grappled with these situations. The first formal treatment of the issue, by Harrison Wagner, analyzed an n-person game in which states have the option to fight battles against each other, either alone or in coalition with others (1986). More powerful states or coalitions win battles against weaker states or coalitions, and if the war continued to an end the weaker side would be extinguished and their resources would be absorbed by the winners. While the game has some interesting implications, the multitude of assumptions needed to define it and the resulting complexity of the game render analysis difficult and call into question the robustness of the findings. Emerson Niou, Peter Ordeshook, and Gregory Rose developed an alternative framework based on "cooperative game theory" that focuses on coalition formation in n-person games, assuming that whatever coalitions are formed can be enforced (1989). Here again, however, the number of specific assumptions necessary to generate a tractable model raises questions about the meaning of the results, as does the overall reliance on the cooperative game-theoretic framework in the anarchic context of international relations. Thus the balance of power problem is one of the most difficult for game theory in security studies.

An even more serious limitation is the possibility that in some cases strategic interaction may not be the central issue. For instance, if misperceptions swamp the evaluative processes of states, game theory may not be helpful in prediction. As an example, Thomas Christensen and Jack Snyder argue that alliance politics before World War I and World War II were dominated by misperception (1990). Before World War I observers believed that the offense was dominant and hence formed tight alliances and hair-trigger military plans. In fact the defense was dominant, and the war degenerated into a stalemate. This shifted perceptions so that observers believed the defense was dominant, whereas in fact the advent of the tank and tactical airpower made possible the blitzkrieg, rendering the world offense dominant once more. Thus the democracies failed to oppose Hitler until it was too late. In both cases, observers failed to appreciate strategic reality and acted on their misperceptions instead. Game theory may help us understand why statesmen act the way they do *given* their misperceptions, but the real work in explaining the events is in accounting for why they harbored the misperception in the first place.

Similarly, if the most important factor in an explanation is a change in preferences, then game theory is also reduced to a supporting role (Jervis 1988). Indeed, two of the most prominent approaches to the study of international relations can be thought of as theories of preference formation. Andrew Moravcsik's (1997) version of liberalism argues that preferences formed at the domestic level tell you most of what you need to know in international relations, while Alexander Wendt's (1999) constructivism is essentially an argument that state interaction shapes their preferences in decisive ways. John Mueller (1989) has argued that as a result of historical learning and other factors, major power war has become "obsolete" in the sense that it is just unthinkably unfashionable, like dueling or human sacrifice. If this is the case, then, once again, strategic considerations would not be the main factor in explaining the decline of warfare.

Conclusion

Rational choice scholarship is especially appropriate for security studies and has contributed greatly to it. The two-actor, high-stakes games that nations play are especially suitable to analysis using game theory. Formal analysis has greatly clarified our understanding of the origins of war, the effect of the structure of the international system on the behavior of states, the democratic peace, arms racing, alliances, and other issues. Many of the most profound insights have been generated from the simplest models, demonstrating the power of a Shaker approach to illuminating fundamental strategic issues. Some issues, such as the balance of power, are harder to analyze, while others, including the origins of state preferences and misperceptions, must be analyzed outside the game-theoretic framework. Current game-theoretic work is, however, constructing a core rationalist theory of international security that will serve future scholars and policymakers as a bedrock tool of analysis in the understanding of the most important issues of war and peace.

Suggested Readings

Fearon, J. D. 1995. Rationalist Explanations for War. *International Organization* 49:379–414.

Kydd, A. 2000. Trust, Reassurance, and Cooperation. *International Organization* 54:325–57.

Powell, R. 1999. *In the Shadow of Power.* Princeton: Princeton University Press.

Schultz, K. A. 1999. Do Democratic Institutions Constrain or Inform? Contrasting Institutional Perspectives on Democracy and War. *International Organization* 53:233–66.

Walt, S. M. 1999. Rigor or Rigor Mortis? Rational Choice and Security Studies. *International Security* 23:5–48, plus the responses in 24 (2).

Notes

I would like to thank the editors, reviewers, Jim Fearon, and Eric Lawrence for helpful comments on earlier drafts.

1. Like all generalizations and models, this one has exceptions. The Shakers were quite innovative and came up with a line of swiveling office chairs and, improbably, even made a swiveling rocker.

2. See O'Neill (1994) for a review of game theory applications to war.

3. Green and Shapiro (1994, 58) lambaste this proposition as an "arbitrary domain restriction." In Aldrich's context (voter turnout) this may be an understandable reaction, but in general the idea makes sense.

4. The most succinct expression of Waltz's views on the subject is in Waltz (1988, esp. 43–44). See also Waltz (1979, esp. 104–10).

5. See Keohane (1986).

6. This is not quite how Grieco himself conceives of his critique—he focuses on the issue of relative gains—but to my mind this is the core that survives the game-theoretic responses by Powell (1991) and Snidal (1991). Powell deals with the problem of modeling war directly. See Powell (1994) for a review of the neoliberal, neorealist debate in the wake of the relative gains episode.

7. Though of course once France was restored by the victors, Germany did face considerable retaliation.

8. Scholars also began to question the link between the search for security and war. Considered carefully, security, or the desire for survival, is actually about as benign a goal as one can hope for in international relations. States that seek security have no real conflict of interest because if they simply agree never to attack each other, they will all live forever in perfect safety, thereby maximizing their utility (Kydd 1993, 1997b; Schweller 1994, 1996). For there to be conflict, therefore, it must be the case that some states are driven by *non*-security-related motivations, like a desire for territory, or that there is *uncertainty* about the motivations of states, so that security seekers are misperceived to be genuinely aggressive. This has led to game-theoretic investigations of how such misperceptions might arise and how they can be overcome through strategies of reassurance (Kydd 1997a, 2000).

9. Note that this is almost the same as Kilgour and Wolinsky-Nahmias's game (chap. 13, this vol.). The model described here differs in that Pakistan can demand any amount of additional terrritory, and that in the incomplete information version, I examine the one-sided uncertainty case where only Pakistan's resolve is unknown.

10. India's payoff for war is $1 - p - c_I$, while its payoff for peace with the new border is $1 - x^1$. The two are equal when $x^1 = p + c_I$.

11. Fearon also identifies two other ways of getting war in a rationalist framework: commitment problems, such as arise in preventive war situations, and issue indivisibilities.

12. These initial coin tosses are conventionally called moves by "Nature," a fictitious nonstrategic player.

13. I assume that $p + c_I > x^1 > p - c_{PL}$, so that the low-cost Pakistan would rather get x^1 than fight.

14. Technically, these predictions fall out of a "mixed strategy" equilibrium in which players randomize over their strategies, not out of the "pure strategy" equilibria considered earlier.

References

Achen, C., and D. Snidal. 1989. Rational Deterrence Theory and Comparative Case Studies. *World Politics* 41 (2): 143–69.

Aldrich, J. H. 1993. Rational Choice and Turnout. *American Journal of Political Science* 37:246–78.

Allan, P., and C. Dupont. 1999. International Relations Theory and Game Theory: Baroque Modeling Choices and Empirical Robustness. *International Political Science Review* 20:23–47.

Allison, G. T. 1971. *Essence of Decision: Explaining the Cuban Missile Crisis.* Boston: Little, Brown.

Axelrod, R. 1984. *The Evolution of Cooperation.* New York: Basic Books.

Blainey, G. 1988. *The Causes of War.* New York: Free Press.

Bueno de Mesquita, B., and D. Lalman. 1992. *War and Reason: Domestic and International Imperatives.* New Haven: Yale University Press.

Bueno de Mesquita, B., J. D. Morrow, R. M. Siverson, and A. Smith. 1999. An Institutional Explanation of the Democratic Peace. *American Political Science Review* 93 (4): 791–807.

Bueno de Mesquita, B., and R. M. Siverson. 1995. War and the Survival of Political Leaders: A Comparative Study of Regime Types and Political Accountability. *American Political Science Review* 89:841–55.

Chan, S. 1997. In Search of the Democratic Peace: Problems and Promise. *Mershon International Studies Review* 41:59–91.

Christensen, T. J., and J. Snyder. 1990. Chain Gangs and Passed Bucks: Predicting Alliance Patterns in Multipolarity. *International Organization* 44 (2): 137–68.

Downs, G. W., and D. M. Rocke. 1990. *Tacit Bargaining, Arms Races, and Arms Control.* Ann Arbor: University of Michigan.

———. 1994. Conflict, Agency, and Gambling for Resurrection: The Principal-Agent Problem Goes to War. *American Journal of Political Science* 38:362–80.

Doyle, M. W. 1983a. Kant, Liberal Legacies, and Foreign Affairs, Part 1. *Philosophy and Public Affairs* 12 (3): 205–35.

———. 1983b. Kant, Liberal Legacies, and Foreign Affairs, Part 2. *Philosophy and Public Affairs* 12 (4): 323–52.

Fearon, J. D. 1993. *Threats to Use Force: Costly Signals and Bargaining in International Crises.* Berkeley: University of California Press.

———. 1995. Rationalist Explanations for War. *International Organization* 49:379–414.

George, A. L., and R. Smoke. 1989. Deterrence and Foreign Policy. *World Politics* 41 (2): 170–82.

Green, D. P., and I. Shapiro. 1994. *Pathologies of Rational Choice Theory: A Critique of Applications in Political Science.* New Haven: Yale University Press.

Grieco, J. 1988. Anarchy and the Limits of Cooperation: A Realist Critique of the Newest Liberal Institutionalism. *International Organization* 42:485–507.

Herz, J. H. 1950. Idealist Internationalism and the Security Dilemma. *World Politics* 2 (2): 157–80.

Iida, K. 1993. When and How Do Domestic Constraints Matter? Uncertainty in International Relations. *Journal of Conflict Resolution* 37 (3): 403–26.

Jervis, R. 1976. *Perception and Misperception in International Politics.* Princeton: Princeton University Press.

———. 1978. Cooperation under the Security Dilemma. *World Politics* 30:167–214.

———. 1988. Realism, Game Theory, and Cooperation. *World Politics* 40 (3): 317–49.

Keohane, R. O. 1984. *After Hegemony: Cooperation and Discord in the World Political Economy.* Princeton: Princeton University Press.

———. 1986. *Neorealism and Its Critics.* New York: Columbia University Press.

Kydd, A. 1993. The Security Dilemma, Game Theory, and World War I. Annual meetings of the American Political Science Association, Washington, DC.

———. 1997a. Game Theory and the Spiral Model. *World Politics* 49:371–400.

———. 1997b. Sheep in Sheep's Clothing: Why Security Seekers Do Not Fight Each Other. *Security Studies* 7:114–55.

———. 2000. Trust, Reassurance, and Cooperation. *International Organization* 54:325–57.

Lebow, R. N. 1981. *Between Peace and War: The Nature of International Crisis.* Baltimore: Johns Hopkins University Press.

Moravcsik, A. 1997. Taking Preferences Seriously: A Liberal Theory of International Politics. *International Organization* 4:513–53.

Morrow, J. D. 1989. Capabilities, Uncertainty, and Resolve: A Limited Information Model of Crisis Bargaining. *American Journal of Political Science* 33 (4): 941–72.

———. 1994. Alliances, Credibility, and Peace Time Costs. *Journal of Conflict Resolution* 38:270–97.

Mueller, J. 1989. *Retreat from Doomsday: The Obsolescence of Major War.* New York: Basic Books.

Niou, E. M. S., P. C. Ordeshook, and G. F. Rose. 1989. *The Balance of Power: Stability in International Systems.* Cambridge: Cambridge University Press.

O'Neill, B. 1994. Game Theory Models of Peace and War. In *Handbook of Game Theory with Economic Applications,* edited by R. J. Aumann and S. Hart. Amsterdam: Elsevier Science.

Oye, K. A. 1986. *Cooperation under Anarchy.* Princeton: Princeton University Press.

Powell, R. 1990. *Nuclear Deterrence Theory: The Problem of Credibility.* Cambridge: Cambridge University Press.

———. 1991. Absolute and Relative Gains in International Relations Theory. *American Political Science Review* 85:1303–20.

———. 1994. Anarchy in International Relations Theory: The Neorealist-Neoliberal Debate. *International Organization* 48 (2): 313–44.

Putnam, R. D. 1988. Diplomacy and Domestic Politics. *International Organization* 42 (3): 427–60.

Richardson, L. F. 1960. *Arms and Insecurity.* Pittsburgh: Boxwood Press.

Rummel, R. J. 1983. Libertarianism and International Violence. *Journal of Conflict Resolution* 27 (1): 27–71.

Russett, B. 1993. *Grasping the Democratic Peace.* Princeton: Princeton University Press.

Sandler, T. 1993. The Economic Theory of Alliances: A Survey. *Journal of Conflict Resolution* 37:446–83.

Schelling, T. 1960. *The Strategy of Conflict.* Cambridge: Harvard University Press.

Schultz, K. A. 1999. Do Democratic Institutions Constrain or Inform? Contrasting Institutional Perspectives on Democracy and War. *International Organization* 53 (2): 233–66.

Schweller, R. L. 1994. Bandwagoning for Profit: Bringing the Revisionist State Back In. *International Security* 19:72–107.

———. 1996. Neorealism's Status Quo Bias: What Security Dilemma? *Security Studies* 5:90–121.

Smith, A. 1998. International Crises and Domestic Politics. *American Political Science Review* 92 (3): 623–38.

Snidal, D. 1991. Relative Gains and the Pattern of International Cooperation. *American Political Science Review* 85:701–26.

Snyder, G., and P. Diesing. 1977. *Conflict among Nations: Bargaining, Decision-Making, and System Structure in International Crises.* Princeton: Princeton University Press.

Wagner, R. H. 1986. The Theory of Games and the Balance of Power. *World Politics* 38:546–76.

Walt, S. M. 1999. Rigor or Rigor Mortis? Rational Choice and Security Studies. *International Security* 23:5–48.

Waltz, K. 1979. *Theory of International Politics.* Reading, MA: Addison-Wesley.

———. 1988. The Origins of War in Neo-Realist Theory. In *The Origin and Prevention of Major Wars,* edited by R. I. Rotberg and T. K. Rabb. Cambridge: Cambridge University Press.

Wendt, A. 1999. *Social Theory of International Politics.* Cambridge: Cambridge University Press.

15. Conclusion: Multimethod Research

Detlef F. Sprinz and Yael Wolinsky-Nahmias

Methodological diversity can promote theory building by questioning core assumptions, proposing alternative explanations, and improving model specification. In this volume, we have attempted to initiate a dialogue across methodological approaches by inviting experts from the different subfields of international relations (IR) to evaluate the merits and limits of methods applied to the study of international political economy, international environmental politics, and international security.

This concluding chapter focuses on three issues. First, we address two methodological problems that are common to the different methods and subfields discussed in the book: self-selection and counterfactual analysis. Second, we show how multiple methods can advance the study of international relations by looking at their contribution to two central debates in the field: the debate over the hegemonic stability theory and the debate about the democratic peace thesis. In the third section we discuss three exemplary studies in international relations that integrate different methods of analysis: Lisa Martin's (1992) *Coercive Cooperation: Explaining Multilateral Economic Sanctions;* Hein Goemans's (2000) *War and Punishment: The Causes of War Termination and the First World War;* and Bruce Bueno de Mesquita's (2002) *Predicting Politics.* We close with some concluding remarks about new trends in the methodology of international relations.

Cross-Methodological Challenges

Selection Bias

The problem of selection bias or self-selection is common to the social sciences and has received much attention in different fields (it also contributed to the award of the Nobel Prize in economics to James J. Heckman in the year 2000). Within political science, Achen (1986) drew early attention to the issue of self-selection, laying the foundation for subsequent work. Selection bias (or self-selection) refers to the problem of estimating the effects of variables given a nonrandom selection of cases. For example, when studying the emergence of international regimes, scholars often concentrate on cases where regimes have emerged, rather than on randomly selected cases that include both successfully established regimes and regimes that have failed to emerge. The problem with studying a nonrandomly selected sample is that the chosen sample of cases may have some important common features that will taint any attempt to identify the causes of regime formation.[1]

Self-selection can have serious consequences in the study of international politics when using case studies, quantitative methods, or even formal modeling.[2] In case studies, focusing on a particular set of cases can bias the theoretical arguments, especially any causal arguments. Self-selection can also limit the scholar's ability to generalize the results of specific cases (see Bennett, chap. 2, and Kacowicz, chap. 5, this vol.). For example, when studying the causes of war, case studies commonly do not consider that many instances of contention between countries do not escalate to armed conflict. This problem is demonstrated by Huth and Allee (chap. 9, this vol.), who present a succession of game-theoretic models, including dispute initiation, challenge the status quo, negotiations, and military escalation game. As each game involves nondeterministic choices, they advocate the use of selection equations in quantitative analyses to estimate who arrives in the sample before undertaking the analysis of the outcome equation. This procedure is analogous to that advanced by Heckman. His research challenges core conjectures of the economic theory of labor, which predicts that only those individuals who find the wages offered worth their activity will actually seek employment. Thus any quantitative analysis of wages and educational status would normally involve only those who are actually employed—omitting those who have chosen not to seek employment. The latter is a result of self-selection and leads to biased (statistical) results. Heckman demonstrates that including the omitted group in the analysis changes the magnitude of covariation between wages and education. Heckman's correction employs a two-step procedure to first estimate the prediction of inclusion in the sample and then use the predicted values along with other factors of primary importance in developing the model of interest.

While selection bias in case studies can be partially overcome by quantitative analysis of a large, randomly chosen set of cases, quantitative studies are not immune to self-selection problems. In the subfield of international political economy, Nooruddin (2002) explores the question of why so few international economic sanctions are successful, even though they often inflict major damage on the target state. He argues that traditional statistical analyses of sanctions overlook the selection effect (i.e., why countries become targets of sanctions in the first case) and that this selection mechanism must be taken into account when examining the results of economic sanctions.

Selection bias also plays a role in formal analysis. Akerlof's (1970) "market for lemons" is a good example of group selection based on a rational choice calculus (see Conybeare, chap. 12, this vol., for more detailed examples). Fearon suggests, in reference to selection effects in international security research, that states select themselves into and out of crises according to their beliefs about an opponent's willingness to use force and their own values for the conflict on the issue at stake. With costly signaling, opportunistic challengers or defenders are more likely to drop out at each stage of the crisis than are more motivated states. Thus, as a crisis proceeds, it becomes increasingly likely that both states involved have high values for conflict on the issues in dispute. In this view, the escalation process of an international crisis gradually separates out more highly motivated states (Fearon 2002, 13–14). Extensive form game-theoretic expositions of a decision problem point to the impact of prior moves, and they sometimes preclude outcomes that are contingent on earlier alternative moves.

Counterfactual Analysis

A second important methodological issue is counterfactual analysis. Counterfactual analysis deals with the outcomes that would have resulted if the explanatory variable had taken on a value other than the one actually observed. For example, a longstanding puzzle for IR scholars has been to explain the emergence of a stable bipolar international system after World War II with the United States and the Soviet Union, each leading a group of nations and significantly affecting their foreign (and sometimes domestic) policies. A common explanation for that phenomenon is the appearance of nuclear weapons that posed an unprecedented threat and thus may have contributed to uniting the Eastern and Western blocs against one another. But some scholars reject that explanation and argue, counterfactually, that the stable bipolar system might well have been created in the absence of nuclear weapons.[3]

James Fearon (1991, 193) argues that counterfactual propositions have an important role in assessing causal arguments and elaborates on several strategies for making counterfactuals a viable part of research. While counterfactuals necessarily involve careful speculation or probablistic reasoning,[4] they must be sufficiently well structured to permit plausible inferences. Tetlock and Belkin (1996, 18) suggest essential standards for the ideal counterfactual, including logical, historical, theoretical, and statistical consistency.[5] Counterfactuals are particularly important as an option for establishing "control cases" in order to make inferences about the plausibility of cause-and-effect relationships (see Bennett, chap. 2, this vol.).

John Odell (chap. 3, this vol.) provides practical guidelines for the application of counterfactuals in case study analysis. Odell suggests creating hypothetical variation in the value of the explanatory variable, using generalizations based on established theories, and comparing the magnitude of effects among explanatory variables. This procedure is particularly useful in single case studies since it creates a series of hypothetical control cases for comparison and thereby strengthens the plausibility of the inferences by the researcher.

Counterfactuals are also useful as a measurement instrument. Sprinz uses counterfactuals to study the effectiveness of international institutions at solving a variety of international problems (see Sprinz, chap. 8, this vol., for details). Using counterfactuals to generate data is quite different from delineating the magnitude of effects of explanatory variables.

The question arises as to whether the if-then logic of interpreting the coefficients of regression estimates is always substantively appropriate with respect to counterfactual reasoning. Assume, for example, that a quantitative study finds that democratic countries do better at protecting their own environment than nondemocratic countries (other factors held constant). Unlike in experimental settings, it cannot be assumed in quasi-experimental settings[6] that the underlying unit of observation can always change its requisite characteristic to form a credible counterfactual (e.g., change from a nondemocracy to a democracy). But even if this were possible, Fearon's caution still holds that "the question . . . is not whether a factor had to occur but whether varying one factor implies changing other factors that *also* would have materially affected the outcome" (1991, 193, emphasis in original).

Finally, as Snidal mentions (chap. 10, this vol.), formal models also use counterfactual reasoning. Simulation models can easily probe the implications of varying initial conditions in a structured way (see Cederman 1996). In game-theoretic models, "off the equilibrium path" expectations can be chosen to establish counterfactuals that should rarely (or never) be observed in actuality if the model is correct. In addition, actions not taken that are consistent with an equilibrium outcome other than the one observed also serve as counterfactuals in game theory (Bueno de Mesquita 1996).

By attending to the possibilities of self-selection and counterfactual analysis, we can strengthen the validity of inferences in the study of international politics. Counterfactuals and self-selection are closely related, because both are connected to unobserved cases that could, if observed, strengthen inferences about the link between cause and effect. Yet selection bias and counterfactuals are conceptually different and have different consequences. Selection bias constrains the analysis by focusing on some cases and excluding others and therefore potentially influencing causal inferences. Counterfactual analysis can add to the analysis by broadening the range of cases to include some relevant cases where an explanatory variable does not exist (or has a different value).[7]

Methodological Diversity and Substantive Debates

Several years ago, Doyle and Ikenberry (1997) argued that the decline of a great theoretical debate in international relations and the ensuing theoretical diversity this creates can have a positive effect on the progress of the field. We agree with this claim and would add that theoretical diversity is most likely to develop when methodological pluralism is widely practiced. Indeed, it has been clear for quite some time that methodological diversity in the study of international politics has been increasing. As we showed in a review of leading journals of international relations (chap. 1, this vol.), many more scholars currently use statistical and formal methods than before. Yet this is not to say that case studies are disappearing from the field; rather it is studies that lack a clear methodological orientation that have become less common.

Taking advantage of the relative strengths of different methods can help advance important debates in international relations. We elaborate on two examples, the debate over hegemonic stability theory and the debate about the democratic peace thesis.

Hegemonic Stability Theory

An enduring problem for scholars of international politics is to explain why countries go to war. However, with the rising importance of the international political economy IR scholars focus increasingly on the circumstances under which countries decide to cooperate with each other. Although the study of international cooperation is closely related to the research on international political economy, the two do not entirely overlap (see Milner, chap. 11, this vol.). Still, one important area of increased cooperation over the last century has been international trade. Early studies of hegemonic stability argued that since free trade and (global) economic stability were public goods, powerful leadership in the international arena was a necessary condition for countries to engage in tariff reductions and economic cooperation (Kindleberger 1973; Krasner 1976; Gilpin 1981). These claims were based on both historical case studies and rational choice analysis. Scholars pointed to empirical evidence such as increased trade liberalization during the nineteenth century when Great Britain had a hegemonic role and following World War II when the United States had a similar role. In contrast, the period between World Wars I and II was marked by the absence of a hegemonic state and by international economic closure and crisis. While these claims seem logical in the context of those particular periods of time, more rigorous analyses raised doubts about their general validity.

Indeed, statistical studies of hegemonic stability theory found a different association between political power and trade policy (see Mansfield, chap. 7, this vol.). Both John Conybeare (1983) and Timothy J. McKeown (1991) found little support for the hypothesis that hegemonic stability affects trade policies. Robert Pahre (1999), studying the international system from 1815 to the present, argued that a hegemonic state was present all throughout that period, though he distinguished between periods of benevolent hegemony and periods of malevolent hegemony. Using regression analysis, Pahre argued that, to the extent that hegemony affected international political economy, it had a malign effect. Mansfield (1994), looking at the period 1850 through 1965, showed that both very high and very low variances of distribution of capabilities are correlated with a high ratio of global trade to global production. Quantitative studies thus raised serious doubts about the main thesis of the hegemonic stability theory.

A different challenge to hegemonic stability theory was presented by Duncan Snidal (1985), who, using a formal model, questioned the necessity of a hegemon for maintaining international cooperation. Snidal showed that a small group ("k group") of states can substitute for a hegemon under certain conditions.

Although many doubts have been raised about hegemonic stability theory, it did introduce political factors into the study of the global economy. The application of different methods to the study of the emergence and sustainability of international economic cooperation had two important effects. At the substantive level, the discourse among scholars using different research methods produced a more comprehensive understanding of the motives of leaders and their decision-making process. At the theoretical level, the use of different methods helped to expose the weaknesses and limits of the theoretical arguments about a hegemonic state being a necessary condition for international economic cooperation.

The Democratic Peace

Another central topic of research in the field of international relations stems from the observation that democratic countries tend not to fight each other, although they are no less likely, in general, to engage in war. This proposition suggests that most wars, therefore, occur either among nondemocratic countries or between democratic countries and nondemocratic countries. As discussed earlier (especially in Kacowicz, chap. 5, and Kydd,

373

chap. 14, this vol.), the democratic peace thesis implies that domestic political structures and values play an important role in explaining international conflict. The argument has been statistically tested and supported by many studies during the 1980s and 1990s (e.g., Maoz and Abdolali 1989; Maoz and Russett 1993; Ray 1995; Chan 1997). While many scholars accept the democratic peace proposition itself, the explanation for this phenomenon remains debatable. As described by Arie Kacowicz (chap. 5, this vol.), case studies have helped identify several possible explanations for the claim that democratic countries tend not to fight each other. Empirically, for much of the twentieth century, the presence of a common external threat in the form of the Soviet Union and the Soviet bloc helped explain peaceful relationships among democratic countries. This explanation is generally consistent with the expectations of realist theories regarding balance of power and alliances. However, while it may be applicable for the Cold War period, it does not explain peace among democracies before and after that period.

Other explanations suggest that democratic countries have a large stake in maintaining long-term commitments to international cooperation, especially as they have become more interdependent economically.[8] Another important line of explanation focuses on shared ideologies and norms among democratic countries. Liberal values and the openness and pluralism that characterize these societies may have a moderating influence on their foreign policy and willingness to use force.

Andrew Kydd (chap. 14, this vol.) discusses the contribution of game theory to the democratic peace research. Kydd points to two main insights. First, game theorists offered a new explanation for the high correlation between regime type and the likelihood of war. That explanation maintains that democratic institutions are more transparent about the true preferences of democratic governments. Therefore, democratic institutions increase government's ability to send credible signals (and threats) and reduce the level of uncertainty in times of crisis. The second contribution of game theory was to devise testable hypotheses for different explanations of the democratic peace thesis. Schultz (1999) offers a sequential crisis bargaining model that shows how the informational qualities of democratic institutions can explain the democratic peace idea better than the alternative explanation that democratic institutions constrain democratic governments that are considering war.

As both the hegemonic stability literature and the democratic peace literature demonstrate, different methods of analysis allow scholars to explore alternative theoretical mechanisms and, most important, to evaluate the validity of different explanations. In both of these debates, the value of using different methods was not simply the addition of alternative explanations (though this is important in itself). Rather, using different research methods helped expose theoretical weaknesses in the arguments and led to better understanding of the phenomenon under investigation.

Multimethod Research in International Relations

Although pursuing multimethod research presents serious challenges for investigators, there is increasing recognition that such an approach can be very effective in studying international politics. Our review of journal articles in international relations (detailed in chap. 1) found that only 4 percent of the articles published in six top IR journals used more than one research method. Yet, several leading scholars in the field have recently published important books that employ multimethod research. We next discuss three exemplary works in international relations that integrate different methodologies: Lisa Martin's (1992) *Coercive Cooperation;* Hein Goemans's (2000) *War and Punishment;* and Bruce Bueno de Mesquita's (2002) *Predicting Politics.* These books cover different substantive areas of international relations and demonstrate how the integration of different research methods in one study can improve the understanding of the issues under investigation.[9]

In *Coercive Cooperation,* Lisa Martin explores the political and institutional conditions leading to the successful imposition of international economic sanctions. In this study, Martin uses game theory, statistical analysis, and case studies to investigate the role of cooperation among the trading partners of the target state. She first offers a deductive framework using formal methods and then establishes statistical associations between variables and investigates case studies that could either confirm or falsify the proposed hypotheses. Martin proposes three different decision-making game models to capture the choices of two countries that are considering the imposition of economic sanctions on a third country. She assumes that states are rational, unitary actors and tries to identify what will foster cooperation between the countries imposing sanctions in each of the games.

Several hypotheses are delineated, including (1) states will be more likely to agree to impose sanctions against a weak, poor target country and (2) cooperation is more likely to decline over time in cases where the United States leads the coalition due to the asymmetry of power among the cooperating states. A key hypothesis, that the involvement of international institutions will encourage cooperation, is supported through a statistical analysis of ninety cases of international cooperation on economic sanctions. The causal mechanism for the effects of varying levels of international cooperation on sanctions is investigated in several case studies, including the economic sanctions against Argentina during the 1982 conflict with Great Britain over the Falkland/Malvinas Islands. In this case, Martin demonstrates the role of an international institution, the European Union, in fostering cooperation among the trading partners of Argentina, under pressure from the United Kingdom. The case studies help to evaluate the hypotheses offered by the different game models as well as the correlations uncovered by the statistical analysis. The case studies confirm the decisive role of international institutions in establishing a credible threat to impose economic sanctions. The study thus illuminates important interconnections between economic and political motivations and policies by integrating different research methods.

A second example of multimethod research is Hein Goemans's *War and Punishment*. Goemans explores the questions of when and why countries decide to end wars, focusing on individual leaders as the relevant decision makers and arguing that domestic politics are a critical factor in leaders' calculations about ending wars. Geomans argues that leaders of different types of regimes will change their war goals as more information is revealed about the costs of war. Leaders will either choose to continue to wage war or agree to a peace settlement, depending on how the terms of the settlement will affect their political future. The author claims that much of the empirical literature on this issue suffers from a selection bias, and he tries to correct for that by using three different research methods. Goemans presents a basic rational choice model of expected utility and offers several hypotheses regarding the strategies that leaders of different regimes will choose as their costs of war vary, especially domestic costs ("punishment"). The hypotheses are tested and supported by statistical analysis based on a cross-national data set that includes characteristics of countries and conflicts. However, the author is quick to admit that the causal direction cannot be firmly established through the statistical analysis, and therefore he complements it with historical case studies focusing on World War I. The case studies demonstrate the main thesis of the book, that a leader's decision to continue or to stop fighting is based, at least partly, on how the terms of settlement will affect his or her political future. Not all possible types of regimes, however, were included in these cases. Thus, the statistical analysis strengthens Goemans's argument by showing the general association between different kinds of regimes and the tendency to terminate war.

Finally, in *Predicting Politics,* Bruce Bueno de Mesquita (2002) demonstrates how multimethod research can advance our understanding of foreign policy. The author uses formal models, quantitative methods, and simulation analysis to explain policy outcomes. He discusses the historical case of the twelfth-century Investiture Struggle between the pope and the European kings over control of the appointment of bishops and over the church income. After reviewing the hypotheses generated by historians, Bueno de Mesquita uses a simple game-theoretic model of the nomination (by the pope) and approval procedure (by the king) for bishops, to develop hypotheses regarding the conditions under which the preferred candidates of the pope or the king were likely to be nominated. Especially if the bishopric were rich rather than poor, kings had disproportionate incentives either to get their preferred candidates approved or to let the bishopric be left vacant—thereby generating additional income for the kingdom. By implication, popes had incentives to retard economic growth policies, whereas kings held the opposite interest—an example of a hypothesis at variance with those advanced by case specialists. Subsequently, Bueno de Mesquita tests the implications of the hypotheses using statistical methods. Any one of the research methods used by Bueno de Mesquita could not have explained past and present events to the same extent. However, taken together, the analytical implications of the formal models, the associations offered by the statistical analysis, and the simulation of a variety of different future states of the world offer a comprehensive framework for analyzing foreign policy decisions.[10]

These three studies are examples of research that dealt with methodological problems by extending the investigation beyond the limits of any one method. All research methods have some weaknesses that may hinder our understanding of cause and effect. Applying different research methods in one study can both expose and help to overcome some of these problems and thus validate the proposed claims.

Summary

An important methodological trend in the study of international relations is the significant increase in the number of quantitative studies, as our survey of leading journals in the field reveals (see chap. 1). This proliferation of quantitative studies, however, did not result in a comparable decrease in the use of any other method. Rather, our survey shows that a second important trend has been a considerable increase in the ratio of articles that have a clear methodological foundation. This increased attention to methods reflects a growing recognition among scholars that systematic and well-structured analysis, based on clear and consistent assumptions, has the potential to further our knowledge of world politics.[11] The growing importance of methodology is also evident in the increased scholarly discourse and the proliferation of methods training in graduate programs and in specialized programs.[12] Consequently, more scholars try to overcome the limits of any single method by using multiple methods as in the three books discussed earlier in this chapter.

One of the messages of this volume is that no one method can address all the challenges of social science research. Recognizing the trade-offs involved in using each method and realizing the advantages one method may have over another for dealing with specific methodological problems are thus key to theory building. Many researchers using case studies aspire to causal arguments, while recognizing the limits of causal modeling based on very small, often nonrandom samples. Some researchers who use formal modeling are beginning to integrate case studies for better evaluation of theoretical claims (Cameron and Morton 2002). Scholars who use quantitative analysis are also showing interest in the insights that game-theoretic models can offer (see Huth and Allee, chap. 9, this vol.).

It is our hope that the use of multiple methods in international relations will continue to grow and that this book will provide an impetus to this trend. Methodological pluralism serves to improve our understanding of policy-making and world events by creating opportunities for scholars to reevaluate their claims and to compensate for methodological weaknesses in any particular approach.

Notes

1. For an exception see Young and Osherenko, *Polar Politics* (1993).

2. A good overview of current modeling of selection effects in international relations can be found in a special issue of *International Interactions* (vol. 28, no. 1 [2002]).

3. Muller (1988).

4. This is referred to as "chancy counterfactuals" in philosophy (see Menzies 2001).

5. The other criteria are clarity and projectability.

6. Experiments use fully randomized assignment of experimental units (e.g., psychology students) to treatments (e.g., stimuli like a medical treatment versus a placebo). In quasi experiments, we also find "treatments, outcome measures, and experimental units, but do not use random assignment to create the comparisons from which treatment-caused change is inferred" (Cook and Campbell 1979, 6). In international relations, we normally have quasi-experimental designs. See Cook and Campbell (1979) and Achen (1986) for discussions of quasi-experimental designs.

7. During work on this book, D. Sprinz received a call that his father had experienced cardiac arrest and had fallen clinically dead. Fortunately, these events occurred while he was at the cardiologist's office. The father was *not* the patient of the cardiologist; rather, he chose to accompany his wife to her cardiac examination. His healthy survival was the outcome of the combination of a treatment counterfactual (being at the cardiologist's office vs. anywhere else) and a self-selection process (caring for his wife).

8. See Charles Lipson (2003).

9. There are other important studies of course. We would like to mention especially David Lake's work, including but not limited to his 1988 *Power, Protection, and Free Trade*.

10. Bueno de Mesquita also developed simulation models to predict policy outcomes (e.g., Bueno de Mesquita and Stokman 1994; Bueno de Mesquita 1994, 2003).

11. The introduction of new journals such as *International Ethics,* where articles published are less likely to use the methods we examine, may have affected this finding.

12. See the appendix for an overview of methods training programs which now cover all three methodologies discussed in this book.

References

Achen, C. 1986. *The Statistical Analysis of Quasi-Experiments.* Berkeley: University of California Press.

Akerlof, G. 1970. The Market for Lemons: Quality Uncertainty and the Market Mechanism. *Quarterly Journal of Economics* 84:488–500.

Bueno de Mesquita, B. 1994. Political Forecasting: An Expected Utility Method. In *European Community Decision-Making: Models, Applications, and Comparisons,* edited by B. Bueno de Mesquita and F. N. Stokman. New Haven: Yale University Press.

———. 1996. Counterfactuals and International Affairs: Some Insights from Game Theory. In *Counterfactual Thought Experiments in World Politics: Logical, Methodological, and Psychological Perspectives,* edited by P. E. Tetlock and A. Belkin. Princeton: Princeton University Press.

———. 2002. *Predicting Politics.* Columbus: Ohio State University Press.

———. 2003. *Principles of International Politics.* 2d ed. Washington, DC: CQ Press.

Bueno de Mesquita, B., and F. N. Stokman, eds. 1994. *European Community Decision-Making: Models, Applications, and Comparisons.* New Haven: Yale University Press.

Cameron, C. M., and R. Morton. 2002. Formal Theory Meets Data. In *Political Science: The State of the Discipline,* edited by I. Katznelson and H. Milner. New York: Norton.

Cederman, L.-E. 1996. Rerunning History: Counterfactual Simulation in World Politics. In *Counterfactual Thought Experiments in World Politics: Logical, Methodological, and Psychological Perspectives,* edited by P. E. Tetlock and A. Belkin. Princeton: Princeton University Press.

Chan, S. 1997. In Search of the Democratic Peace: Problems and Promise. *Mershon International Studies Review* 41:59–91.

Conybeare, J. A. C. 1983. Tariff Protection in Developed and Developing Countries: A Cross-Sectional and Longitudinal Analysis. *International Organization* 37:441–67.

Cook, T. D., and D. T. Campbell. 1979. *Quasi-Experimentation: Design and Analysis Issues for Field Settings.* Boston: Houghton Mifflin.

Doyle, M. W., and G. J. Ikenberry, eds. 1997. *New Thinking in International Relations Theory.* Boulder: Westview.

Fearon, J. D. 1991. Counterfactuals and Hypothesis Testing in Political Science. *World Politics* 43 (2): 169–95.

———. 2002. Selection Effects and Deterrence. *International Interactions* 28 (1): 5–29.

Gilpin, R. 1981. *War and Change in World Politics.* Cambridge: Cambridge University Press.

Goemans, H. 2000. *War and Punishment: The Causes of War Termination and the First World War.* Princeton: Princeton University Press.

Kindleberger, C. P. 1973. *The World in Depression, 1929–1939.* Berkeley: University of California Press.

Conclusion

Krasner, S. D. 1976. State Power and the Structure of Foreign Trade. *World Politics* 28:317–47.

Lake, D. 1988. *Power, Protection, and Free Trade.* Ithaca: Cornell University Press.

Lipson, C. 2003. *Reliable Partners! How Democracies Have Made a Separate Peace.* Princeton: Princeton University Press.

Mansfield, E. D. 1994. *Power, Trade, and War.* Princeton: Princeton University Press.

Maoz, Z., and N. Abdolali. 1989. Regime Type and International Conflict. *Journal of Conflict Resolution* 33:3–35.

Maoz, Z., and B. Russett. 1993. Normative and Structural Causes of Democratic Peace, 1946–86. *American Political Science Review* 87 (3): 624–38.

Martin, L. L. 1992. *Coercive Cooperation: Explaining Multilateral Economic Sanctions.* Princeton: Princeton University Press.

McKeown, T. J. 1991. A Liberal Trade Order? The Long-Run Pattern of Imports to the Advanced Capitalist States. *International Studies Quarterly* 35:151–72.

Menzies, P. 2001. Counterfactual Theories of Causation. In *The Stanford Encyclopedia of Philosophy,* edited by E. N. Zalta (summer edition). http://plato.Stanford.edu/archives/sum2001.

Muller, J. 1988. The Essential Irrelevance of Nuclear Weapons: Stability in the Postwar World. *International Security* 13:55–79.

Nooruddin, I. 2002. Modeling Selection Bias in Studies of Sanctions Efficacy. *International Interactions* 28 (1): 59–75.

Pahre, R. 1999. *Leading Questions: How Hegemony Affects the International Political Economy.* Ann Arbor: University of Michigan Press.

Ray, L. 1995. *Democracy and International Conflict: An Evaluation of the Democratic Peace Proposition.* Columbia: University of South Carolina Press.

Schultz, K. A. 1999. Do Democratic Institutions Constrain or Inform? Contrasting Institutional Perspectives on Democracy and War. *International Organization* 53 (2): 233–66.

Snidal, D. 1985. The Limits of Hegemonic Stability Theory. *International Organization* 39:579–614.

Tetlock, P. E., and A. Belkin, eds. 1996. *Counterfactual Thought Experiments in World Politics: Logical, Methodological, and Psychological Perspectives.* Princeton: Princeton University Press.

Young, O. R., and G. Osherenko, eds. 1993. *Polar Politics: Creating International Environmental Regimes.* Ithaca: Cornell University Press.

Appendix

1. Resources on the Internet

Methods in General

Social Science Information Gateway (SOSIG), University of Bristol, UK. Section on Methodology
  http://sosig.esrc.bris.ac.uk/social_science_general/social_science_ methodology/
  Internet information gateway to research resources both for quantitative and qualitative methodology. Includes article collections, individual papers, bibliographic databases, data resources and educational materials.

"Research Methods Knowledge Base" by William Trochim (Cornell University)
  http://trochim.human.cornell.edu/kb/
  A comprehensive web-based textbook that addresses topics found in typical introductory undergraduate or graduate course in social research methods.

Quantitative Research and Formal Modeling

The Society for Political Methodology and the Political Methodology Section of the American Political Science Association
  http://polmeth.wustl.edu
  Webpage of the (quantitative) political methodology section of the American Political Science Association (APSA). Offers a gateway to the electronic paper-archive, links to the APSA newsletter *The Methodologist* and its Journal *Political Analysis.* The site also offers a section on computing resources.

Richard Tucker, Vanderbilt University
http://www.vanderbilt.edu/~rtucker/polisci/
A comprehensive listing of materials and links on quantitative methods and formal modeling.

Qualitative Methodology

American Political Science Association Section on Qualitative Methodology
http://www.asu.edu/clas/polisci/cqrm/QualitativeMethodsAPSA.html
Offers newsletter, mailing lists, and syllabi.

Fuzzy Set / Qualitative Comparative Analysis (FS/QCA)
http://www.u.arizona.edu/~cragin/fsqca.htm
Downloadable version of the FS/QCA software developed in conjunction with the work of Charles Ragin.

Small-N Compass / Systematic Cross-Case Analysis
http://www.compasss.org/
Information about training and software related to cross-case analysis for small-N studies.

University of Colorado at Denver: Link Collection on Qualitative Methodology
http://carbon.cudenver.edu/~mryder/itc_data/pract_res.html
A broad range of sources on various types of qualitative reasearch as well as links to sources.

Andrew Bennett's Homepage
http://www.georgetown.edu/bennett/
Contains a paper collection and a link to his course on qualitative research methods.

The Qualitative Report Online (Edited by Ronald J. Chenail)
http://www.nova.edu/ssss/QR/
Online journal dedicated to qualitative research in general; published since 1990.

2. Training Programs in Methodology

The Merriam Program in Formal Theory, University of Illinois at
  Urbana-Champaign
  http://csf.colorado.edu/isa/ssip/merfrml.html
  Overview of program on training in formal theory.

Essex Summer School in Social Science Data Analysis and Collection
  http://www.essex.ac.uk/methods
  European-based training program, mostly in quantitative methodol-
    ogy for social scientists.

Summer Program in Quantitative Methods, Inter-University Consortium
  for Political and Social Research.
  http://www.icpsr.umich.edu/training/summer/index.html
  U.S.-based summer program in quantitative methodology for social
    scientists.

The Inter-University Consortium on Qualitative Research Methods
  http://www.asu.edu/clas/polisci/cqrm/
  Information about summer programs on qualitative political science
    methodology, newsletter, syllabi, and mailing list.

Summer Program on Empirical Implications of Theoretical Models
  http://www.cbrss.harvard.edu/eitm.htm
  http://www.isr.umich.edu/cps/eitm/eitm.html
  Held from 2002–2005 at Harvard University, the University of
    Michigan, Duke University, and the University of California,
    Berkeley: National Science Foundation-funded summer programs
    on a rotating basis. Combines formal models with empirical
    research in political science.

Contributors

Todd Allee is Assistant Professor of Political Science at the University of Illinois at Urbana-Champaign. His current research focuses on the role of the World Trade Organization in reducing trade conflict and domestic political motivations for seeking international adjudication of trade and other disputes. He is the coauthor, with Paul Huth, of *The Democratic Peace and Territorial Conflict in the Twentieth Century* (2003).

Andrew Bennett is Associate Professor of Government at Georgetown University. His research specialties include qualitative research methods, Soviet and Russian military interventions, alliance burden sharing, and American foreign policy. His most recent book, coauthored with Alexander L. George, is *Case Studies and Theory Development* (forthcoming).

Thomas Bernauer is Associate Professor of International Relations at the Swiss Federal Institute of Technology (ETH) in Zurich. His research and teaching focus on international political economy and international environmental policy. His publications include *Genes, Trade and Regulation* (2003), *Staaten im Weltmarkt* (*States in the World Market,* 2000), and numerous articles in journals and edited books.

Bear F. Braumoeller is Assistant Professor of Government at Harvard University. His research specialties and publications focus on international relations theory, security studies, and statistical methods. He has a special interest in great power politics, especially those involving Russia and the United States, and is currently at work on a new systemic theory of international politics.

John A. C. Conybeare is Professor of Political Science at the University of Iowa. His research and publications are primarily in international political economy, including the politics of trade policy, the microeconomics of military alliances, global common property issues, the motivations for certain forms of violence (terrorism and privateering) and, most recently, the politics of international mergers in the automobile industry.

Paul Huth is Professor of Political Science and Senior Research Scientist at the University of Michigan, where he teaches international relations. His research and publications center on the escalation and resolution of international disputes. His most recent book (coauthored with Todd Allee) is *The Democratic Peace and Territorial Conflict in the Twentieth Century* (2003).

Arie M. Kacowicz is Senior Lecturer in International Relations at the Hebrew University of Jerusalem, Israel. He is the author of *Peaceful Territorial Change* (1994) and *Zones of Peace in the Third World* (1998) and coeditor of *Stable Peace among Nations* (2000). He has recently completed a book manuscript, *The Impact of Norms in the International Society: The Latin American Experience, 1881–2002.*

D. Marc Kilgour is Professor of Mathematics at Wilfrid Laurier University, Waterloo, Ontario, Canada, and Director of the Laurier Centre for Military, Strategic, and Disarmament Studies. His major research interests include cross-disciplinary analysis of decisions. He has applied game theory to various political science and international relations topics, including arms control, environmental management, negotiation, voting, and coalition formation. His most recent book is *Perfect Deterrence* (coauthored with Frank Zagare, 2000).

Andrew Kydd is Assistant Professor of Government at Harvard University. His research interests focus on game-theoretic analysis of international security issues such as arms racing, conflict, and trust. He is especially interested in the interaction among state motivations, beliefs about motivations, and international behavior. He has published articles in leading political science journals and is currently finishing a book manuscript on the role of trust in the Cold War.

Edward D. Mansfield is Hum Rosen Professor of Political Science and Director of the Christopher H. Browne Center for International Politics at the University of Pennsylvania. He is the author of *Power, Trade, and War*

(1994), coauthor with Jack Snyder of *Democratization and War* (forthcoming), and coeditor with Helen Milner of *The Political Economy of Economic Regionalism* (1997).

Helen V. Milner, James T. Shotwell Professor of International Relations at Columbia University, specializes in international and comparative political economy. Her most recent books include *Political Science: The State of the Discipline III* (coedited with Ira Katznelson, 2002), *Interests, Institutions and Information: Domestic Politics and International Relations* (1997), and *The Political Economy of Economic Regionalism* (coedited with Edward Mansfield, 1997).

Ronald Mitchell is Associate Professor of Political Science at the University of Oregon. His research and teaching focus on international relations and the effectiveness of international institutions. His publications include *Intentional Oil Pollution at Sea: Environmental Policy and Treaty Compliance* (1994), articles in *International Organization, International Studies Quarterly,* and *Global Governance,* and chapters in numerous edited volumes.

John S. Odell is Professor of International Relations at the University of Southern California, where he teaches international relations and research methods. His most recent book is *Negotiating the World Economy* (2000). His research explores the process of negotiation over international economic issues. He coordinates a research network on economic negotiations, on the Web at www-rcf.usc.edu/~odell/ENN.

Anne E. Sartori is Assistant Professor of Politics and Charles G. Osgood Preceptor at Princeton University. Her research interests include international conflict and cooperation and the statistical testing of game-theoretic models. She is the author of *Deterrence by Diplomacy* (forthcoming) as well as articles on diplomacy and on statistical methods.

Duncan Snidal is Associate Professor of Political Science and Public Policy at the University of Chicago and Director of the Program on International Politics, Economics, and Security (PIPES). His research and publications focus on international cooperation and institutions with a recent emphasis on the development of international legalization and the design of international institutions.

Contributors

Detlef F. Sprinz is a Senior Fellow with the Department of Global Change and Social Systems of the Potsdam Institute for Climate Impact Research (PIK) and an adjunct member of the Faculty of Economics and Social Science, University of Potsdam, Germany. His research and publications encompass international regimes and their effectiveness, international environmental policy, and modeling political decisions. He is coeditor of *International Relations and Global Climate Change* (with Urs Luterbacher, 2001).

Yael Wolinsky-Nahmias is Senior Lecturer and Associate Chair of the department of Political Science at Northwestern University. Her research and teaching interests are in international relations and environmental politics. She is currently conducting research on environmental NGOs and on state and local ballot initiatives for land preservation in the United States.

Name Index

Subject Index

Subject Index

effects of economic development on, 178

effects of regime type on, 178

effects of trade on, 91–92, 186

increasing importance of, 317

International environmental regimes, 87, 88, 89, 91, 92, 97, 178, 182, 317, 318

effectiveness of, 90, 97, 182–84, 185, 186, 326

emergence of, 182, 185, 326

International institutions, 3, 14, 61, 66, 170, 250, 265, 267, 268, 271, 279, 284, 376

International organizations, 3, 5, 56, 87, 306, 307

International political economy (IPE)

defined, 153, 266–69

and foreign economic policy, 62, 276–78

growth of quantitative studies of, 153–54

and international cooperation, 278–80

and political conflict, 164–66

system-level analysis of, 154

See also International trade; Preferential trading agreements

International regimes, 2, 11, 56, 58, 73, 83, 85, 87, 88, 89, 93, 97, 177, 185, 278, 282, 321, 368

effectiveness of, 83, 85, 90, 178, 184, 186

formation of, 58, 83, 85, 98–99, 178, 368

International security. *See* Security studies

International trade

effects of alliances on, 157–62, 170–71

effects of hegemony on, 154–57, 170–71, 274

effects of political-military relations on, 164–66, 170–71, 173n

factoral models of, 276–77

as a public good, 274–75, 299

sectoral models of, 277–78

Interviews, 28, 94, 97

Iraq invasion of Kuwait (1990), 117

Ireland, 112, 114

Israel, 112, 117, 246, 306, 310, 331

Jordan, 331, 336

Jordan River, 258, 331, 332, 335

Kashmir, 13, 350–53, 355

Korea, 117, 357

Korean War, 117

Kuwait, 117

Kyoto Conference on Climate Change (1997), 307. *See also* Climate change

Leadership, 61, 203, 214, 275, 372

Lebanon, 331

Logit models, 211, 214, 215, 217

London, 61, 65

Measurement error, 24, 30, 33, 36, 50n, 194, 202, 215–18, 219

Measurement problems, 293, 296

direct, 186, 187

indirect, 186

See also Measurement error

Method of agreement. *See* Case study methods, method of agreement

Method of difference. *See* Case study methods, method of difference

Methodology, trends in, 5–8, 187–88, 344–45

Mexico, 73, 298

Microeconomics
  assumptions of, 291
  defined, 290
  and war (*see* War, microeconomic
    explanations of)
Middle East, 13, 117
Military balance, 215
Military intervention, 26–28, 112,
  117
Models
  advantages and limitations of,
    231–33, 236
  defined, 227–28
  empirical testing of, 237
  mathematical, 227, 228, 235
  specification, 133–39, 187, 214
  types of, 234
  See also Formal methods/models
Monetary policies, 3, 12, 56, 62, 68,
  73n, 265, 276, 278, 282, 305,
  306
Montreal Protocol on ozone-depleting
  substances (1987), 96, 97
Moral hazard, 305, 306
Multicollinearity, 182, 189n
Multimethod research. *See* Cross-methods (multimethod) research
Multiple equilibria, 45, 138–39, 251,
  252, 253, 254, 312, 334, 337

NAFTA (North American Free Trade
  Agreement), 90, 162, 298, 299,
  321
Nash equilibrium, 248, 254, 270,
  271, 337, 339n
Negotiations, 12, 13, 56, 57, 61, 63,
  65, 66, 68, 73, 81, 83, 88, 94,
  95, 247, 317, 331, 359
  over the environment, 95, 318, 319,
  320–25, 329, 339
  as a stage of international conflict

(*see* International conflict,
  stages of)
NGOs (nongovernmental organizations), 3, 82, 85, 88, 98–99, 321
Nixon, Richard, 59
Nondirected dyads, 204–5, 207
Normal form game. *See* Game theory
  models, normal form vs. extensive form
Norms, 63, 85, 86, 109, 110, 118,
  133, 147n, 205, 206, 207, 302,
  309, 328, 346, 357, 374
Nuclear crises, 112, 116
  deterrence, 3, 119, 236
  weapons, 135, 236, 300, 305, 370

Observations, 5, 10, 35, 57, 67, 88,
  94, 95, 96, 98, 99, 100, 165,
  203, 204, 206, 207, 217, 310,
  371
  defined, 42
  nonindependent, 12, 194, 201, 210,
    212–15, 219
  number of, 20, 41, 68, 69, 70, 86,
    88, 89, 90, 100, 140, 141
  outliers, 189n
  selection of, 89–93, 96, 102n
  single, 42, 208
  "within-case," 75n
OPEC (Organization of Petroleum
  Exporting Countries), 290, 292,
  299, 303, 310
Ozone layer, 317, 321, 327
  depletion of, 93, 97, 317, 321
  effects of regime type on, 89, 321
  See also Montreal Protocol

Pakistan, 13, 130, 350–58, 363n
Parsimony, 19, 38, 39, 108, 232
Path dependency, 19, 34, 38–39, 44,
  108, 111